Navigating the ELPS in the English Language Arts and Reading Classroom

Using the Standards to Improve Instruction for English Language Learners

By: John Seidlitz

with contributions from Valerie Auer and Marcy Voss

Seidlitz Education
56 Via Regalo
San Clemente, CA 92673

ISBN 978-0-9822078-4-0

For related titles and support materials visit www.johnseidlitzcom.

Table of Contents

English Language Learners in Texas and the New Proficiency Standards 5

How to Use this Manual 6

Introduction (subsection a) 9

District Responsibilities (subsection b) 15

- *Understanding the ELPS Framework* 18
- *ELPS District Implementation Checklist* 20
- *ELPS Aligned Walk-Through Observation* 22

Cross-Curricular Student Expectations (subsection c) 25

- *ELPS Integration Plan for Teachers* 32
- *Seven Steps to Building a Language-Rich Interactive Classroom* 33
- *Language Objectives Aligned to Student Expectations* 34
- *ELPS Lesson Plan Template* 35
- *ELPS Lesson Plan Activity Guide* 36
- *English Language Arts and Reading Lessons that Promote Language Development for English Language Learners*
    - Sample Elementary Lesson: Sequencing 37
    - Sample Middle School Lesson: Point of VIew 38
    - Sample High School Lesson: Tone/Mood through Dialogue 39
- *ELAR TEKS/ELPS Side-by-Sides*
    - *Kindergarten* 41
    - *First-Grade* 53
    - *Second Grade* 69
    - *Third Grade* 83
    - *Fourth Grade* 97
    - *Fifth Grade* 111
    - *Sixth Grade* 127
    - *Seventh Grade* 141
    - *Eighth Grade* 155
    - *Ninth Grade* 169
    - *Tenth Grade* 183
    - *Eleventh Grade* 197
    - *Twelfth Grade* 213
- *Sentence Stems and Activities Aligned to Student Expectations* 229

Language Proficiency Level Descriptors (subsection d) 245

Guide to Terms and Activities 261

Bibliography 275

This page is intentionally left blank.

English Language Learners in Texas and the New Proficiency Standards

Research into what works for English Language Learners indicates that one of the keys to success is a consistent focus on content area language acquisition (Gibbons, P., 2002; Samway, K., 2006; Echevarria, Vogt, Short, 2008; Zweirs, J., 2008). This approach emphasizes the need to intentionally make content comprehensible while developing academic language skills for students acquiring English as a second language. It also requires that academic language instruction be integrated into all areas of instruction so that all teachers of ELLs understand their role as teachera of content and language.

In 1998, the second language acquisition (ESL) standards were adopted as part of the Texas Essential Knowledge and Skills for Spanish Language Arts and English Language Arts. These standards included student expectations and descriptions of proficiency levels for reading, writing, listening, and speaking for students at various levels of language proficiency. Because these standards were only integrated into English and Spanish language arts, few content area teachers made use of them when planning instruction for English Language Learners.

In 2006, the Texas Education Agency assembled a group to review and revise the ESL standards. The result was the new English Language Proficiency Standards that went into effect in December of 2007. The standards describe the instruction that districts need to provide for English Language Learners to successfully master both content area knowledge and academic language. Unlike the former ESL standards, the new standards clearly indicate that the ELPS are to be integrated into *each subject of the required curriculum.* The new ELPS contain a brief introduction into what kind of instruction is required for English Language Learners, an outline of district responsibilities, cross curricular student expectations, and language proficiency level descriptors.

Although integrating the ELPS into content areas will take time and effort for Texas educators, the new standards provide a unique opportunity to improve instruction for English Language Learners. The purpose of this manual is to provide resources and tools that will help make the process of implementation easier for administrators, specialists, and teachers who serve English learners in classrooms across Texas.

How to Use this Manual

This manual is designed to help teachers, administrators and specialists use the ELPS (*http://www.tea.state.tx.us/rules/tac/chapter074/ch074a.html*) to improve instruction for English Language Learners. It is divided into four sections corresponding to the four sections of the English Language Proficiency Standards:

- (a) Introduction
- (b) District responsibilities
- (c) Cross-curricular student expectations
- (d) Language proficiency level descriptors

Each section begins with the text of the subsection of chapter 74.4 (TAC) that the tools and resources will address. This is followed by an assessment of current levels of understanding and implementation. The assessment is designed to guide administrators, educators, and specialists through a process of deciding which tools and resources will best meet their current needs. The assessment is followed by tools for understanding the meaning of the document as well as templates for implementing changes at the classroom, campus, and district levels that align with the new standards.

Section (a) addresses the introduction to the *English Language Proficiency Standards (2008).* The section includes summaries of the introduction (subsection a), district responsibilities (subsection b), the student expectations (subsection c), and the language proficiency level descriptors (subsection d). The summaries are followed by a handout listing reasons why the ELPS are significant to the instruction of English Language Learners in Texas.

Section (b) outlines district responsibilities discussed in the ELPS. The first set of tools is designed to help educators understand the ELPS framework for English proficiency. They help clarify specific terms found in chapter 74.4. The terms ***communicated, sequenced,*** and ***scaffolded*** that describe ***linguistically accommodated instruction*** and the terms ***focused, targeted, and systematic*** that describe high-quality, second-language acquisition instruction are discussed. The next set of tools includes an implementation checklist and a series of planning, observation, and coaching tools that can be used to meet the needs of teachers and administrators implementing ELPS at the classroom or campus level.

Section (c) addresses cross-curricular student expectations. The tools are designed to help educators integrate the ELPS into content-area instruction. A quick guide to reading the new standards is included as well as specific lesson planning templates and sample lessons aligned to the ELPS. An ELPS Integration Plan for Teachers walks educators through a process for creating lesson plans that target academic language and concept development. Another tool outlines a seven-step process for using the ELPS to create a language-rich, interactive classroom. The last tool in this section is a comprehensive guide for planning instruction using the ELPS which includes activities and suggested sentence stems to address each of the standards.

Section (d) contains tools and resources for planning instruction based on students' language proficiency levels. A summary of each language level and specific strategies corresponding to each proficiency level as well as tools for differentiating instruction are provided. The section does not include tools for formal assessment of English Language Learners nor linguistic accommodations for English learners taking the Linguistically Accommodated Testing (LAT). These can be found at the Texas Education Agency website here: http://portals.tea.state.tx.us/page.aspx?id=568.

Guide to Terms and Activities: This section contains a description of each of the activities and strategies mentioned in the manual as well as references for further research on the activity.

This page is intentionally left blank.

Introduction

(subsection a)

Chapter 74. Curriculum Requirements:
Subchapter A. Required Curriculum

§74.4. English Language Proficiency Standards

http://www.tea.state.tx.us/rules/tac/chapter074/ch074a.html

(a) Introduction.

(1) The English language proficiency standards in this section outline English language proficiency level descriptors and student expectations for English language learners (ELLs). School districts shall implement this section as an integral part of each subject in the required curriculum. The English language proficiency standards are to be published along with the Texas Essential Knowledge and Skills (TEKS) for each subject in the required curriculum.

(2) In order for ELLs to be successful, they must acquire both social and academic language proficiency in English. Social language proficiency in English consists of the English needed for daily social interactions. Academic language proficiency consists of the English needed to think critically, understand and learn new concepts, process complex academic material, and interact and communicate in English academic settings.

(3) Classroom instruction that effectively integrates second-language acquisition with quality content-area instruction ensures that ELLs acquire social and academic language proficiency in English, learn the knowledge and skills in the TEKS, and reach their full academic potential.

(4) Effective instruction in second-language acquisition involves giving ELLs opportunities to listen, speak, read, and write at their current levels of English development while gradually increasing the linguistic complexity of the English they read and hear, and are expected to speak and write.

(5) The cross-curricular second-language acquisition skills in subsection (c) of this section apply to ELLs in Kindergarten - Grade 12.

(6) The English language proficiency levels of beginning, intermediate, advanced, and advanced high are not grade-specific. ELLs may exhibit different proficiency levels within the language domains of listening, speaking, reading, and writing. The proficiency level descriptors outlined in subsection (d) of this section show the progression of second-language acquisition from one proficiency level to the next and serve as a road map to help content-area teachers instruct ELLs commensurate with students' linguistic needs.

ELPS Awareness Self-Assessment

Rate the current level of awareness of the English Language Proficiency standards at your district or campus.

A: Always
M: Mostly
S: Sometimes
N: Never

Indicator	A	M	S	N	Comments/Questions
Teachers of ELLs are aware of the unique needs of ELLs to acquire social language skills for social interaction.					
Teachers of ELLs are aware of the unique needs of ELLs to acquire academic language necessary for academic tasks.					
Teachers of ELLs are aware of the need to integrate language and content instruction to ensure that ELLs acquire social and academic English.					
Teachers of ELLs receive staff development on the unique needs of ELLs to acquire social and academic English.					
ELLs are assessed for their language proficiency level upon entry into the district.					
Teachers of ELLs are aware of the language levels of their students on the initial district assessment and on the TELPAS.					
Administrators, teachers, and specialists are aware of the need to integrate the cross-curricular student expectations of the ELPS into content-area instruction.					

Summaries of ELPS*
Introduction, District Responsibilities, and Student Expectations
(subsection a,b,c)

Introduction	District Responsibilities
a1: Part of required curriculum for each subject including **proficiency standards** and **level descriptors** a2: ELLs need social and academic English language proficiency to be successful a3: Instruction must integrate **social and academic English** in content areas a4: ELLs must read, write, listen, and speak in increasing complexity a5: Student Expectations of ELPS apply to K - 12 students a6: Level descriptors are not grade - specific and serve as a road map	b1: Identify students' proficiency levels using proficiency-level descriptors b2: Provide **linguistically accommodated** content instruction (communicated, sequenced, scaffolded) b3: Provide linguistically accommodated content-based language instruction b4: Focused, targeted, and systematic language instruction for beginning and intermediate ELLs (Grade 3 or higher)
Learning Strategies	
c1A: Use prior knowledge to learn new language c1B: Monitor language with self-corrective techniques c1C: Use techniques to learn new vocabulary c1D: Speak using learning strategies	c1E: Use and reuse new, basic, and academic language to internalize language c1F: Use accessible language to learn new language c1G: Distinguish formal and informal English c1H: Expand repertoire of language learning strategies
Listening	**Speaking**
c2A: Distinguish sound and intonation c2B: Recognize English sound system in new vocabulary c2C: Learn new language heard in classroom interactions and instruction c2D: Monitor understanding and seek clarification c2E: Use visual, contextual linguistic support to confirm and enhance understanding c2F: Derive meaning from a variety of media c2G: Understand general meaning, main points, and details c2H: Understand implicit ideas and information c2I: Demonstrate listening comprehension	c3A: Practice using English sound system in new vocabulary c3B: Use new vocabulary in stories, descriptions, and classroom communication c3C: Speak using a variety of sentence structures c3D: Speak using grade-level content-area vocabulary in context c3E: Share in cooperative groups c3F: Ask and give information using high-frequency and content-area vocabulary c3G: Express opinions, ideas, and feelings c3H: Narrate, describe, and explain c3I: Adapt spoken language for formal and informal purposes c3J: Respond orally to information from a variety of media sources
Reading	**Writing**
c4A: Learn relationships of sounds and letters in English c4B: Recognize directionality of English text c4C: Develop sight vocabulary and language structures c4D: Use prereading supports c4E: Read linguistically accommodated content-area materials c4F: Use visual and contextual supports to read text c4G: Show comprehension of English text individually and in groups c4H: Read silently with comprehension c4I: Show comprehension through basic reading skills c4J: Show comprehension through inferential skills c4K: Show comprehension through analytical skills	c5A: Learn relationships between sounds and letters when writing c5B: Write using newly acquired vocabulary c5C: Spell familiar English words c5D: Edit writing c5E: Employ complex grammatical structures c5F: Write using variety of sentence structures and words c5G: Narrate, describe, and explain in writing

* *These summaries must be used in conjunction with cross-curricular student expectations when planning instruction.*

Summaries of ELPS: Proficiency Level Descriptors*
(subsection d)

Level	Listening (*d1: K-12*) *The student comprehends . . .*	Speaking (*d2: K-12*) *The student speaks . . .*	Reading (*d4: 2-12*) *The student reads . . .*	Writing (*d6: 2-12*) *The student writes . . .*
Beginning (A)	1A(i) few **simple conversations** with linguistic support 1A(ii) **modified conversation** 1A(iii) few words, **does not seek clarification**, watches others for cues	2A(i) using **single words and short phrases** with practiced material; tends to give up on attempts 2A(ii) using **limited bank of key vocabulary** 2A(iii) with **recently practiced, familiar material** 2A(iv) with frequent **errors** that hinder communication 2A(v) with **pronunciation that inhibits communication**	4A(i) little except recently practiced terms, **environmental print**, high-frequency words, **concrete words represented by pictures** 4A(ii) **slowly, word by word** 4A(iii) with very limited sense of English structure 4A(iv) with comprehension of **practiced, familiar text** 4A(v) with need for **visuals and prior knowledge** 4A(vi) modified and **adapted text**	6A(i) with **little ability to use English** 6A(ii) **without focus** and coherence, conventions, organization, or voice 6A(iii) labels, lists, and copies of printed text and **high-frequency words/phrases**, short and simple, practiced sentences primarily in **present tense with frequent errors** that hinder or prevent understanding
Intermediate (B)	1B(i) unfamiliar language with **linguistic supports** and adaptations 1B(ii) unmodified conversation with **key words** and phrases 1B(iii) with **requests for clarification** by asking speaker to repeat, slow down, or rephrase speech	2B(i) **with simple messages** and hesitation to think about meaning 2B(ii) using **basic vocabulary** 2B(iii) with **simple sentence structures** and present tense 2B(iv) with **errors** that inhibit unfamiliar communication 2B(v) with **pronunciation generally understood** by those familiar with English language learners	4B(i) **wider range of topics:** and everyday academic language 4B(ii) **slowly** and **rereads** 4B(iii) basic language structures 4B(iv) simple sentences **with visual cues, pretaught vocabulary** and **interaction** 4B(v) **grade-level texts** with difficulty 4B(vi) at high level with **linguistic accommodation**	6B(i) with **limited ability to use English** in content-area writing 6B(ii) best on **topics that are highly familiar** with simple English 6B(iii) with **simple oral tone in messages**, high-frequency vocabulary, loosely connected text, repetition of ideas, **mostly in the present tense**, undetailed descriptions, and **frequent errors**
Advanced (C)	1C(i) with some processing time, **visuals, verbal cues, and gestures; for unfamiliar conversations** 1C(ii) most unmodified interaction 1C(iii) with occasional **requests** for the speaker to slow down, repeat, rephrase, and **clarify meaning**	2C(i) in conversations with some **pauses to restate, repeat, and clarify** 2C(ii) using **content-based and abstract terms** on familiar topics 2C(iii) with **past, present, and future** 2C(iv) using **complex sentences** and grammar with some errors 2C(v) with **pronunciation usually understood** by most	4C(i) abstract grade-appropriate text 4C(ii) **longer phrases and familiar sentences** appropriately 4C(iii) while developing the ability to construct meaning from text 4C(iv) at **high-comprehension** level with **linguistic support** for unfamiliar topics and to clarify meaning	6C(i) grade-appropriate **ideas with second-language support** 6C(ii) with extra need for second-language **support when topics are technical and abstract** 6C(iii) with a grasp of basic English usage and some understanding of complex usage with **emerging grade-appropriate vocabulary** and a more academic tone
Advanced High (D)	1D(i) longer **discussions on unfamiliar topics** 1D(ii) spoken information nearly **comparable to native speaker** 1D(iii) with few requests for speaker to slow down, repeat, or rephrase	2D(i) in **extended discussions** with few pauses 2D(ii) using **abstract, content-based vocabulary** except low-frequency terms; using idioms 2D(iii) with grammar **nearly comparable to native speaker** 2D(iv) with **few errors** blocking communication 2D(v) **occasional mispronunciation**	4D(i) **nearly comparable to native speakers** 4D(ii) **grade-appropriate familiar text** appropriately 4D(iii) while constructing meaning at near-native ability level 4D(iv) with high-level comprehension with **minimal linguistic support**	6D(i) grade-appropriate **content-area ideas with little need for** linguistic **support** 6D(ii) develop and demonstrate **grade-appropriate** writing 6D(iii) nearly **comparable to native speakers** with clarity and precision, with **occasional difficulties** and with naturalness of language.

****These summaries are not appropriate to use in formally identifying student proficiency levels for TELPAS. TELPAS assessment and training materials are provided by the Texas Education Agency Student Assessment Division**: http://www.tea.state.tx.us/index3.aspx?id=3300&menu_id3=793*

Why the ELPS?

1. English Language Learners benefit from content-area instruction that is accommodated to their need for comprehensible input (Krashen, 1983; Echevarria, Vogt, and Short, 2008).

2. English Language Learners benefit from academic language instruction integrated into content-area instruction (Crandall, 1987; Snow et. al. 1989).

3. English Language Learners benefit from programs that hold high expectations for students for academic success (Collier, 1992; Lucas et al, 1990, Samway & McKeon 2007).

4. Language proficiency standards provide a common framework for integrating language and content instruction for English Language Learners (Short, 2000).

District Responsibilities

(subsection b)

§74.4. English Language Proficiency Standards

http://www.tea.state.tx.us/rules/tac/chapter074/ch074a.html

(b) School district responsibilities. In fulfilling the requirements of this section, school districts shall:

(1) identify the student's English language proficiency levels in the domains of listening, speaking, reading and writing in accordance with the proficiency level descriptors for the beginning, intermediate, advanced, and advanced high levels delineated in subsection (d) of this section;

(2) provide instruction in the knowledge and skills of the foundation and enrichment curriculum in a manner that is linguistically accommodated (communicated, sequenced, and scaffolded) commensurate with the student's levels of English language proficiency to ensure that the student learns the knowledge and skills in the required curriculum;

(3) provide content-based instruction including the cross-curricular second-language acquisition essential knowledge and skills in subsection (c) of this section in a manner that is linguistically accommodated to help the student acquire English language proficiency; and

(4) provide intensive and ongoing foundational second-language acquisition instruction to ELLs in Grade 3 or higher who are at the beginning or intermediate level of English language proficiency in listening, speaking, reading, and/or writing as determined by the state's English language proficiency assessment system. These ELLs require focused, targeted, and systematic second-language acquisition instruction to provide them with the foundation of English language vocabulary, grammar, syntax, and English mechanics necessary to support content-based instruction and accelerated learning of English.

ELPS Implementation Self-Assessment

Rate the current level of implementation of the English Language Proficiency Standards at your district or campus.

A: Always
M: Mostly
S: Sometimes
N: Never

Understanding the ELPS Framework: (1)

Indicator	A	M	S	N	Comments/Questions
Teachers of ELLs receive sufficient training on how to provide ELL instruction in social and academic English.					
Teachers of ELLs receive sufficient training on how to differentiate instruction based on the language levels of English Language Learners.					
Teachers of ELLs integrate language and content-area instruction in their lesson plans.					
Teachers of ELLs provide linguistically accommodated instruction to meet the language proficiency levels of their English Language Learners .					
ELLs have opportunities to read and write in academic English during content-area instruction.					
ELLs have opportunities to listen and speak using academic English during content-area instruction.					
The cross-curricular student expectations are being integrated into existing curriculum frameworks.					
The cross-curricular student expectations are being integrated into content-area lesson plans.					

Understanding the ELPS Framework: (1)
Linguistically Accommodated Instruction

Curriculum for ELLs must be:	What is it?	What are some examples?
Communicated	Comprehensible input is used to convey the meaning of key concepts to students. (Krashen, 1983)	• Visuals, TPR (Total Physical Response), and other techniques to communicate key concepts • Clear explanation of academic tasks • Speech appropriate for language level • Use of Native Language Resources (Echevarria, Vogt, Short, 2008)
Sequenced	Instruction is differentiated to align with the progression of students' language development level. (Hill & Flynn, 2006)	• Differentiate language and content instruction • Target use of supplementary materials and resources • Preteach social and academic vocabulary necessary for interaction and classroom tasks (Hill & Flynn, 2006)
Scaffolded	ELLs receive structured support that leads to independent acquisition of language and content knowledge. (Echevarria, Vogt, Short, 2008)	• **Oral scaffolding:** recasting, paraphrasing, wait time, etc. • **Procedural scaffolding:** moving from whole class to group, to individual tasks. • **Instructional scaffolding:** providing students concrete structures such as sentence and paragraph frames, patterns, and models. (Echevarria, Vogt, & Short, 2008)

Understanding the ELPS Framework: (2)

Foundations of Second-Language Acquisition Instruction for Beginning and Intermediate ELLs Grades 3 - 12

"Make sure the system for second-language acquisition instruction focuses on the target."

Second-language acquisition instruction must be:	What is it?	What are some examples?
Focused	**Concentrated effort centered on student acquisition** of vocabulary, grammar, syntax, and English mechanics necessary to support content-based instruction and accelerated learning of English	• Explicit instruction in English vocabulary and language structures • Lesson plans with cross-curricular student expectations from the ELPS • Use of sentence structures of increasing complexity in vocabulary, grammar, and syntax
Targeted	**Specific goals and objectives** align with vocabulary, grammar, syntax, and English mechanics necessary to support content-based instruction and accelerated learning of English	• Content objectives for ELLs align with the TEKS • Language objectives for ELLs align with ELPS and language skills necessary for TEKS • Formal and informal assessments align with content and language assessments
Systematic	**Well-organized structure** in place to ensure students acquire vocabulary, grammar, syntax, and English mechanics necessary to support content-based instruction and accelerated learning of English.	• ELPS integrated into district curriculum frameworks • **Comprehensive plan for students in Grades 3 - 12 at beginner or intermediate** level for integrating language and content instruction • Comprehensive plan for assessing the implementation of focused, targeted instruction for beginner and intermediate students in Grades 3 - 12 • Periodic review of progress of ELLs through formal and informal assessment

ELPS District Implementation Checklist

Goal	We will have met this goal when . . .	Steps	Person(s) Responsible	Dates/Deadlines
Administrators and specialists integrate ELPS into ongoing professional development and evaluation.				
Staff understands the importance of TELPAS and other formal assessments to identify language levels of ELLs.				
Staff understands the need for ELLs to develop social and academic English.				
Staff understands methods for providing linguistically accommodated instruction for ELLs.				
Staff understands cross-curricular student expectations.				
Staff develops a plan for systematic academic language development for ELLs.				
Teachers include ELPS in lesson plans in core content areas.				

Two Key Questions for Assessing Quality Instruction for ELLs

Do English learners understand the key content concepts *(aligned to TEKS)*?	Are English Language Learners developing their ability to read, write, listen, and speak in academic English about content concepts *(in ways described in the ELPS)*?

ELPS Aligned Walk-Through Observation

Observer: Class:
Teacher: Date:

Indicator	Comments/Questions
☐ Content and language objectives posted	
☐ Evidence of explicit vocabulary instruction	
☐ Evidence of variety of techniques to make content comprehensible	
☐ Evidence of reading and writing in academic English	
☐ Evidence of student/student interaction focusing on lesson concepts	
☐ Specific instructional interventions for ELLs appropriate to students' language levels (sentence stems, native language resources, word banks, low-risk environment for language production, etc.)	

ELPS Aligned Lesson Observation

Observer: Class:
Teacher: Date:

Indicator	Comments/Questions
☐ Teacher posts and explains clearly defined content objectives aligned to the TEKS to ELLs.	
☐ Teacher posts and explains clearly defined language objectives aligned to the ELPS to ELLs.	
☐ Teacher clearly communicates key concepts, words, phrases, and directions for instructional tasks to ELLs (*using visuals, gestures, native language resources, etc., as needed*).	
☐ Teacher differentiates instruction *(alters instruction, language demands, and assessment)* to align with the students' language development level.	
☐ Teacher provides verbal and procedural scaffolding for ELLs *(sentence stems, modeling, instructional strategies, etc.)*.	
☐ Teacher provides opportunities for students to read and write using academic English.	
☐ Teacher provides opportunities for ELLs to listen and speak using academic and social English.	
☐ ELLs demonstrate understanding of content and language objectives.	

ELPS Aligned Lesson Observation Coaching Tool

Observer:
Teacher:

Class:
Date:

Indicator	Comments/Questions
☐ Teacher posts and explains clearly defined content objectives aligned to the TEKS to ELLs.	• Are the objectives posted? • Do ELLs understand the objectives? • Are the objectives aligned with the TEKS? • Does the lesson align with the objectives?
☐ Teacher posts and explains clearly defined language objectives aligned to the ELPS to ELLs.	• Are the objectives posted? • Do ELLs understand the objectives? • Are the objectives aligned with the ELPS? • Does the lesson align with the objectives?
☐ Teacher clearly communicates key concepts, words, phrases, and directions for instructional tasks to English learners *(using visuals, gestures, native language resources, etc., as needed).*	• Do ELLs understand the key concepts? • Does the teacher explicitly teach key concept-area vocabulary? • Does the teacher teach ELLs specific words and phrases necessary for instructional tasks? • Do ELLs show a clear understanding of instructional tasks?
☐ Teacher differentiates instruction *(alters instruction, language demands, and assessment)* to align with the students' language development level.	• Is the teacher aware of the students' language levels? • Are instructions, assignments, and assessments appropriate for the students' level of language development?
☐ Teacher provides verbal and procedural scaffolding for ELLs *(sentence stems, modeling, instruction in strategies, etc.).*	• Does the teacher provide models, examples, and structures that enable ELLs to work toward independence? • Do ELLs use specific strategies when they need clarification about content or language?
☐ Teacher provides opportunities for students to read and write using academic English.	• Do ELLs read academic English during the lesson? • Do ELLs write during the lesson? • Are ELLs supported in finding ways to enable them to read and write during the lesson?
☐ Teacher provides opportunities for ELLs to listen and speak using academic and social English.	• Do ELLs listen and speak using social English? • Do ELLs use content-area vocabulary during classroom interactions? • Do ELLs use academic English structures during classroom interactions?
☐ ELLs demonstrate understanding of content and language objectives.	• Are ELLs assessed throughout the lesson for understanding of content and language?

Cross-Curricular Student Expectations

(subsection c)

§74.4. English Language Proficiency Standards

http://www.tea.state.tx.us/rules/tac/chapter074/ch074a.html

(c) Cross-curricular Student Expectations

(1) Cross-curricular second-language acquisition/learning strategies. The ELL uses language learning strategies to develop an awareness of his or her own learning processes in all content-areas. In order for the ELL to meet grade-level learning expectations across the foundation and enrichment curriculum, all instruction delivered in English must be linguistically accommodated (communicated, sequenced, and scaffolded) commensurate with the student's level of English language proficiency. The student is expected to:

(A) use prior knowledge and experiences to understand meanings in English;

(B) monitor oral and written language production and employ self-corrective techniques or other resources;

(C) use strategic learning techniques such as concept mapping, drawing, memorizing, comparing, contrasting, and reviewing to acquire basic and grade-level vocabulary;

(D) speak using learning strategies such as requesting assistance, employing non-verbal cues, and using synonyms and circumlocution (conveying ideas by defining or describing when exact English words are not known);

(E) internalize new, basic, and academic language by using and reusing it in meaningful ways in speaking and writing activities that build concept and language attainment;

(F) use accessible language and learn new and essential language in the process;

(G) demonstrate an increasing ability to distinguish between formal and informal English and an increasing knowledge of when to use each one commensurate with grade-level learning expectations; and

(H) develop and expand repertoire of learning strategies such as reasoning inductively or deductively, looking for patterns in language, and analyzing sayings and expressions commensurate with grade-level learning expectations.

(2) Cross-curricular second-language acquisition/listening. The ELL listens to a variety of speakers including teachers, peers, and electronic media to gain an increasing level of comprehension of newly acquired language in all content areas. ELLs may be at the beginning, intermediate, advanced, or advanced high stage of English language acquisition in listening. In order for the ELL to meet grade-level learning expectations across the foundation and enrichment curriculum, all instruction delivered in English must be linguistically accommodated (communicated, sequenced, and scaffolded) commensurate with the student's level of English language proficiency. The student is expected to:

(A) distinguish sounds and intonation patterns of English with increasing ease;

(B) recognize elements of the English sound system in newly acquired vocabulary such as long and short vowels, silent letters, and consonant clusters;

(C) learn new language structures, expressions, and basic and academic vocabulary heard during classroom instruction and interactions;

(D) monitor understanding of spoken language during classroom instruction and interactions and seek clarification as needed;

(E) use visual, contextual, and linguistic support to enhance and confirm understanding of increasingly complex and elaborated spoken language;

(F) listen to and derive meaning from a variety of media such as audio tape, video, DVD, and CD-ROM to build and reinforce concept and language attainment;

(G) understand the general meaning, main points, and important details of spoken language ranging from situations in which topics, language, and contexts are familiar to unfamiliar;

(H) understand implicit ideas and information in increasingly complex spoken language commensurate with grade-level learning expectations; and

(I) demonstrate listening comprehension of increasingly complex spoken English by following directions, retelling or summarizing spoken messages, responding to questions and requests, collaborating with peers, and taking notes commensurate with content and grade-level needs.

(3) Cross-curricular second-language acquisition/speaking. The ELL speaks in a variety of modes for a variety of purposes with an awareness of different language registers (formal/informal) using vocabulary with increasing fluency and accuracy in language arts and all content areas. ELLs may be at the beginning, intermediate, advanced, or advanced high stage of English language acquisition in speaking. In order for the ELL to meet grade-level learning expectations across the foundation and enrichment curriculum, all instruction delivered in English must be linguistically accommodated (communicated, sequenced, and scaffolded) commensurate with the student's level of English language proficiency. The student is expected to:

(A) practice producing sounds of newly acquired vocabulary such as long and short vowels, silent letters, and consonant clusters to pronounce English words in a manner that is increasingly comprehensible;

(B) expand and internalize initial English vocabulary by learning and using high-frequency English words necessary for identifying and describing people, places, and objects, by retelling simple stories and basic information represented or supported by pictures, and by learning and using routine language needed for classroom communication;

(C) speak using a variety of grammatical structures, sentence lengths, sentence types, and connecting words with increasing accuracy and ease as more English is acquired;

(D) speak using grade-level content-area vocabulary in context to internalize new English words and build academic language proficiency;

(E) share information in cooperative learning interactions;

(F) ask and give information ranging from using a very limited bank of high-frequency, high-need, concrete vocabulary, including key words and expressions needed for basic communication in academic and social contexts, to using abstract and content-based vocabulary during extended speaking assignments;

(G) express opinions, ideas, and feelings ranging from communicating single words and short phrases to participating in extended discussions on a variety of social and grade-appropriate academic topics;

(H) narrate, describe, and explain with increasing specificity and detail as more English is acquired;

(I) adapt spoken language appropriately for formal and informal purposes; and

(J) respond orally to information presented in a wide variety of print, electronic, audio, and visual media to build and reinforce concept and language attainment.

(4) Cross-curricular second-language acquisition/reading. The ELL reads a variety of texts for a variety of purposes with an increasing level of comprehension in all content areas. ELLs may be at the beginning, intermediate, advanced, or advanced high stage of English language acquisition in reading. In order for the ELL to meet grade-level learning expectations across the foundation and enrichment curriculum, all instruction delivered in English must be linguistically accommodated (communicated, sequenced, and scaffolded) commensurate with the student's level of English language proficiency. For Kindergarten and Grade 1, certain of these student expectations apply to text read aloud for students not yet at the stage of decoding written text. The student is expected to:

(A) learn relationships between sounds and letters of the English language and decode (sound out) words using a combination of skills such as recognizing sound-letter relationships and identifying cognates, affixes, roots, and base words;

(B) recognize directionality of English reading such as left to right and top to bottom;

(C) develop basic sight vocabulary, derive meaning of environmental print, and comprehend English vocabulary and language structures used routinely in written classroom materials;

(D) use prereading supports such as graphic organizers, illustrations, and pretaught topic-related vocabulary and other prereading activities to enhance comprehension of written text;

(E) read linguistically accommodated content-area material with a decreasing need for linguistic accommodations as more English is learned;

(F) use visual and contextual support and support from peers and teachers to read grade-appropriate content-area text, to enhance and confirm understanding, and to develop vocabulary, to grasp language structures, and to tap background knowledge needed to comprehend increasingly challenging language;

(G) demonstrate comprehension of increasingly complex English by participating in shared reading, retelling or summarizing material, responding to questions, and taking notes commensurate with content-area and grade-level needs;

(H) read silently with increasing ease and comprehension for longer periods;

(I) demonstrate English comprehension and expand reading skills by employing basic reading skills such as demonstrating understanding of supporting ideas and details in text and graphic sources, summarizing text, and distinguishing main ideas from details commensurate with content-area needs;

(J) demonstrate English comprehension and expand reading skills by employing inferential skills such as predicting, making connections between ideas, drawing inferences and conclusions from text and graphic sources, and finding supporting text evidence commensurate with content-area needs; and

(K) demonstrate English comprehension and expand reading skills by employing analytical skills such as evaluating written information and performing critical analyses commensurate with content-area and grade level needs.

(5) Cross-curricular second-language acquisition/writing. The ELL writes in a variety of forms with increasing accuracy to effectively address a specific purpose and audience in all content areas. ELLs may be at the beginning, intermediate, advanced, or advanced high stage of English language acquisition in writing. In order for the ELL to meet grade-level learning expectations across foundation

and enrichment curriculum, all instruction delivered in English must be linguistically accommodated (communicated, sequenced, and scaffolded) commensurate with the student's level of English language proficiency. For Kindergarten and Grade 1, certain of these student expectations do not apply until the student has reached the stage of generating original written text using a standard writing system. The student is expected to:

(A) learn relationships between sounds and letters of the English language to represent sounds when writing in English;

(B) write using newly acquired basic vocabulary and content-based grade-level vocabulary;

(C) spell familiar English words with increasing accuracy, and employ English spelling patterns and rules with increasing accuracy as more English is acquired;

(D) edit writing for standard grammar and usage, including subject-verb agreement, pronoun agreement, and appropriate verb tenses commensurate with grade-level expectations as more English is acquired;

(E) employ increasingly complex grammatical structures in content-area writing commensurate with grade-level expectations, such as:

(i) using correct verbs, tenses, and pronouns/antecedents;

(ii) using possessive case (apostrophe *s*) correctly; and

(iii) using negatives and contractions correctly;

(F) write using a variety of grade-appropriate sentence lengths, patterns, and connecting words to combine phrases, clauses, and sentences in increasingly accurate ways as more English is acquired; and

(G) narrate, describe, and explain with increasing specificity and detail to fulfill content-area writing needs as more English is acquired.

ELPS Integration into Lesson Planning: Self-Assessment

Rate the current level of integration of the English Language Proficiency standards in your lessons.

A: Always
M: Mostly
S: Sometimes
N: Never

Indicator	A	M	S	N	Comments/Questions
I am aware of my district and school's program goals for ELLs.					
I am aware of specific instructional strategies to support ELLs in attaining English language proficiency.					
Students have opportunities to interact socially in my classroom.					
Students interact using academic English about key concepts in my classroom.					
Students read and write using academic English in my classroom.					
I set language objectives for my students.					
I have integrated the ELPS student expectations into my lessons.					
English learners have opportunities to build vocabulary and concept knowledge.					

How to Read the Cross-Curricular Student Expectations

Cross-curricular student expectations are organized into five categories for second-language acquisition:

1. learning strategies
2. listening
3. speaking
4. reading
5. writing

The knowledge and skills statement describes the intentions of the student expectations included in this section.

5) **Cross-curricular second-language acquisition/writing.** *The ELL writes in a variety of forms with increasing accuracy to effectively address a specific purpose and audience in all content areas. ELLs may be at the beginning, intermediate, advanced, or advanced high stage of English language acquisition in writing. In order for the ELL to meet grade-level learning expectations across foundation and enrichment curriculum, all instruction delivered in English must be linguistically accommodated (communicated, sequenced, and scaffolded) commensurate with the student's level of English language proficiency.* **For Kindergarten and Grade 1, certain of these student expectations do not apply until the student has reached the stage of generating original written text using a standard writing system.** *The student is expected to:*

(A) learn relationships between sounds and letters of the English language to represent sounds when writing in English;

(B) write using newly acquired basic vocabulary and content-based grade-level vocabulary;

(C) spell familiar English words with increasing accuracy, and employ English spelling patterns and rules with increasing accuracy as more English is acquired;

(D) edit writing for standard grammar and usage, including subject-verb agreement, pronoun agreement, and appropriate verb tenses commensurate with grade-level expectations as more English is acquired.

Note that some student expectations do not apply for students at early levels of literacy.

Each student expectation is listed individually by letter. These expectations can be used for creating curriculum frameworks, creating and documenting lesson plans, and writing language objectives for English Language Learners.

ELPS Integration Plan for Teachers

1. Identify language proficiency levels of all ELLs.

2. Identify appropriate linguistic accommodations and strategies for differentiating instruction.

3. Take steps to build a language-rich, interactive.

4. Identify cross-curricular student expectations of the ELPS (subsection c) that could be integrated as language objectives into existing content-area instruction.

5. Create focused lesson plans that target academic language and concept development.

Seven Steps to Building a Language-Rich Interactive Classroom

1. Teach students language and strategies to use when they don't know what to say.	1B Monitor language with self-corrective techniques 1D Speak using learning strategies 1F Use accessible language to learn new language 1H Expand repertoire of learning strategies to acquire new language 2D Monitor understanding and seek clarification 2E Use linguistic support to confirm and enhance understanding
2. Encourage students to speak in complete sentences.	1G Distinguish formal and informal English 3A Practice speaking using English sound system in new vocabulary 3C Speak using a variety of sentence structures 3D Speak using grade-level vocabulary in context 3F Speak using common and content-area vocabulary 3I Use oral language for formal and informal purposes
3. Randomize and rotate who is called on so students of all language levels can participate.	1G Distinguish formal and informal English 3A Practice speaking using English sound system in new vocabulary 3C Speak using a variety of sentence structures 3D Speak using grade-level vocabulary in context 3F Speak using common and content-area vocabulary 3I Use oral language for formal and informal purposes
4. Use response signals for students to monitor their own comprehension.	1B Monitor language with self-corrective techniques 2D Monitor understanding and seek clarification 2E Use linguistic support to confirm and enhance understanding 2I Demonstrate listening comprehension
5. Use visuals and a focus on vocabulary to build background.	1A Use prior knowledge to learn new language 1C Use techniques to learn new vocabulary 2A Distinguish sound and intonation 2B Recognize English sound system in new vocabulary 2F Derive meaning from a variety of media 3J Respond orally to a variety of media sources 4A Learn relationships of sounds and letters in English 4C Develop sight vocabulary and language structures 5C Spell familiar English words
6. Have students participate in structured reading activities.	4B Recognize directionality of English text 4D Use prereading supports 4E Read linguistically accommodated materials 4F Use visual and contextual supports to read text 4G Show comprehension of English text individually and in groups 4H Read silently with comprehension 4I Show comprehension through basic reading skills 4J Show comprehension through inferential skills 4K Show comprehension through analytical skills
7. Have students participate in structured conversation and writing activities.	**Conversation** 1E Use and reuse basic and academic language 2C Learn language heard in interactions and instruction 2H Understand implicit ideas and information 2G Understand general meaning, main points, and details of spoken language 3B Use new vocabulary in stories, descriptions, and classroom communication 3G Orally express opinions, ideas, and feelings 3E Share in cooperative groups 3H Orally narrate, describe, and explain **Writing** 5A Learn relationships between sounds and letters when writing 5B Write using newly acquired vocabulary 5D Edit writing 5E Employ complex grammatical structures 5F Write using variety of sentence structures and words 5G Narrate, describe, and explain in writing

Language Objectives Aligned to Cross-Curricular Student Expectations
(subsection c)

Learning Strategies	
1A: Use what they know about ___ to predict the meaning of . . . 1B: Check how well they are able to say . . . 1C: Use ___ to learn new vocabulary about . . . 1D: Use strategies such as ___ to discuss . . .	1E: Use and reuse the words/phrases ___ in a discussion/writing activity about . . . 1F: Use the phrase ___ to learn the meaning of . . . 1G: Use formal/informal English to describe . . . 1H: Use strategies such as ___ to learn the meaning of . . .

Listening	Speaking
2A: Recognize correct pronunciation of . . . 2B: Recognize sounds used in the words . . . 2C: Identify words and phrases heard in a discussion about . . . 2D: Check for understanding by . . . /Seek help by . . . 2E: Use supports such as ___ to enhance understanding of . . . 2F: Use ___ (media source) to learn/review . . . 2G: Describe general meaning, main points, and details heard in . . . 2H: Identify implicit ideas and information heard in . . . 2I: Demonstrate listening comprehension by . . .	3A: Pronounce the words ___ correctly. 3B: Use new vocabulary about ___ in stories, pictures, descriptions, and/or classroom communication . . . 3C: Speak using a variety of types of sentence stems about . . . 3D: Speak using the words ___ about . . . 3E: Share in cooperative groups about . . . 3F: Ask and give information using the words . . . 3G: Express opinions, ideas, and feelings about ___ using the words/phrases . . . 3H: Narrate, describe, and explain . . . 3I: Use formal/informal English to say . . . 3J: Respond orally to information from a variety of media sources about . . .

Reading	Writing
4A: Identify relationships between sounds and letters by . . . 4B: Recognize directionality of English text. 4C: Recognize the words/phrases . . . 4D: Use prereading supports such as ___ to understand . . . 4E: Read materials about ___ with support of simplified text/visuals/word banks as needed. 4F: Use visual and contextual supports to read . . . 4G: Show comprehension of English text about . . . 4H: Demonstrate comprehension of text read silently by . . . 4I: Show comprehension of text about ___ through basic reading skills such as . . . 4J: Show comprehension of text/graphic sources about ___ through inferential skills such as . . . 4K: Show comprehension of text about ___ through analytical skills such as . . .	5A: Learn relationships between sounds and letters when writing about . . . 5B: Write using newly acquired vocabulary about . . . 5C: Spell English words such as . . . 5D: Edit writing about . . . 5E: Use simple and complex sentences to write about . . . 5F: Write using a variety of sentence frames and selected vocabulary about . . . 5G: Narrate, describe, and explain in writing about . . .

ELPS Lesson Plan Template

Grade: ______________________ Topic: ______________________

Subject: ______________________ Date: ______________________

Content Objective *(Aligned with TEKS)*:	Language Objective *(Aligned with ELPS)*:
Vocabulary:	Visuals, Materials, & Texts:

Activities	Review & Checks for Understanding: *(Response Signals, Writing, Self-Assessment, Student Products, etc.)*
Activating Prior Knowledge *(Processes, Stems, and Strategies)*: Building Vocabulary and Concept Knowledge *(Processes, Stems, and Strategies)*: Structured Conversation and Writing *(Processes, Stems, and Strategies)*:	

ELPS Lesson Plan Activity Guide
(subsection c)

Instructional Strategies	ELPS Student Expectation Summaries	Classroom Strategies/Techniques	
Activating Prior Knowledge	1A Use prior knowledge to learn new language 1F Use accessible language to learn new language 4D Use prereading supports 4E Read linguistically accommodated content-area materials 4F Use visual, contextual, and peer supports to read text	• Anticipation Guides • Advance Organizers • Backwards Bookwalk • Chunking Input • Graphic Organizers	• KWL • Manipulatives • Prediction Café • Scanning • Vis. Literacy Frames • Visuals/Video
Building Vocabulary and Concept Knowledge	1C Use techniques to learn new vocabulary 1E Use and reuse basic and academic language 1H Expand repertoire of learning strategies to acquire language 2B Recognize English sound system in new vocabulary 2F Derive meaning from a variety of media 3A Practice speaking using English sound system in new vocabulary 3B Use new vocabulary in oral communication 4A Learn relationships of sounds and letters in English 4B Recognize directionality of English text 4C Develop sight vocabulary and language structures 4G Show comprehension of English text individually and in groups 4H Read silently with comprehension 4I Show comprehension through basic reading skills 4J Show comprehension through inferential skills 4K Show comprehension through analytical skills	• Affixes, Roots, and Cognates • Cloze Sentences • Concept Attainment • Comprehension Strategies • DRTA • Expert/Novice • Hi-lo readers Homophone/ Homograph Sort	• List/Sort/Label • Nonlinguistic Rep. • QtA • QAR • SQP2RS • Self-Assessment of Word Knowledge • Word Analysis • Think Alouds • Word Generation • Word Sorts • Word Walls
Structured Conversation	1B Monitor language with self-corrective techniques 1D Speak using learning strategies 1G Distinguish between formal and informal English 2A Distinguish sound and intonation 2C Learn language heard in interactions and instruction 2D Monitor understanding and seek clarification 2E Use support to confirm and enhance understanding 2G Understand general meaning, main points, and details 2H Understand implicit ideas and information 2I Demonstrate listening comprehension 3C Speak using a variety of sentence structures 3D Speak using grade-level, content-area vocabulary in context 3E Share in cooperative groups 3F Ask and give information using common and content-area vocabulary 3G Orally Express opinions, ideas, and feelings 3H Orally Narrate, describe, and explain 3I Use oral language for formal and informal purposes 3J Respond orally to a variety of media sources	• Accountable Conversation Stems • Instr. Conversation • Literature Circles • Num. Heads Together • Perspective-Based Activities • Question Answer Relationship (QAR)	• QSSSA • Response Triads • Reciprocal Teaching • Structured Conv. • Structured Academic Controversy • Think, Pair, Share, • Tiered Resp. Stems • W.I.T.
Writing	5A Learn relationships between sounds and letters when writing 5B Write using basic and content-area vocabulary 5C Spell familiar English words accurately 5D Edit writing for standard grammar and usage 5E Employ complex grammatical structures in content area 5F Write using variety of sentence structures and words 5G Narrate, describe, and explain in writing	• Book Reviews • Contextualized Grammar Instruction • Daily Oral Language • Double Entry Journals • Draw & Write • Genre Analysis and Imitation • Learning Logs • RAFT	• Scaffolded Paragraph Writing • Sentence Stems • Sentence Mark Up • Sentence Sorts • Summary Frames • Unit Study for ELLs • Writing Process • Writing Scaffolds

ELPS Lesson Plan Sample (Elementary)

Grade: 3rd **Topic:** Sequencing

Subject: English Language Arts **Date:**

Content Objective *(Aligned with TEKS)*:	**Language Objective *(Aligned with ELPS)*:**
(8A) SWBAT sequence the plot's main events and provide evidence from the text *Why Mosquitoes Buzz in People's Ears* to support their understanding	2(I) SWBAT demonstrate listening comprehension by sequencing information shared orally.
Vocabulary: First, order, next, then, before, after, finally, last. Text Specific Vocabulary: (*Why Mosquitoes . . .*) Nonsense, plotting, mischief, duty, warn, satisfy, danger, annoyed, frightened, startled, guilty conscience	**Visuals, Materials, & Texts:** Suggested English Book: *Why Mosquitoes Buzz in People's Ears* by Verna Aardema Suggested Spanish Book: *Que Monton De Tamales* (Too Many Tamales) by Gary Soto Poster paper, crayons or colored pencils, large chart paper, index cards

Activities	**Review & Checks for Understanding:** *(Response Signals, Writing, Self-Assessment, Student Products, etc.)*
Activating Prior Knowledge *(Processes, Stems, and Strategies)*: Have students think of their daily schedule. *What do you do first in the morning? *What are the events of your day? Discuss using sequencing words (first, order, next, then, before, after, finally, last) and make a class list to serve as a visual reminder for the Think, Pair, Share activity.	
Think, Pair, Share Have students pair with a partner and explain their daily schedule using complete sentences. **The first thing I do is . . .* **Then I . . . before I . . .* **Finally, the last thing I do . . .* Then have students write each event of their daily schedule on an index card and then trade them with their partner. Their partner will read the cards and put them in the correct chronological order. Then have the pair share the information about each other to the class.	Students raise hands to indicate they are ready to share a sentence stem.
Building Vocabulary and Concept Knowledge *(Processes, Stems, and Strategies)*: Introduce new vocabulary (both sequence vocabulary and text-specific) and as a class, create a simple definition and record on chart paper. Have students add new vocabulary to their Personal Dictionary or Word Study Book. Add new vocabulary to the Word Wall to aid in student comprehension of vocabulary and as a visual reminder.	Students record new vocabulary in their Personal Dictionaries.
Read the book *Why Mosquitoes Buzz in People's Ears* as the students actively listen. Then discuss the story and sequence the events on the chart paper, explaining the role of each animal throughout the book.	Students actively listen to the story.
Have students work in pairs or trios and assign them an animal from the story (mosquito, iguana, snake, rabbit, crow, monkey, owlet, Mother Owl, and King Lion). Each group will create a poster of their animal and write at least two sentences, using the new vocabulary words, to describe their animal's role in the story. *The first event that happened was . . . *After that the next event that occurred was . . . *At last the final event was . . . For example: **Mosquito** The **first** event that happened was the mosquito saw a farmer with a giant yam. **Then** the mosquito told the iguana what he had seen. **Iguana** The iguana thought it was such **nonsense**. **After** that he put sticks in his ears and went off into the woods.	Students select a sentence stem to begin writing and to incorporate the lesson's vocabulary. Students successfully write their animal's account in sequential order.
Structured Conversation and Writing *(Processes, Stems, and Strategies)*: Once the students are finished with their posters, they will present them to the class in sequential order and then post their poster as a visual reminder of the story. *My animal was . . . the event that occurred was . . . and this caused . . . *A vocabulary term I used in my writing today was . . . which means . . . *A term I heard my peers use today was . . . which means . . . Then, individually, have students create a complete sequence of events for the entire story, using the posters as a guide for their writing. Allow students to conduct a Gallery Walk to view the posters of their classmates to ensure the correct sequence. Share!	Students engage in sharing sentence stems as directed.

ELPS Lesson Plan Sample (Middle School)

Grade: 7th **Topic:** Point of View

Subject: English Language Arts **Date:**

Content Objective *(Aligned with TEKS)*: (6C) SWBAT analyze different forms of point of view, including first-person, third-person omniscient, and third-person limited.	**Language Objective *(Aligned with ELPS)*:** 4(K) SWBAT show comprehension of text about *The Three Little Pigs* through analytical skills such as evaluating and defending a position.
Vocabulary: First person, third person, perspective, debate, defend **Text Specific Vocabulary:** neighbor, spoil, impolite, framed, villain, victim, fault	**Visuals, Materials, & Texts:** Suggested Texts: *The Three Little Pigs* and *The True Story of the Three Little Pigs*

Activities

Review & Checks for Understanding: *(Response Signals, Writing, Self-Assessment, Student Products, etc.)*

Activating Prior Knowledge *(Processes, Stems, and Strategies)*:

Discuss first person and third person as a class and record pronouns that would be used in each category on a T-Chart and display as a visual reminder.

First Person	Third Person
I, we, us, our, me	he, him, they them, she, her

Have students think of a time they had a personal conflict with another person.

*Have you ever been accused of doing something wrong?
*Have you ever had to defend your actions?

Review & Checks: Students engage in the classroom discussion of pronouns.

Have students write a first-person account paragraph to describe their response to the question(s). Then pair students and have them share their paragraph with their partner. The partner will then rewrite the paragraph in third person by changing the appropriate pronouns.

Review & Checks: Students write their personal account of a conflict using first person.

Building Vocabulary and Concept Knowledge *(Processes, Stems, and Strategies)*:

Introduce new vocabulary, and as a class, create a simple definition and record on chart paper. Have students add new vocabulary to their Personal Dictionary or Word Study Book. Add new vocabulary to the Word Wall to aid in student comprehension of vocabulary and assist as a visual reminder.

Review & Checks: Students raise hands to show they are ready to share their third-person paragraph;

Read the stories of *The Three Little Pigs* and *The True Story of the Three Little Pigs* to the class as they actively listen. Once both stories are read, present the two points of view of the same event. These are the wolf's point of view and the pig's point of view of what happened when the houses were destroyed and two of the pigs were consumed.

Conduct a Ranking Activity and have the students line up according to whom they believe is telling the truth–the wolf or the pig. Have one side of the room represent the wolf, the other side the pig, and an imaginary line in between for those who are not sure what side to believe–they can be in the middle or leaning toward one side or the other.

Choose a person who is completely for the wolf and allow him/her to explain why the wolf is telling the truth and then have someone from the other side to defend the pig. Once both sides have had the opportunity to defend a side, allow the students to change their ranking. Be sure students are using complete sentences to defend their character.

*I believe the . . . is telling the truth because
*The . . . is guilty because . . .

Review & Checks: Students participate in a Total Response Signal–Ranking Activity.

Structured Conversation and Writing *(Processes, Stems, and Strategies)*:

<u>T-Chart, Pair, Debate</u>

Pair students with someone from the opposing side of the Ranking Activity. Together, have them complete a T-Chart, each filling in their chosen character's point of view–the wolf's side or the pig's side. Students will then defend their positions beginning with their sentence stems and debate the issues by writing out a script together of their dialogue. Allow students to perform their skit to the class as they defend their character's point of view.

Review & Checks: Students give reasons for defending their point of view;

<u>Writing</u>

Students will choose their favorite fairy tale and tell the story from another character's point of view. They may choose to be the Wicked Stepmother in *Cinderella* and tell the story from her perspective. (e.g. My husband dies and his slightly deranged daughter, who talks to mice and believes in Fairy Godmothers, expects to live in my house rent-free!)

Have the students follow the writing process as they first brainstorm ideas and then begin their first draft. Once they have completed their first draft, allow students to pair with a partner and read their version of the fairy tale. The partner will listen and provide feedback using the following stems:

*One thing I noticed in your story was . . .
*I really enjoyed the part when . . .
*One thing that might improve the story is . . .

Review & Checks: Students use sentence stems to pair, read, listen, and provide feedback to a peer regarding their writing.

ELPS Lesson Plan Sample (High School)

Grade: 10th **Topic:** Tone/Mood through Dialogue

Subject: English Language Arts **Date:**

Content Objective *(Aligned with TEKS)*:	**Language Objective *(Aligned with ELPS)*:**
(14A) SWBAT write using devices such as sensory details that define the mood or tone.	3(E) SWBAT share in cooperative groups about how to change a narrative paragraph into a dialogue
Vocabulary: Tone, mood, appreciative compassionate, humorous ambivalent, empathetic, condescending, pessimistic, pretentious, melancholy, mischievous, miserable, speculative, contemptuous, elated, horrified, etc.	**Visuals, Materials, & Texts:** Poster paper, magazine or newspaper pictures, chart paper, *Tone & Mood Words* Video (http://www.youtube.com/watch?v=jDUhDV-72S0)

Activities	**Review & Checks for Understanding:** *(Response Signals, Writing, Self-Assessment, Student Products, etc.)*
Activating Prior Knowledge *(Processes, Stems, and Strategies)* Introduce tone and mood through dialogue by reading two quotations to the students and compare the tone and mood of each passage from *Romeo and Juliet*. 1) *See, how she leans her cheek upon her hand! O that I were a glove upon that hand, That I might touch that cheek!* 2) *A glooming peace this morning with it brings. The sun for sorrow will not show his head. Go hence and have more talk of these sad things; Some shall be pardon'd, and some punished;* *What words help determine the mood? *How are the passages different? *What is the tone of the speaker?	Students raise hands to indicate they are ready to share a sentence stem.
Building Vocabulary and Concept Knowledge *(Processes, Stems, and Strategies)*: Create a list of tone and mood words, both positive and negative, and record them as a visual reminder. Have the students watch the video at http://www.youtube.com/watch?v=jDUhDV-72S0 and then have them create a visual representation of the words on their tone/mood list.	Students create a visual representation of a tone/mood word.
Introduce new vocabulary and as a class, create a simple definition and record on chart paper. Have students add new vocabulary to their Personal Dictionary or Word Study Book. Add new vocabulary to the Word Wall to aid in student comprehension of vocabulary and assist as a visual reminder. Using a narrative paragraph model, for the students, how to change the narrative paragraph into dialogue. Explain the correct punctuation in writing dialogue and demonstrate how to properly transform a narrative piece into dialogue.	Students transform the narrative piece to dialogue using different tone/mood words.
Working in pairs, the students will then take the same paragraph and again transform it to dialogue, but change the mood and tone by using their new vocabulary words. Assign each group a different tone/mood to convey through the use of dialogue and allow them to share their interpretations with the class.	Students create dialogues to go with pictures and determine the tone/mood of the image.
Structured Conversation and Writing *(Processes, Stems, and Strategies)*: Working in pairs or trios, give each group a picture from a magazine or newspaper and have them create a dialogue to go with their picture. They must use words from their word list to assist in setting the tone/mood of the dialogue. Then create a Gallery Walk and have the pictures posted around the room. Make photo copies of all the dialogues and give each group a copy of all the dialogues. They must read through all the dialogues and then determine which picture matches which dialogue. Then have each group read their dialogue as they reveal which picture is the match.	Students participate in a Gallery Walk.

This page is intentionally left blank.

ELAR TEKS and ELPS Side-by-Side
Kindergarten

Kindergarten ELAR TEKS	ELPS
(1) Reading/Beginning Reading Skills/Print Awareness. Students understand how English is written and printed. Students are expected to:	
(A) recognize that spoken words can be represented by print for communication;	4 (C) develop basic sight vocabulary, derive meaning of environmental print, and comprehend English vocabulary and language structures used routinely in written classroom materials
(B) identify upper and lower-case letters;	4 (A) learn relationships between sounds and letters of the English language and decode (sound out) words using a combination of skills such as recognizing sound-letter relationships and identifying cognates, affixes, roots, and base words
(C) demonstrate the one-to-one correspondence between a spoken word and a printed word in text;	4 (A) learn relationships between sounds and letters of the English language and decode (sound out) words using a combination of skills such as recognizing sound-letter relationships and identifying cognates, affixes, roots, and base words
(D) recognize the difference between a letter and a printed word;	4 (A) learn relationships between sounds and letters of the English language and decode (sound out) words using a combination of skills such as recognizing sound-letter relationships and identifying cognates, affixes, roots, and base words
(E) recognize that sentences are comprised of words separated by spaces and demonstrate the awareness of word boundaries (e.g., through kinesthetic or tactile actions such as clapping and jumping);	1 (H) develop and expand repertoire of learning strategies such as reasoning inductively or deductively, looking for patterns in language, and analyzing sayings and expressions commensurate with grade-level learning expectations
(F) hold a book right-side up, turn its pages correctly, and know that reading moves from top to bottom and left to right; and	4 (B) recognize directionality of English reading such as left to right and top to bottom
(G) identify different parts of a book (e.g., front and back covers, title page).	*No ELPS Correlation*
(2) Reading/Beginning Reading Skills/ Phonological Awareness. Students display phonological awareness. Students are expected to:	
(A) identify a sentence made up of a group of words;	*No ELPS Correlation*
(B) identify syllables in spoken words;	2 (A) distinguish sounds and intonation patterns of English with increasing ease
(C) orally generate rhymes in response to spoken words (e.g., "What rhymes with hat?");	3 (A) practice producing sounds of newly acquired vocabulary such as long and short vowels, silent letters, and consonant clusters to pronounce English words in a manner that is increasingly comprehensible
(D) distinguish orally presented rhyming pairs of words from non-rhyming pairs;	2 (A) distinguish sounds and intonation patterns of English with increasing ease

Kindergarten ELAR TEKS	ELPS
(2) cont . . . (E) recognize spoken alliteration or groups of words that begin with the same spoken onset or initial sound (e.g., "baby boy bounces the ball");	2 (A) distinguish sounds and intonation patterns of English with increasing ease
(F) blend spoken onsets and rhymes to form simple words (e.g., onset/c/ and rhyme/at/ make cat);	3 (A) practice producing sounds of newly acquired vocabulary such as long and short vowels, silent letters, and consonant clusters to pronounce English words in a manner that is increasingly comprehensible
(G) blend spoken phonemes to form one-syllable words (e.g.,/m/ . . . /a/ . . . /n/ says man);	3 (A) practice producing sounds of newly acquired vocabulary such as long and short vowels, silent letters, and consonant clusters to pronounce English words in a manner that is increasingly comprehensible
(H) isolate the initial sound in one-syllable spoken words; and	2 (A) distinguish sounds and intonation patterns of English with increasing ease
(I) segment spoken one-syllable words into two to three phonemes (e.g., dog: /d/ . . . /o/. . . /g/).	2 (A) distinguish sounds and intonation patterns of English with increasing ease
(3) Reading/Beginning Reading Skills/Phonics. Students use the relationships between letters and sounds, spelling patterns, and morphological analysis to decode written English. Students are expected to:	
(A) identify the common sounds that letters represent;	2 (A) distinguish sounds and intonation patterns of English with increasing ease 2 (B) recognize elements of the English sound system in newly acquired vocabulary such as long and short vowels, silent letters, and consonant clusters
(B) use knowledge of letter-sound relationships to decode regular words in text and independent of content (e.g., VC, CVC, CCVC, and CVCC words);	4 (A) learn relationships between sounds and letters of the English language and decode (sound out) words using a combination of skills such as recognizing sound-letter relationships and identifying cognates, affixes, roots, and base words
(C) recognize that new words are created when letters are changed, added, or deleted; and	4 (A) learn relationships between sounds and letters of the English language and decode (sound out) words using a combination of skills such as recognizing sound-letter relationships and identifying cognates, affixes, roots, and base words
(D) identify and read at least 25 high-frequency words from a commonly used list.	4 (C) develop basic sight vocabulary, derive meaning of environmental print, and comprehend English vocabulary and language structures used routinely in written classroom materials

(4) *Reading/Beginning Reading/Strategies. Students comprehend a variety of texts drawing on useful strategies as needed. Students are expected to:*	
Kindergarten ELAR TEKS	**ELPS**
(4) cont . . . (A) predict what might happen next in text based on the cover, title, and illustrations; and	4 (J) demonstrate English comprehension and expand reading skills by employing inferential skills such as predicting, making connections between ideas, drawing inferences and conclusions from text and graphic sources, and finding supporting text evidence commensurate with content-area needs
(B) ask and respond to questions about texts read aloud.	3 (F) ask and give information ranging from using a very limited bank of high-frequency, high-need, concrete vocabulary, including key words and expressions needed for basic communication in academic and social contexts, to using abstract and content-based vocabulary during extended speaking assignments 4 (G) demonstrate comprehension of increasingly complex English by participating in shared reading, retelling or summarizing material, responding to questions, and taking notes commensurate with content area and grade level needs
5) *Reading/Vocabulary Development. Students understand new vocabulary and use it correctly when reading and writing. Students are expected to:*	
(A) identify and use words that name actions, directions, positions, sequences, and locations;	1 (E) internalize new, basic and, academic language by using and reusing it in meaningful ways in speaking and writing activities that build concept and language attainment 4 (C) develop basic sight vocabulary, derive meaning of environmental print, and comprehend English vocabulary and language structures used routinely in written classroom materials
(B) recognize that compound words are made up of shorter words;	4 (A) learn relationships between sounds and letters of the English language and decode (sound out) words using a combination of skills such as recognizing sound-letter relationships and identifying cognates, affixes, roots, and base words

(C) identify and sort pictures of objects into conceptual categories (e.g., colors, shapes, textures); and	1 (E) internalize new, basic, and academic language by using and reusing it in meaningful ways in speaking and writing activities that build concept and language attainment 3 (B) expand and internalize initial English vocabulary by learning and using high-frequency English words necessary for identifying and describing people, places, and objects, by retelling simple stories and basic information represented or supported by pictures, and by learning and using routine language needed for classroom communication

Kindergarten ELAR TEKS	**ELPS**
(5) cont . . . (D) use a picture dictionary to find words.	1 (B) monitor oral and written language production and employ self-corrective techniques or other resources 1 (C) use strategic learning techniques such as concept mapping, drawing, memorizing, comparing, contrasting, and reviewing to acquire basic and grade-level vocabulary 4 (F) use visual and contextual support and support from peers and teachers to read grade-appropriate content area text, enhance and confirm understanding, and develop vocabulary, grasp of language structures, and background knowledge needed to comprehend increasingly challenging language
(6) *Reading/Comprehension of Literary Text/Theme and Genre. Students analyze, make inferences, and draw conclusions about theme and genre in different cultural, historical, and contemporary contexts and provide evidence from the text to support their understanding. Students are expected to:*	
(A) identify elements of a story including setting, character, and key events;	4 (K) demonstrate English comprehension and expand reading skills by employing analytical skills such as evaluating written information and performing critical analyses commensurate with content-area and grade-level needs
(B) discuss the big idea (theme) of a well-known folktale or fable and connect it to personal experience;	4 (I) demonstrate English comprehension and expand reading skills by employing basic reading skills such as demonstrating understanding of supporting ideas and details in text and graphic sources, summarizing text, and distinguishing main ideas from details commensurate with content-area needs 4 (J) demonstrate English comprehension and expand reading skills by employing inferential skills such as predicting, making connections between ideas,

	drawing inferences and conclusions from text and graphic sources, and finding supporting text evidence commensurate with content-area needs
(C) recognize sensory details; and	4 (K) demonstrate English comprehension and expand reading skills by employing analytical skills such as evaluating written information and performing critical analyses commensurate with content-area and grade-level needs
(D) recognize recurring phrases and characters in traditional fairy tales, lullabies, and folktales from various cultures	1 (H) develop and expand repertoire of learning strategies such as reasoning inductively or deductively, looking for patterns in language, and analyzing sayings and expressions commensurate with grade-level learning expectations 4 (K) demonstrate English comprehension and expand reading skills by employing analytical skills such as evaluating written information and performing critical analyses commensurate with content-area and grade-level needs

Kindergarten ELAR TEKS	ELPS
(7) *Reading/Comprehension of Literary Text/Poetry. Students understand, make inferences and draw conclusions about the structure and elements of poetry and provide evidence from text to support their understanding. Students are expected to respond to rhythm and rhyme in poetry by identifying a regular beat and similarities in word sounds.*	2 (A) distinguish sounds and intonation patterns of English with increasing ease 3 (H) narrate, describe, and explain with increasing specificity and detail as more English is acquired 4 (J) demonstrate English comprehension and expand reading skills by employing inferential skills such as predicting, making connections between ideas, drawing inferences and conclusions from text and graphic sources, and finding supporting text evidence commensurate with content-area needs
(8) *Reading/Comprehension of Literary Text/Fiction. Students understand, make inferences and draw conclusions about the structure and elements of fiction and provide evidence from text to support their understanding. Students are expected to:*	
(A) retell a main event from a story read aloud; and	2 (I) demonstrate listening comprehension of increasingly complex spoken English by following directions, retelling or summarizing spoken messages, responding to questions and requests, collaborating with peers, and taking notes commensurate with content and grade-level needs. 4 (G) demonstrate comprehension of increasingly complex English by participating in shared reading, retelling or summarizing material, responding to questions, and taking notes commensurate with content-area and grade-level needs 4 (J) demonstrate English comprehension and expand reading skills by employing inferential skills such as predicting, making connections between ideas, drawing inferences and conclusions from text and graphic sources, and finding supporting text evidence commensurate with content-area needs
(B) describe characters in a story and the reasons for	4 (K) demonstrate English comprehension and expand

their actions.	reading skills by employing analytical skills such as evaluating written information and performing critical analyses commensurate with content-area and grade-level needs
(9) Reading/Comprehension of Informational Text/Culture and History. Students analyze, make inferences and draw conclusions about the author's purpose in cultural, historical, and contemporary contexts and provide evidence from the text to support their understanding. Students are expected to identify the topic of an informational text heard.	4 (I) demonstrate English comprehension and expand reading skills by employing basic reading skills such as demonstrating understanding of supporting ideas and details in text and graphic sources, summarizing text, and distinguishing main ideas from details commensurate with content-area needs 4 (J) demonstrate English comprehension and expand reading skills by employing inferential skills such as predicting, making connections between ideas, drawing inferences and conclusions from text and graphic sources, and finding supporting text evidence commensurate with content-area needs
Kindergarten ELAR TEKS	**ELPS**
(9) cont . . .	4 (K) demonstrate English comprehension and expand reading skills by employing analytical skills such as evaluating written information and performing critical analyses commensurate with content-area and grade-level needs
(10) Reading/Comprehension of Informational Text/Expository Text. Students analyze, make inferences and draw conclusions about expository text, and provide evidence from text to support their understanding. Students are expected to:	
(A) identify the topic and details in expository text heard or read, referring to the words and/or illustrations;	2 (G) understand the general meaning, main points, and important details of spoken language ranging from situations in which topics, language, and contexts are familiar to unfamiliar 4 (E) read linguistically accommodated content-area material with a decreasing need for linguistic accommodations as more English is learned 4 (I) demonstrate English comprehension and expand reading skills by employing basic reading skills such as demonstrating understanding of supporting ideas and details in text and graphic sources, summarizing text, and distinguishing main ideas from details commensurate with content-area needs
(B) retell important facts in a text, heard or read;	2 (I) demonstrate listening comprehension of increasingly complex spoken English by following directions, retelling or summarizing spoken messages, responding to questions and requests, collaborating with peers, and taking notes commensurate with content and grade-level needs 4 (G) demonstrate comprehension of increasingly complex English by participating in shared reading, retelling or summarizing material, responding to questions, and taking notes commensurate with

	content-area and grade-level needs
(C) discuss the ways authors group information in text; and	4 (K) demonstrate English comprehension and expand reading skills by employing analytical skills such as evaluating written information and performing critical analyses commensurate with content-area and grade-level needs
(D) use titles and illustrations to make predictions about text.	4 (D) use prereading supports such as graphic organizers, illustrations, and pretaught topic-related vocabulary and other prereading activities to enhance comprehension of written text 4 (J) demonstrate English comprehension and expand reading skills by employing inferential skills such as predicting, making connections between ideas, drawing inferences and conclusions from text and graphic sources, and finding supporting text evidence commensurate with content-area needs

Kindergarten ELAR TEKS	ELPS
(11) Reading/Comprehension of Informational Text/Procedural Texts. Students understand how to glean and use information in procedural texts and documents. Students are expected to:	
(A) follow pictorial directions (e.g., recipes, science experiments); and	1 (A) use prior knowledge and experiences to understand meanings in English 4 (F) use visual and contextual support and support from peers and teachers to read grade-appropriate content-area text, enhance and confirm understanding, and develop vocabulary, grasp of language structures, and background knowledge needed to comprehend increasingly challenging language
(B) identify the meaning of specific signs (e.g., traffic signs, warning signs).	1 (A) use prior knowledge and experiences to understand meanings in English 4 (C) develop basic sight vocabulary, derive meaning of environmental print, and comprehend English vocabulary and language structures used routinely in written classroom materials
(12) Reading/Media Literacy. Students use comprehension skills to analyze how words, images, graphics, and sounds work together in various forms to impact meaning. Students continue to apply earlier standards with greater depth in increasingly more complex texts. Students (with adult assistance) are expected	

to:	
(A) identify different forms of media (e.g., advertisements, newspapers, radio programs); and	2 (F) listen to and derive meaning from a variety of media such as audio tape, video, DVD, and CD-ROM to build and reinforce concept and language attainment
(B) identify techniques used in media (e.g., sound, movement).	2 (F) listen to and derive meaning from a variety of media such as audio tape, video, DVD, and CD-ROM to build and reinforce concept and language attainment
Reading/Media Literacy - No Correlation	4 (H) read silently with increasing ease and comprehension for longer periods

Kindergarten ELAR TEKS	ELPS
(13) Writing/Writing Process. Students use elements of the writing process (planning, drafting, revising, editing, and publishing) to compose text. Students (with adult assistance) are expected to:	
(A) plan a first draft by generating ideas for writing through class discussion;	5 (B) write using newly acquired basic vocabulary and content-based grade-level vocabulary
(B) develop drafts by sequencing the action or details in the story;	5 (G) narrate, describe, and explain with increasing specificity and detail to fulfill content-area writing needs as more English is acquired
(C) revise drafts by adding details or sentences;	5 (D) edit writing for standard grammar and usage, including subject-verb agreement, pronoun agreement, and appropriate verb tenses commensurate with grade-level expectations as more English is acquired
(D) edit drafts by leaving spaces between letters and words; and	5 (D) edit writing for standard grammar and usage, including subject-verb agreement, pronoun agreement, and appropriate verb tenses commensurate with grade-level expectations as more English is acquired
(E) share writing with others.	3 (C) speak using a variety of grammatical structures, sentence lengths, sentence types, and connecting words with increasing accuracy and ease as more English is acquired 3(E) share information in cooperative learning interactions
(14) Writing/Literary Texts. Students write literary texts to express their ideas and feelings about real or imagined people, events, and ideas. Students are expected to:	
(A) dictate or write sentences to tell a story and put the sentences in chronological sequence; and	5 (G) narrate, describe, and explain with increasing specificity and detail to fulfill content area writing needs as more English is acquired

(B) write short poems.	1 (E) internalize new, basic, and academic language by using and reusing it in meaningful ways in speaking and writing activities that build concept and language attainment 5 (B) write using newly acquired basic vocabulary and content-based grade-level vocabulary
(15) Writing/Expository and Procedural Texts. Students write expository and procedural or work-related texts to communicate ideas and information to specific audiences for specific purposes. Students are expected to dictate or write information for lists, captions, or invitations.	5 (F) write using a variety of grade-appropriate sentence lengths, patterns, and connecting words to combine phrases, clauses, and sentences in increasingly accurate ways as more English is acquired
Kindergarten ELAR TEKS	**ELPS**
(16) Oral and Written Conventions/Conventions. Students understand the function of and use the conventions of academic language when speaking and writing. Students continue to apply earlier standards with greater complexity. Students are expected to:	
(A) understand and use the following parts of speech in the context of reading, writing, and speaking (with adult assistance): (i) past and future tenses when speaking; (ii) nouns (singular/plural); (iii) descriptive words; (iv) prepositions and simple prepositional phrases appropriately when speaking or writing (e.g., in, on, under, over); and (v) pronouns (e.g., I, me);	5 (E) employ increasingly complex grammatical structures in content-area writing commensurate with grade-level expectations, such as: (i) using correct verbs, tenses, and pronouns / antecedents (ii) using possessive case (apostrophes) correctly and (iii) using negatives and contractions correctly
(B) speak in complete sentences to communicate; and	3 (C) speak using a variety of grammatical structures, sentence lengths, sentence types, and connecting words with increasing accuracy and ease as more English is acquired
(C) use complete simple sentences.	5 (F) write using a variety of grade-appropriate sentence lengths, patterns, and connecting words to combine phrases, clauses, and sentences in increasingly accurate ways as more English is acquired
(17) Oral and Written Conventions/Handwriting, Capitalization, and Punctuation. Students write legibly and use appropriate capitalization and punctuation conventions in their compositions. Students are expected to:	
(A) form upper- and lower-case letters legibly using the basic conventions of print (left-to-right and top-to-bottom progression);	5 (A) learn relationships between sounds and letters of the English language to represent sounds when writing in English

(B) capitalize the first letter in a sentence; and	5 (D) edit writing for standard grammar and usage, including subject-verb agreement, pronoun agreement, and appropriate verb tenses commensurate with grade-level expectations as more English is acquired
(C) use punctuation at the end of a sentence.	5 (D) edit writing for standard grammar and usage, including subject-verb agreement, pronoun agreement, and appropriate verb tenses commensurate with grade-level expectations as more English is acquired
(18) Oral and Written Conventions/Spelling. Students spell correctly. Students are expected to:	
Kindergarten ELAR TEKS	**ELPS**
(18) cont . . . (A) use phonological knowledge to match sounds to letters;	5 (A) learn relationships between sounds and letters of the English language to represent sounds when writing in English
(B) use letter-sound correspondences to spell consonant-vowel-consonant (CVC) words (e.g., "cut"); and	5 (C) spell familiar English words with increasing accuracy, and employ English spelling patterns and rules with increasing accuracy as more English is acquired
(C) write one's own name.	5 (A) learn relationships between sounds and letters of the English language to represent sounds when writing in English
(19) Research/Research Plan. Students ask open-ended research questions and develop a plan for answering them. Students (with adult assistance) are expected to:	
(A) ask questions about topics of class-wide interest; and	1 (F) use accessible language and learn new and essential language in the process 3 (F) ask and give information ranging from using a very limited bank of high-frequency, high-need, concrete vocabulary, including key words and expressions needed for basic communication in academic and social contexts, to using abstract and content-based vocabulary during extended speaking assignments
(B) decide what sources or people in the classroom, school, library, or home can answer these questions	*No ELPS Correlation*
(20) Research/Gathering Sources. Students determine, locate, and explore the full range of relevant sources addressing a research question and systematically record the information they gather. Students (with adult assistance) are expected to:	

(A) gather evidence from provided text sources; and	4 (J) demonstrate English comprehension and expand reading skills by employing inferential skills such as predicting, making connections between ideas, drawing inferences and conclusions from text and graphic sources, and finding supporting text evidence commensurate with content-area needs
(B) use pictures in conjunction with writing when documenting research.	4 (F) use visual and contextual support and support from peers and teachers to read grade-appropriate content-area text, enhance and confirm understanding, and develop vocabulary, grasp of language structures, and background knowledge needed to comprehend increasingly challenging language 4 (J) demonstrate English comprehension and expand reading skills by employing inferential skills such as predicting, making connections between ideas, drawing inferences and conclusions from text and graphic sources, and finding supporting text evidence commensurate with content-area needs

Kindergarten ELAR TEKS	ELPS
(21) Listening and Speaking/Listening. Students use comprehension skills to listen attentively to others in formal and informal settings. Students continue to apply earlier standards with greater complexity. Students are expected to:	
(A) listen attentively by facing speakers and asking questions to clarify information; and	2 (D) monitor understanding of spoken language during classroom instruction and interactions and seek clarification as needed 2 (H) understand implicit ideas and information in increasingly complex spoken language commensurate with grade-level learning expectations 3 (F) ask and give information ranging from using a very limited bank of high-frequency, high-need, concrete vocabulary, including key words and expressions needed for basic communication in academic and social contexts, to using abstract and content-based vocabulary during extended speaking assignments
(B) follow oral directions that involve a short related sequence of actions.	2 (E) use visual, contextual, and linguistic support to enhance and confirm understanding of increasingly complex and elaborated spoken language 2 (G) understand the general meaning, main points, and important details of spoken language ranging from situations in which topics, language, and contexts are familiar to unfamiliar 2 (I) demonstrate listening comprehension of increasingly complex spoken English by following directions, retelling or summarizing spoken messages, responding to questions and requests, collaborating with peers, and taking notes commensurate with content and grade-level needs

(22) *Listening and Speaking/Speaking. Students speak clearly and to the point, using the conventions of language. Students continue to apply earlier standards with greater complexity. Students are expected to share information and ideas by speaking audibly and clearly using the conventions of language.*	1 (D) speak using learning strategies such as requesting assistance, employing nonverbal cues, and using synonyms and circumlocution (conveying ideas by defining or describing when exact English words are not known) 3 (B) expand and internalize initial English vocabulary by learning and using high-frequency English words necessary for identifying and describing people, places, and objects, by retelling simple stories and basic information represented or supported by pictures, and by learning and using routine language needed for classroom communication 3 (D) speak using grade-level content-area vocabulary in context to internalize new English words and build academic language proficiency
Kindergarten ELAR TEKS	**ELPS**
(22) cont . . .	3 (F) ask and give information ranging from using a very limited bank of high-frequency, high-need, concrete vocabulary, including key words and expressions needed for basic communication in academic and social contexts, to using abstract and content-based vocabulary during extended speaking assignments 3 (G) express opinions, ideas, and feelings ranging from communicating single words and short phrases to participating in extended discussions on a variety of social and grade-appropriate academic topics 3 (H) narrate, describe, and explain with increasing specificity and detail as more English is acquired 3 (I) adapt spoken language appropriately for formal and informal purposes 3 (J) respond orally to information presented in a wide variety of print, electronic, audio, and visual media to build and reinforce concept and language attainment
(23) *Listening and Speaking/Teamwork. Students work productively with others in teams. Students continue to apply earlier standards with greater complexity. Students are expected to follow agreed-upon rules for discussion, including taking turns and speaking one at a time.*	3 (E) share information in cooperative learning interactions 2 (I) demonstrate listening comprehension of increasingly complex spoken English by following directions, retelling or summarizing spoken messages, responding to questions and requests, collaborating with peers, and taking notes 1 (B) monitor oral and written language production and employ self-corrective techniques or other resources 1 (G) demonstrate an increasing ability to distinguish between formal and informal English and an increasing knowledge of when to use each one commensurate with grade-level learning expectations

ELAR TEKS and ELPS Side-by-Side
First-Grade

First-Grade ELAR TEKS	ELPS
(1) Reading/Beginning Reading Skills/Print Awareness. Students understand how English is written and printed. Students are expected to:	
(A) recognize that spoken words are represented in written English by specific sequences of letters;	4 (A) learn relationships between sounds and letters of the English language and decode (sound out) words using a combination of skills such as recognizing sound-letter relationships and identifying cognates, affixes, roots, and base words
(B) identify upper and lower-case letters;	4 (A) learn relationships between sounds and letters of the English language and decode (sound out) words using a combination of skills such as recognizing sound-letter relationships and identifying cognates, affixes, roots, and base words
(C) sequence the letters of the alphabet;	*No ELPS Correlation*
(D) recognize the distinguishing features of a sentence (e.g., capitalization of first word, ending punctuation);	1 (H) develop and expand repertoire of learning strategies such as reasoning inductively or deductively, looking for patterns in language, and analyzing sayings and expressions commensurate with grade-level learning expectations
(E) read texts by moving from top to bottom of the page and tracking words from left to right with return sweep; and	4(B) recognize directionality of English reading such as left to right and top to bottom
(F) identify the information that different parts of a book provide (e.g., title, author, illustrator, table of contents).	*No ELPS Correlation*
(2) Reading/Beginning Reading Skills/Phonological Awareness. Students display phonological awareness. Students are expected to:	
(A) orally generate a series of original rhyming words using a variety of phonograms (e.g., *ake, ant, ain*) and consonant blends (e.g., *bl, st, tr*);	3 (A) practice producing sounds of newly acquired vocabulary such as long and short vowels, silent letters, and consonant clusters to pronounce English words in a manner that is increasingly comprehensible 4 (A) learn relationships between sounds and letters of the English language and decode (sound out) words using a combination of skills such as recognizing sound-letter relationships and identifying cognates, affixes, roots, and base words
B) distinguish between long and short vowel sounds in spoken one-syllable words (e.g., *bit/bite*);	2 (A) distinguish sounds and intonation patterns of English with increasing ease 2 (B) recognize elements of the English sound system in newly acquired vocabulary such as long and short vowels, silent letters, and consonant clusters 4 (A) learn relationships between sounds and letters of the English language and decode (sound out) words using a combination of skills such as recognizing sound-letter relationships and identifying cognates, affixes, roots, and base words

First-Grade ELAR TEKS	ELPS
(2) cont . . . (C) recognize the change in a spoken word when a specified phoneme is added, changed, or removed (e.g., /b/l/o/w/ to/g/l/o/w/);	2 (A) distinguish sounds and intonation patterns of English with increasing ease 2 (B) recognize elements of the English sound system in newly acquired vocabulary such as long and short vowels, silent letters, and consonant clusters 4 (A) learn relationships between sounds and letters of the English language and decode (sound out) words using a combination of skills such as recognizing sound-letter relationships and identifying cognates, affixes, roots, and base words
(D) blend spoken phonemes to form one and two-syllable words, including consonant blends (e.g., spr);	3 (A) practice producing sounds of newly acquired vocabulary such as long and short vowels, silent letters, and consonant clusters to pronounce English words in a manner that is increasingly comprehensible 4 (A) learn relationships between sounds and letters of the English language and decode (sound out) words using a combination of skills such as recognizing sound-letter relationships and identifying cognates, affixes, roots, and base words
(E) isolate initial, medial, and final sounds in one-syllable spoken words; and	2 (A) distinguish sounds and intonation patterns of English with increasing ease 2 (B) recognize elements of the English sound system in newly acquired vocabulary such as long and short vowels, silent letters, and consonant clusters
(F) segment spoken one-syllable words of three to five phonemes into individual phonemes (e.g., splat =/s/p/l/a/t/).	3 (A) practice producing sounds of newly acquired vocabulary such as long and short vowels, silent letters, and consonant clusters to pronounce English words in a manner that is increasingly comprehensible
(3) *Reading/Beginning Reading Skills/Phonics. Students use the relationships between letters and sounds, spelling patterns, and morphological analysis to decode written English. Students will continue to apply earlier standards with greater depth in increasingly more complex texts. Students are expected to:*	

First-Grade ELAR TEKS	ELPS
(3) cont . . . (A) decode words in context and in isolation by applying common letter-sound correspondences, including: (i) single letters (consonants) including b, c=/k/, c=/s/, d, f, g=/g/ (hard), g=/j/ (soft), h, j, k, l, m, n, p, qu=/kw/, r, s=/s/, s=/z/, t, v, w, x=/ks/, y, and z; (ii) single letters (vowels) including short a, short e, short i, short o, short u, long a (a-e), long e (e), long i (i-e), long o (o-e), long u (u-e), y=long e, and y=long i; (iii) consonant blends (e.g., bl, st); (iv) consonant digraphs including ch, tch, sh, th=as in thing, wh, ng, ck, kn, -dge, and ph; (v) vowel digraphs including oo as in foot, oo as in moon, ea as in eat, ea as in bread, ee, ow as in how, ow as in snow, ou as in out, ay,ai, aw, au, ew, oa, ie as in chief, ie as in pie, and -igh; and (vi) vowel diphthongs including oy, oi, ou, and ow;	2 (B) recognize elements of the English sound system in newly acquired vocabulary such as long and short vowels, silent letters, and consonant clusters 4 (A) learn relationships between sounds and letters of the English language and decode (sound out) words using a combination of skills such as recognizing sound-letter relationships and identifying cognates, affixes, roots, and base words
(B) combine sounds from letters and common spelling patterns (e.g., consonant blends, long and shortvowel patterns) to create recognizable words;	4 (A) learn relationships between sounds and letters of the English language and decode (sound out) words using a combination of skills such as recognizing sound-letter relationships and identifying cognates, affixes, roots, and base words 5 (A) learn relationships between sounds and letters of the English language to represent sounds when writing in English 5 (C) spell familiar English words with increasing accuracy, and employ English spelling patterns and rules with increasing accuracy as more English is acquired
(C) use common syllabication patterns to decode words, including: (i) closed syllable (CVC) (e.g., mat, rab-bit); (ii) open syllable (CV) (e.g., he, ba-by); (iii) final stable syllable (e.g., ap-ple, a-ble); (iv) vowel-consonant-silent "e" words (VCe) (e.g., kite, hide); (v) vowel digraphs and diphthongs (e.g., boy-hood, oat-meal); and (vi) r-controlled vowel sounds (e.g., tar); including er, ir, ur, ar, and or);	1 (H) develop and expand repertoire of learning strategies such as reasoning inductively or deductively, looking for patterns in language, and analyzing sayings and expressions commensurate with grade-level learning expectations 2 (B) recognize elements of the English sound system in newly acquired vocabulary such as long and short vowels, silent letters, and consonant clusters 4 (A) learn relationships between sounds and letters of the English language and decode (sound out) words using a combination of skills such as recognizing sound-letter relationships and identifying cognates, affixes, roots, and base words
(D) decode words with common spelling patterns (e.g., -ink, -onk, -ick);	4 (A) learn relationships between sounds and letters of the English language and decode (sound out) words using a combination of skills such as recognizing sound-letter relationships and identifying cognates, affixes, roots, and base words 5 (C) spell familiar English words with increasing accuracy, and employ English spelling patterns and rules with increasing accuracy as more English is acquired
(E) read base words with inflectional endings (e.g., plurals, past tenses);	4 (A) learn relationships between sounds and letters of the English language and decode (sound out) words using a combination of skills such as recognizing sound-letter relationships and identifying cognates, affixes, roots, and base words
(F) use knowledge of the meaning of base words to identify and read common compound words (e.g., football, popcorn, daydream);	1 (A) use prior knowledge and experiences to understand meanings in English

First-Grade ELAR TEKS	ELPS
(3)(F) cont . . .	4 (A) learn relationships between sounds and letters of the English language and decode (sound out) words using a combination of skills such as recognizing sound-letter relationships and identifying cognates, affixes, roots, and base words
(G) identify and read contractions (e.g., isn't, can't);	1 (H) develop and expand repertoire of learning strategies such as reasoning inductively or deductively, looking for patterns in language, and analyzing sayings and expressions commensurate with grade-level learning expectations 4 (C) develop basic sight vocabulary, derive meaning of environmental print, and comprehend English vocabulary and language structures used routinely in written classroom materials
(H) identify and read at least 100 high-frequency words from a commonly used list; and	4 (C) develop basic sight vocabulary, derive meaning of environmental print, and comprehend English vocabulary and language structures used routinely in written classroom materials
(I) monitor accuracy of decoding.	1 (B) monitor oral and written language production and employ self-corrective techniques or other resources
(4) Reading/Beginning Reading/Strategies. Students comprehend a variety of texts drawing on useful strategies as needed. Students are expected to:	
(A) confirm predictions about what will happen next in text by "reading the part that tells"	4 (J) demonstrate English comprehension and expand reading skills by employing inferential skills such as predicting, making connections between ideas, drawing inferences and conclusions from text and graphic sources, and finding supporting text evidence commensurate with content-area needs
(B) ask relevant questions, seek clarification, and locate facts and details about stories and other texts; and	3 (F) ask and give information ranging from using a very limited bank of high-frequency, high-need, concrete vocabulary, including key words and expressions needed for basic communication in academic and social contexts, to using abstract and content-based vocabulary during extended speaking assignments 4 (I) demonstrate English comprehension and expand reading skills by employing basic reading skills such as demonstrating understanding of supporting ideas and details in text and graphic sources, summarizing text, and distinguishing main ideas from details commensurate with content-area needs
(C) establish purpose for reading selected texts and monitor comprehension, making corrections and adjustments when that understanding breaks down (e.g., identifying clues, using background knowledge, generating questions, rereading a portion aloud).	4 (F) use visual and contextual support and support from peers and teachers to read grade-appropriate content-area text, enhance and confirm understanding, and develop vocabulary, grasp of language structures, and background knowledge needed to comprehend increasingly challenging language

First-Grade ELAR TEKS	ELPS
(4)(C) cont . . .	4 (J) demonstrate English comprehension and expand reading skills by employing inferential skills such as predicting, making connections between ideas, drawing inferences and conclusions from text and graphic sources, and finding supporting text evidence commensurate with content-area needs
(5) *Reading/Fluency. Students read grade-level text with fluency and comprehension. Students are expected to read aloud grade-level appropriate text with fluency (rate, accuracy, expression, appropriate phrasing) and comprehension.*	4 (E) read linguistically accommodated content-area material with a decreasing need for linguistic accommodations as more English is learned 4 (H) read silently with increasing ease and comprehension for longer periods
(6) *Reading/Vocabulary Development. Students understand new vocabulary and use it when reading and writing. Students are expected to:*	
(A) identify words that name actions (verbs) and words that name persons, places, or things (nouns);	1 (E) internalize new, basic, and academic language by using and reusing it in meaningful ways in speaking and writing activities that build concept and language attainment
(B) determine the meaning of compound words using knowledge of the meaning of their individual component words (e.g., lunchtime);	1 (F) use accessible language and learn new and essential language in the process 4 (A) learn relationships between sounds and letters of the English language and decode (sound out) words using a combination of skills such as recognizing sound-letter relationships and identifying cognates, affixes, roots, and base words
(C) determine what words mean from how they are used in a sentence, either heard or read;	4 (F) use visual and contextual support and support from peers and teachers to read grade-appropriate content-area text, to enhance and confirm understanding, and to develop vocabulary, to grasp language structures, and to tap background knowledge needed to comprehend increasingly challenging language
(D) identify and sort words into conceptual categories (e.g., opposites, living things);	1 (C) use strategic learning techniques such as concept mapping, drawing, memorizing, comparing, contrasting, and reviewing to acquire basic and grade-level vocabulary 1 (E) internalize new, basic, and academic language by using and reusing it in meaningful ways in speaking and writing activities that build concept and language attainment
(E) alphabetize a series of words to the first or second letter and use a dictionary to find words.	1 (B) monitor oral and written language production and employ self-corrective techniques or other resources

First-Grade ELAR TEKS	ELPS
(7) *Reading/Comprehension of Literary Text/Theme and Genre. Students analyze, make inferences and draw conclusions about theme and genre in different cultural, historical, and contemporary contexts and provide evidence from the text to support their understanding. Students are expected to:*	
(A) connect the meaning of a well-known story or fable to personal experiences; and	1 (A) use prior knowledge and experiences to understand meanings in English 4 (J) demonstrate English comprehension and expand reading skills by employing inferential skills such as predicting, making connections between ideas, drawing inferences and conclusions from text and graphic sources, and finding supporting text evidence commensurate with content-area needs
(B) explain the function of recurring phrases (e.g., "Once upon a time" or "They lived happily ever after") in traditional folk and fairy tales.	1 (H) develop and expand repertoire of learning strategies such as reasoning inductively or deductively, looking for patterns in language, and analyzing sayings and expressions commensurate with grade-level learning expectations 4 (I) demonstrate English comprehension and expand reading skills by employing basic reading skills such as demonstrating understanding of supporting ideas and details in text and graphic sources and summarizing
(8) *Reading/Comprehension of Literary Text/Poetry. Students understand, make inferences and draw conclusions about the structure and elements of poetry and provide evidence from text to support their understanding. Students are expected to respond to and use rhythm, rhyme, and alliteration in poetry.*	1 (H) develop and expand repertoire of learning strategies such as reasoning inductively or deductively, looking for patterns in language, and analyzing sayings and expressions commensurate with grade-level learning expectations 4 (J) demonstrate English comprehension and expand reading skills by employing inferential skills such as predicting, making connections between ideas, drawing inferences and conclusions from text and graphic sources, and finding supporting text evidence commensurate with content-area needs
(9) *Reading/Comprehension of Literary Text/Fiction. Students understand, make inferences, and draw conclusions about the structure and elements of fiction and provide evidence from text to support their understanding. Students are expected to:*	
(A) describe the plot (problem and solution) and retell a story's beginning, middle, and end with attention to the sequence of events; and	4 (G) demonstrate comprehension of increasingly complex English by participating in shared reading, retelling or summarizing material, responding to questions, and taking notes commensurate with content-area and grade-level needs
(B) describe characters in a story and the reasons for their actions and feelings.	4 (K) demonstrate English comprehension and expand reading skills by employing analytical skills such as evaluating written information and performing critical analyses commensurate with content-area and grade-

	level needs
First-Grade ELAR TEKS	**ELPS**
(10) *Reading/Comprehension of Literary Text/Literary Nonfiction. Students understand, make inferences and draw conclusions about the varied structural patterns and features of literary nonfiction and respond by providing evidence from text to support their understanding. Students are expected to determine whether a story is true or fantasy and explain why.*	4 (J) demonstrate English comprehension and expand reading skills by employing inferential skills such as predicting, making connections between ideas, drawing inferences and conclusions from text and graphic sources, and finding supporting text evidence commensurate with content-area needs
(11) *Reading/Comprehension of Literary Text/Sensory Language. Students understand, make inferences, and draw conclusions about how an author's sensory language creates imagery in literary text and provide evidence from text to support their understanding. Students are expected to recognize sensory details in literary text.*	1 (H) develop and expand repertoire of learning strategies such as reasoning inductively or deductively, looking for patterns in language, and analyzing sayings and expressions commensurate with grade-level learning expectations 4 (J) demonstrate English comprehension and expand reading skills by employing inferential skills such as predicting, making connections between ideas, drawing inferences and conclusions from text and graphic sources, and finding supporting text evidence commensurate with content-area needs
(12) *Reading/Comprehension of Text/Independent Reading. Students read independently for sustained periods of time and produce evidence of their reading. Students are expected to read independently for a sustained period of time.*	4 (E) read linguistically accommodated content-area material with a decreasing need for linguistic accommodations as more English is learned 4 (H) read silently with increasing ease and comprehension for longer periods
(13) *Reading/Comprehension of Informational Text/Culture and History. Students analyze, make inferences, and draw conclusions about the author's purpose in cultural, historical, and contemporary contexts and provide evidence from the text to support their understanding. Students are expected to identify the topic and explain the author's purpose in writing about the text.*	4 (J) demonstrate English comprehension and expand reading skills by employing inferential skills such as predicting, making connections between ideas, drawing inferences and conclusions from text and graphic sources, and finding supporting text evidence commensurate with content-area needs 4 (K) demonstrate English comprehension and expand reading skills by employing analytical skills such as evaluating written information and performing critical analyses commensurate with content-area and grade-level needs
(14) *Reading/Comprehension of Informational Text/Expository Text. Students analyze, make inferences and draw conclusions about expository text and provide evidence from text to*	

support their understanding. Students are expected to:	
First-Grade ELAR TEKS	**ELPS**
(14) cont . . . (A) restate the main idea, heard or read;	4 (I) demonstrate English comprehension and expand reading skills by employing basic reading skills such as demonstrating understanding of supporting ideas and details in text and graphic sources, summarizing text, and distinguishing main ideas from details commensurate with content-area needs
(B) identify important facts or details in text, heard or read;	4 (I) demonstrate English comprehension and expand reading skills by employing basic reading skills such as demonstrating understanding of supporting ideas and details in text and graphic sources, summarizing text, and distinguishing main ideas from details commensurate with content-area needs
(C) retell the order of events in a text by referring to the words and/or illustrations; and	4 (G) demonstrate comprehension of increasingly complex English by participating in shared reading, retelling or summarizing material, responding to questions, and taking notes commensurate with content-area and grade-level needs
(D) use text features (e.g., title, tables of contents, illustrations) to locate specific information in text.	4 (I) demonstrate English comprehension and expand reading skills by employing basic reading skills such as demonstrating understanding of supporting ideas and details in text and graphic sources, summarizing text, and distinguishing main ideas from details commensurate with content-area needs
(15) Reading/Comprehension of Informational Text/Procedural Texts. Students understand how to glean and use information in procedural texts and documents. Students are expected to:	
(A) follow written multistep directions with picture cues to assist with understanding;	4 (D) use prereading supports such as graphic organizers, illustrations, and pretaught topic-related vocabulary and other prereading activities to enhance comprehension of written text 4 (E) read linguistically accommodated content-area material with a decreasing need for linguistic accommodations as more English is learned

(B) explain the meaning of specific signs and symbols (e.g., map features).	1 (A) use prior knowledge and experiences to understand meanings in English

First-Grade ELAR TEKS	ELPS
(16) Reading/Media Literacy. Students use comprehension skills to analyze how words, images, graphics, and sounds work together in various forms to impact meaning. Students continue to apply earlier standards with greater depth in increasingly more complex texts. Students are expected to:	
(A) recognize different purposes of media (e.g., informational, entertainment) (with adult assistance); and	2 (F) listen to and derive meaning from a variety of media such as audio tape, video, DVD, and CD-ROM to build and reinforce concept and language attainment
(B) identify techniques used in media (e.g., sound, movement).	2 (F) listen to and derive meaning from a variety of media such as audio tape, video, DVD, and CD-ROM to build and reinforce concept and language attainment

(17) Writing/Writing Process. Students use elements of the writing process (planning, drafting, revising, editing, and publishing) to compose text. Students are expected to:	
(A) plan a first draft by generating ideas for writing (e.g., drawing, sharing ideas, listing key ideas);	1 (C) use strategic learning techniques such as concept mapping, drawing, memorizing, comparing, contrasting, and reviewing to acquire basic and grade-level vocabulary 3 (E) share in cooperative learning interactions 5 (B) write using newly acquired basic vocabulary and content-based grade-level vocabulary
(B) develop drafts by sequencing ideas through writing sentences;	5 (F) write using a variety of grade-appropriate sentence lengths, patterns, and connecting words to combine phrases, clauses, and sentences in increasingly accurate ways as more English is acquired

(C) revise drafts by adding or deleting a word, phrase, or sentence;	5 (D) edit writing for standard grammar and usage, including subject-verb agreement, pronoun agreement, and appropriate verb tenses commensurate with grade-level expectations as more English is acquired
(D) edit drafts for grammar, punctuation, and spelling using a teacher-developed rubric;	5 (D) edit writing for standard grammar and usage, including subject-verb agreement, pronoun agreement, and appropriate verb tenses commensurate with grade-level expectations as more English is acquired 5 (E) employ increasingly complex grammatical structures in content-area writing commensurate with grade-level expectations, such as: (i) using correct verbs, tenses, and pronouns / antecedents (ii) using possessive case (apostrophes) correctly (iii) using negatives and contractions correctly
First-Grade ELAR TEKS	**ELPS**
(17) cont . . . (E) publish and share writing with others.	3 (C) speak using a variety of grammatical structures, sentence lengths, sentence types, and connecting words with increasing accuracy and ease as more English is acquired 3 (E) Share in cooperative learning interactions
(18) Writing/Literary Texts. Students write literary texts to express their ideas and feelings about real or imagined people, events, and ideas. Students are expected to:	
(A) write brief stories that include a beginning, middle, and end;	5 (F) write using a variety of grade-appropriate sentence lengths, patterns, and connecting words to combine phrases, clauses, and sentences in increasingly accurate ways as more English is acquired 5 (G) narrate, describe, and explain with increasing specificity and detail to fulfill content-area writing needs as more English is acquired
(B) write short poems that convey sensory details.	1 (E) internalize new, basic, and academic language by using and reusing it in meaningful ways in speaking and writing activities that build concept and language attainment 5 (B) write using newly acquired basic vocabulary and content-based grade-level vocabulary
(19) Writing/Expository and Procedural Texts. Students write expository and procedural or work-related texts to communicate ideas and information to specific audiences for specific	

purposes. Students are expected to:	
(A) write brief compositions about topics of interest to the student;	5 (F) write using a variety of grade-appropriate sentence lengths, patterns, and connecting words to combine phrases, clauses, and sentences in increasingly accurate ways as more English is acquired 5 (G) narrate, describe, and explain with increasing specificity and detail to fulfill content-area writing needs as more English is acquired
(B) write short letters that put ideas in a chronological or logical sequence and use appropriate conventions (e.g., date, salutation, closing); and	5 (F) write using a variety of grade-appropriate sentence lengths, patterns, and connecting words to combine phrases, clauses, and sentences in increasingly accurate ways as more English is acquired; 5 (G) narrate, describe, and explain with increasing specificity and detail to fulfill content-area writing needs as more English is acquired
(C) write brief comments on literary or informational texts.	5 (F) write using a variety of grade-appropriate sentence lengths, patterns, and connecting words to combine phrases, clauses, and sentences in increasingly accurate ways as more English is acquired 5 (G) narrate, describe, and explain with increasing specificity and detail to fulfill content-area writing needs as more English is acquired

First-Grade ELAR TEKS	ELPS
(20) Oral and Written Conventions/Conventions. Students understand the function of and use the conventions of academic language when speaking and writing. Students continue to apply earlier standards with greater complexity. Students are expected to:	
(A) understand and use the following parts of speech in the context of reading, writing, and speaking: (i) verbs (past, present, and future); (ii) nouns (singular/plural, common/proper); (iii) adjectives (e.g., descriptive: green, tall); (iv) adverbs (e.g., time: before, next); (v) prepositions and prepositional phrases; (vi) pronouns (e.g., I, me); (vii) time-order transition words;	5 (E) employ increasingly complex grammatical structures in content-area writing commensurate with grade-level expectations, such as: (i) using correct verbs, tenses, and pronouns / antecedents (ii) using possessive case (apostrophes) correctly (iii) using negatives and contractions correctly 5 (F) write using a variety of grade-appropriate sentence lengths, patterns, and connecting words to combine phrases, clauses, and sentences in increasingly accurate ways as more English is acquired
(B) speak in complete sentences with correct subject-verb agreement;	3 (C) speak using a variety of grammatical structures, sentence lengths, sentence types, and connecting words with increasing accuracy and ease as more English is acquired
(C) ask questions with appropriate subject-verb inversion.	3 (F) ask and give information ranging from using a very limited bank of high-frequency, high-need, concrete vocabulary, including key words and expressions needed for basic communication in academic and social contexts, to using abstract and content-based vocabulary during extended speaking assignments
(21) Oral and Written Conventions/Handwriting, Capitalization, and Punctuation. Students write	

legibly and use appropriate capitalization and punctuation conventions in their compositions. Students are expected to:	
(A) form upper and lower-case letters legibly in text, using the basic conventions of print (left-to-right and top-to-bottom progression), including spacing between words and sentences;	5 (A) learn relationships between sounds and letters of the English language to represent sounds when writing in English
(B) recognize and use basic capitalization for: (i) the beginning of sentences; (ii) the pronoun "I"; (iii) names of people;	5 (C) spell familiar English words with increasing accuracy, and employ English spelling patterns and rules with increasing accuracy as more English is acquired
(C) recognize and use punctuation marks at the end of declarative, exclamatory, and interrogative sentences.	*No ELPS Correlation*
(22) Oral and Written Conventions/Spelling. Students spell correctly. Students are expected to:	
First-Grade ELAR TEKS	**ELPS**
(22) cont . . . (A) use phonological knowledge to match sounds to letters to construct known words;	5 (A) learn relationships between sounds and letters of the English language to represent sounds when writing in English
(B) use letter-sound patterns to spell: (i) consonant-vowel-consonant (CVC) words; (ii) consonant-vowel-consonant-silent e (CVCe) words (e.g., "hope"); (iii) one-syllable words with consonant blends (e.g., "drop")	5 (A) learn relationships between sounds and letters of the English language to represent sounds when writing in English 5 (C) spell familiar English words with increasing accuracy, and employ English spelling patterns and rules with increasing accuracy as more English is acquired
(C) spell high-frequency words from a commonly used list;	5 (C) spell familiar English words with increasing accuracy, and employ English spelling patterns and rules with increasing accuracy as more English is acquired
(D) spell base words with inflectional endings (e.g., adding "s" to make words plurals); and	5 (C) spell familiar English words with increasing accuracy, and employ English spelling patterns and rules with increasing accuracy as more English is acquired
(E) use resources to find correct spellings.	1 (B) monitor oral and written language production and employ self-corrective techniques or other resources
(23) Research/Research Plan. Students ask open-ended research questions and develop a plan for answering them. Students (with adult assistance) are expected to:	
(A) generate a list of topics of class-wide interest and formulate open-ended questions about one or two of the topics; and	3 (F) ask and give information ranging from using a very limited bank of high-frequency, high-need, concrete vocabulary, including key words and expressions needed for basic communication in academic and social contexts, to using abstract and content-based vocabulary

	4 (K) demonstrate English comprehension and expand reading skills by employing analytical skills such as evaluating written information and performing critical analyses commensurate with content-area and grade-level needs during extended speaking assignments;
(B) decide what sources of information might be relevant to answer these questions.	2 (I) demonstrate listening comprehension of increasingly complex spoken English by following directions, retelling or summarizing spoken messages, responding to questions and requests, collaborating with peers, and taking notes commensurate with content and grade-level needs
(24) Research/Gathering Sources. Students determine, locate, and explore the full range of relevant sources addressing a research question and systematically record the information they gather. Students (with adult assistance) are expected to:	
First-Grade ELAR TEKS	**ELPS**
(24) cont . . . (A) gather evidence from available sources (natural and personal) as well as from interviews with local experts;	2 (D) monitor understanding of spoken language during classroom instruction and interactions and seek clarification as needed 4 (J) demonstrate English comprehension and expand reading skills by employing inferential skills such as predicting, making connections between ideas, drawing inferences and conclusions from text and graphic sources, and finding supporting text evidence commensurate with content-area needs
(B) use text features (e.g., table of contents, alphabetized index) in age-appropriate reference works (e.g., picture dictionaries) to locate information; and	4 (D) use prereading supports such as graphic organizers, illustrations, and pretaught topic-related vocabulary and other prereading activities to enhance comprehension of written text 4 (E) read linguistically accommodated content-area material with a decreasing need for linguistic accommodations as more English is learned
(C) record basic information in simple visual formats (e.g., notes, charts, picture graphs, diagrams).	1 (C) use strategic learning techniques such as concept mapping, drawing, memorizing, comparing, contrasting, and reviewing to acquire basic and grade-level vocabulary
(25) Research/Synthesizing Information. Students clarify research questions and evaluate and synthesize collected information. Students (with adult assistance) are expected to revise the topic as a result of answers to initial research questions.	4 (J) demonstrate English comprehension and expand reading skills by employing inferential skills such as predicting, making connections between ideas, drawing inferences and conclusions from text and graphic sources, and finding supporting text evidence commensurate with content-area needs
(26) Research/Organizing and Presenting Ideas. Students organize and present their ideas and	5 (G) narrate, describe, and explain with increasing specificity and detail to fulfill content-area writing needs as more English is acquired

information according to the purpose of the research and their audience. Students (with adult assistance) are expected to create a visual display or dramatization to convey the results of the research.	4 (F) use visual and contextual support and support from peers and teachers to read grade-appropriate content-area text, to enhance and confirm understanding, and to develop vocabulary, to grasp language structures, and to tap background knowledge needed to comprehend increasingly challenging language
(27) *Listening and Speaking/Listening. Students use comprehension skills to listen attentively to others in formal and informal settings. Students continue to apply earlier standards with greater complexity. Students are expected to:*	
(A) listen attentively to speakers and ask relevant questions to clarify information; and	2 (D) monitor understanding of spoken language during classroom instruction and interactions and seek clarification as needed

First-Grade ELAR TEKS	**ELPS**
(27)(A) cont . . .	2 (I) demonstrate listening comprehension of increasingly complex spoken English by following directions, retelling or summarizing spoken messages, responding to questions and requests, collaborating with peers, and taking notes commensurate with content and grade-level needs 3 (F) ask and give information ranging from using a very limited bank of high-frequency, high-need, concrete vocabulary, including key words and expressions needed for basic communication in academic and social contexts, to using abstract and content-based vocabulary during extended speaking assignments
(B) follow, restate, and give oral instructions that involve a short related sequence of actions.	2 (E) use visual, contextual, and linguistic support to enhance and confirm understanding of increasingly complex and elaborated spoken language 2 (G) understand the general meaning, main points, and important details of spoken language ranging from situations in which topics, language, and contexts are familiar to unfamiliar 2 (H) understand implicit ideas and information in increasingly complex spoken language commensurate with grade-level learning expectations 2 (I) demonstrate listening comprehension of increasingly complex spoken English by following directions, retelling or summarizing spoken messages, responding to questions and requests, collaborating with peers, and taking notes commensurate with content and grade-level needs 3 (F) ask and give information ranging from using a very limited bank of high-frequency, high-need, concrete vocabulary, including key words and expressions needed for basic communication in academic and social contexts, to using abstract and content-based vocabulary during extended speaking assignments

(28) Listening and Speaking/Speaking. Students speak clearly and to the point, using the conventions of language. Students continue to apply earlier standards with greater complexity. Students are expected to share information and ideas about the topic under discussion, speaking clearly at an appropriate pace, using the conventions of language.	1 (D) speak using learning strategies such as requesting assistance, employing nonverbal cues, and using synonyms and circumlocution (conveying ideas by defining or describing when exact English words are not known) 3 (B) expand and internalize initial English vocabulary by learning and using high-frequency English words necessary for identifying and describing people, places, and objects, by retelling simple stories and basic information represented or supported by pictures, and by learning and using routine language needed for classroom communication 3 (C) speak using a variety of grammatical structures, sentence lengths, sentence types, and connecting words with increasing accuracy and ease as more English is acquired 3 (D) speak using grade-level content-area vocabulary in context to internalize new English words and build academic language proficiency

First-Grade ELAR TEKS	ELPS
(28) cont . . .	3 (G) express opinions, ideas, and feelings ranging from communicating single words and short phrases to participating in extended discussions on a variety of social and grade-appropriate academic topics; 3 (H) narrate, describe, and explain with increasing specificity and detail as more English is acquired 3 (I) adapt spoken language appropriately for formal and informal purposes 3 (J) respond orally to information presented in a wide variety of print, electronic, audio, and visual media to build and reinforce concept and language attainment
(29) Listening and Speaking/Teamwork. Students work productively with others in teams. Students continue to apply earlier standards with greater complexity. Students are expected to follow agreed-upon rules for discussion, including listening to others, speaking when recognized, and making appropriate contributions.	1 (B) monitor oral and written language production and employ self-corrective techniques or other resources; 1 (G) demonstrate an increasing ability to distinguish between formal and informal English and an increasing knowledge of when to use each one commensurate with grade-level learning expectations 2 (I) demonstrate listening comprehension of increasingly complex spoken English by following directions, retelling or summarizing spoken messages, responding to questions and requests, collaborating with peers, and taking notes 3 (E) share information in cooperative learning interactions

This page is intentionally left blank.

ELAR TEKS and ELPS Side-by-Side
Second Grade

Second-Grade ELAR TEKS	ELPS
1) Reading/Beginning Reading Skills/Print Awareness. Students understand how English is written and printed. Students are expected to distinguish features of a sentence (e.g., capitalization of first word, ending punctuation, commas, quotation marks).	4(B) recognize directionality of English reading such as left to right and top to bottom 4 (E) read linguistically accommodated content area material with a decreasing need for linguistic accommodations as more English is learned
(2) Reading/Beginning Reading Skills/Phonics. Students use the relationships between letters and sounds, spelling patterns, and morphological analysis to decode written English. Students will continue to apply earlier standards with greater depth in increasingly more complex texts. Students are expected to:	
(A) decode multisyllabic words in context and independent of context by applying common letter-sound correspondences including: (i) single letters (consonants and vowels); (ii) consonant blends (e.g., thr, spl); (iii) consonant digraphs (e.g., ng, ck, ph); and (iv) vowel digraphs (e.g., ie, ue, ew) and diphthongs (e.g., oi, ou);	2 (A) distinguish sounds and intonation patterns of English with increasing ease 2 (B) recognize elements of the English sound system in newly acquired vocabulary, such as long and short vowels, silent letters, and consonant clusters 4 (A) learn relationships between sounds and letters of the English language and decode (sound out) words using a combination of skills such as recognizing sound-letter relationships and identifying cognates, affixes, roots, and base words
(B) use common syllabication patterns to decode words including: (i) closed syllable (CVC) (e.g., pic-nic, mon-ster); (ii) open syllable (CV) (e.g., ti-ger); (iii) final stable syllable (e.g., sta-tion, tum-ble); (iv) vowel-consonant-silent "e" words (VCe) (e.g., in-vite, cape); (v) r-controlled vowels (e.g., per-fect, cor-ner); and (vi) vowel digraphs and diphthongs (e.g., boy-hood, oat-meal);	4 (A) learn relationships between sounds and letters of the English language and decode (sound out) words using a combination of skills such as recognizing sound-letter relationships and identifying cognates, affixes, roots, and base words
(C) decode words by applying knowledge of common spelling patterns (e.g., *ight, ant*);	5 (C) spell familiar English words with increasing accuracy, and employ English spelling patterns and rules with increasing accuracy as more English is acquired
(D) read words with common prefixes (e.g., *un, dis*) and suffixes (e.g., *ly, less, ful*);	4 (A) learn relationships between sounds and letters of the English language and decode (sound out) words using a combination of skills such as recognizing sound-letter relationships and identifying cognates, affixes, roots, and base words
(E) identify and read abbreviations (e.g., Mr., Ave.);	4 (C) develop basic sight vocabulary, derive meaning of environmental print, and comprehend English vocabulary and language structures used routinely in written classroom materials

Second-Grade ELAR TEKS	ELPS
(2) cont . . . (F) identify and read contractions (e.g., haven't, it's);	1 (H) develop and expand repertoire of learning strategies such as reasoning inductively or deductively, looking for patterns in language, and analyzing sayings and expressions commensurate with grade-level learning expectations 4 (C) develop basic sight vocabulary, derive meaning of environmental print, and comprehend English vocabulary and language structures used routinely in written classroom materials
(G) identify and read at least 300 high-frequency words from a commonly used list; and	4 (C) develop basic sight vocabulary, derive meaning of environmental print, and comprehend English vocabulary and language structures used routinely in written classroom materials
(H) monitor accuracy of decoding.	1 (B) monitor oral and written language production and employ self-corrective techniques or other resources
(3) Reading/Beginning Reading/Strategies. Students comprehend a variety of texts drawing on useful strategies as needed. Students are expected to:	
(A) use ideas (e.g., illustrations, titles, topic sentences, key words, and foreshadowing) to make and confirm predictions;	4 (D) use prereading supports such as graphic organizers, illustrations, and pretaught topic-related vocabulary and other prereading activities to enhance comprehension of written text 4 (J) demonstrate English comprehension and expand reading skills by employing inferential skills such as predicting, making connections between ideas, drawing inferences and conclusions from text and graphic sources, and finding supporting text evidence commensurate with content-area needs
(B) ask relevant questions, seek clarification, and locate facts and details about stories and other texts and support answers with evidence from text; and	3 (F) ask and give information ranging from using a very limited bank of high-frequency, high-need, concrete vocabulary, including key words and expressions needed for basic communication in academic and social contexts, to using abstract and content-based vocabulary during extended speaking assignments 4 (I) demonstrate English comprehension and expand reading skills by employing basic reading skills such as demonstrating understanding of supporting ideas and details in text and graphic sources, summarizing text, and distinguishing main ideas from details commensurate with content-area needs
(C) establish purpose for reading selected texts and monitor comprehension, making corrections and adjustments when that understanding breaks down (e.g., identifying clues, using background knowledge, generating questions, rereading a portion aloud).	4 (F) use visual and contextual support and support from peers and teachers to read grade-appropriate content-area text, enhance and confirm understanding, and develop vocabulary, grasp of language structures, and background knowledge needed to comprehend increasingly challenging language 4 (J) demonstrate English comprehension and expand reading skills by employing inferential skills such as predicting, making connections between ideas, drawing inferences and conclusions from text and graphic sources, and finding supporting text evidence commensurate with content-area needs

Second-Grade ELAR TEKS	ELPS
(4) Reading/Fluency. Students read grade-level text with fluency and comprehension. Students are expected to read aloud grade-level appropriate text with fluency (rate, accuracy, expression, appropriate phrasing) and comprehension.	4 (E) read linguistically accommodated content-area material with a decreasing need for linguistic accommodations as more English is learned 4 (H) read silently with increasing ease and comprehension for longer periods
(5) Reading/Vocabulary Development. Students understand new vocabulary and use it when reading and writing. Students are expected to:	
(A) use prefixes and suffixes to determine the meaning of words (e.g., allow/disallow);	4 (A) learn relationships between sounds and letters of the English language and decode (sound out) words using a combination of skills such as recognizing sound-letter relationships and identifying cognates, affixes, roots, and base words 4 (C) develop basic sight vocabulary, derive meaning of environmental print, and comprehend English vocabulary and language structures used routinely in written classroom materials
(B) use context to determine the relevant meaning of unfamiliar words or multiple-meaning words;	1 (F) use accessible language and learn new and essential language in the process 4 (F) use visual and contextual support and support from peers and teachers to read grade-appropriate content-area text, to enhance and confirm understanding, and to develop vocabulary, to grasp language structures, and to tap background knowledge needed to comprehend increasingly challenging language
(C) identify and use common words that are opposite (antonyms) or similar (synonyms) in meaning; and	1 (E) internalize new, basic, and academic language by using and reusing it in meaningful ways in speaking and writing activities that build concept and language attainment 1 (C) use strategic learning techniques such as concept mapping, drawing, memorizing, comparing, contrasting, and reviewing to acquire basic and grade-level vocabulary 3 (B) expand and internalize initial English vocabulary by learning and using high-frequency English words necessary for identifying and describing people, places, and objects, by retelling simple stories and basic information represented or supported by pictures, and by learning and using routine language needed for classroom communication
(D) alphabetize a series of words and use a dictionary or a glossary to find words.	1 (B) monitor oral and written language production and employ self-corrective techniques or other resources

Second-Grade ELAR TEKS	ELPS
(6) *Reading/Comprehension of Literary Text/Theme and Genre. Students analyze, make inferences and draw conclusions about theme and genre in different cultural, historical, and contemporary contexts and provide evidence from the text to support their understanding. Students are expected to:*	4 (J) demonstrate English comprehension and expand reading skills by employing inferential skills such as predicting, making connections between ideas, drawing inferences and conclusions from text and graphic sources, and finding supporting text evidence commensurate with content-area needs 4 (K) demonstrate English comprehension and expand reading skills by employing analytical skills such as evaluating written information and performing critical analyses commensurate with content-area and grade-level needs
(A) identify moral lessons as themes in well-known fables, legends, myths, or stories; and	4 (K) demonstrate English comprehension and expand reading skills by employing analytical skills such as evaluating written information and performing critical analyses commensurate with content-area and grade-level needs
(B) compare different versions of the same story in traditional and contemporary folktales with respect to their characters, settings, and plot.	1 (C) use strategic learning techniques such as concept mapping, drawing, memorizing, comparing, contrasting, and reviewing to acquire basic and grade-level vocabulary 4 (K) demonstrate English comprehension and expand reading skills by employing analytical skills such as evaluating written information and performing critical analyses commensurate with content-area and grade-level needs
(7) *Reading/Comprehension of Literary Text/Poetry. Students understand, make inferences, and draw conclusions about the structure and elements of poetry and provide evidence from text to support their understanding. Students are expected to describe how rhyme, rhythm, and repetition interact to create images in poetry.*	4 (J) demonstrate English comprehension and expand reading skills by employing inferential skills such as predicting, making connections between ideas, drawing inferences and conclusions from text and graphic sources, and finding supporting text evidence commensurate with content-area needs
(8) *Reading/Comprehension of Literary Text/Drama. Students understand, make inferences, and draw conclusions about the structure and elements of drama and provide evidence from text to support their understanding. Students are expected to identify the elements of dialogue and use them in informal plays.*	1 (H) develop and expand repertoire of learning strategies such as reasoning inductively or deductively, looking for patterns in language, and analyzing sayings and expressions commensurate with grade-level learning expectations 4 (J) demonstrate English comprehension and expand reading skills by employing inferential skills such as predicting, making connections between ideas, drawing inferences and conclusions from text and graphic sources, and finding supporting text evidence commensurate with content-area needs
(9) *Reading/Comprehension of Literary Text/Fiction. Students understand, make inferences and draw conclusions about the structure and elements of fiction and provide evidence from text to support their understanding. Students are expected to:*	

Second-Grade ELAR TEKS	ELPS
(9) cont . . . (A) describe similarities and differences in the plots and settings of several works by the same author; and	1 (C) use strategic learning techniques such as concept mapping, drawing, memorizing, comparing, contrasting, and reviewing to acquire basic and grade-level vocabulary 4 (K) demonstrate English comprehension and expand reading skills by employing analytical skills such as evaluating written information and performing critical analyses commensurate with content-area and grade-level needs
(B) describe main characters in works of fiction, including their traits, motivations, and feelings.	4 (J) demonstrate English comprehension and expand reading skills by employing inferential skills such as predicting, making connections between ideas, drawing inferences and conclusions from text and graphic sources, and finding supporting text evidence commensurate with content-area needs 4 (K) demonstrate English comprehension and expand reading skills by employing analytical skills such as evaluating written information and performing critical analyses commensurate with content-area and grade-level needs
(10) Reading/Comprehension of Literary Text/Literary Nonfiction. Students understand, make inferences and draw conclusions about the varied structural patterns and features of literary nonfiction and respond by providing evidence from text to support their understanding. Students are expected to distinguish between fiction and nonfiction.	4 (J) demonstrate English comprehension and expand reading skills by employing inferential skills such as predicting, making connections between ideas, drawing inferences and conclusions from text and graphic sources, and finding supporting text evidence commensurate with content-area needs 4 (K) demonstrate English comprehension and expand reading skills by employing analytical skills such as evaluating written information and performing critical analyses commensurate with content-area and grade-level needs
(11) Reading/Comprehension of Literary Text/Sensory Language. Students understand, make inferences, and draw conclusions about how an author's sensory language creates imagery in literary text and provides evidence from text to support their understanding. Students are expected to recognize that some words and phrases have literal and nonliteral meanings (e.g., take steps).	1 (H) develop and expand repertoire of learning strategies such as reasoning inductively or deductively, looking for patterns in language, and analyzing sayings and expressions commensurate with grade-level learning expectations 4 (J) demonstrate English comprehension and expand reading skills by employing inferential skills such as predicting, making connections between ideas, drawing inferences and conclusions from text and graphic sources, and finding supporting text evidence commensurate with content-area needs
(12) Reading/Comprehension of Text/Independent Reading. Students read independently for sustained periods of time and produce evidence of their reading. Students are expected to read independently for a sustained period of time and paraphrase what the reading was about, maintaining meaning.	4 (E) read linguistically accommodated content-area material with a decreasing need for linguistic accommodations as more English is learned 4 (H) read silently with increasing ease and comprehension for longer periods

Second-Grade ELAR TEKS	ELPS
(13) *Reading/Comprehension of Informational Text/Culture and History. Students analyze, make inferences and draw conclusions about the author's purpose in cultural, historical, and contemporary contexts and provide evidence from the text to support their understanding. Students are expected to identify the topic and explain the author's purpose in writing the text.*	4 (J) demonstrate English comprehension and expand reading skills by employing inferential skills such as predicting, making connections between ideas, drawing inferences and conclusions from text and graphic sources, and finding supporting text evidence commensurate with content-area needs
(14) *Reading/Comprehension of Informational Text/Expository Text. Students analyze, make inferences, and draw conclusions about and understand expository text and provide evidence from text to support their understanding. Students are expected to:*	
(A) identify the main idea in a text and distinguish it from the topic;	4 (I) demonstrate English comprehension and expand reading skills by employing basic reading skills such as demonstrating understanding of supporting ideas and details in text and graphic sources, summarizing text, and distinguishing main ideas from details commensurate with content-area needs
(B) locate the facts that are clearly stated in a text;	4 (I) demonstrate English comprehension and expand reading skills by employing basic reading skills such as demonstrating understanding of supporting ideas and details in text and graphic sources, summarizing text, and distinguishing main ideas from details commensurate with content-area needs
(C) describe the order of events or ideas in a text; and	4 (G) demonstrate comprehension of increasingly complex English by participating in shared reading, retelling or summarizing material, responding to questions, and taking notes commensurate with content-area and grade-level needs 4 (K) demonstrate English comprehension and expand reading skills by employing analytical skills such as evaluating written information and performing critical analyses commensurate with content-area and grade-level needs
(D) use text features (e.g., table of contents, index, headings) to locate specific information in text.	4 (D) use prereading supports such as graphic organizers, illustrations, and pretaught topic-related vocabulary and other prereading activities to enhance comprehension of written text
(15) *Reading/Comprehension of Informational Text/Procedural Text. Students understand how to glean and use information in procedural texts and documents. Students are expected to:*	

Second-Grade ELAR TEKS	ELPS
(15) cont . . . (A) follow written multistep directions; and	4 (D) use prereading supports such as graphic organizers, illustrations, and pretaught topic-related vocabulary and other prereading activities to enhance comprehension of written text 4 (E) read linguistically accommodated content-area material with a decreasing need for linguistic accommodations as more English is learned
(B) use common graphic features to assist in the interpretation of text (e.g., captions, illustrations).	4 (D) use prereading supports such as graphic organizers, illustrations, and pretaught topic-related vocabulary and other prereading activities to enhance comprehension of written text
(16) Reading/Media Literacy. Students use comprehension skills to analyze how words, images, graphics, and sounds work together in various forms to impact meaning. Students continue to apply earlier standards with greater depth in increasingly more complex texts. Students are expected to:	
(A) recognize different purposes of media (e.g., informational, entertainment);	2 (F) listen to and derive meaning from a variety of media such as audio tape, video, DVD, and CD-ROM to build and reinforce concept and language attainment
(B) describe techniques used to create media messages (e.g., sound, graphics); and	2 (F) listen to and derive meaning from a variety of media such as audio tape, video, DVD, and CD-ROM to build and reinforce concept and language attainment
(C) identify various written conventions for using digital media (e.g., e-mail, website, video game).	1 (H) develop and expand repertoire of learning strategies such as reasoning inductively or deductively, looking for patterns in language, and analyzing sayings and expressions commensurate with grade-level learning expectations
(17) Writing/Writing Process. Students use elements of the writing process (planning, drafting, revising, editing, and publishing) to compose text. Students are expected to:	
(A) plan a first draft by generating ideas for writing (e.g., drawing, sharing ideas, listing key ideas);	1 (C) use strategic learning techniques such as concept mapping, drawing, memorizing, comparing, contrasting, and reviewing to acquire basic and grade-level vocabulary 1 (E) internalize new, basic, and academic language by using and reusing it in meaningful ways in speaking and writing activities that build concept and language attainment 3 (E) share in cooperative learning interactions
(B) develop drafts by sequencing ideas through writing sentences;	5 (B) write using newly acquired basic vocabulary and content-based grade-level vocabulary

Second-Grade ELAR TEKS	ELPS
(17)(B) cont . . .	5 (F) write using a variety of grade-appropriate sentence lengths, patterns, and connecting words to combine phrases, clauses, and sentences in increasingly accurate ways as more English is acquired
(C) revise drafts by adding or deleting words, phrases, or sentences;	5 (D) edit writing for standard grammar and usage, including subject-verb agreement, pronoun agreement, and appropriate verb tenses commensurate with grade-level expectations as more English is acquired
(D) edit drafts for grammar, punctuation, and spelling using a teacher-developed rubric; and	5 (D) edit writing for standard grammar and usage, including subject-verb agreement, pronoun agreement, and appropriate verb tenses commensurate with grade-level expectations as more English is acquired
(E) publish and share writing with others.	3 (C) speak using a variety of grammatical structures, sentence lengths, sentence types, and connecting words with increasing accuracy and ease as more English is acquired
(18) Writing/Literary Texts. Students write literary texts to express their ideas and feelings about real or imagined people, events, and ideas. Students are expected to:	
(A) write brief stories that include a beginning, middle, and end; and	5 (F) write using a variety of grade-appropriate sentence lengths, patterns, and connecting words to combine phrases, clauses, and sentences in increasingly accurate ways as more English is acquired 5 (G) narrate, describe, and explain with increasing specificity and detail to fulfill content-area writing needs as more English is acquired
(B) write short poems that convey sensory details.	1 (E) internalize new, basic, and academic language by using and reusing it in meaningful ways in speaking and writing activities that build concept and language attainment
(19) Writing/Expository and Procedural Texts. Students write expository and procedural or work-related texts to communicate ideas and information to specific audiences for specific purposes. Students are expected to:	
(A) write brief compositions about topics of interest to the student;	5 (F) write using a variety of grade-appropriate sentence lengths, patterns, and connecting words to combine phrases, clauses, and sentences in increasingly accurate ways as more English is acquired 5 (G) narrate, describe, and explain with increasing specificity and detail to fulfill content-area writing needs as more English is acquired
(B) write short letters that put ideas in a chronological or logical sequence and use appropriate conventions (e.g., date, salutation, closing); and	5 (F) write using a variety of grade-appropriate sentence lengths, patterns, and connecting words to combine phrases, clauses, and sentences in increasingly accurate ways as more English is acquired

Second-Grade ELAR TEKS	ELPS
(19)(B) cont . . .	5 (G) narrate, describe, and explain with increasing specificity and detail to fulfill content-area writing needs as more English is acquired
(C) write brief comments on literary or informational texts.	5 (F) write using a variety of grade-appropriate sentence lengths, patterns, and connecting words to combine phrases, clauses, and sentences in increasingly accurate ways as more English is acquired 5 (G) narrate, describe, and explain with increasing specificity and detail to fulfill content-area writing needs as more English is acquired
(20) Writing/Persuasive Texts. Students write persuasive texts to influence the attitudes or actions of a specific audience on specific issues. Students are expected to write persuasive statements about issues that are important to the student for the appropriate audience in the school, home, or local community.	5 (F) write using a variety of grade-appropriate sentence lengths, patterns, and connecting words to combine phrases, clauses, and sentences in increasingly accurate ways as more English is acquired; and 5 (G) narrate, describe, and explain with increasing specificity and detail to fulfill content-area writing needs as more English is acquired
(21) Oral and Written Conventions/Conventions. Students understand the function of and use the conventions of academic language when speaking and writing. Students continue to apply earlier standards with greater complexity. Students are expected to:	
(A) understand and use the following parts of speech in the context of reading, writing, and speaking: (i) verbs (past, present, and future); (ii) nouns (singular/plural, common/proper); (iii) adjectives (e.g., descriptive: old, wonderful; articles: a, an, the); (iv) adverbs (e.g., time: before, next; manner: carefully, beautifully); (v) prepositions and prepositional phrases; (vi) pronouns (e.g., he, him); and (vii) time-order transition words;	5 (E) employ increasingly complex grammatical structures in content-area writing commensurate with grade-level expectations, such as: (i) using correct verbs, tenses, and pronouns / antecedents (ii) using possessive case (apostrophes) correctly (iii) using negatives and contractions correctly 5 (F) write using a variety of grade-appropriate sentence lengths, patterns, and connecting words to combine phrases, clauses, and sentences in increasingly accurate ways as more English is acquired
(B) use complete sentences with correct subject-verb agreement; and	5 (D) edit writing for standard grammar and usage, including subject-verb agreement, pronoun agreement, and appropriate verb tenses commensurate with grade-level expectations as more English is acquired;
(C) distinguish among declarative and interrogative sentences.	1 (H) develop and expand repertoire of learning strategies such as reasoning inductively or deductively, looking for patterns in language, and analyzing sayings and expressions commensurate with grade-level learning expectations

Second-Grade ELAR TEKS	ELPS
(22) Oral and Written Conventions/Handwriting, Capitalization, and Punctuation. Students write legibly and use appropriate capitalization and punctuation conventions in their compositions. Students are expected to:	
(A) write legibly leaving appropriate margins for readability;	5 (E) employ increasingly complex grammatical structures in content-area writing commensurate with grade-level expectations, such as: (i) using correct verbs, tenses, and pronouns / antecedents (ii) using possessive case (apostrophes) correctly (iii) using negatives and contractions correctly
(B) use capitalization for: (i) proper nouns; (ii) months and days of the week; and (iii) the salutation and closing of a letter; and	5 (C) spell familiar English words with increasing accuracy, and employ English spelling patterns and rules with increasing accuracy as more English is acquired
(C) recognize and use punctuation marks, including: (i) ending punctuation in sentences; (ii) apostrophes and contractions; and (iii) apostrophes and possessives.	*No ELPS Correlation*
(23) Oral and Written Conventions/Spelling. Students spell correctly. Students are expected to:	
(A) use phonological knowledge to match sounds to letters to construct unknown words;	5 (A) learn relationships between sounds and letters of the English language to represent sounds when writing in English
(B) spell words with common orthographic patterns and rules: (i) complex consonants (e.g., hard and soft c and g, ck); (ii) r-controlled vowels; (iii) long vowels (e.g., VCe-hope); and (iv) vowel digraphs (e.g., oo-book, fool, ee-feet), diphthongs (e.g., ou-out, ow-cow, oi-coil, oy-toy);	5 (C) spell familiar English words with increasing accuracy, and employ English spelling patterns and rules with increasing accuracy as more English is acquired
(C) spell high-frequency words from a commonly used list;	5 (C) spell familiar English words with increasing accuracy, and employ English spelling patterns and rules with increasing accuracy as more English is acquired
(D) spell base words with inflectional endings (e.g., -ing and -ed);	5 (C) spell familiar English words with increasing accuracy, and employ English spelling patterns and rules with increasing accuracy as more English is acquired
(E) spell simple contractions (e.g., isn't, aren't, can't); and	5 (C) spell familiar English words with increasing accuracy, and employ English spelling patterns and rules with increasing accuracy as more English is acquired
(F) use resources to find correct spellings.	1 (B) monitor oral and written language production and employ self-corrective techniques or other resources

Second-Grade ELAR TEKS	ELPS
(24) *Research/Research Plan. Students ask open-ended research questions and develop a plan for answering them. Students are expected to:*	
(A) generate a list of topics of class-wide interest and formulate open-ended questions about one or two of the topics; and	3 (F) ask and give information ranging from using a very limited bank of high-frequency, high-need, concrete vocabulary, including key words and expressions needed for basic communication in academic and social contexts, to using abstract and content-based vocabulary during extended speaking assignments
(B) decide what sources of information might be relevant to answer these questions.	2 (I) demonstrate listening comprehension of increasingly complex spoken English by following directions, retelling or summarizing spoken messages, responding to questions and requests, collaborating with peers, and taking notes commensurate with content and grade-level needs 4 (K) demonstrate English comprehension and expand reading skills by employing analytical skills such as evaluating written information and performing critical analyses commensurate with content-area and grade-level needs
(25) *Research/Gathering Sources. Students determine, locate, and explore the full range of relevant sources addressing a research question and systematically record the information they gather. Students are expected to:*	
(A) gather evidence from available sources (natural and personal) as well as from interviews with local experts;	3 (F) ask and give information ranging from using a very limited bank of high-frequency, high-need, concrete vocabulary, including key words and expressions needed for basic communication in academic and social contexts, to using abstract and content-based vocabulary during extended speaking assignments
(B) use text features (e.g., table of contents, alphabetized index, headings) in age-appropriate reference works (e.g., picture dictionaries) to locate information; and	4 (D) use prereading supports such as graphic organizers, illustrations, and pretaught topic-related vocabulary and other prereading activities to enhance comprehension of written text
(C) record basic information in simple visual formats (e.g., notes, charts, picture graphs, diagrams).	1 (C) use strategic learning techniques such as concept mapping, drawing, memorizing, comparing, contrasting, and reviewing to acquire basic and grade-level vocabulary
(26) *Research/Synthesizing Information. Students clarify research questions and evaluate and synthesize collected information. Students are expected to revise the topic as a result of answers to initial research questions.*	4 (J) demonstrate English comprehension and expand reading skills by employing inferential skills such as predicting, making connections between ideas, drawing inferences and conclusions from text and graphic sources, and finding supporting text evidence commensurate with content area needs

Second-Grade ELAR TEKS	ELPS
(27) Research/Organizing and Presenting Ideas. Students organize and present their ideas and information according to the purpose of the research and their audience. Students (with adult assistance) are expected to create a visual display or dramatization to convey the results of the research.	4 (F) use visual and contextual support and support from peers and teachers to read grade-appropriate content-area text, to enhance and confirm understanding, and to develop vocabulary, to grasp language structures, and to tap background knowledge needed to comprehend increasingly challenging language 5 (G) narrate, describe, and explain with increasing specificity and detail to fulfill content-area writing needs as more English is acquired
(28) Listening and Speaking/Listening. Students use comprehension skills to listen attentively to others in formal and informal settings. Students continue to apply earlier standards with greater complexity. Students are expected to:	
(A) listen attentively to speakers and ask relevant questions to clarify information; and	2 (D) monitor understanding of spoken language during classroom instruction and interactions and seek clarification as needed 2 (I) demonstrate listening comprehension of increasingly complex spoken English by following directions, retelling or summarizing spoken messages, responding to questions and requests, collaborating with peers, and taking notes commensurate with content and grade-level needs 3 (F) ask and give information ranging from using a very limited bank of high-frequency, high-need, concrete vocabulary, including key words and expressions needed for basic communication in academic and social contexts, to using abstract and content-based vocabulary during extended speaking assignments
(B) follow, restate, and give oral instructions that involve a short related sequence of actions.	2 (E) use visual, contextual, and linguistic support to enhance and confirm understanding of increasingly complex and elaborated spoken language 2 (G) understand the general meaning, main points, and important details of spoken language ranging from situations in which topics, language, and contexts are familiar to unfamiliar 2 (H) understand implicit ideas and information in increasingly complex spoken language commensurate with grade-level learning experiences 2 (I) demonstrate listening comprehension of increasingly complex spoken English by following directions, retelling or summarizing spoken messages, responding to questions and requests, collaborating with peers, and taking notes commensurate with content and grade-level needs 3 (F) ask and give information ranging from using a very limited bank of high-frequency, high-need, concrete vocabulary, including key words and expressions needed for basic communication in academic and social contexts, to using abstract and content-based vocabulary during extended speaking assignments expectations

Second-Grade ELAR TEKS	ELPS
(29) *Listing and Speaking/Speaking. Students speak clearly and to the point, using the conventions of language. Students continue to apply earlier standards with greater complexity. Students are expected to share information and ideas that focus on the topic under discussion, speaking clearly at an appropriate pace, using the conventions of language.*	1 (D) speak using learning strategies such as requesting assistance, employing non-verbal cues, and using synonyms and circumlocution (conveying ideas by defining or describing when exact English words are not known) 2 (C) learn new language structures, expressions, and basic and academic vocabulary heard during classroom instruction and interactions 3 (A) practice producing sounds of newly acquired vocabulary such as long and short vowels, silent letters, and consonant clusters to pronounce English words in a manner that is increasingly comprehensible 3 (B) expand and internalize initial English vocabulary by learning and using high-frequency English words necessary for identifying and describing people, places, and objects, by retelling simple stories and basic information represented or supported by pictures, and by learning and using routine language needed for classroom communication 3 (C) speak using a variety of grammatical structures, sentence lengths, sentence types, and connecting words with increasing accuracy and ease as more English is acquired 3 (D) speak using grade-level content-area vocabulary in context to internalize new English words and build academic language proficiency 3 (G) express opinions, ideas, and feelings ranging from communicating single words and short phrases to participating in extended discussions on a variety of social and grade-appropriate academic topics 3 (H) narrate, describe, and explain with increasing specificity and detail as more English is acquired 3 (I) adapt spoken language appropriately for formal and informal purposes 3 (J) respond orally to information presented in a wide variety of print, electronic, audio, and visual media to build and reinforce concept attainment
(30) *Listening and Speaking/Teamwork. Students work productively with others in teams. Students continue to apply earlier standards with greater complexity. Students are expected to follow agreed-upon rules for discussion, including listening to others, speaking when recognized, and making appropriate contributions.*	1 (A) use prior knowledge and experiences to understand meanings in English 1 (B) monitor oral and written language production and employ self-corrective techniques or other resources 1 (G) demonstrate an increasing ability to distinguish between formal and informal English and an increasing knowledge of when to use each one commensurate with grade-level learning expectations 2 (I) demonstrate listening comprehension of increasingly complex spoken English by following directions, retelling or summarizing spoken messages, responding to questions and requests, collaborating with peers, and taking notes 3 (E) share information in cooperative learning interactions

This page is intentionally left blank.

ELAR TEKS and ELPS Side-by-Side
Third-Grade

Third-Grade ELAR TEKS	ELPS
(1) *Reading/Beginning Reading Skills/Phonics. Students use the relationships between letters and sounds, spelling patterns, and morphological analysis to decode written English. Students are expected to:*	
(A) decode multisyllabic words in context and independent of context by applying common spelling patterns including: (i) dropping the final "e" and add endings such as -ing, -ed, or -able (e.g., use, using, used, usable); (ii) doubling final consonants when adding an ending (e.g., hop to hopping); (iii) changing the final "y" to "i" (e.g., baby to babies); (iv) using knowledge of common prefixes and suffixes (e.g., *dis, ly*); and (v) using knowledge of derivational affixes (e.g., *de, ful, able*);	2 (A) distinguish sounds and intonation patterns of English with increasing ease 2 (B) recognize elements of the English sound system in newly acquired vocabulary such as long and short vowels, silent letters, and consonant clusters 4 (A) learn relationships between sounds and letters of the English language and decode (sound out) words using a combination of skills such as recognizing sound-letter relationships and identifying cognates, affixes, roots, and base words
(B) use common syllabication patterns to decode words including: (i) closed syllable (CVC) (e.g., mag-net, splen-did); (ii) open syllable (CV) (e.g., ve-to); (iii) final stable syllable (e.g., puz-zle, con-trac-tion); (iv) r-controlled vowels (e.g., fer-ment, car-pool); and (v) vowel digraphs and diphthongs (e.g., ei-ther);	4 (A) learn relationships between sounds and letters of the English language and decode (sound out) words using a combination of skills such as recognizing sound-letter relationships and identifying cognates, affixes, roots, and base words
(C) decode words applying knowledge of common spelling patterns (e.g., -eigh, -ought);	5 (C) spell familiar English words with increasing accuracy, and employ English spelling patterns and rules with increasing accuracy as more English is acquired
(D) identify and read contractions (e.g., I'd, won't); and	1 (H) develop and expand repertoire of learning strategies such as reasoning inductively or deductively, looking for patterns in language, and analyzing sayings and expressions commensurate with grade-level learning expectations 4 (C) develop basic sight vocabulary, derive meaning of environmental print, and comprehend English vocabulary and language structures used routinely in written classroom materials
(E) monitor accuracy in decoding.	1 (B) monitor oral and written language production and employ self-corrective techniques or other resources;
(2) *Reading/Beginning Reading/Strategies. Students comprehend a variety of texts drawing on useful strategies as needed. Students are expected to:*	

Third-Grade ELAR TEKS	ELPS
(2) cont . . . (A) use ideas (e.g., illustrations, titles, topic sentences, key words, and foreshadowing clues) to make and confirm predictions;	4 (D) use prereading supports such as graphic organizers, illustrations, and pretaught topic-related vocabulary and other prereading activities to enhance comprehension of written text 4 (J) demonstrate English comprehension and expand reading skills by employing inferential skills such as predicting, making connections between ideas, drawing inferences and conclusions from text and graphic sources, and finding supporting text evidence commensurate with content-area needs
(B) ask relevant questions, seek clarification, and locate facts and details about stories and other texts and support answers with evidence from text; and	3 (F) ask and give information ranging from using a very limited bank of high-frequency, high-need, concrete vocabulary, including key words and expressions needed for basic communication in academic and social contexts, to using abstract and content-based vocabulary during extended speaking assignments 4 (I) demonstrate English comprehension and expand reading skills by employing basic reading skills such as demonstrating understanding of supporting ideas and details in text and graphic sources, summarizing text, and distinguishing main ideas from details commensurate with content-area needs
(C) establish purpose for reading selected texts and monitor comprehension, making corrections and adjustments when that understanding breaks down (e.g., identifying clues, using background knowledge, generating questions, rereading a portion aloud).	4 (I) demonstrate English comprehension and expand reading skills by employing basic reading skills such as demonstrating understanding of supporting ideas and details in text and graphic sources, summarizing text, and distinguishing main ideas from details commensurate with content-area needs
(3) Reading/Fluency. Students read grade-level text with fluency and comprehension. Students are expected to read aloud grade-level appropriate text with fluency (rate, accuracy, expression, appropriate phrasing) and comprehension.	4 (E) read linguistically accommodated content area material with a decreasing need for linguistic accommodations as more English is learned 4 (H) read silently with increasing ease and comprehension for longer periods
(4) Reading/Vocabulary Development. Students understand new vocabulary and use it when reading and writing. Students are expected to:	
(A) identify the meaning of common prefixes (e.g., *in, dis)* and suffixes (e.g., *full, less*), and know how they change the meaning of roots;	4 (A) learn relationships between sounds and letters of the English language and decode (sound out) words using a combination of skills such as recognizing sound-letter relationships and identifying cognates, affixes, roots, and base words;
(B) use context to determine the relevant meaning of unfamiliar words or distinguish among multiple meaning words and homographs;	1 (F) use accessible language and learn new and essential language in the process 4 (F) use visual and contextual support and support from peers and teachers to read grade-appropriate content-area text, enhance and confirm understanding, and develop vocabulary, grasp of language structures, and background knowledge needed to comprehend increasingly challenging language

Third-Grade ELAR TEKS	ELPS
(4) cont . . . (C) identify and use antonyms, synonyms, homographs, and homophones;	3 (B) expand and internalize initial English vocabulary by learning and using high-frequency English words necessary for identifying and describing people, places, and objects, by retelling simple stories and basic information represented or supported by pictures, and by learning and using routine language needed for classroom communication;
(D) identify and apply playful uses of language (e.g., tongue twisters, palindromes, riddles); and	1 (H) develop and expand repertoire of learning strategies such as reasoning inductively or deductively, looking for patterns in language, and analyzing sayings and expressions commensurate with grade-level learning expectations
(E) alphabetize a series of words to the third letter and use a dictionary or a glossary to determine the meanings, syllabication, and pronunciation of unknown words.	1 (B) monitor oral and written language production and employ self-corrective techniques or other resources
(5) *Reading/Comprehension of Literary Text/Theme and Genre. Students analyze, make inferences and draw conclusions about theme and genre in different cultural, historical, and contemporary contexts and provide evidence from the text to support their understanding. Students are expected to:*	
(A) paraphrase the themes and supporting details of fables, legends, myths, or stories; and	4 (I) demonstrate English comprehension and expand reading skills by employing basic reading skills such as demonstrating understanding of supporting ideas and details in text and graphic sources, summarizing text, and distinguishing main ideas from details commensurate with content-area needs 4 (K) demonstrate English comprehension and expand reading skills by employing analytical skills such as evaluating written information and performing critical analyses commensurate with content-area and grade-level needs
(B) compare and contrast the settings in myths and traditional folktales.	1 (C) use strategic learning techniques such as concept mapping, drawing, memorizing, comparing, contrasting, and reviewing to acquire basic and grade-level vocabulary 4 (K) demonstrate English comprehension and expand reading skills by employing analytical skills such as evaluating written information and performing critical analyses commensurate with content-area and grade-level needs

Third-Grade ELAR TEKS	ELPS
(6) *Reading/Comprehension of Literary Text/Poetry. Students understand, make inferences, and draw conclusions about the structure and elements of poetry and provide evidence from text to support their understanding. Students are expected to describe the characteristics of various forms of poetry and how they create imagery (e.g., narrative poetry, lyrical poetry, humorous poetry, free verse).*	1 (H) develop and expand repertoire of learning strategies such as reasoning inductively or deductively, looking for patterns in language, and analyzing sayings and expressions commensurate with grade-level learning expectations 4 (J) demonstrate English comprehension and expand reading skills by employing inferential skills such as predicting, making connections between ideas, drawing inferences and conclusions from text and graphic sources, and finding supporting text evidence commensurate with content-area needs
(7) *Reading/Comprehension of Literary Text/Drama. Students understand, make inferences, and draw conclusions about the structure and elements of drama and provide evidence from text to support their understanding. Students are expected to explain the elements of plot and character as presented through dialogue in scripts that are read, viewed, written, or performed.*	3 (H) narrate, describe, and explain with increasing specificity and detail as more English is acquired 4 (J) demonstrate English comprehension and expand reading skills by employing inferential skills such as predicting, making connections between ideas, drawing inferences and conclusions from text and graphic sources, and finding supporting text evidence commensurate with content-area needs
(8) *Reading/Comprehension of Literary Text/Fiction. Students understand, make inferences, and draw conclusions about the structure and elements of fiction and provide evidence from text to support their understanding. Students are expected to:*	
(A) sequence and summarize the plot's main events and explain their influence on future events;	4 (I) demonstrate English comprehension and expand reading skills by employing basic reading skills such as demonstrating understanding of supporting ideas and details in text and graphic sources, summarizing text, and distinguishing main ideas from details commensurate with content area-needs 4 (K) demonstrate English comprehension and expand reading skills by employing analytical skills such as evaluating written information and performing critical analyses commensurate with content-area and grade-level needs
(B) describe the interaction of characters including their relationships and the changes they undergo; and	4 (K) demonstrate English comprehension and expand reading skills by employing analytical skills such as evaluating written information and performing critical analyses commensurate with content-area and grade-level needs
(C) identify whether the narrator or speaker of a story is first or third person.	*No ELPS Correlation*

Third-Grade ELAR TEKS	ELPS
(9) *Reading/Comprehension of Literary Text/Literary Nonfiction. Students understand, make inferences, and draw conclusions about the varied structural patterns and features of literary nonfiction and respond by providing evidence from text to support their understanding. Students are expected to explain the difference in point of view between a biography and autobiography.*	4 (J) demonstrate English comprehension and expand reading skills by employing inferential skills such as predicting, making connections between ideas, drawing inferences and conclusions from text and graphic sources, and finding supporting text evidence commensurate with content-area needs 4 (K) demonstrate English comprehension and expand reading skills by employing analytical skills such as evaluating written information and performing critical analyses commensurate with content-area and grade-level needs
(10) *Reading/Comprehension of Literary Text/Sensory Language. Students understand, make inferences and draw conclusions about how an author's sensory language creates imagery in literary text and provide evidence from text to support their understanding. Students are expected to identify language that creates a graphic visual experience and appeals to the senses.*	1 (H) develop and expand repertoire of learning strategies such as reasoning inductively or deductively, looking for patterns in language, and analyzing sayings and expressions commensurate with grade-level learning expectations 4 (J) demonstrate English comprehension and expand reading skills by employing inferential skills such as predicting, making connections between ideas, drawing inferences and conclusions from text and graphic sources, and finding supporting text evidence commensurate with content-area needs
(11) *Reading/Comprehension of Text/Independent Reading. Students read independently for sustained periods of time and produce evidence of their reading. Students are expected to read independently for a sustained period of time and paraphrase what the reading was about, maintaining meaning and logical order (e.g., generate a reading log or journal; participate in book talks).*	4 (E) read linguistically accommodated content-area material with a decreasing need for linguistic accommodations as more English is learned 4 (H) read silently with increasing ease and comprehension for longer periods 4 (I) demonstrate English comprehension and expand reading skills by employing basic reading skills such as demonstrating understanding of supporting ideas and details in text and graphic sources, summarizing text, and distinguishing main ideas from details commensurate with content-area needs
(12) *Reading/Comprehension of Informational Text/Culture and History. Students analyze, make inferences, and draw conclusions about the author's purpose in cultural, historical, and contemporary contexts and provide evidence from the text to support their understanding. Students are expected to identify the topic and locate the author's stated purposes in writing the text.*	4 (J) demonstrate English comprehension and expand reading skills by employing inferential skills such as predicting, making connections between ideas, drawing inferences and conclusions from text and graphic sources, and finding supporting text evidence commensurate with content-area needs 4 (K) demonstrate English comprehension and expand reading skills by employing analytical skills such as evaluating written information and performing critical analyses commensurate with content-area and grade-level needs

Third-Grade ELAR TEKS	ELPS
(13) *Reading/Comprehension of Informational Text/Expository Text. Students analyze, make inference,s and draw conclusions about expository text and provide evidence from text to support their understanding. Students are expected to:*	
(A) identify the details or facts that support the main idea;	4 (I) demonstrate English comprehension and expand reading skills by employing basic reading skills such as demonstrating understanding of supporting ideas and details in text and graphic sources, summarizing text, and distinguishing main ideas from details commensurate with content-area needs
(B) draw conclusions from the facts presented in text and support those assertions with textual evidence;	4 (J) demonstrate English comprehension and expand reading skills by employing inferential skills such as predicting, making connections between ideas, drawing inferences and conclusions from text and graphic sources, and finding supporting text evidence commensurate with content-area needs
(C) identify explicit cause and effect relationships among ideas in texts; and	4 (K) demonstrate English comprehension and expand reading skills by employing analytical skills such as evaluating written information and performing critical analyses commensurate with content-area and grade-level needs
(D) use text features (e.g., bold print, captions, key words, italics) to locate information and make and verify predictions about contents of text.	4 (D) use prereading supports such as graphic organizers, illustrations, and pretaught topic-related vocabulary and other prereading activities to enhance comprehension of written text
(14) *Reading/Comprehension of Informational Text/Persuasive Text. Students analyze, make inferences, and draw conclusions about persuasive text and provide evidence from text to support their analyses. Students are expected to identify what the author is trying to persuade the reader to think or do.*	4 (J) demonstrate English comprehension and expand reading skills by employing inferential skills such as predicting, making connections between ideas, drawing inferences and conclusions from text and graphic sources, and finding supporting text evidence commensurate with content-area needs 4 (K) demonstrate English comprehension and expand reading skills by employing analytical skills such as evaluating written information and performing critical analyses commensurate with content-area and grade-level needs
(15) *Reading/Comprehension of Informational Text/Procedural Texts. Students understand how to glean and use information in procedural texts and documents. Students are expected to:*	
(A) follow and explain a set of written multistep directions; and	4 (E) read linguistically accommodated content-area material with a decreasing need for linguistic accommodations as more English is learned 4 (D) use prereading supports such as graphic organizers, illustrations, and pretaught topic-related vocabulary and other prereading activities to enhance comprehension of written text

Third-Grade ELAR TEKS	ELPS
(15) cont . . . (B) locate and use specific information in graphic features of text.	4 (D) use prereading supports such as graphic organizers, illustrations, and pretaught topic-related vocabulary and other prereading activities to enhance comprehension of written text 4 (F) use visual and contextual support and support from peers and teachers to read grade-appropriate content-area text, to enhance and confirm understanding, and to develop vocabulary, to grasp language structures, and to tap background knowledge needed to comprehend increasingly challenging language
(16) *Reading/Media Literacy. Students use comprehension skills to analyze how words, images, graphics, and sounds work together in various forms to impact meaning. Students will continue to apply earlier standards with greater depth in increasingly more complex texts. Students are expected to:*	
(A) understand how communication changes when moving from one genre of media to another;	2 (F) listen to and derive meaning from a variety of media such as audio tape, video, DVD, and CD-ROM to build and reinforce concept and language attainment 3 (I) adapt spoken language appropriately for formal and informal purposes
(B) explain how various design techniques used in media influence the message (e.g., shape, color, sound); and	4 (I) demonstrate English comprehension and expand reading skills by employing basic reading skills such as demonstrating understanding of supporting ideas and details in text and graphic sources, summarizing text, and distinguishing main ideas from details commensurate with content area needs
(C) compare various written conventions used for digital media (e.g., language in an informal e-mail vs. language in a web-based news article).	1 (C) use strategic learning techniques such as concept mapping, drawing, memorizing, comparing, contrasting, and reviewing to acquire basic and grade-level vocabulary 3 (I) adapt spoken language appropriately for formal and informal purposes 4 (K) demonstrate English comprehension and expand reading skills by employing analytical skills such as evaluating written information and performing critical analyses commensurate with content-area and grade-level needs
Reading/Media Literacy - No Correlation	**4(B) recognize directionality of English reading such as left to right and top to bottom**
(17) *Writing/Writing Process. Students use elements of the writing process (planning, drafting, revising, editing, and publishing) to compose text. Students are expected to:*	

Third-Grade ELAR TEKS	ELPS
(17) cont . . . (A) plan a first draft by selecting a genre appropriate for conveying the intended meaning to an audience and generating ideas through a range of strategies (e.g., brainstorming, graphic organizers, logs, journals);	1 (C) use strategic learning techniques such as concept mapping, drawing, memorizing, comparing, contrasting, and reviewing to acquire basic and grade-level vocabulary 1 (E) internalize new, basic, and academic language by using and reusing it in meaningful ways in speaking and writing activities that build concept and language attainment 3 (E) share in cooperative learning interactions
(B) develop drafts by categorizing ideas and organizing them into paragraphs;	1 (C) use strategic learning techniques such as concept mapping, drawing, memorizing, comparing, contrasting, and reviewing to acquire basic and grade-level vocabulary 1 (E) internalize new, basic, and academic language by using and reusing it in meaningful ways in speaking and writing activities that build concept and language attainment 5 (F) write using a variety of grade-appropriate sentence lengths, patterns, and connecting words to combine phrases, clauses, and sentences in increasingly accurate ways as more English is acquired
(C) revise drafts for coherence, organization, use of simple and compound sentences, and audience;	5 (F) write using a variety of grade-appropriate sentence lengths, patterns, and connecting words to combine phrases, clauses, and sentences in increasingly accurate ways as more English is acquired
(D) edit drafts for grammar, mechanics, and spelling using a teacher-developed rubric; and	5 (D) edit writing for standard grammar and usage, including subject-verb agreement, pronoun agreement, and appropriate verb tenses commensurate with grade-level expectations as more English is acquired
(E) publish written work for a specific audience.	3 (E) share in cooperative learning interactions
(18) Writing/Literary Texts. Students write literary texts to express their ideas and feelings about real or imagined people, events, and ideas. Students are expected to:	
(A) write imaginative stories that build the plot to a climax and contain details about the characters and setting; and	5 (F) write using a variety of grade-appropriate sentence lengths, patterns, and connecting words to combine phrases, clauses, and sentences in increasingly accurate ways as more English is acquired; and 5 (G) narrate, describe, and explain with increasing specificity and detail to fulfill content-area writing needs as more English is acquired
(B) write poems that convey sensory details using the conventions of poetry (e.g., rhyme, meter, patterns of verse).	1 (E) internalize new, basic, and academic language by using and reusing it in meaningful ways in speaking and writing activities that build concept and language attainment 5 (B) write using newly acquired basic vocabulary and content-based grade-level vocabulary

Third-Grade ELAR TEKS	ELPS
(19) *Writing. Students write about their own experiences. Students are expected to write about important personal experiences.*	1 (A) use prior knowledge and experiences to understand meanings in English 5 (F) write using a variety of grade-appropriate sentence lengths, patterns, and connecting words to combine phrases, clauses, and sentences in increasingly accurate ways as more English is acquired 5 (G) narrate, describe, and explain with increasing specificity and detail to fulfill content-area writing needs as more English is acquired
(20) *Writing/Expository and Procedural Texts. Students write expository and procedural or work-related texts to communicate ideas and information to specific audiences for specific purposes. Students are expected to:*	
(A) create brief compositions that: (i) establish a central idea in a topic sentence; (ii) include supporting sentences with simple facts, details, and explanations; and (iii) contain a concluding statement;	5 (F) write using a variety of grade-appropriate sentence lengths, patterns, and connecting words to combine phrases, clauses, and sentences in increasingly accurate ways as more English is acquired
(B) write letters whose language is tailored to the audience and purpose (e.g., a thank you note to a friend) and that use appropriate conventions (e.g., date, salutation, closing); and	1 (G) demonstrate an increasing ability to distinguish between formal and informal English and an increasing knowledge of when to use each one commensurate with grade-level learning expectation 5 (F) write using a variety of grade-appropriate sentence lengths, patterns, and connecting words to combine phrases, clauses, and sentences in increasingly accurate ways as more English is acquired 5 (G) narrate, describe, and explain with increasing specificity and detail to fulfill content-area writing needs as more English is acquired
(C) write responses to literary or expository texts that demonstrate an understanding of the text.	4 (K) demonstrate English comprehension and expand reading skills by employing analytical skills such as evaluating written information and performing critical analyses commensurate with content-area and grade-level needs 5 (B) write using newly acquired basic vocabulary and content-based grade-level vocabulary 5 (F) write using a variety of grade-appropriate sentence lengths, patterns, and connecting words to combine phrases, clauses, and sentences in increasingly accurate ways as more English is acquired 5 (G) narrate, describe, and explain with increasing specificity and detail to fulfill content-area writing needs as more English is acquired
(21) *Writing/Persuasive Texts. Students write persuasive texts to influence the attitudes or actions of a specific audience on specific issues. Students are expected to write persuasive essays for appropriate audiences that establish a position and use supporting details.*	5 (F) write using a variety of grade-appropriate sentence lengths, patterns, and connecting words to combine phrases, clauses, and sentences in increasingly accurate ways as more English is acquired 5 (G) narrate, describe, and explain with increasing specificity and detail to fulfill content-area writing needs as more English is acquired

Third-Grade ELAR TEKS	ELPS
(22) Oral and Written Conventions/Conventions. Students understand the function of and use the conventions of academic language when speaking and writing. Students continue to apply earlier standards with greater complexity. Students are expected to:	
(A) use and understand the function of the following parts of speech in the context of reading, writing, and speaking: (i) verbs (past, present, and future); (ii) nouns (singular/plural, common/proper); (iii) adjectives (e.g., descriptive: wooden, rectangular; limiting: this, that; articles: a, an, the); (iv) adverbs (e.g., time: before, next; manner: carefully, beautifully); (v) prepositions and prepositional phrases; (vi) possessive pronouns (e.g., his, hers, theirs); (vii) coordinating conjunctions (e.g., and, or, but); and (viii) time-order transition words and transitions that indicate a conclusion;	5 (E) employ increasingly complex grammatical structures in content-area writing commensurate with grade-level expectations, such as: (i) using correct verbs, tenses, and pronouns / antecedents (ii) using possessive case (apostrophes) correctly (iii) using negatives and contractions correctly 5 (F) write using a variety of grade-appropriate sentence lengths, patterns, and connecting words to combine phrases, clauses, and sentences in increasingly accurate ways as more English is acquired
(B) use the complete subject and the complete predicate in a sentence; and	5 (F) write using a variety of grade-appropriate sentence lengths, patterns, and connecting words to combine phrases, clauses, and sentences in increasingly accurate ways as more English is acquired
(C) use complete simple and compound sentences with correct subject-verb agreement.	5 (D) edit writing for standard grammar and usage, including subject-verb agreement, pronoun agreement, and appropriate verb tenses commensurate with grade-level expectations as more English is acquired 5 (E) employ increasingly complex grammatical structures in content-area writing commensurate with grade-level expectations, such as: (i) using correct verbs, tenses, and pronouns / antecedents (ii) using possessive case (apostrophes) correctly (iii) using negatives and contractions correctly
(23) Oral and Written Conventions/Handwriting, Capitalization, and Punctuation. Students write legibly and use appropriate capitalization and punctuation conventions in their compositions. Students are expected to:	
(A) write legibly in cursive script with spacing between words in a sentence;	5 (B) write using newly acquired basic vocabulary and content-based grade-level vocabulary
(B) use capitalization for: (i) geographical names and places; (ii) historical periods; and (iii) official titles of people;	5 (C) spell familiar English words with increasing accuracy, and employ English spelling patterns and rules with increasing accuracy as more English is acquired 5 (D) edit writing for standard grammar and usage, including subject-verb agreement, pronoun agreement, and appropriate verb tenses

Third Grade ELAR TEKS	ELPS
(23) cont . . . (C) recognize and use punctuation marks including: (i) apostrophes in contractions and possessives; (ii) commas in series and dates; and	5 (C) spell familiar English words with increasing accuracy, and employ English spelling patterns and rules with increasing accuracy as more English is acquired
(D) use correct mechanics including paragraph indentations.	5 (C) spell familiar English words with increasing accuracy, and employ English spelling patterns and rules with increasing accuracy as more English is acquired
(24) Oral and Written Conventions/Spelling. Students spell correctly. Students are expected to:	
(A) use knowledge of letter sounds, word parts, word segmentation, and syllabication to spell;	5 (A) learn relationships between sounds and letters of the English language to represent sounds when writing in English
(B) spell words with more advanced orthographic patterns and rules: (i) consonant doubling when adding an ending; (ii) dropping final "e" when endings are added (e.g., *ing, ed*); (iii) changing "y" to "i" before adding an ending; (iv) double consonants in middle of words; (v) complex consonants (e.g., *scr, dge, tch*); and (vi) abstract vowels (e.g., ou as in *could, touch, through, bought*);	5 (C) spell familiar English words with increasing accuracy, and employ English spelling patterns and rules with increasing accuracy as more English is acquired
(C) spell high-frequency and compound words from a commonly used list;	5 (C) spell familiar English words with increasing accuracy, and employ English spelling patterns and rules with increasing accuracy as more English is acquired
(D) spell words with common syllable constructions (e.g., closed, open, final stable syllable);	5 (C) spell familiar English words with increasing accuracy, and employ English spelling patterns and rules with increasing accuracy as more English is acquired
(E) spell single syllable homophones (e.g., bear/bare; week/weak; road/rode);	5 (C) spell familiar English words with increasing accuracy, and employ English spelling patterns and rules with increasing accuracy as more English is acquired
(F) spell complex contractions (e.g., should've, won't); and	5 (C) spell familiar English words with increasing accuracy, and employ English spelling patterns and rules with increasing accuracy as more English is acquired
(G) use print and electronic resources to find and check correct spellings.	1 (B) monitor oral and written language production and employ self-corrective techniques or other resources
(25) Research/Research Plan. Students ask open-ended research questions and develop a plan for answering them. Students are expected to:	
(A) generate research topics from personal interests or by brainstorming with others, narrow to one topic, and formulate open-ended questions about the major research topic; and	1 (E) internalize new, basic, and academic language by using and reusing it in meaningful ways in speaking and writing activities that build concept and language attainment 3 (G) express opinions, ideas, and feelings ranging from communicating single words and short phrases to participating in extended discussions on a variety of social and grade-appropriate academic topics

Third-Grade ELAR TEKS	ELPS
(25) cont . . . (B) generate a research plan for gathering relevant information (e.g., surveys, interviews, encyclopedias) about the major research question.	*No ELPS Correlation*
(26) Research/Gathering Sources. Students determine, locate, and explore the full range of relevant sources addressing a research question and systematically record the information they gather. Students are expected to:	
(A) follow the research plan to collect information from multiple sources of information, both oral and written, including: (i) student-initiated surveys, on-site inspections, and interviews; (ii) data from experts, reference texts, and online searches; and (iii) visual sources of information (e.g., maps, timelines, graphs) where appropriate;	2 (E) use visual, contextual, and linguistic support to enhance and confirm understanding of increasingly complex and elaborated spoken language 3 (F) ask and give information ranging from using a very limited bank of high-frequency, high-need, concrete vocabulary, including key words and expressions needed for basic communication in academic and social contexts, to using abstract and content-based vocabulary during extended speaking assignments 4 (D) use prereading supports such as graphic organizers, illustrations, and pretaught topic-related vocabulary and other prereading activities to enhance comprehension of written text
(B) use skimming and scanning techniques to identify data by looking at text features (e.g., bold print, captions, key words, italics);	4 (D) use prereading supports such as graphic organizers, illustrations, and pretaught topic-related vocabulary and other prereading activities to enhance comprehension of written text
(C) take simple notes and sort evidence into provided categories or an organizer;	4 (G) demonstrate comprehension of increasingly complex English by participating in shared reading, retelling or summarizing material, responding to questions, and taking notes commensurate with content-area and grade-level needs
(D) identify the author, title, publisher, and publication year of sources; and	*No ELPS Correlation*
(E) differentiate between paraphrasing and plagiarism and identify the importance of citing valid and reliable sources.	*No ELPS Correlation*
(27) Research/Synthesizing Information. Students clarify research questions and evaluate and synthesize collected information. Students are expected to improve the focus of research as a result of consulting expert sources (e.g., reference librarians and local experts on the topic).	4 (F) use visual and contextual support and support from peers and teachers to read grade-appropriate content-area text, to enhance and confirm understanding, to develop vocabulary, to grasp language structures, and to tap background knowledge needed to comprehend increasingly challenging language 4 (J) demonstrate English comprehension and expand reading skills by employing inferential skills such as predicting, making connections between ideas, drawing inferences and conclusions from text and graphic sources, and finding supporting text evidence commensurate with content area needs

Third-Grade ELAR TEKS	ELPS
(28) *Research/Organizing and Presenting Ideas. Students organize and present their ideas and information according to the purpose of the research and their audience. Students are expected to draw conclusions through a brief written explanation and create a works-cited page from notes, including the author, title, publisher, and publication year for each source used.*	4 (J) demonstrate English comprehension and expand reading skills by employing inferential skills such as predicting, making connections between ideas, drawing inferences and conclusions from text and graphic sources, and finding supporting text evidence commensurate with content-area needs
(29) *Listening and Speaking/Listening. Students use comprehension skills to listen attentively to others in formal and informal settings. Students continue to apply earlier standards with greater complexity. Students are expected to:*	
(A) listen attentively to speakers, ask relevant questions, and make pertinent comments; and	2 (D) monitor understanding of spoken language during classroom instruction and interactions and seek clarification as needed 2 (I) demonstrate listening comprehension of increasingly complex spoken English by following directions, retelling or summarizing spoken messages, responding to questions and requests, collaborating with peers, and taking notes commensurate with content and grade-level needs 3 (F) ask and give information ranging from using a very limited bank of high-frequency, high-need, concrete vocabulary, including key words and expressions needed for basic communication in academic and social contexts, to using abstract and content-based vocabulary during extended speaking assignments
(B) follow, restate, and give oral instructions that involve a series of related sequences of action.	2 (G) understand the general meaning, main points, and important details of spoken language ranging from situations in which topics, language, and contexts are familiar to unfamiliar 2 (H) understand implicit ideas and information in increasingly complex spoken language commensurate with grade-level learning expectations 2 (I) demonstrate listening comprehension of increasingly complex spoken English by following directions, retelling or summarizing spoken messages, responding to questions and requests, collaborating with peers, and taking notes commensurate with content and grade-level needs 3 (F) ask and give information ranging from using a very limited bank of high-frequency, high-need, concrete vocabulary, including key words and expressions needed for basic communication in academic and social contexts, to using abstract and content-based vocabulary during extended speaking assignments

Third-Grade ELAR TEKS	ELPS
(30) Listening and Speaking/Speaking. Students speak clearly and to the point, using the conventions of language. Students continue to apply earlier standards with greater complexity. Students are expected to speak coherently about the topic under discussion, employing eye contact, speaking rate, volume, enunciation, and the conventions of language to communicate ideas effectively.	1 (D) speak using learning strategies such as requesting assistance, employing nonverbal cues, and using synonyms and circumlocution 2 (C) learn new language structures, expressions, and basic and academic vocabulary heard during classroom instruction and interactions 3 (B) expand and internalize initial English vocabulary by learning and using high-frequency English words necessary for identifying and describing people, places, and objects, by retelling simple stories and basic information represented or supported by pictures, and by learning and using routine language needed for classroom communication 3 (C) speak using a variety of grammatical structures, sentence lengths, sentence types, and connecting words with increasing accuracy and ease as more English is acquired 3 (D) speak using grade-level content-area vocabulary in context to internalize new English words and build academic language proficiency 3 (G) express opinions, ideas, and feelings ranging from communicating single words and short phrases to participating in extended discussions on a variety of social and grade-appropriate academic topics 3 (H) narrate, describe, and explain with increasing specificity and detail as more English is acquired 3 (I) adapt spoken language appropriately for formal and informal purposes 3 (J) respond orally to information presented in a wide variety of print, electronic, audio, and visual media to build and reinforce concept and language attainment
(31) Listening and Speaking/Teamwork. Students work productively with others in teams. Students continue to apply earlier standards with greater complexity. Students are expected to participate in teacher- and student-led discussions by posing and answering questions with appropriate detail and by providing suggestions that build upon the ideas of others.	1 (B) monitor oral and written language production and employ self-corrective techniques or other resources 1 (G) demonstrate an increasing ability to distinguish between formal and informal English and an increasing knowledge of when to use each one commensurate with grade-level learning expectations 2 (I) demonstrate listening comprehension of increasingly complex spoken English by following directions, retelling or summarizing spoken messages, responding to questions and requests, collaborating with peers, and taking notes 3 (E) share information in cooperative learning interactions
Listening and Speaking/Teamwork – No Correlation	**2 (A) distinguish sounds and intonation patterns of English with increasing ease** **2 (B) recognize elements of the English sound system in newly acquired vocabulary such as long and short vowels, silent letters, and consonant clusters** **3 (A) practice producing sounds of newly acquired vocabulary such as long and short vowels, silent letters, and consonant clusters to pronounce English words in a manner that is increasingly comprehensible**

ELAR TEKS and ELPS Side-by-Side
Fourth-Grade

Fourth-Grade ELAR TEKS	ELPS
(1) *Reading/Fluency. Students read grade-level text with fluency and comprehension. Students are expected to read aloud grade-level stories with fluency (rate, accuracy, expression, appropriate phrasing) and comprehension.*	4 (E) read linguistically accommodated content-area material with a decreasing need for linguistic accommodations as more English is learned 4 (H) read silently with increasing ease and comprehension for longer periods
(2) *Reading/Vocabulary Development. Students understand new vocabulary and use it when reading and writing. Students are expected to:*	
(A) determine the meaning of grade-level academic English words derived from Latin, Greek, or other linguistic roots and affixes;	4 (A) learn relationships between sounds and letters of the English language and decode (sound out) words using a combination of skills such as recognizing sound-letter relationships and identifying cognates, affixes, roots, and base words 4 (C) develop basic sight vocabulary, derive meaning of environmental print, and comprehend English vocabulary and language structures used routinely in written classroom materials
(B) use the context of the sentence (e.g., in-sentence example or definition) to determine the meaning of unfamiliar words or multiple meaning words;	1 (F) use accessible language and learn new and essential language in the process 4 (F) use visual and contextual support and support from peers and teachers to read grade-appropriate content-area text, to enhance and confirm understanding, to develop vocabulary, to grasp language structures, and to tap background knowledge needed to comprehend increasingly challenging language
(C) complete analogies using knowledge of antonyms and synonyms (e.g., boy:girl as male: ____ or girl:woman as boy: _____);	1 (C) use strategic learning techniques such as concept mapping, drawing, memorizing, comparing, contrasting, and reviewing to acquire basic and grade-level vocabulary
(D) identify the meaning of common idioms; and	1 (G) demonstrate an increasing ability to distinguish between formal and informal English and an increasing knowledge of when to use each one commensurate with grade-level learning expectations 1 (H) develop and expand repertoire of learning strategies such as reasoning inductively or deductively, looking for patterns in language, and analyzing sayings and expressions commensurate with grade-level learning expectations
(E) use a dictionary or glossary to determine the meanings, syllabication, and pronunciation of unknown words.	1 (B) monitor oral and written language production and employ self-corrective techniques or other resources

Fourth-Grade ELAR TEKS	ELPS
(3) *Reading/Comprehension of Literary Text/Theme and Genre. Students analyze, make inferences, and draw conclusions about theme and genre in different cultural, historical, and contemporary contexts and provide evidence from the text to support their understanding. Students are expected to:*	
(A) summarize and explain the lesson or message of a work of fiction as its theme; and	4 (G) demonstrate comprehension of increasingly complex English by participating in shared reading, retelling or summarizing material, responding to questions, and taking notes commensurate with content-area and grade-level needs 4 (I) demonstrate English comprehension and expand reading skills by employing basic reading skills such as demonstrating understanding of supporting ideas and details in text and graphic sources, summarizing text, and distinguishing main ideas from details commensurate with content-area needs
(B) compare and contrast the adventures or exploits of characters (e.g., the trickster) in traditional and classical literature.	1 (C) use strategic learning techniques such as concept mapping, drawing, memorizing, comparing, contrasting, and reviewing to acquire basic and grade-level vocabulary 4 (K) demonstrate English comprehension and expand reading skills by employing analytical skills such as evaluating written information and performing critical analyses commensurate with content-area and grade-level needs
(4) *Reading/Comprehension of Literary Text/Poetry. Students understand, make inferences, and draw conclusions about the structure and elements of poetry and provide evidence from text to support their understanding. Students are expected to explain how the structural elements of poetry (e.g., rhyme, meter, stanzas, line breaks) relate to form (e.g., lyrical poetry, free verse).*	1 (H) develop and expand repertoire of learning strategies such as reasoning inductively or deductively, looking for patterns in language, and analyzing sayings and expressions commensurate with grade-level learning expectations 4 (J) demonstrate English comprehension and expand reading skills by employing inferential skills such as predicting, making connections between ideas, drawing inferences and conclusions from text and graphic sources, and finding supporting text evidence commensurate with content-area needs
(5) *Reading/Comprehension of Literary Text/Drama. Students understand, make inferences, and draw conclusions about the structure and elements of drama and provide evidence from text to support their understanding. Students are expected to describe the structural elements particular to dramatic literature.*	4 (J) demonstrate English comprehension and expand reading skills by employing inferential skills such as predicting, making connections between ideas, drawing inferences and conclusions from text and graphic sources, and finding supporting text evidence commensurate with content-area needs

Fourth-Grade ELAR TEKS	ELPS
(6) *Reading/Comprehension of Literary Text/Fiction. Students understand, make inferences and draw conclusions about the structure and elements of fiction and provide evidence from text to support their understanding. Students are expected to:*	
(A) sequence and summarize the plot's main events and explain their influence on future events;	4 (G) demonstrate comprehension of increasingly complex English by participating in shared reading, retelling or summarizing material, responding to questions, and taking notes commensurate with content-area and grade-level needs 4 (I) demonstrate English comprehension and expand reading skills by employing basic reading skills such as demonstrating understanding of supporting ideas and details in text and graphic sources, summarizing text, and distinguishing main ideas from details commensurate with content-area needs
(B) describe the interaction of characters including their relationships and the changes they undergo; and	4 (J) demonstrate English comprehension and expand reading skills by employing inferential skills such as predicting, making connections between ideas, drawing inferences and conclusions from text and graphic sources, and finding supporting text evidence commensurate with content-area needs 4 (K) demonstrate English comprehension and expand reading skills by employing analytical skills such as evaluating written information and performing critical analyses commensurate with content-area and grade-level needs
(C) identify whether the narrator or speaker of a story is first or third person.	*No ELPS Correlation*
(7) *Reading/Comprehension of Literary Text/Literary Nonfiction. Students understand, make inferences and draw conclusions about the varied structural patterns and features of literary nonfiction and provide evidence from text to support their understanding. Students are expected to identify similarities and differences between the events and characters' experiences in a fictional work and the actual events and experiences described in an author's biography or autobiography.*	4 (J) demonstrate English comprehension and expand reading skills by employing inferential skills such as predicting, making connections between ideas, drawing inferences and conclusions from text and graphic sources, and finding supporting text evidence commensurate with content-area needs 4 (K) demonstrate English comprehension and expand reading skills by employing analytical skills such as evaluating written information and performing critical analyses commensurate with content-area and grade-level needs
(8) *Reading/Comprehension of Literary Text/Sensory Language. Students understand, make inferences and draw conclusions about how an author's sensory language creates imagery in literary text and provide evidence from text to support their understanding. Students are expected to identify the author's use of similes and metaphors to produce imagery.*	1 (H) develop and expand repertoire of learning strategies such as reasoning inductively or deductively, looking for patterns in language, and analyzing sayings and expressions commensurate with grade-level learning expectations 4 (J) demonstrate English comprehension and expand reading skills by employing inferential skills such as predicting, making connections between ideas, drawing inferences and conclusions from text and graphic sources, and finding supporting text evidence commensurate with content-area needs

Fourth-Grade ELAR TEKS	ELPS
(9) *Reading/Comprehension of Text/Independent Reading. Students read independently for sustained periods of time and produce evidence of their reading. Students are expected to read independently for a sustained period of time and paraphrase what the reading was about, maintaining meaning and logical order (e.g., generate a reading log or journal; participate in book talks).*	4 (E) read linguistically accommodated content-area material with a decreasing need for linguistic accommodations as more English is learned 4 (H) read silently with increasing ease and comprehension for longer periods 4 (I) demonstrate English comprehension and expand reading skills by employing basic reading skills such as demonstrating understanding of supporting ideas and details in text and graphic sources, summarizing text, and distinguishing main ideas from details commensurate with content-area needs
(10) *Reading/Comprehension of Informational Text/Culture and History. Students analyze, make inferences and draw conclusions about the author's purpose in cultural, historical, and contemporary contexts and provide evidence from the text to support their understanding. Students are expected to explain the difference between a stated and an implied purpose for an expository text.*	4 (J) demonstrate English comprehension and expand reading skills by employing inferential skills such as predicting, making connections between ideas, drawing inferences and conclusions from text and graphic sources, and finding supporting text evidence commensurate with content-area needs 4 (K) demonstrate English comprehension and expand reading skills by employing analytical skills such as evaluating written information and performing critical analyses commensurate with content-area and grade-level needs
(11) *Reading/Comprehension of Informational Text/Expository Text. Students analyze, make inferences and draw conclusions about expository text and provide evidence from text to support their understanding. Students are expected to:*	
(A) summarize the main idea and supporting details in text in ways that maintain meaning;	4 (G) demonstrate comprehension of increasingly complex English by participating in shared reading, retelling or summarizing material, responding to questions, and taking notes commensurate with content-area and grade-level needs 4 (I) demonstrate English comprehension and expand reading skills by employing basic reading skills such as demonstrating understanding of supporting ideas and details in text and graphic sources, summarizing text, and distinguishing main ideas from details commensurate with content-area needs
(B) distinguish fact from opinion in a text and explain how to verify what is a fact;	4 (K) demonstrate English comprehension and expand reading skills by employing analytical skills such as evaluating written information and performing critical analyses commensurate with content-area and grade-level needs
(C) describe explicit and implicit relationships among ideas in texts organized by cause-and-effect, sequence, or comparison; and	4 (J) demonstrate English comprehension and expand reading skills by employing inferential skills such as predicting, making connections between ideas, drawing inferences and conclusions from text and graphic sources, and finding supporting text evidence commensurate with content-area needs

Fourth-Grade ELAR TEKS	ELPS
(11) (C) cont . . .	4 (K) demonstrate English comprehension and expand reading skills by employing analytical skills such as evaluating written information and performing critical analyses commensurate with content-area and grade-level needs
(D) use multiple text features (e.g., guide words, topic and concluding sentences) to gain an overview of the contents of text and to locate information.	4 (D) use prereading supports such as graphic organizers, illustrations, and pretaught topic-related vocabulary and other prereading activities to enhance comprehension of written text
(12) Reading/Comprehension of Informational Text/Persuasive Text. Students analyze, make inferences, and draw conclusions about persuasive text and provide evidence from text to support their analysis. Students are expected to explain how an author uses language to present information to influence what the reader thinks or does.	4 (J) demonstrate English comprehension and expand reading skills by employing inferential skills such as predicting, making connections between ideas, drawing inferences and conclusions from text and graphic sources, and finding supporting text evidence commensurate with content-area needs 4 (K) demonstrate English comprehension and expand reading skills by employing analytical skills such as evaluating written information and performing critical analyses commensurate with content-area and grade-level needs
(13) Reading/Comprehension of Informational Text/Procedural Texts. Students understand how to glean and use information in procedural texts and documents. Students are expected to:	
(A) determine the sequence of activities needed to carry out a procedure (e.g., following a recipe); and	4 (F) use visual and contextual support and support from peers and teachers to read grade-appropriate content-area text, enhance and confirm understanding, and develop vocabulary, grasp of language structures, and background knowledge needed to comprehend increasingly challenging language
(B) explain factual information presented graphically (e.g., charts, diagrams, graphs, illustrations).	4 (D) use prereading supports such as graphic organizers, illustrations, and pretaught topic-related vocabulary and other prereading activities to enhance comprehension of written text 4 (F) use visual and contextual support and support from peers and teachers to read grade-appropriate content-area text, to enhance and confirm understanding, to develop vocabulary, to grasp language structures, and to tap background knowledge needed to comprehend increasingly challenging language
(14) Reading/Media Literacy. Students use comprehension skills to analyze how words, images, graphics, and sounds work together in various forms to impact meaning. Students continue to apply earlier standards with greater depth in increasingly more complex texts. Students are expected to:	

Fourth-Grade ELAR TEKS	ELPS
(14) cont . . . (A) explain the positive and negative impacts of advertisement techniques used in various genres of media to impact consumer behavior;	2 (F) listen to and derive meaning from a variety of media such as audio tape, video, DVD, and CD-ROM to build and reinforce concept and language attainment; 4 (K) demonstrate English comprehension and expand reading skills by employing analytical skills such as evaluating written information and performing critical analyses commensurate with content-area and grade-level needs
(B) explain how various design techniques used in media influence the message (e.g., pacing, close-ups, sound effects); and	*No ELPS Correlation*
(C) compare various written conventions used for digital media (e.g., language in an informal e-mail vs. language in a Web-based news article).	1 (G) demonstrate an increasing ability to distinguish between formal and informal English and an increasing knowledge of when to use each one commensurate with grade-level learning expectations 4 (K) demonstrate English comprehension and expand reading skills by employing analytical skills such as evaluating written information and performing critical analyses commensurate with content-area and grade-level needs
Reading/Media Literacy – No Correlation	**4(B) recognize directionality of English reading such as left to right and top to bottom** **4 (E) read linguistically accommodated content-area material with a decreasing need for linguistic accommodations as more English is learned**
(15) Writing/Writing Process. Students use elements of the writing process (planning, drafting, revising, editing, and publishing) to compose text. Students are expected to:	
(A) plan a first draft by selecting a genre appropriate for conveying the intended meaning to an audience and generating ideas through a range of strategies (e.g., brainstorming, graphic organizers, logs, journals);	1 (C) use strategic learning techniques such as concept mapping, drawing, memorizing, comparing, contrasting, and reviewing to acquire basic and grade-level vocabulary 1 (E) internalize new, basic, and academic language by using and reusing it in meaningful ways in speaking and writing activities that build concept and language attainment 3 (E) share in cooperative learning interactions
(B) develop drafts by categorizing ideas and organizing them into paragraphs;	1 (C) use strategic learning techniques such as concept mapping, drawing, memorizing, comparing, contrasting, and reviewing to acquire basic and grade-level vocabulary 1 (E) internalize new, basic, and academic language by using and reusing it in meaningful ways in speaking and writing activities that build concept and language attainment 5 (F) write using a variety of grade-appropriate sentence lengths, patterns, and connecting words to combine phrases, clauses, and sentences in increasingly accurate ways as more English is acquired
(C) revise drafts for coherence, organization, use of simple and compound sentences, and audience;	5 (F) write using a variety of grade-appropriate sentence lengths, patterns, and connecting words to combine phrases, clauses, and sentences in increasingly accurate ways as more English is acquired

Fourth-Grade ELAR TEKS	ELPS
(15) cont . . . (D) edit drafts for grammar, mechanics, and spelling using a teacher-developed rubric; and	5 (D) edit writing for standard grammar and usage, including subject-verb agreement, pronoun agreement, and appropriate verb tenses commensurate with grade-level expectations as more English is acquired
(E) revise final draft in response to feedback from peers and teacher and publish written work for a specific audience.	4 (F) use visual and contextual support and support from peers and teachers to read grade-appropriate content-area text, to enhance and confirm understanding, to develop vocabulary, to grasp language structures, and to tap background knowledge needed to comprehend increasingly challenging language
(16) Writing/Literary Texts. Students write literary texts to express their ideas and feelings about real or imagined people, events, and ideas. Students are expected to:	
(A) write imaginative stories that build the plot to a climax and contain details about the characters and setting; and	5 (B) write using newly acquired basic vocabulary and content-based grade-level vocabulary 5 (F) write using a variety of grade-appropriate sentence lengths, patterns, and connecting words to combine phrases, clauses, and sentences in increasingly accurate ways as more English is acquired 5 (G) narrate, describe, and explain with increasing specificity and detail to fulfill content-area writing needs as more English is acquired
(B) write poems that convey sensory details using the conventions of poetry (e.g., rhyme, meter, patterns of verse).	1 (E) internalize new, basic, and academic language by using and reusing it in meaningful ways in speaking and writing activities that build concept and language attainment 5 (B) write using newly acquired basic vocabulary and content-based grade-level vocabulary
(17) Writing. Students write about their own experiences. Students are expected to write about important personal experiences.	5 (F) write using a variety of grade-appropriate sentence lengths, patterns, and connecting words to combine phrases, clauses, and sentences in increasingly accurate ways as more English is acquired 5 (G) narrate, describe, and explain with increasing specificity and detail to fulfill content-area writing needs as more English is acquired
(18) Writing/Expository and Procedural Texts. Students write expository and procedural or work-related texts to communicate ideas and information to specific audiences for specific purposes. Students are expected to:	

Fourth-Grade ELAR TEKS	ELPS
(18) cont . . . (A) create brief compositions that: (i) establish a central idea in a topic sentence; (ii) include supporting sentences with simple facts, details, and explanations; and (iii) contain a concluding statement;	5 (B) write using newly acquired basic vocabulary and content-based grade-level vocabulary 5 (F) write using a variety of grade-appropriate sentence lengths, patterns, and connecting words to combine phrases, clauses, and sentences in increasingly accurate ways as more English is acquired 5 (G) narrate, describe, and explain with increasing specificity and detail to fulfill content-area writing needs as more English is acquired
(B) write letters whose language is tailored to the audience and purpose (e.g., a thank you note to a friend) and that use appropriate conventions (e.g., date, salutation, closing); and	2 (E) use visual, contextual, and linguistic support to enhance and confirm understanding of increasingly complex and elaborated spoken language 5 (F) write using a variety of grade-appropriate sentence lengths, patterns, and connecting words to combine phrases, clauses, and sentences in increasingly accurate ways as more English is acquired
(C) write responses to literary or expository texts and provide evidence from the text to demonstrate understanding.	5 (F) write using a variety of grade-appropriate sentence lengths, patterns, and connecting words to combine phrases, clauses, and sentences in increasingly accurate ways as more English is acquired
(19) Writing/Persuasive Texts. Students write persuasive texts to influence the attitudes or actions of a specific audience on specific issues. Students are expected to write persuasive essays for appropriate audiences that establish a position and use supporting details.	5 (F) write using a variety of grade-appropriate sentence lengths, patterns, and connecting words to combine phrases, clauses, and sentences in increasingly accurate ways as more English is acquired 5 (G) narrate, describe, and explain with increasing specificity and detail to fulfill content-area writing needs as more English is acquired
(20) Oral and Written Conventions/Conventions. Students understand the function of and use the conventions of academic language when speaking and writing. Students continue to apply earlier standards with greater complexity. Students are expected to:	
(A) use and understand the function of the following parts of speech in the context of reading, writing, and speaking: (i) verbs (irregular verbs); (ii) nouns (singular/plural, common/proper); (iii) adjectives (e.g., descriptive, including purpose: sleeping bag, frying pan) and their comparative and superlative forms (e.g., fast, faster, fastest); (iv) adverbs (e.g., frequency: usually, sometimes; intensity: almost, a lot); (v) prepositions and prepositional phrases to convey location, time, direction, or to provide details;	5 (E) employ increasingly complex grammatical structures in content-area writing commensurate with grade-level expectations, such as: (i) using correct verbs, tenses, and pronouns / antecedents (ii) using possessive case (apostrophe s) correctly (iii) using negatives and contractions correctly 5 (F) write using a variety of grade-appropriate sentence lengths, patterns, and connecting words to combine phrases, clauses, and sentences in increasingly accurate ways as more English is acquired

Fourth-Grade ELAR TEKS	ELPS
(20) (A) cont . . . (vi) reflexive pronouns (e.g., myself, ourselves); (vii) correlative conjunctions (e.g., either/or, neither/nor); and (viii) use time-order transition words and transitions that indicate a conclusion;	5 (E) employ increasingly complex grammatical structures in content-area writing commensurate with grade-level expectations, such as: (i) using correct verbs, tenses, and pronouns / antecedents (ii) using possessive case (apostrophe s) correctly (iii) using negatives and contractions correctly 5 (F) write using a variety of grade-appropriate sentence lengths, patterns, and connecting words to combine phrases, clauses, and sentences in increasingly accurate ways as more English is acquired
(B) use the complete subject and the complete predicate in a sentence; and	5 (F) write using a variety of grade-appropriate sentence lengths, patterns, and connecting words to combine phrases, clauses, and sentences in increasingly accurate ways as more English is acquired
(C) use complete simple and compound sentences with correct subject-verb agreement.	5 (D) edit writing for standard grammar and usage, including subject-verb agreement, pronoun agreement, and appropriate verb tenses commensurate with grade-level expectations as more English is acquired 5 (E) employ increasingly complex grammatical structures in content-area writing commensurate with grade-level expectations, such as: (i) using correct verbs, tenses, and pronouns / antecedents (ii) using possessive case (apostrophes) correctly (iii) using negatives and contractions correctly
(21) Oral and Written Conventions/Handwriting, Capitalization, and Punctuation. Students write legibly and use appropriate capitalization and punctuation conventions in their compositions. Students are expected to:	
(A) write legibly by selecting cursive script or manuscript printing as appropriate;	5 (B) write using newly acquired basic vocabulary and content-based grade-level vocabulary
(B) use capitalization for: (i) historical events and documents; (ii) titles of books, stories, and essays; and (iii) languages, races, and nationalities; and	5 (C) spell familiar English words with increasing accuracy, and employ English spelling patterns and rules with increasing accuracy as more English is acquired 5 (D) edit writing for standard grammar and usage, including subject-verb agreement, pronoun agreement, and appropriate verb tenses
(C) recognize and use punctuation marks including: (i) commas in compound sentences; and (ii) quotation marks.	5 (E) employ increasingly complex grammatical structures in content-area writing commensurate with grade-level expectations, such as: (i) using correct verbs, tenses, and pronouns / antecedents (ii) using possessive case (apostrophes) correctly (iii) using negatives and contractions correctly

Fourth-Grade ELAR TEKS	ELPS
(22) Oral and Written Conventions/Spelling. Students spell correctly. Students are expected to:	
(A) spell words with more advanced orthographic patterns and rules: (i) plural rules (e.g., words ending in f as in *leaf, leaves*; adding es); (ii) irregular plurals (e.g., *man/men, foot/feet, child/children*); (iii) double consonants in middle of words; (iv) other ways to spell sh (e.g., *sion, tion, cian*); and (v) silent letters (e.g., *knee, wring*);	5 (C) spell familiar English words with increasing accuracy, and employ English spelling patterns and rules with increasing accuracy as more English is acquired
(B) spell base words and roots with affixes (e.g., *ion, ment, ly, dis, pre*);	5 (C) spell familiar English words with increasing accuracy, and employ English spelling patterns and rules with increasing accuracy as more English is acquired
(C) spell commonly used homophones (e.g., *there, they're, their; two, too, to*); and	5 (C) spell familiar English words with increasing accuracy, and employ English spelling patterns and rules with increasing accuracy as more English is acquired
(D) use spelling patterns and rules and print and electronic resources to determine and check correct spellings.	1 (B) monitor oral and written language production and employ self-corrective techniques or other resources 5 (C) spell familiar English words with increasing accuracy, and employ English spelling patterns and rules with increasing accuracy as more English is acquired
Oral and Written Conventions/Spelling – No Correlation	**5 (A) learn relationships between sounds and letters of the English language to represent sounds when writing in English**
(23) Research/Research Plan. Students ask open-ended research questions and develop a plan for answering them. Students are expected to:	
(A) generate research topics from personal interests or by brainstorming with others, narrow to one topic, and formulate open-ended questions about the major research topic; and	1 (E) internalize new, basic, and academic language by using and reusing it in meaningful ways in speaking and writing activities that build concept and language attainment 3 (G) express opinions, ideas, and feelings ranging from communicating single words and short phrases to participating in extended discussions on a variety of social and grade-appropriate academic topics
(B) generate a research plan for gathering relevant information (e.g., surveys, interviews, encyclopedias) about the major research question.	*No ELPS Correlation*
(24) Research/Gathering Sources. Students determine, locate, and explore the full range of relevant sources addressing a research question and systematically record the information they gather. Students are expected to:	

Fourth-Grade ELAR TEKS	ELPS
(24) cont . . . (A) follow the research plan to collect information from multiple sources of information both oral and written, including: (i) student-initiated surveys, on-site inspections, and interviews; (ii) data from experts, reference texts, and online searches; and (iii) visual sources of information (e.g., maps, timelines, graphs) where appropriate;	2 (E) use visual, contextual, and linguistic support to enhance and confirm understanding of increasingly complex and elaborated spoken language 3 (F) ask and give information ranging from using a very limited bank of high-frequency, high-need, concrete vocabulary, including key words and expressions needed for basic communication in academic and social contexts, to using abstract and content-based vocabulary during extended speaking assignments 4 (D) use prereading supports such as graphic organizers, illustrations, and pretaught topic-related vocabulary and other prereading activities to enhance comprehension of written text
(B) use skimming and scanning techniques to identify data by looking at text features (e.g., bold print, italics);	1 (C) use strategic learning techniques such as concept mapping, drawing, memorizing, comparing, contrasting, and reviewing to acquire basic and grade-level vocabulary 4 (D) use prereading supports such as graphic organizers, illustrations, and pretaught topic-related vocabulary and other prereading activities to enhance comprehension of written text
(C) take simple notes and sort evidence into provided categories or an organizer;	4 (G) demonstrate comprehension of increasingly complex English by participating in shared reading, retelling or summarizing material, responding to questions, and taking notes commensurate with content-area and grade-level needs
(D) identify the author, title, publisher, and publication year of sources; and	*No ELPS Correlation*
(E) differentiate between paraphrasing and plagiarism and identify the importance of citing valid and reliable sources.	*No ELPS Correlation*
(25) *Research/Synthesizing Information. Students clarify research questions and evaluate and synthesize collected information. Students are expected to improve the focus of research as a result of consulting expert sources (e.g., reference librarians and local experts on the topic).*	4 (F) use visual and contextual support and support from peers and teachers to read grade-appropriate content-area text, enhance and confirm understanding, and develop vocabulary, grasp of language structures, and background knowledge needed to comprehend increasingly challenging language 4 (J) demonstrate English comprehension and expand reading skills by employing inferential skills such as predicting, making connections between ideas, drawing inferences and conclusions from text and graphic sources, and finding supporting text evidence commensurate with content-area needs
(26) *Research/Organizing and Presenting Ideas. Students organize and present their ideas and information according to the purpose of the research and their audience. Students are expected to draw conclusions through a brief written explanation and create a works-cited page from notes, including the author, title, publisher, and publication year for each source used.*	4 (J) demonstrate English comprehension and expand reading skills by employing inferential skills such as predicting, making connections between ideas, drawing inferences and conclusions from text and graphic sources, and finding supporting text evidence commensurate with content-area needs

Fourth-Grade ELAR TEKS	ELPS
(27) Listening and Speaking/Listening. Students use comprehension skills to listen attentively to others in formal and informal settings. Students continue to apply earlier standards with greater complexity. Students are expected to:	
(A) listen attentively to speakers, ask relevant questions, and make pertinent comments; and	2 (D) monitor understanding of spoken language during classroom instruction and interactions and seek clarification as needed 2 (I) demonstrate listening comprehension of increasingly complex spoken English by following directions, retelling or summarizing spoken messages, responding to questions and requests, collaborating with peers, and taking notes commensurate with content and grade-level needs 3 (F) ask and give information ranging from using a very limited bank of high-frequency, high-need, concrete vocabulary, including key words and expressions needed for basic communication in academic and social contexts, to using abstract and content-based vocabulary during extended speaking assignments
(B) follow, restate, and give oral instructions that involve a series of related sequences of action.	2 (G) understand the general meaning, main points, and important details of spoken language ranging from situations in which topics, language, and contexts are familiar to unfamiliar 2 (H) understand implicit ideas and information in increasingly complex spoken language commensurate with grade-level learning expectations 2 (I) demonstrate listening comprehension of increasingly complex spoken English by following directions, retelling or summarizing spoken messages, responding to questions and requests, collaborating with peers, and taking notes commensurate with content and grade-level needs 3 (F) ask and give information ranging from using a very limited bank of high-frequency, high-need, concrete vocabulary, including key words and expressions needed for basic communication in academic and social contexts, to using abstract and content-based vocabulary during extended speaking assignments

Fourth-Grade ELAR TEKS	ELPS
(28) *Listening and Speaking/Speaking. Students speak clearly and to the point, using the conventions of language. Students continue to apply earlier standards with greater complexity. Students are expected to express an opinion supported by accurate information, employing eye contact, speaking rate, volume, and enunciation, and the conventions of language to communicate ideas effectively.*	1 (D) speak using learning strategies such as requesting assistance, employing nonverbal cues, and using synonyms and circumlocution 2 (C) learn new language structures, expressions, and basic and academic vocabulary heard during classroom instruction and interactions 3 (B) expand and internalize initial English vocabulary by learning and using high-frequency English words necessary for identifying and describing people, places, and objects, by retelling simple stories and basic information represented or supported by pictures, and by learning and using routine language needed for classroom communication 3 (C) speak using a variety of grammatical structures, sentence lengths, sentence types, and connecting words with increasing accuracy and ease as more English is acquired 3 (D) speak using grade-level content-area vocabulary in context to internalize new English words and build academic language proficiency 3 (G) express opinions, ideas, and feelings ranging from communicating single words and short phrases to participating in extended discussions on a variety of social and grade-appropriate academic topics 3 (H) narrate, describe, and explain with increasing specificity and detail as more English is acquired 3 (I) adapt spoken language appropriately for formal and informal purposes 3 (J) respond orally to information presented in a wide variety of print, electronic, audio, and visual media to build and reinforce concept and language attainment
Listening and Speaking / Speaking – No Correlation	**2 (A) distinguish sounds and intonation patterns of English with increasing ease**
	2 (B) recognize elements of the English sound system in newly acquired vocabulary such as long and short vowels, silent letters, and consonant clusters
	3 (A) practice producing sounds of newly acquired vocabulary such as long and short vowels, silent letters, and consonant clusters to pronounce English words in a manner that is increasingly comprehensible
(29) *Listening and Speaking/Teamwork. Students work productively with others in teams. Students continue to apply earlier standards with greater complexity. Students are expected to participate in teacher- and student-led discussions by posing and answering questions with appropriate detail and by providing suggestions that build upon the ideas of others.*	1 (B) monitor oral and written language production and employ self-corrective techniques or other resources 1 (G) demonstrate an increasing ability to distinguish between formal and informal English and an increasing knowledge of when to use each one commensurate with grade-level learning expectations 2 (I) demonstrate listening comprehension of increasingly complex spoken English by following directions, retelling or summarizing spoken messages, responding to questions and requests, collaborating with peers, and taking notes 3 (E) share information in cooperative learning interactions

This page is intentionally left blank.

ELAR TEKS and ELPS Side-by-Side
Fifth-Grade

Fifth-Grade ELAR TEKS	ELPS
(1) Reading/Fluency. Students read grade-level text with fluency and comprehension. Students are expected to read aloud grade-level stories with fluency (rate, accuracy, expression, appropriate phrasing) and comprehension.	4 (E) read linguistically accommodated content-area material with a decreasing need for linguistic accommodations as more English is learned 4 (H) read silently with increasing ease and comprehension for longer periods
(2) Reading/Vocabulary Development. Students understand new vocabulary and use it when reading and writing. Students are expected to:	
(A) determine the meaning of grade-level academic English words derived from Latin, Greek, or other linguistic roots and affixes;	4 (A) learn relationships between sounds and letters of the English language and decode (sound out) words using a combination of skills such as recognizing sound-letter relationships and identifying cognates, affixes, roots, and base words 4 (C) develop basic sight vocabulary, derive meaning of environmental print, and comprehend English vocabulary and language structures used routinely in written classroom materials
(B) use context (e.g., in-sentence restatement) to determine or clarify the meaning of unfamiliar or multiple meaning words;	1 (F) use accessible language and learn new and essential language in the process 4 (F) use visual and contextual support and support from peers and teachers to read grade-appropriate content-area text, to enhance and confirm understanding, to develop vocabulary, to grasp language structures, and to tap background knowledge needed to comprehend increasingly challenging language
(C) produce analogies with known antonyms and synonyms;	1 (C) use strategic learning techniques such as concept mapping, drawing, memorizing, comparing, contrasting, and reviewing to acquire basic and grade-level vocabulary
(D) identify and explain the meaning of common idioms, adages, and other sayings; and	1 (G) demonstrate an increasing ability to distinguish between formal and informal English and an increasing knowledge of when to use each one commensurate with grade-level learning expectations 1 (H) develop and expand repertoire of learning strategies such as reasoning inductively or deductively, looking for patterns in language, and analyzing sayings and expressions commensurate with grade-level learning expectations
(E) use a dictionary, a glossary, or a thesaurus (printed or electronic) to determine the meanings, syllabication, pronunciations, alternate word choices, and parts of speech of words.	1 (B) monitor oral and written language production and employ self-corrective techniques or other resources

Fifth-Grade ELAR TEKS	ELPS
(3) *Reading/Comprehension of Literary Text/Theme and Genre. Students analyze, make inferences and draw conclusions about theme and genre in different cultural, historical, and contemporary contexts and provide evidence from the text to support their understanding. Students are expected to:*	
(A) compare and contrast the themes or moral lessons of several works of fiction from various cultures;	1 (C) use strategic learning techniques such as concept mapping, drawing, memorizing, comparing, contrasting, and reviewing to acquire basic and grade-level vocabulary 4 (K) demonstrate English comprehension and expand reading skills by employing analytical skills such as evaluating written information and performing critical analyses commensurate with content-area and grade-level needs
(B) describe the phenomena explained in origin myths from various cultures; and	4 (J) demonstrate English comprehension and expand reading skills by employing inferential skills such as predicting, making connections between ideas, drawing inferences and conclusions from text and graphic sources, and finding supporting text evidence commensurate with content-area needs
(C) explain the effect of a historical event or movement on the theme of a work of literature.	4 (J) demonstrate English comprehension and expand reading skills by employing inferential skills such as predicting, making connections between ideas, drawing inferences and conclusions from text and graphic sources, and finding supporting text evidence commensurate with content-area needs
(4) *Reading/Comprehension of Literary Text/Poetry. Students understand, make inferences and draw conclusions about the structure and elements of poetry and provide evidence from text to support their understanding. Students are expected to analyze how poets use sound effects (e.g., alliteration, internal rhyme, onomatopoeia, rhyme scheme) to reinforce meaning in poems.*	1 (H) develop and expand repertoire of learning strategies such as reasoning inductively or deductively, looking for patterns in language, and analyzing sayings and expressions commensurate with grade-level learning expectations 4 (J) demonstrate English comprehension and expand reading skills by employing inferential skills such as predicting, making connections between ideas, drawing inferences and conclusions from text and graphic sources, and finding supporting text evidence commensurate with content-area needs
(5) *Reading/Comprehension of Literary Text/Drama. Students understand, make inferences and draw conclusions about the structure and elements of drama and provide evidence from text to support their understanding. Students are expected to analyze the similarities and differences between an original text and its dramatic adaptation.*	4 (J) demonstrate English comprehension and expand reading skills by employing inferential skills such as predicting, making connections between ideas, drawing inferences and conclusions from text and graphic sources, and finding supporting text evidence commensurate with content-area needs

Fifth-Grade ELAR TEKS	ELPS
(6) *Reading/Comprehension of Literary Text/Fiction. Students understand, make inferences, and draw conclusions about the structure and elements of fiction and provide evidence from text to support their understanding. Students are expected to:*	
(A) describe incidents that advance the story or novel, explaining how each incident gives rise to or foreshadows future events;	4 (J) demonstrate English comprehension and expand reading skills by employing inferential skills such as predicting, making connections between ideas, drawing inferences and conclusions from text and graphic sources, and finding supporting text evidence commensurate with content-area needs 4 (K) demonstrate English comprehension and expand reading skills by employing analytical skills such as evaluating written information and performing critical analyses commensurate with content-area and grade-level needs
(B) explain the roles and functions of characters in various plots, including their relationships and conflicts; and	4 (J) demonstrate English comprehension and expand reading skills by employing inferential skills such as predicting, making connections between ideas, drawing inferences and conclusions from text and graphic sources, and finding supporting text evidence commensurate with content-area needs 4 (K) demonstrate English comprehension and expand reading skills by employing analytical skills such as evaluating written information and performing critical analyses commensurate with content-area and grade-level needs
(C) explain different forms of third-person points of view in stories.	4 (K) demonstrate English comprehension and expand reading skills by employing analytical skills such as evaluating written information and performing critical analyses commensurate with content-area and grade-level needs
(7) *Reading/Comprehension of Literary Text/Literary Nonfiction. Students understand, make inferences, and draw conclusions about the varied structural patterns and features of literary nonfiction and provide evidence from text to support their understanding. Students are expected to identify the literary language and devices used in biographies and autobiographies, including how authors present major events in a person's life.*	1 (H) develop and expand repertoire of learning strategies such as reasoning inductively or deductively, looking for patterns in language, and analyzing sayings and expressions commensurate with grade-level learning expectations 4 (J) demonstrate English comprehension and expand reading skills by employing inferential skills such as predicting, making connections between ideas, drawing inferences and conclusions from text and graphic sources, and finding supporting text evidence commensurate with content-area needs 4 (K) demonstrate English comprehension and expand reading skills by employing analytical skills such as evaluating written information and performing critical analyses commensurate with content-area and grade-level needs

Fifth-Grade ELAR TEKS	ELPS
(8) *Reading/Comprehension of Literary Text/Sensory Language. Students understand, make inferences and draw conclusions about how an author's sensory language creates imagery in literary text and provide evidence from text to support their understanding. Students are expected to evaluate the impact of sensory details, imagery, and figurative language in literary text.*	4 (J) demonstrate English comprehension and expand reading skills by employing inferential skills such as predicting, making connections between ideas, drawing inferences and conclusions from text and graphic sources, and finding supporting text evidence commensurate with content-area needs
(9) *Reading/Comprehension of Text/Independent Reading. Students read independently for sustained periods of time and produce evidence of their reading. Students are expected to read independently for a sustained period of time and summarize or paraphrase what the reading was about, maintaining meaning and logical order (e.g., generate a reading log or journal; participate in book talks).*	4 (E) read linguistically accommodated content-area material with a decreasing need for linguistic accommodations as more English is learned 4 (H) read silently with increasing ease and comprehension for longer periods 4 (I) demonstrate English comprehension and expand reading skills by employing basic reading skills such as demonstrating understanding of supporting ideas and details in text and graphic sources, summarizing text, and distinguishing main ideas from details commensurate with content-area needs
(10) *Reading/Comprehension of Informational Text/Culture and History. Students analyze, make inferences and draw conclusions about the author's purpose in cultural, historical, and contemporary contexts and provide evidence from the text to support their understanding. Students are expected to draw conclusions from the information presented by an author and evaluate how well the author's purpose was achieved.*	4 (J) demonstrate English comprehension and expand reading skills by employing inferential skills such as predicting, making connections between ideas, drawing inferences and conclusions from text and graphic sources, and finding supporting text evidence commensurate with content-area needs 4 (K) demonstrate English comprehension and expand reading skills by employing analytical skills such as evaluating written information and performing critical analyses commensurate with content-area and grade-level needs
(11) *Reading/Comprehension of Informational Text/Expository Text. Students analyze, make inferences, and draw conclusions about expository text and provide evidence from text to support their understanding. Students are expected to:*	

(A) summarize the main ideas and supporting details in a text in ways that maintain meaning and logical order;	4 (G) demonstrate comprehension of increasingly complex English by participating in shared reading, retelling or summarizing material, responding to questions, and taking notes commensurate with content-area and grade-level needs 4 (I) demonstrate English comprehension and expand reading skills by employing basic reading skills such as demonstrating understanding of supporting ideas and details in text and graphic sources, summarizing text, and distinguishing main ideas from details commensurate with content-area needs

Fifth-Grade ELAR TEKS	**ELPS**
(11) cont . . . (B) determine the facts in text and verify them through established methods;	4 (I) demonstrate English comprehension and expand reading skills by employing basic reading skills such as demonstrating understanding of supporting ideas and details in text and graphic sources, summarizing text, and distinguishing main ideas from details commensurate with content-area needs
(C) analyze how the organizational pattern of a text (e.g., cause and effect, compare/contrast, sequential order, logical order, classification schemes) influences the relationships among the ideas;	4 (K) demonstrate English comprehension and expand reading skills by employing analytical skills such as evaluating written information and performing critical analyses commensurate with content-area and grade-level needs
(D) use multiple text features and graphics to gain an overview of the contents of text and to locate information; and	4 (D) use prereading supports such as graphic organizers, illustrations, and pretaught topic-related vocabulary and other prereading activities to enhance comprehension of written text
(E) synthesize and make logical connections between ideas within a text and across two or three texts representing similar or different genres.	1 (H) develop and expand repertoire of learning strategies such as reasoning inductively or deductively, looking for patterns in language, and analyzing sayings and expressions 4 (J) demonstrate English comprehension and expand reading skills by employing inferential skills such as predicting, making connections between ideas, drawing inferences and conclusions from text and graphic sources, and finding supporting text evidence commensurate with content-area needs
(12) Reading/Comprehension of Informational Text/Persuasive Text. Students analyze, make inferences, and draw conclusions about persuasive text and provide evidence from text to support their analysis. Students are expected to:	
(A) identify the author's viewpoint or position and explain the basic relationships among ideas (e.g., parallelism, comparison, causality) in the argument; and	4 (J) demonstrate English comprehension and expand reading skills by employing inferential skills such as predicting, making connections between ideas, drawing inferences and conclusions from text and graphic sources, and finding supporting text evidence commensurate with content-area needs
(B) recognize exaggerated, contradictory, or misleading statements in text.	4 (K) demonstrate English comprehension and expand reading skills by employing analytical skills such as evaluating written information and performing critical analyses commensurate with content-area and grade-level needs

(13) Reading/Comprehension of Informational Text/Procedural Texts. Students understand how to glean and use information in procedural texts and documents. Students are expected to:	
Fifth-Grade ELAR TEKS	**ELPS**
(13) cont . . . (A) interpret details from procedural text to complete a task, solve a problem, or perform procedures; and	4 (I) demonstrate English comprehension and expand reading skills by employing basic reading skills such as demonstrating understanding of supporting ideas and details in text and graphic sources, summarizing text, and distinguishing main ideas from details commensurate with content-area needs
(B) interpret factual or quantitative information presented in maps, charts, illustrations, graphs, timelines, tables, and diagrams.	4 (D) use prereading supports such as graphic organizers, illustrations, and pretaught topic-related vocabulary and other prereading activities to enhance comprehension of written text 4 (F) use visual and contextual support and support from peers and teachers to read grade-appropriate content-area text, to enhance and confirm understanding, to develop vocabulary, to grasp language structures, and to tap background knowledge needed to comprehend increasingly challenging language 4 (I) demonstrate English comprehension and expand reading skills by employing basic reading skills such as demonstrating understanding of supporting ideas and details in text and graphic sources, summarizing text, and distinguishing main ideas from details commensurate with content-area needs
(14) Reading/Media Literacy. Students use comprehension skills to analyze how words, images, graphics, and sounds work together in various forms to impact meaning. Students continue to apply earlier standards with greater depth in increasingly more complex texts. Students are expected to:	
(A) explain how messages conveyed in various forms of media are presented differently (e.g., documentaries, online information, televised news);	2 (F) listen to and derive meaning from a variety of media such as audio tape, video, DVD, and CD-ROM to build and reinforce concept and language attainment 4 (K) demonstrate English comprehension and expand reading skills by employing analytical skills such as evaluating written information and performing critical analyses commensurate with content-area and grade-level needs
(B) consider the difference in techniques used in media (e.g., commercials, documentaries, news);	1 (H) develop and expand repertoire of learning strategies such as reasoning inductively or deductively, looking for patterns in language, and analyzing sayings and expressions commensurate with grade-level learning expectations

	4 (K) demonstrate English comprehension and expand reading skills by employing analytical skills such as evaluating written information and performing critical analyses commensurate with content-area and grade-level needs
(C) identify the point of view of media presentations; and	4 (K) demonstrate English comprehension and expand reading skills by employing analytical skills such as evaluating written information and performing critical analyses commensurate with content-area and grade-level needs
Fifth-Grade ELAR TEKS	**ELPS**
(14) cont . . . (D) analyze various digital media venues for levels of formality and informality.	4 (K) demonstrate English comprehension and expand reading skills by employing analytical skills such as evaluating written information and performing critical analyses commensurate with content-area and grade-level needs
Reading/Media Literacy – No Correlation	**4(B) recognize directionality of English reading such as left to right and top to bottom**
(15) Writing/Writing Process. Students use elements of the writing process (planning, drafting, revising, editing, and publishing) to compose text. Students are expected to:	
(A) plan a first draft by selecting a genre appropriate for conveying the intended meaning to an audience, determining appropriate topics through a range of strategies (e.g., discussion, background reading, personal interests, interviews), and developing a thesis or controlling idea;	1 (C) use strategic learning techniques such as concept mapping, drawing, memorizing, comparing, contrasting, and reviewing to acquire basic and grade-level vocabulary 1 (E) internalize new, basic, and academic language by using and reusing it in meaningful ways in speaking and writing activities that build concept and language attainment 3 (E) share in cooperative learning interactions 3 (G) express opinions, ideas, and feelings ranging from communicating single words and short phrases to participating in extended discussions on a variety of social and grade-appropriate academic topics
(B) develop drafts by choosing an appropriate organizational strategy (e.g., sequence of events, cause-and-effect, compare/contrast) and building on ideas to create a focused, organized, and coherent piece of writing;	1 (C) use strategic learning techniques such as concept mapping, drawing, memorizing, comparing, contrasting, and reviewing to acquire basic and grade-level vocabulary 5 (F) write using a variety of grade-appropriate sentence lengths, patterns, and connecting words to combine phrases, clauses, and sentences in increasingly accurate ways as more English is acquired
(C) revise drafts to clarify meaning, enhance style, include simple and compound sentences, and improve transitions by adding, deleting, combining, and rearranging sentences or larger units of text after rethinking how well questions of purpose, audience, and genre have been addressed;	5 (F) write using a variety of grade-appropriate sentence lengths, patterns, and connecting words to combine phrases, clauses, and sentences in increasingly accurate ways as more English is acquired
(D) edit drafts for grammar, mechanics, and spelling; and	5 (D) edit writing for standard grammar and usage, including subject-verb agreement, pronoun agreement, and appropriate verb tenses commensurate with grade-level expectations as more English is acquired

(E) revise final draft in response to feedback from peers and teacher and publish written work for appropriate audiences.	3 (E) share information in cooperative learning interactions 4 (F) use visual and contextual support and support from peers and teachers to read grade-appropriate content-area text, enhance and confirm understanding, to develop vocabulary, to grasp language structures, and to tap background knowledge needed to comprehend increasingly challenging language

Fifth-Grade ELAR TEKS	ELPS
(16) Writing/Literary Texts. Students write literary texts to express their ideas and feelings about real or imagined people, events, and ideas. Students are expected to:	
(A) write imaginative stories that include: (i) a clearly defined focus, plot, and point of view; (ii) a specific, believable setting created through the use of sensory details; and (iii) dialogue that develops the story; and	5 (F) write using a variety of grade-appropriate sentence lengths, patterns, and connecting words to combine phrases, clauses, and sentences in increasingly accurate ways as more English is acquired 5 (G) narrate, describe, and explain with increasing specificity and detail to fulfill content-area writing needs as more English is acquired
(B) write poems using: (i) poetic techniques (e.g., alliteration, onomatopoeia); (ii) figurative language (e.g., similes, metaphors); and (iii) graphic elements (e.g., capital letters, line length).	1 (E) internalize new, basic, and academic language by using and reusing it in meaningful ways in speaking and writing activities that build concept and language attainment 5 (B) write using newly acquired basic vocabulary and content-based grade-level vocabulary
(17) Writing. Students write about their own experiences. Students are expected to write a personal narrative that conveys thoughts and feelings about an experience.	5 (F) write using a variety of grade-appropriate sentence lengths, patterns, and connecting words to combine phrases, clauses, and sentences in increasingly accurate ways as more English is acquired 5 (G) narrate, describe, and explain with increasing specificity and detail to fulfill content-area writing needs as more English is acquired
(18) Writing/Expository and Procedural Texts. Students write expository and procedural or work-related texts to communicate ideas and information to specific audiences for specific purposes. Students are expected to:	
(A) create multiparagraph essays to convey information about the topic that: (i) present effective introductions and concluding paragraphs; (ii) guide and inform the reader's understanding of key ideas and evidence; (iii) include specific facts, details, and examples in an appropriately organized structure; and (iv) use a variety of sentence structures and	5 (B) write using newly acquired basic vocabulary and content-based grade-level vocabulary 5 (F) write using a variety of grade-appropriate sentence lengths, patterns, and connecting words to combine phrases, clauses, and sentences in increasingly accurate ways as more English is acquired 5 (G) narrate, describe, and explain with increasing specificity and detail to fulfill content-area writing needs as more English is acquired

transitions to link paragraphs;	
(B) write formal and informal letters that convey ideas, include important information, demonstrate a sense of closure, and use appropriate conventions (e.g., date, salutation, closing); and	1 (G) demonstrate an increasing ability to distinguish between formal and informal English and an increasing knowledge of when to use each one commensurate with grade-level learning expectations 5 (F) write using a variety of grade-appropriate sentence lengths, patterns, and connecting words to combine phrases, clauses, and sentences in increasingly accurate ways as more English is acquired

Fifth-Grade ELAR TEKS	**ELPS**
(18) (B) cont . . .	5 (G) narrate, describe, and explain with increasing specificity and detail to fulfill content-area writing needs as more English is acquired
(C) write responses to literary or expository texts and provide evidence from the text to demonstrate understanding	5 (F) write using a variety of grade-appropriate sentence lengths, patterns, and connecting words to combine phrases, clauses, and sentences in increasingly accurate ways as more English is acquired 5 (G) narrate, describe, and explain with increasing specificity and detail to fulfill content-area writing needs as more English is acquired
(19) ***Writing/Persuasive Texts. Students write persuasive texts to influence the attitudes or actions of a specific audience on specific issues. Students are expected to write persuasive essays for appropriate audiences that establish a position and include sound reasoning, detailed and relevant evidence, and consideration of alternatives.***	5 (F) write using a variety of grade-appropriate sentence lengths, patterns, and connecting words to combine phrases, clauses, and sentences in increasingly accurate ways as more English is acquired 5 (G) narrate, describe, and explain with increasing specificity and detail to fulfill content-area writing needs as more English is acquired
(20) ***Oral and Written Conventions/Conventions. Students understand the function of and use the conventions of academic language when speaking and writing. Students continue to apply earlier standards with greater complexity. Students are expected to:***	

(A) use and understand the function of the following parts of speech in the context of reading, writing, and speaking: (i) verbs (irregular verbs and active voice); (ii) collective nouns (e.g., class, public); (iii) adjectives (e.g., descriptive, including origins: French windows, American cars) and their comparative and superlative forms (e.g., good, better, best); (iv) adverbs (e.g., frequency: usually, sometimes; intensity: almost, a lot); (v) prepositions and prepositional phrases to convey location, time, direction, or to provide details; (vi) indefinite pronouns (e.g., all, both, nothing, anything); (vii) subordinating conjunctions (e.g., while, because, although, if); and (viii) transitional words (e.g., also, therefore);	5 (E) employ increasingly complex grammatical structures in content-area writing commensurate with grade-level expectations, such as: (i) using correct verbs, tenses, and pronouns / antecedents (ii) using possessive case (apostrophes) correctly (iii) using negatives and contractions correctly
(B) use the complete subject and the complete predicate in a sentence; and	*No ELPS Correlations*
Fifth-Grade ELAR TEKS	**ELPS**
(20) cont . . . (C) use complete simple and compound sentences with correct subject-verb agreement.	5 (E) employ increasingly complex grammatical structures in content-area writing commensurate with grade-level expectations, such as: (i) using correct verbs, tenses, and pronouns / antecedents (ii) using possessive case (apostrophes) correctly (iii) using negatives and contractions correctly 5 (F) write using a variety of grade-appropriate sentence lengths, patterns, and connecting words to combine phrases, clauses, and sentences in increasingly accurate ways as more English is acquired
(21) Oral and Written Conventions/Handwriting, Capitalization, and Punctuation. Students write legibly and use appropriate capitalization and punctuation conventions in their compositions. Students are expected to:	
(A) use capitalization for: (i) abbreviations; (ii) initials and acronyms; and (iii) organizations;	5 (C) spell familiar English words with increasing accuracy, and employ English spelling patterns and rules with increasing accuracy as more English is acquired 5 (D) edit writing for standard grammar and usage, including subject-verb agreement, pronoun agreement, and appropriate verb tenses
(B) recognize and use punctuation marks including: (i) commas in compound sentences; and (ii) proper punctuation and spacing for quotations; and	5 (E) employ increasingly complex grammatical structures in content-area writing commensurate with grade-level expectations, such as: (i) using correct verbs, tenses, and pronouns / antecedents (ii) using possessive case (apostrophes) correctly (iii) using negatives and contractions correctly

(C) use proper mechanics, including italics and underlining for titles and emphasis.	5 (E) employ increasingly complex grammatical structures in content-area writing commensurate with grade-level expectations, such as: (i) using correct verbs, tenses, and pronouns / antecedents (ii) using possessive case (apostrophes) correctly (iii) using negatives and contractions correctly
(22) Oral and Written Conventions/Spelling. Students spell correctly. Students are expected to:	
(A) spell words with more advanced orthographic patterns and rules: (i) consonant changes (e.g., /t/ to/sh/ in *select, selection*;/k/ to/sh/ in *music, musician*); (ii) vowel changes (e.g., long to short in *crime, criminal*; long to schwa in *define, definition; short to schwa in legality, legal*); and (iii) silent and sounded consonants (e.g., *haste, hasten; sign, signal; condemn, condemnation*);	5 (C) spell familiar English words with increasing accuracy, and employ English spelling patterns and rules with increasing accuracy as more English is acquired

Fifth-Grade ELAR TEKS	ELPS
(22) cont . . . (B) spell words with: (i) Greek Roots (e.g., *tele, photo, graph, meter*); (ii) Latin Roots (e.g., *spec, scrib, rupt, port, ject, dict*); (iii) Greek suffixes (e.g., *ology, phobia, ism, ist*); and (iv) Latin derived suffixes (e.g., *able, ible; ance, ence*);	5 (C) spell familiar English words with increasing accuracy, and employ English spelling patterns and rules with increasing accuracy as more English is acquired
(C) differentiate between commonly confused terms (e.g., *its, it's; affect, effect);*	5 (E) employ increasingly complex grammatical structures in content-area writing commensurate with grade-level expectations, such as: (i) using correct verbs, tenses, and pronouns / antecedents (ii) using possessive case (apostrophes) correctly (iii) using negatives and contractions correctly
(D) use spelling patterns and rules and print and electronic resources to determine and check correct spellings; and	1 (B) monitor oral and written language production and employ self-corrective techniques or other resources 5 (C) spell familiar English words with increasing accuracy, and employ English spelling patterns and rules with increasing accuracy as more English is acquired 5 (D) edit writing for standard grammar and usage, including subject-verb agreement, pronoun agreement, and appropriate verb tenses commensurate with grade-level expectations as more English is acquired
(E) know how to use the spell-check function in word processing while understanding its limitations.	1 (B) monitor oral and written language production and employ self-corrective techniques or other resources
Oral and Written Conventions/Spelling – No Correlation	**5 (A) learn relationships between sounds and letters of the English language to represent sounds when writing in English**
(23) Research/Research Plan. Students ask open-ended research questions and develop a plan for answering them. Students are expected to:	

(A) brainstorm, consult with others, decide upon a topic, and formulate open-ended questions to address the major research topic; and	1 (E) internalize new, basic, and academic language by using and reusing it in meaningful ways in speaking and writing activities that build concept and language attainment 3 (F) ask and give information ranging from using a very limited bank of high-frequency, high-need, concrete vocabulary, including key words and expressions needed for basic communication in academic and social contexts, to using abstract and content-based vocabulary during extended speaking assignments 3 (G) express opinions, ideas, and feelings ranging from communicating single words and short phrases to participating in extended discussions on a variety of social and grade-appropriate academic topics
(B) generate a research plan for gathering relevant information about the major research question.	*No ELPS Correlation*

Fifth-Grade ELAR TEKS	ELPS
(24) Research/Gathering Sources. Students determine, locate, and explore the full range of relevant sources addressing a research question and systematically record the information they gather. Students are expected to:	
(A) follow the research plan to collect data from a range of print and electronic resources (e.g., reference texts, periodicals, webpages, online sources) and data from experts;	3 (F) ask and give information ranging from using a very limited bank of high-frequency, high-need, concrete vocabulary, including key words and expressions needed for basic communication in academic and social contexts, to using abstract and content-based vocabulary during extended speaking assignments
(B) differentiate between primary and secondary sources;	*No ELPS Correlation*
(C) record data, utilizing available technology (e.g., word processors) in order to see the relationships between ideas, and convert graphic/visual data (e.g., charts, diagrams, timelines) into written notes;	2 (E) use visual, contextual, and linguistic support to enhance and confirm understanding of increasingly complex and elaborated spoken language 4 (G) demonstrate comprehension of increasingly complex English by participating in shared reading, retelling or summarizing material, responding to questions, and taking notes commensurate with content-area and grade-level needs
(D) identify the source of notes (e.g., author, title, page number) and record bibliographic information concerning those sources according to a standard format; and	*No ELPS Correlation*
(E) differentiate between paraphrasing and plagiarism and identify the importance of citing valid and reliable sources.	*No ELPS Correlation*
(25) Research/Synthesizing Information. Students clarify research questions and evaluate and synthesize collected information. Students are	

expected to:	
(A) refine the major research question, if necessary, guided by the answers to a secondary set of questions; and	4 (F) use visual and contextual support and support from peers and teachers to read grade-appropriate content-area text, to enhance and confirm understanding, to develop vocabulary, to grasp language structures, and to tap background knowledge needed to comprehend increasingly challenging language
(B) evaluate the relevance, validity, and reliability of sources for the research.	4 (J) demonstrate English comprehension and expand reading skills by employing inferential skills such as predicting, making connections between ideas, drawing inferences and conclusions from text and graphic sources, and finding supporting text evidence commensurate with content-area needs

Fifth-Grade ELAR TEKS	ELPS
(26) Research/Organizing and Presenting Ideas. Students organize and present their ideas and information according to the purpose of the research and their audience. Students are expected to synthesize the research into a written or an oral presentation that:	
(A) compiles important information from multiple sources;	4 (J) demonstrate English comprehension and expand reading skills by employing inferential skills such as predicting, making connections between ideas, drawing inferences and conclusions from text and graphic sources, and finding supporting text evidence commensurate with content-area needs
(B) develops a topic sentence, summarizes findings, and uses evidence to support conclusions;	5 (F) write using a variety of grade-appropriate sentence lengths, patterns, and connecting words to combine phrases, clauses, and sentences in increasingly accurate ways as more English is acquired 5 (G) narrate, describe, and explain with increasing specificity and detail to fulfill content-area writing needs as more English is acquired
(C) presents the findings in a consistent format; and	5 (G) narrate, describe, and explain with increasing specificity and detail to fulfill content-area writing needs as more English is acquired
(D) uses quotations to support ideas and an appropriate form of documentation to acknowledge sources (e.g., bibliography, works cited).	*No ELPS Correlation*
(27) Listening and Speaking/Listening. Students use comprehension skills to listen attentively to others in formal and informal settings. Students continue to apply earlier standards with greater complexity. Students are expected to:	

(A) listen to and interpret a speaker's messages (both verbal and nonverbal) and ask questions to clarify the speaker's purpose or perspective;	2 (D) monitor understanding of spoken language during classroom instruction and interactions and seek clarification as needed 2 (I) demonstrate listening comprehension of increasingly complex spoken English by following directions, retelling or summarizing spoken messages, responding to questions and requests, collaborating with peers, and taking notes commensurate with content and grade-level needs 3 (F) ask and give information ranging from using a very limited bank of high-frequency, high-need, concrete vocabulary, including key words and expressions needed for basic communication in academic and social contexts, to using abstract and content-based vocabulary during extended speaking assignments
(B) follow, restate, and give oral instructions that include multiple action steps; and	2 (G) understand the general meaning, main points, and important details of spoken language ranging from situations in which topics, language, and contexts are familiar to unfamiliar

Fifth-Grade ELAR TEKS	**ELPS**
(27)(B) cont . . .	2 (H) understand implicit ideas and information in increasingly complex spoken language commensurate with grade-level learning expectations 2 (I) demonstrate listening comprehension of increasingly complex spoken English by following directions, retelling or summarizing spoken messages, responding to questions and requests, collaborating with peers, and taking notes commensurate with content and grade-level needs 3 (F) ask and give information ranging from using a very limited bank of high-frequency, high-need, concrete vocabulary, including key words and expressions needed for basic communication in academic and social contexts, to using abstract and content-based vocabulary during extended speaking assignments
(C) determine both main and supporting ideas in the speaker's message.	2 (G) understand the general meaning, main points, and important details of spoken language ranging from situations in which topics, language, and contexts are familiar to unfamiliar
Listening and Speaking/Listening – No Correlation	**2 (A) distinguish sounds and intonation patterns of English with increasing ease**
	2 (B) recognize elements of the English sound system in newly acquired vocabulary such as long and short vowels, silent letters, and consonant clusters
(28) Listening and Speaking/Speaking. Students speak clearly and to the point, using the conventions of language. Students continue to apply earlier standards with greater complexity. Students are expected to give organized presentations employing eye contact, speaking rate, volume, enunciation, natural gestures, and conventions of language to communicate ideas effectively.	1 (D) speak using learning strategies such as requesting assistance, employing nonverbal cues, and using synonyms and circumlocution 2 (C) learn new language structures, expressions, and basic and academic vocabulary heard during classroom instruction and interactions 3 (B) expand and internalize initial English vocabulary by learning and using high-frequency English words necessary for identifying and describing people, places, and objects, by retelling simple stories and

	basic information represented or supported by pictures, and by learning and using routine language needed for classroom communication 3 (C) speak using a variety of grammatical structures, sentence lengths, sentence types, and connecting words with increasing accuracy and ease as more English is acquired 3 (D) speak using grade-level content-area vocabulary in context to internalize new English words and build academic language proficiency 3 (G) express opinions, ideas, and feelings ranging from communicating single words and short phrases to participating in extended discussions on a variety of social and grade-appropriate academic topics 3 (H) narrate, describe, and explain with increasing specificity and detail as more English is acquired; 3 (I) adapt spoken language appropriately for formal and informal purposes 3 (J) respond orally to information presented in a wide variety of print, electronic, audio, and visual media to build and reinforce concept and language attainment;

Fifth-Grade ELAR TEKS	ELPS
Listening and Speaking/Speaking – No Correlation	**3 (A) practice producing sounds of newly acquired vocabulary such as long and short vowels, silent letters, and consonant clusters to pronounce English words in a manner that is increasingly comprehensible**
(29) Listening and Speaking/Teamwork. Students work productively with others in teams. Students continue to apply earlier standards with greater complexity. Students are expected to participate in student-led discussions by eliciting and considering suggestions from other group members and by identifying points of agreement and disagreement.	1 (B) monitor oral and written language production and employ self-corrective techniques or other resources 1 (G) demonstrate an increasing ability to distinguish between formal and informal English and an increasing knowledge of when to use each one commensurate with grade-level learning expectations 2 (I) demonstrate listening comprehension of increasingly complex spoken English by following directions, retelling or summarizing spoken messages, responding to questions and requests, collaborating with peers, and taking notes 3 (E) share information in cooperative learning interactions

This page is intentionally left blank.

ELAR TEKS and ELPS Side-by-Side
Sixth-Grade

Sixth-Grade ELAR TEKS	ELPS
(1) *Reading/Fluency. Students read grade-level text with fluency and comprehension. Students are expected to adjust fluency when reading aloud grade-level text based on the reading purpose and the nature of the text.*	4 (E) read linguistically accommodated content-area material with a decreasing need for linguistic accommodations as more English is learned 4 (H) read silently with increasing ease and comprehension for longer periods
(2) *Reading/Vocabulary Development. Students understand new vocabulary and use it when reading and writing. Students are expected to:*	
(A) determine the meaning of grade-level academic English words derived from Latin, Greek, or other linguistic roots and affixes;	4 (A) learn relationships between sounds and letters of the English language and decode (sound out) words using a combination of skills such as recognizing sound-letter relationships and identifying cognates, affixes, roots, and base words 4 (C) develop basic sight vocabulary, derive meaning of environmental print, and comprehend English vocabulary and language structures used routinely in written classroom materials
(B) use context (e.g., cause and effect or compare/contrast organizational text structures) to determine or clarify the meaning of unfamiliar or multiple meaning words;	1 (F) use accessible language and learn new and essential language in the process 4 (F) use visual and contextual support and support from peers and teachers to read grade-appropriate content-area text, to enhance and confirm understanding, to develop vocabulary, to grasp language structures, and to tap background knowledge needed to comprehend increasingly challenging language
(C) complete analogies that describe part to whole or whole to part (e.g., ink:pen as page: ____ or pen:ink as book: ____);	1 (C) use strategic learning techniques such as concept mapping, drawing, memorizing, comparing, contrasting, and reviewing to acquire basic and grade-level vocabulary
(D) explain the meaning of foreign words and phrases commonly used in written English (e.g., RSVP, que sera sera); and	1 (H) develop and expand repertoire of learning strategies such as reasoning inductively or deductively, looking for patterns in language, and analyzing sayings and expressions commensurate with grade-level learning expectations
(E) use a dictionary, a glossary, or a thesaurus (printed or electronic) to determine the meanings, syllabication, pronunciations, alternate word choices, and parts of speech of words.	1 (B) monitor oral and written language production and employ self-corrective techniques or other resources

Sixth-Grade ELAR TEKS	ELPS
(3) *Reading/Comprehension of Literary Text/Theme and Genre. Students analyze, make inferences and draw conclusions about theme and genre in different cultural, historical, and contemporary contexts and provide evidence from the text to support their understanding. Students are expected to:*	
(A) infer the implicit theme of a work of fiction, distinguishing theme from the topic;	4 (J) demonstrate English comprehension and expand reading skills by employing inferential skills such as predicting, making connections between ideas, drawing inferences and conclusions from text and graphic sources, and finding supporting text evidence commensurate with content-area needs
(B) analyze the function of stylistic elements (e.g., magic helper, rule of three) in traditional and classical literature from various cultures; and	4 (K) demonstrate English comprehension and expand reading skills by employing analytical skills such as evaluating written information and performing critical analyses commensurate with content-area and grade-level needs
(C) compare and contrast the historical and cultural settings of two literary works.	1 (C) use strategic learning techniques such as concept mapping, drawing, memorizing, comparing, contrasting, and reviewing to acquire basic and grade-level vocabulary 4 (K) demonstrate English comprehension and expand reading skills by employing analytical skills such as evaluating written information and performing critical analyses commensurate with content-area and grade-level needs
(4) *Reading/Comprehension of Literary Text/Poetry. Students understand, make inferences and draw conclusions about the structure and elements of poetry and provide evidence from text to support their understanding. Students are expected to explain how figurative language (e.g., personification, metaphors, similes, hyperbole) contributes to the meaning of a poem.*	1 (H) develop and expand repertoire of learning strategies such as reasoning inductively or deductively, looking for patterns in language, and analyzing sayings and expressions commensurate with grade-level learning expectations 4 (J) demonstrate English comprehension and expand reading skills by employing inferential skills such as predicting, making connections between ideas, drawing inferences and conclusions from text and graphic sources, and finding supporting text evidence commensurate with content-area needs
(5) *Reading/Comprehension of Literary Text/Drama. Students understand, make inferences, and draw conclusions about the structure and elements of drama and provide evidence from text to support their understanding. Students are expected to explain the similarities and differences in the setting, characters, and plot of a play and those in a film based upon the same story line.*	4 (J) demonstrate English comprehension and expand reading skills by employing inferential skills such as predicting, making connections between ideas, drawing inferences and conclusions from text and graphic sources, and finding supporting text evidence commensurate with content-area needs

Sixth-Grade ELAR TEKS	ELPS
(6) *Reading/Comprehension of Literary Text/Fiction. Students understand, make inferences, and draw conclusions about the structure and elements of fiction and provide evidence from text to support their understanding. Students are expected to:*	
(A) summarize the elements of plot development (e.g., rising action, turning point, climax, falling action, denouement) in various works of fiction;	4 (G) demonstrate comprehension of increasingly complex English by participating in shared reading, retelling or summarizing material, responding to questions, and taking notes commensurate with content-area and grade-level needs
(B) recognize dialect and conversational voice and explain how authors use dialect to convey character; and	1 (H) develop and expand repertoire of learning strategies such as reasoning inductively or deductively, looking for patterns in language, and analyzing sayings and expressions commensurate with grade-level learning expectations 4 (K) demonstrate English comprehension and expand reading skills by employing analytical skills such as evaluating written information and performing critical analyses commensurate with content-area and grade-level needs
(C) describe different forms of point of view, including first and third person.	4 (K) demonstrate English comprehension and expand reading skills by employing analytical skills such as evaluating written information and performing critical analyses commensurate with content-area and grade-level needs
(7) *Reading/Comprehension of Literary Text/Literary Nonfiction. Students understand, make inferences and draw conclusions about the varied structural patterns and features of literary nonfiction and provide evidence from text to support their understanding. Students are expected to identify the literary language and devices used in memoirs and personal narratives and compare their characteristics with those of an autobiography.*	1 (H) develop and expand repertoire of learning strategies such as reasoning inductively or deductively, looking for patterns in language, and analyzing sayings and expressions commensurate with grade-level learning expectations 4 (J) demonstrate English comprehension and expand reading skills by employing inferential skills such as predicting, making connections between ideas, drawing inferences and conclusions from text and graphic sources, and finding supporting text evidence commensurate with content-area needs 4 (K) demonstrate English comprehension and expand reading skills by employing analytical skills such as evaluating written information and performing critical analyses commensurate with content-area and grade-level needs
(8) *Reading/Comprehension of Literary Text/Sensory Language. Students understand, make inferences, and draw conclusions about how an author's sensory language creates imagery in literary text and provide evidence from text to support their understanding. Students are expected to explain how authors create meaning through stylistic elements and figurative language emphasizing the use of personification, hyperbole, and refrains.*	1 (H) develop and expand repertoire of learning strategies such as reasoning inductively or deductively, looking for patterns in language, and analyzing sayings and expressions commensurate with grade-level learning expectations 4 (J) demonstrate English comprehension and expand reading skills by employing inferential skills such as predicting, making connections between ideas, drawing inferences and conclusions from text and graphic sources, and finding supporting text evidence commensurate with content-area needs

Sixth-Grade ELAR TEKS	ELPS
(9) Reading/Comprehension of Informational Text/Culture and History. Students analyze, make inferences, and draw conclusions about the author's purpose in cultural, historical, and contemporary contexts and provide evidence from the text to support their understanding. Students are expected to compare and contrast the stated or implied purposes of different authors writing on the same topic.	4 (J) demonstrate English comprehension and expand reading skills by employing inferential skills such as predicting, making connections between ideas, drawing inferences and conclusions from text and graphic sources, and finding supporting text evidence commensurate with content-area needs 4 (K) demonstrate English comprehension and expand reading skills by employing analytical skills such as evaluating written information and performing critical analyses commensurate with content-area and grade-level needs
(10) Reading/Comprehension of Informational Text/Expository Text. Students analyze, make inferences, and draw conclusions about expository text and provide evidence from text to support their understanding. Students are expected to:	
(A) summarize the main ideas and supporting details in text, demonstrating an understanding that a summary does not include opinions;	4 (G) demonstrate comprehension of increasingly complex English by participating in shared reading, retelling or summarizing material, responding to questions, and taking notes commensurate with content-area and grade-level needs 4 (I) demonstrate English comprehension and expand reading skills by employing basic reading skills such as demonstrating understanding of supporting ideas and details in text and graphic sources, summarizing text, and distinguishing main ideas from details commensurate with content-area needs
(B) explain whether facts included in an argument are used for or against an issue;	4 (K) demonstrate English comprehension and expand reading skills by employing analytical skills such as evaluating written information and performing critical analyses commensurate with content-area and grade-level needs
(C) explain how different organizational patterns (e.g., proposition and support, problem and solution) develop the main idea and the author's viewpoint; and	1 (H) develop and expand repertoire of learning strategies such as reasoning inductively or deductively, looking for patterns in language, and analyzing sayings and expressions 4 (J) demonstrate English comprehension and expand reading skills by employing inferential skills such as predicting, making connections between ideas, drawing inferences and conclusions from text and graphic sources, and finding supporting text evidence commensurate with content-area needs
(D) synthesize and make logical connections between ideas within a text and across two or three texts representing similar or different genres.	1 (H) develop and expand repertoire of learning strategies such as reasoning inductively or deductively, looking for patterns in language, and analyzing sayings and expressions 4 (J) demonstrate English comprehension and expand reading skills by employing inferential skills such as predicting, making connections between ideas, drawing inferences and conclusions from text and graphic sources, and finding supporting text evidence commensurate with content-area needs

Sixth-Grade ELAR TEKS	ELPS
(11) *Reading/Comprehension of Informational Text/Persuasive Text. Students analyze, make inferences, and draw conclusions about persuasive text and provide evidence from text to support their analyses. Students are expected to:*	
(A) compare and contrast the structure and viewpoints of two different authors writing for the same purpose, noting the stated claim and supporting evidence; and	1 (C) use strategic learning techniques such as concept mapping, drawing, memorizing, comparing, contrasting, and reviewing to acquire basic and grade-level vocabulary 4 (K) demonstrate English comprehension and expand reading skills by employing analytical skills such as evaluating written information and performing critical analyses commensurate with content-area and grade-level needs
(B) identify faulty reasoning used in persuasive texts.	1 (H) develop and expand repertoire of learning strategies such as reasoning inductively or deductively, looking for patterns in language, and analyzing sayings and expressions 4 (J) demonstrate English comprehension and expand reading skills by employing inferential skills such as predicting, making connections between ideas, drawing inferences and conclusions from text and graphic sources, and finding supporting text evidence commensurate with content-area needs 4 (K) demonstrate English comprehension and expand reading skills by employing analytical skills such as evaluating written information and performing critical analyses commensurate with content-area and grade-level needs
(12) *Reading/Comprehension of Informational Text/Procedural Texts. Students understand how to glean and use information in procedural texts and documents. Students are expected to:*	
(A) follow multitasked instructions to complete a task, solve a problem, or perform procedures; and	4 (F) use visual and contextual support and support from peers and teachers to read grade-appropriate content-area text, to enhance and confirm understanding, to develop vocabulary, to grasp language structures, and to tap background knowledge needed to comprehend increasingly challenging language
(B) interpret factual, quantitative, or technical information presented in maps, charts, illustrations, graphs, timelines, tables, and diagrams.	4 (D) use prereading supports such as graphic organizers, illustrations, and pretaught topic-related vocabulary and other prereading activities to enhance comprehension of written text 4 (F) use visual and contextual support and support from peers and teachers to read grade-appropriate content-area text, to enhance and confirm understanding, to develop vocabulary, to grasp language structures, and to tap background knowledge needed to comprehend increasingly challenging language

Sixth-Grade ELAR TEKS	ELPS
(13) Reading/Media Literacy. Students use comprehension skills to analyze how words, images, graphics, and sounds work together in various forms to impact meaning. Students will continue to apply earlier standards with greater depth in increasingly more complex texts. Students are expected to:	
(A) explain messages conveyed in various forms of media;	2 (F) listen to and derive meaning from a variety of media such as audio tape, video, DVD, and CD-ROM to build and reinforce concept and language attainment 4 (I) demonstrate English comprehension and expand reading skills by employing basic reading skills such as demonstrating understanding of supporting ideas and details in text and graphic sources, summarizing text, and distinguishing main ideas from details commensurate with content-area needs 4 (K) demonstrate English comprehension and expand reading skills by employing analytical skills such as evaluating written information and performing critical analyses commensurate with content-area and grade-level needs
(B) recognize how various techniques influence viewers' emotions;	4 (K) demonstrate English comprehension and expand reading skills by employing analytical skills such as evaluating written information and performing critical analyses commensurate with content-area and grade-level needs
(C) critique persuasive techniques (e.g., testimonials, bandwagon appeal) used in media messages; and	2 (F) listen to and derive meaning from a variety of media such as audio tape, video, DVD, and CD ROM to build and reinforce concept and language attainment 4 (K) demonstrate English comprehension and expand reading skills by employing analytical skills such as evaluating written information and performing critical analyses commensurate with content-area and grade-level needs
(D) analyze various digital media venues for levels of formality and informality.	2 (F) listen to and derive meaning from a variety of media such as audio tape, video, DVD, and CD-ROM to build and reinforce concept and language attainment 4 (K) demonstrate English comprehension and expand reading skills by employing analytical skills such as evaluating written information and performing critical analyses commensurate with content-area and grade-level needs
Reading/Media Literacy – No Correlation	**4(B) recognize directionality of English reading such as left to right and top to bottom**
	4 (E) read linguistically accommodated content-area material with a decreasing need for linguistic accommodations as more English is learned
(14) Writing/Writing Process. Students use elements of the writing process (planning, drafting, revising, editing, and publishing) to compose text. Students are expected to:	

Sixth-Grade ELAR TEKS	ELPS
(14) cont . . . (A) plan a first draft by selecting a genre appropriate for conveying the intended meaning to an audience, determining appropriate topics through a range of strategies (e.g., discussion, background reading, personal interests, interviews), and developing a thesis or controlling idea;	1 (C) use strategic learning techniques such as concept mapping, drawing, memorizing, comparing, contrasting, and reviewing to acquire basic and grade-level vocabulary 1 (E) internalize new, basic, and academic language by using and reusing it in meaningful ways in speaking and writing activities that build concept and language attainment 3 (E) share in cooperative learning interactions 3 (G) express opinions, ideas, and feelings ranging from communicating single words and short phrases to participating in extended discussions on a variety of social and grade-appropriate academic topics
(B) develop drafts by choosing an appropriate organizational strategy (e.g., sequence of events, cause and effect, compare/contrast) and building on ideas to create a focused, organized, and coherent piece of writing;	1 (C) use strategic learning techniques such as concept mapping, drawing, memorizing, comparing, contrasting, and reviewing to acquire basic and grade-level vocabulary 5 (F) write using a variety of grade-appropriate sentence lengths, patterns, and connecting words to combine phrases, clauses, and sentences in increasingly accurate ways as more English is acquired
(C) revise drafts to clarify meaning, enhance style, include simple and compound sentences, and improve transitions by adding, deleting, combining, and rearranging sentences or larger units of text after rethinking how well questions of purpose, audience, and genre have been addressed	5 (F) write using a variety of grade-appropriate sentence lengths, patterns, and connecting words to combine phrases, clauses, and sentences in increasingly accurate ways as more English is acquired
(D) edit drafts for grammar, mechanics, and spelling; and	5 (D) edit writing for standard grammar and usage, including subject-verb agreement, pronoun agreement, and appropriate verb tenses commensurate with grade-level expectations as more English is acquired
(E) revise final draft in response to feedback from peers and teacher and publish written work for appropriate audiences.	4 (F) use visual and contextual support and support from peers and teachers to read grade-appropriate content-area text, to enhance and confirm understanding, to develop vocabulary, to grasp language structures, and to tap background knowledge needed to comprehend increasingly challenging language 5 (D) edit writing for standard grammar and usage, including subject-verb agreement, pronoun agreement, and appropriate verb tenses commensurate with grade-level expectations as more English is acquired
(15) *Writing/Literary Texts. Students write literary texts to express their ideas and feelings about real or imagined people, events, and ideas. Students are expected to:*	
(A) write imaginative stories that include:	5 (F) write using a variety of grade-appropriate sentence lengths, patterns, and connecting words to combine phrases, clauses, and sentences in increasingly accurate ways as more English is acquired 5 (G) narrate, describe, and explain with increasing specificity and detail to fulfill content-area writing needs as more English is acquired

Sixth-Grade ELAR TEKS	ELPS
(15) (A) cont . . . (i) a clearly defined focus, plot, and point of view; (ii) a specific, believable setting created through the use of sensory details; and (iii) dialogue that develops the story; and	5 (F) write using a variety of grade-appropriate sentence lengths, patterns, and connecting words to combine phrases, clauses, and sentences in increasingly accurate ways as more English is acquired 5 (G) narrate, describe, and explain with increasing specificity and detail to fulfill content-area writing needs as more English is acquired
(B) write poems using: (i) poetic techniques (e.g., alliteration, onomatopoeia); (ii) figurative language (e.g., similes, metaphors); and (iii) graphic elements (e.g., capital letters, line length).	1 (E) internalize new, basic, and academic language by using and reusing it in meaningful ways in speaking and writing activities that build concept and language attainment
(16) Writing. Students write about their own experiences. Students are expected to write a personal narrative that has a clearly defined focus and communicates the importance of or reasons for actions and/or consequences.	5 (F) write using a variety of grade-appropriate sentence lengths, patterns, and connecting words to combine phrases, clauses, and sentences in increasingly accurate ways as more English is acquired 5 (G) narrate, describe, and explain with increasing specificity and detail to fulfill content-area writing needs as more English is acquired
(17) Writing/Expository and Procedural Texts. Students write expository and procedural or work-related texts to communicate ideas and information to specific audiences for specific purposes. Students are expected to:	
(A) create multiparagraph essays to convey information about a topic that: (i) present effective introductions and concluding paragraphs; (ii) guide and inform the reader's understanding of key ideas and evidence; (iii) include specific facts, details, and examples in an appropriately organized structure; and (iv) use a variety of sentence structures and transitions to link paragraphs;	5 (B) write using newly acquired basic vocabulary and content-based grade-level vocabulary 5 (F) write using a variety of grade-appropriate sentence lengths, patterns, and connecting words to combine phrases, clauses, and sentences in increasingly accurate ways as more English is acquired 5 (G) narrate, describe, and explain with increasing specificity and detail to fulfill content-area writing needs as more English is acquired
(B) write informal letters that convey ideas, include important information, demonstrate a sense of closure, and use appropriate conventions (e.g., date, salutation, closing);	1 (G) demonstrate an increasing ability to distinguish between formal and informal English and an increasing knowledge of when to use each one commensurate with grade-level learning expectations 5 (B) write using newly acquired basic vocabulary 5 (F) write using a variety of grade-appropriate sentence lengths, patterns, and connecting words to combine phrases, clauses, and sentences in increasingly accurate ways as more English is acquired 5 (G) narrate, describe, and explain with increasing specificity and detail to fulfill content-area writing needs as more English is acquired

Sixth-Grade ELAR TEKS	ELPS
(17) cont . . . (C) write responses to literary or expository texts and provide evidence from the text to demonstrate understanding; and	5 (B) write using newly acquired basic vocabulary 5 (G) narrate, describe, and explain with increasing specificity and detail to fulfill content-area writing needs as more English is acquired
(D) produce a multimedia presentation involving text and graphics using available technology.	5 (F) write using a variety of grade-appropriate sentence lengths, patterns, and connecting words to combine phrases, clauses, and sentences in increasingly accurate ways as more English is acquired 5 (G) narrate, describe, and explain with increasing specificity and detail to fulfill content-area writing needs as more English is acquired
(18) Writing/Persuasive Texts. Students write persuasive texts to influence the attitudes or actions of a specific audience on specific issues. Students are expected to write persuasive essays for appropriate audiences that establish a position and include sound reasoning, detailed and relevant evidence, and consideration of alternatives.	5 (B) write using newly acquired basic vocabulary 5 (F) write using a variety of grade-appropriate sentence lengths, patterns, and connecting words to combine phrases, clauses, and sentences in increasingly accurate ways as more English is acquired 5 (G) narrate, describe, and explain with increasing specificity and detail to fulfill content-area writing needs as more English is acquired
(19) Oral and Written Conventions/Conventions. Students understand the function of and use the conventions of academic language when speaking and writing. Students will continue to apply earlier standards with greater complexity. Students are expected to:	
(A) use and understand the function of the following parts of speech in the context of reading, writing, and speaking: (i) verbs (irregular verbs and active and passive voice); (ii) noncount nouns (e.g., rice, paper); (iii) predicate adjectives (She is intelligent.) and their comparative and superlative forms (e.g., many, more, most); (iv) conjunctive adverbs (e.g., consequently, furthermore, indeed); (v) prepositions and prepositional phrases to convey location, time, direction, or to provide details; (vi) indefinite pronouns (e.g., all, both, nothing, anything); (vii) subordinating conjunctions (e.g., while, because, although, if); and (viii) transitional words and phrases that demonstrate an understanding of the function of the transition related to the organization of the writing (e.g., on the contrary, in addition to);	5 (E) employ increasingly complex grammatical structures in content-area writing commensurate with grade-level expectations, such as: (i) using correct verbs, tenses, and pronouns / antecedents (ii) using possessive case (apostrophes) correctly (iii) using negatives and contractions correctly 5 (F) write using a variety of grade-appropriate sentence lengths, patterns, and connecting words to combine phrases, clauses, and sentences in increasingly accurate ways as more English is acquired

Sixth-Grade ELAR TEKS	ELPS
(19) cont . . . (B) differentiate between the active and passive voice and know how to use them both; and	1 (H) develop and expand repertoire of learning strategies such as reasoning inductively or deductively, looking for patterns in language, and analyzing sayings and expressions commensurate with grade-level learning expectations
(C) use complete simple and compound sentences with correct subject-verb agreement.	5 (E) employ increasingly complex grammatical structures in content-area writing commensurate with grade-level expectations, such as: (i) using correct verbs, tenses, and pronouns / antecedents (ii) using possessive case (apostrophes) correctly (iii) using negatives and contractions correctly 5 (F) write using a variety of grade-appropriate sentence lengths, patterns, and connecting words to combine phrases, clauses, and sentences in increasingly accurate ways as more English is acquired
(20) Oral and Written Conventions/Handwriting, Capitalization, and Punctuation. Students write legibly and use appropriate capitalization and punctuation conventions in their compositions. Students are expected to:	
(A) use capitalization for: (i) abbreviations; (ii) initials and acronyms; and (iii) organizations;	5 (C) spell familiar English words with increasing accuracy, and employ English spelling patterns and rules with increasing accuracy as more English is acquired 5 (D) edit writing for standard grammar and usage, including subject-verb agreement, pronoun agreement, and appropriate verb tenses 5 (F) write using a variety of grade-appropriate sentence lengths, patterns, and connecting words to combine phrases, clauses, and sentences in increasingly accurate ways as more English is acquired
(B) recognize and use punctuation marks including: (i) commas in compound sentences; (ii) proper punctuation and spacing for quotations; and (iii) parentheses, brackets, and ellipses (to indicate omissions and interruptions or incomplete statements); and	5 (E) employ increasingly complex grammatical structures in content-area writing commensurate with grade-level expectations, such as: (i) using correct verbs, tenses, and pronouns / antecedents; (ii) using possessive case (apostrophes) correctly (iii) using negatives and contractions correctly
(C) use proper mechanics including italics and underlining for titles of books.	5 (C) spell familiar English words with increasing accuracy, and employ English spelling patterns and rules with increasing accuracy as more English is acquired
(21) Oral and Written Conventions/Spelling. Students spell correctly. Students are expected to:	
(A) differentiate between commonly confused terms (e.g., its, it's; affect, effect);	5 (C) spell familiar English words with increasing accuracy, and employ English spelling patterns and rules with increasing accuracy as more English is acquired
(B) use spelling patterns and rules and print and electronic resources to determine and check correct spellings; and	5 (C) spell familiar English words with increasing accuracy, and employ English spelling patterns and rules with increasing accuracy as more English is acquired

Sixth-Grade ELAR TEKS	ELPS
(21) cont . . . (C) know how to use the spell-check function in word processing while understanding its limitations.	1 (B) monitor oral and written language production and employ self-corrective techniques or other resources
Oral and Written Conventions / Spelling – No Correlation	**5 (A) learn relationships between sounds and letters of the English language to represent sounds when writing in English**
(22) Research/Research Plan. Students ask open-ended research questions and develop a plan for answering them. Students are expected to:	
(A) brainstorm, consult with others, decide upon a topic, and formulate open-ended questions to address the major research topic; and	1 (E) internalize new, basic, and academic language by using and reusing it in meaningful ways in speaking and writing activities that build concept and language attainment 3 (F) ask and give information ranging from using a very limited bank of high-frequency, high-need, concrete vocabulary, including key words and expressions needed for basic communication in academic and social contexts, to using abstract and content-based vocabulary during extended speaking assignments 3 (G) express opinions, ideas, and feelings ranging from communicating single words and short phrases to participating in extended discussions on a variety of social and grade-appropriate academic topics
(B) generate a research plan for gathering relevant information about the major research question.	*No ELPS Correlation*
(23) Research/Gathering Sources. Students determine, locate, and explore the full range of relevant sources addressing a research question and systematically record the information they gather. Students are expected to:	
(A) follow the research plan to collect data from a range of print and electronic resources (e.g., reference texts, periodicals, webpages, online sources) and data from experts;	3 (F) ask and give information ranging from using a very limited bank of high-frequency, high-need, concrete vocabulary, including key words and expressions needed for basic communication in academic and social contexts, to using abstract and content-based vocabulary during extended speaking assignments
(B) differentiate between primary and secondary sources;	*No ELPS Correlation*
(C) record data, utilizing available technology (e.g., word processors) in order to see the relationships between ideas, and convert graphic/visual data (e.g., charts, diagrams, timelines) into written notes;	2 (E) use visual, contextual, and linguistic support to enhance and confirm understanding of increasingly complex and elaborated spoken language; 4 (G) demonstrate comprehension of increasingly complex English by participating in shared reading, retelling or summarizing material, responding to questions, and taking notes commensurate with content-area and grade level needs
(D) identify the source of notes (e.g., author, title, page number) and record bibliographic information concerning those sources according to a standard format; and	*No ELPS Correlation*

Sixth-Grade ELAR TEKS	ELPS
(23) cont . . . (E) differentiate between paraphrasing and plagiarism and identify the importance of citing valid and reliable sources.	*No ELPS Correlation*
(24) Research/Synthesizing Information. Students clarify research questions and evaluate and synthesize collected information. Students are expected to:	
(A) refine the major research question, if necessary, guided by the answers to a secondary set of questions; and	4 (F) use visual and contextual support and support from peers and teachers to read grade-appropriate content-area text, to enhance and confirm understanding, to develop vocabulary, to grasp language structures, and to tap background knowledge needed to comprehend increasingly challenging language
(B) evaluate the relevance and reliability of sources for the research.	4 (K) demonstrate English comprehension and expand reading skills by employing analytical skills such as evaluating written information and performing critical analyses commensurate with content-area and grade-level needs
(25) Research/Organizing and Presenting Ideas. Students organize and present their ideas and information according to the purpose of the research and their audience. Students are expected to synthesize the research into a written or an oral presentation that:	
(A) compiles important information from multiple sources;	4 (J) demonstrate English comprehension and expand reading skills by employing inferential skills such as predicting, making connections between ideas, drawing inferences and conclusions from text and graphic sources, and finding supporting text evidence commensurate with content-area needs
(B) develops a topic sentence, summarizes findings, and uses evidence to support conclusions;	5 (F) write using a variety of grade-appropriate sentence lengths, patterns, and connecting words to combine phrases, clauses, and sentences in increasingly accurate ways as more English is acquired 5 (G) narrate, describe, and explain with increasing specificity and detail to fulfill content-area writing needs as more English is acquired
(C) presents the findings in a consistent format; and	5 (G) narrate, describe, and explain with increasing specificity and detail to fulfill content-area writing needs as more English is acquired
(D) uses quotations to support ideas and an appropriate form of documentation to acknowledge sources (e.g., bibliography, works cited).	*No ELPS Correlation*

Sixth-Grade ELAR TEKS	ELPS
(26) Listening and Speaking/Listening. Students will use comprehension skills to listen attentively to others in formal and informal settings. Students will continue to apply earlier standards with greater complexity. Students are expected to:	
(A) listen to and interpret a speaker's messages (both verbal and nonverbal) and ask questions to clarify the speaker's purpose and perspective;	2 (D) monitor understanding of spoken language during classroom instruction and interactions and seek clarification as needed 2 (I) demonstrate listening comprehension of increasingly complex spoken English by following directions, retelling or summarizing spoken messages, responding to questions and requests, collaborating with peers, and taking notes commensurate with content and grade-level needs 3 (F) ask and give information ranging from using a very limited bank of high-frequency, high-need, concrete vocabulary, including key words and expressions needed for basic communication in academic and social contexts, to using abstract and content-based vocabulary during extended speaking assignments
(B) follow and give oral instructions that include multiple action steps; and	2 (E) use visual, contextual, and linguistic support to enhance and confirm understanding of increasingly complex and elaborated spoken language 2 (G) understand the general meaning, main points, and important details of spoken language ranging from situations in which topics, language, and contexts are familiar to unfamiliar 2 (H) understand implicit ideas and information in increasingly complex spoken language commensurate with grade-level learning expectations 2 (I) demonstrate listening comprehension of increasingly complex spoken English by following directions, retelling or summarizing spoken messages, responding to questions and requests, collaborating with peers, and taking notes commensurate with content and grade-level needs 3 (F) ask and give information ranging from using a very limited bank of high-frequency, high-need, concrete vocabulary, including key words and expressions needed for basic communication in academic and social contexts, to using abstract and content-based vocabulary during extended speaking assignments
(C) paraphrase the major ideas and supporting evidence in formal and informal presentations.	2 (G) understand the general meaning, main points, and important details of spoken language ranging from situations in which topics, language, and contexts are familiar to unfamiliar 2 (I) demonstrate listening comprehension of increasingly complex spoken English by following directions, retelling or summarizing spoken messages, responding to questions and requests, collaborating with peers, and taking notes commensurate with content and grade-level needs

Sixth-Grade ELAR TEKS	ELPS
Listening and Speaking/Listening – No Correlation	**2 (A) distinguish sounds and intonation patterns of English with increasing ease** **2 (B) recognize elements of the English sound system in newly acquired vocabulary such as long and short vowels, silent letters, and consonant clusters**
(27) Listening and Speaking/Speaking. Students speak clearly and to the point, using the conventions of language. Students will continue to apply earlier standards with greater complexity. Students are expected to give an organized presentation with a specific point of view, employing eye contact, speaking rate, volume, enunciation, natural gestures, and conventions of language to communicate ideas effectively.	1 (D) speak using learning strategies such as requesting assistance, employing nonverbal cues, and using synonyms and circumlocution 2 (C) learn new language structures, expressions, and basic and academic vocabulary heard during classroom instruction and interactions 3 (B) expand and internalize initial English vocabulary by learning and using high-frequency English words necessary for identifying and describing people, places, and objects, by retelling simple stories and basic information represented or supported by pictures, and by learning and using routine language needed for classroom communication 3 (C) speak using a variety of grammatical structures, sentence lengths, sentence types, and connecting words with increasing accuracy and ease as more English is acquired 3 (D) speak using grade-level content-area vocabulary in context to internalize new English words and build academic language proficiency 3 (G) express opinions, ideas, and feelings ranging from communicating single words and short phrases to participating in extended discussions on a variety of social and grade-appropriate academic topics 3 (H) narrate, describe, and explain with increasing specificity and detail as more English is acquired 3 (I) adapt spoken language appropriately for formal and informal purposes 3 (J) respond orally to information presented in a wide variety of print, electronic, audio, and visual media to build and reinforce concept and language attainment
Listening and Speaking/Speaking – No Correlation	**3 (A) practice producing sounds of newly acquired vocabulary such as long and short vowels, silent letters, and consonant clusters to pronounce English words in a manner that is increasingly comprehensible**
(28) Listening and Speaking/Teamwork. Students work productively with others in teams. Students will continue to apply earlier standards with greater complexity. Students are expected to participate in student-led discussions by eliciting and considering suggestions from other group members and by identifying points of agreement and disagreement.	1 (B) monitor oral and written language production and employ self-corrective techniques or other resources 2 (I) demonstrate listening comprehension of increasingly complex spoken English by following directions, retelling or summarizing spoken messages, responding to questions and requests, collaborating with peers, and taking notes 3 (E) share information in cooperative learning interactions

ELAR TEKS and ELPS Side-by-Side
Seventh-Grade

Seventh-Grade ELAR TEKS	ELPS
(1) *Reading/Fluency. Students read grade-level text with fluency and comprehension. Students are expected to adjust fluency when reading aloud grade-level text based on the reading purpose and the nature of the text.*	4 (E) read linguistically accommodated content-area material with a decreasing need for linguistic accommodations as more English is learned 4 (H) read silently with increasing ease and comprehension for longer periods
(2) *Reading/Vocabulary Development. Students understand new vocabulary and use it when reading and writing. Students are expected to:*	
(A) determine the meaning of grade-level academic English words derived from Latin, Greek, or other linguistic roots and affixes;	4 (A) learn relationships between sounds and letters of the English language and decode (sound out) words using a combination of skills such as recognizing sound-letter relationships and identifying cognates, affixes, roots, and base words 4 (C) develop basic sight vocabulary, derive meaning of environmental print, and comprehend English vocabulary and language structures used routinely in written classroom materials
(B) use context (within a sentence and in larger sections of text) to determine or clarify the meaning of unfamiliar or ambiguous words;	1 (F) use accessible language and learn new and essential language in the process 4 (F) use visual and contextual support and support from peers and teachers to read grade-appropriate content-area text, to enhance and confirm understanding, to develop vocabulary, to grasp language structures, and to tap background knowledge needed to comprehend increasingly challenging language
(C) complete analogies that describe part to whole or whole to part;	1 (C) use strategic learning techniques such as concept mapping, drawing, memorizing, comparing, contrasting, and reviewing to acquire basic and grade-level vocabulary
(D) identify the meaning of foreign words commonly used in written English with emphasis on Latin and Greek words (e.g., habeas corpus, E Pluribus Unum, bona fide, nemesis); and	1 (H) develop and expand repertoire of learning strategies such as reasoning inductively or deductively, looking for patterns in language, and analyzing sayings and expressions commensurate with grade-level learning expectations
(E) use a dictionary, a glossary, or a thesaurus (printed or electronic) to determine the meanings, syllabication, pronunciations, alternate word choices, and parts of speech of English words.	1 (B) monitor oral and written language production and employ self-corrective techniques or other resources
(3) *Reading/Comprehension of Literary Text/Theme and Genre. Students analyze, make inferences, and draw conclusions about theme and genre in different cultural, historical, and contemporary contexts and provide evidence from the text to support their understanding. Students are expected to:*	

Seventh-Grade ELAR TEKS	ELPS
(3) cont . . . (A) describe multiple themes in a work of fiction;	4 (J) demonstrate English comprehension and expand reading skills by employing inferential skills such as predicting, making connections between ideas, drawing inferences and conclusions from text and graphic sources, and finding supporting text evidence commensurate with content-area needs
(B) describe conventions in myths and epic tales (e.g., extended simile, the quest, the hero's tasks, circle stories); and	4 (K) demonstrate English comprehension and expand reading skills by employing analytical skills such as evaluating written information and performing critical analyses commensurate with content-area and grade-level needs
(C) analyze how place and time influence the theme or message of a literary work.	4 (K) demonstrate English comprehension and expand reading skills by employing analytical skills such as evaluating written information and performing critical analyses commensurate with content-area and grade-level needs
(4) Reading/Comprehension of Literary Text/Poetry. Students understand, make inferences, and draw conclusions about the structure and elements of poetry and provide evidence from text to support their understanding. Students are expected to analyze the importance of graphical elements (e.g., capital letters, line length, word position) on the meaning of a poem.	4 (J) demonstrate English comprehension and expand reading skills by employing inferential skills such as predicting, making connections between ideas, drawing inferences and conclusions from text and graphic sources, and finding supporting text evidence commensurate with content-area needs 4 (K) demonstrate English comprehension and expand reading skills by employing analytical skills such as evaluating written information and performing critical analyses commensurate with content-area and grade-level needs
(5) Reading/Comprehension of Literary Text/Drama. Students understand, make inferences and draw conclusions about the structure and elements of drama and provide evidence from text to support their understanding. Students are expected to explain a playwright's use of dialogue and stage directions.	4 (J) demonstrate English comprehension and expand reading skills by employing inferential skills such as predicting, making connections between ideas, drawing inferences and conclusions from text and graphic sources, and finding supporting text evidence commensurate with content-area needs
(6) Reading/Comprehension of Literary Text/Fiction. Students understand, make inferences, and draw conclusions about the structure and elements of fiction and provide evidence from text to support their understanding. Students are expected to:	
(A) explain the influence of the setting on plot development;	4 (J) demonstrate English comprehension and expand reading skills by employing inferential skills such as predicting, making connections between ideas, drawing inferences and conclusions from text and graphic sources, and finding supporting text evidence commensurate with content-area needs

Seventh-Grade ELAR TEKS	ELPS
(6) cont . . . (B) analyze the development of the plot through the internal and external responses of the characters, including their motivations and conflicts; and	4 (J) demonstrate English comprehension and expand reading skills by employing inferential skills such as predicting, making connections between ideas, drawing inferences and conclusions from text and graphic sources, and finding supporting text evidence commensurate with content-area needs 4 (K) demonstrate English comprehension and expand reading skills by employing analytical skills such as evaluating written information and performing critical analyses commensurate with content-area and grade-level needs
(C) analyze different forms of point of view, including first-person, third-person omniscient, and third-person limited.	4 (K) demonstrate English comprehension and expand reading skills by employing analytical skills such as evaluating written information and performing critical analyses commensurate with content-area and grade-level needs
(7) Reading/Comprehension of Literary Text/Literary Nonfiction. Students understand, make inferences, and draw conclusions about the varied structural patterns and features of literary nonfiction and provide evidence from text to support their understanding. Students are expected to describe the structural and substantive differences between an autobiography or a diary and a fictional adaptation of it.	4 (J) demonstrate English comprehension and expand reading skills by employing inferential skills such as predicting, making connections between ideas, drawing inferences and conclusions from text and graphic sources, and finding supporting text evidence commensurate with content-area needs 4 (K) demonstrate English comprehension and expand reading skills by employing analytical skills such as evaluating written information and performing critical analyses commensurate with content-area and grade-level needs
(8) Reading/Comprehension of Literary Text/Sensory Language. Students understand, make inferences, and draw conclusions about how an author's sensory language creates imagery in literary text and provide evidence from text to support their understanding. Students are expected to determine the figurative meaning of phrases and analyze how an author's use of language creates imagery, appeals to the senses, and suggests mood.	4 (J) demonstrate English comprehension and expand reading skills by employing inferential skills such as predicting, making connections between ideas, drawing inferences and conclusions from text and graphic sources, and finding supporting text evidence commensurate with content-area needs
(9) Reading/Comprehension of Informational Text/Culture and History. Students analyze, make inferences, and draw conclusions about the author's purpose in cultural, historical, and contemporary contexts and provide evidence from the text to support their understanding. Students are expected to explain the difference between the theme of a literary work and the author's purpose in an expository text.	4 (J) demonstrate English comprehension and expand reading skills by employing inferential skills such as predicting, making connections between ideas, drawing inferences and conclusions from text and graphic sources, and finding supporting text evidence commensurate with content-area needs 4 (K) demonstrate English comprehension and expand reading skills by employing analytical skills such as evaluating written information and performing critical analyses commensurate with content-area and grade-level needs

Seventh-Grade ELAR TEKS	ELPS
(10) Reading/Comprehension of Informational Text/Expository Text. Students analyze, make inferences, and draw conclusions about expository text and provide evidence from text to support their understanding. Students are expected to:	
(A) evaluate a summary of the original text for accuracy of the main ideas, supporting details, and overall meaning;	4 (I) demonstrate English comprehension and expand reading skills by employing basic reading skills such as demonstrating understanding of supporting ideas and details in text and graphic sources, summarizing text, and distinguishing main ideas from details commensurate with content-area needs
(B) distinguish factual claims from commonplace assertions and opinions;	4 (K) demonstrate English comprehension and expand reading skills by employing analytical skills such as evaluating written information and performing critical analyses commensurate with content-area and grade-level needs
(C) use different organizational patterns as guides for summarizing and forming an overview of different kinds of expository text; and	1 (H) develop and expand repertoire of learning strategies such as reasoning inductively or deductively, looking for patterns in language, and analyzing sayings and expressions 4 (I) demonstrate English comprehension and expand reading skills by employing basic reading skills such as demonstrating understanding of supporting ideas and details in text and graphic sources, summarizing text, and distinguishing main ideas from details commensurate with content-area needs
(D) synthesize and make logical connections between ideas within a text and across two or three texts representing similar or different genres, and support those findings with textual evidence.	1 (H) develop and expand repertoire of learning strategies such as reasoning inductively or deductively, looking for patterns in language, and analyzing sayings and expressions 4 (J) demonstrate English comprehension and expand reading skills by employing inferential skills such as predicting, making connections between ideas, drawing inferences and conclusions from text and graphic sources, and finding supporting text evidence commensurate with content-area needs
(11) Reading/Comprehension of Informational Text/Persuasive Text. Students analyze, make inferences, and draw conclusions about persuasive text and provide evidence from text to support their analysis. Students are expected to:	
(A) analyze the structure of the central argument in contemporary policy speeches (e.g., argument by cause and effect, analogy, authority) and identify the different types of evidence used to support the argument; and	4 (J) demonstrate English comprehension and expand reading skills by employing inferential skills such as predicting, making connections between ideas, drawing inferences and conclusions from text and graphic sources, and finding supporting text evidence commensurate with content-area needs 4 (K) demonstrate English comprehension and expand reading skills by employing analytical skills such as evaluating written information and performing critical

	analyses commensurate with content-area and grade-level needs
Seventh-Grade ELAR TEKS	**ELPS**
(11) cont . . . (B) identify such rhetorical fallacies as ad hominem, exaggeration, stereotyping, or categorical claims in persuasive texts.	1 (H) develop and expand repertoire of learning strategies such as reasoning inductively or deductively, looking for patterns in language, and analyzing sayings and expressions 4 (K) demonstrate English comprehension and expand reading skills by employing analytical skills such as evaluating written information and performing critical analyses commensurate with content-area and grade-level needs
(12) Reading/Comprehension of Informational Text/Procedural Texts. Students understand how to glean and use information in procedural texts and documents. Students are expected to:	
(A) follow multidimensional instructions from text to complete a task, solve a problem, or perform procedures; and	4 (J) demonstrate English comprehension and expand reading skills by employing inferential skills such as predicting, making connections between ideas, drawing inferences and conclusions from text and graphic sources, and finding supporting text evidence commensurate with content-area needs
(B) explain the function of the graphical components of a text.	4 (D) use prereading supports such as graphic organizers, illustrations, and pretaught topic-related vocabulary and other prereading activities to enhance comprehension of written text 4 (F) use visual and contextual support and support from peers and teachers to read grade-appropriate content-area text, to enhance and confirm understanding, to develop vocabulary, to grasp language structures, and to tap background knowledge needed to comprehend increasingly challenging language
(13) Reading/Media Literacy. Students use comprehension skills to analyze how words, images, graphics, and sounds work together in various forms to impact meaning. Students will continue to apply earlier standards with greater depth in increasingly more complex texts. Students are expected to:	
(A) interpret both explicit and implicit messages in various forms of media;	2 (F) listen to and derive meaning from a variety of media such as audio tape, video, DVD, and CD-ROM to build and reinforce concept and language attainment 4 (I) demonstrate English comprehension and expand reading skills by employing basic reading skills such as demonstrating understanding of supporting ideas and details in text and graphic sources, summarizing text, and distinguishing main ideas from details commensurate with content-area needs 4 (K) demonstrate English comprehension and expand reading skills by employing analytical skills such as evaluating written information and performing critical

	analyses commensurate with content-area and grade-level needs
Seventh-Grade ELAR TEKS	**ELPS**
(13) cont . . . (B) interpret how visual and sound techniques (e.g., special effects, camera angles, lighting, music) influence the message;	2 (F) listen to and derive meaning from a variety of media such as audio tape, video, DVD, and CD-ROM to build and reinforce concept and language attainment
(C) evaluate various ways media influences and informs audiences; and	2 (F) listen to and derive meaning from a variety of media such as audio tape, video, DVD, and CD-ROM to build and reinforce concept and language attainment 4 (J) demonstrate English comprehension and expand reading skills by employing inferential skills such as predicting, making connections between ideas, drawing inferences and conclusions from text and graphic sources, and finding supporting text evidence commensurate with content-area needs 4 (K) demonstrate English comprehension and expand reading skills by employing analytical skills such as evaluating written information and performing critical analyses commensurate with content-area and grade-level needs
(D) assess the correct level of formality and tone for successful participation in various digital media.	1 (G) demonstrate an increasing ability to distinguish between formal and informal English and an increasing knowledge of when to use each one commensurate with grade-level learning expectations 2 (F) listen to and derive meaning from a variety of media such as audio tape, video, DVD, and CD ROM to build and reinforce concept and language attainment
Reading/Media Literacy – No Correlation	**4(B) recognize directionality of English reading such as left to right and top to bottom** **4 (E) read linguistically accommodated content-area material with a decreasing need for linguistic accommodations as more English is learned**
(14) Writing/Writing Process. Students use elements of the writing process (planning, drafting, revising, editing, and publishing) to compose text. Students are expected to:	
(A) plan a first draft by selecting a genre appropriate for conveying the intended meaning to an audience, determining appropriate topics through a range of strategies (e.g., discussion, background reading, personal interests, interviews), and developing a thesis or controlling idea;	1 (A) use prior knowledge and experiences to understand meanings in English 3 (G) express opinions, ideas, and feelings ranging from communicating single words and short phrases to participating in extended discussions on a variety of social and grade-appropriate academic topics 5 (B) write using newly acquired basic vocabulary and content-based grade-level vocabulary

(B) develop drafts by choosing an appropriate organizational strategy (e.g., sequence of events, cause-and-effect, compare/contrast) and building on ideas to create a focused, organized, and coherent piece of writing;	1 (C) use strategic learning techniques such as concept mapping, drawing, memorizing, comparing, contrasting, and reviewing to acquire basic and grade-level vocabulary 5 (F) write using a variety of grade-appropriate sentence lengths, patterns, and connecting words to combine phrases, clauses, and sentences in increasingly accurate ways as more English is acquired

Seventh-Grade ELAR TEKS	ELPS
(14) cont . . . (C) revise drafts to ensure precise word choice and vivid images; consistent point of view; use of simple, compound, and complex sentences; internal and external coherence; and the use of effective transitions after rethinking how well questions of purpose, audience, and genre have been addressed;	5 (D) edit writing for standard grammar and usage, including subject-verb agreement, pronoun agreement, and appropriate verb tenses commensurate with grade-level expectations as more English is acquired 5 (F) write using a variety of grade-appropriate sentence lengths, patterns, and connecting words to combine phrases, clauses, and sentences in increasingly accurate ways as more English is acquired
(D) edit drafts for grammar, mechanics, and spelling; and	5 (D) edit writing for standard grammar and usage, including subject-verb agreement, pronoun agreement, and appropriate verb tenses commensurate with grade-level expectations as more English is acquired
(E) revise final draft in response to feedback from peers and teacher and publish written work for appropriate audiences.	4 (F) use visual and contextual support and support from peers and teachers to read grade-appropriate content-area text, to enhance and confirm understanding, to develop vocabulary, to grasp language structures, and to tap background knowledge needed to comprehend increasingly challenging language
(15) Writing/Literary Texts. Students write literary texts to express their ideas and feelings about real or imagined people, events, and ideas. Students are expected to:	
(A) write an imaginative story that: (i) sustains reader interest; (ii) includes well-paced action and an engaging story line; (iii) creates a specific, believable setting through the use of sensory details; (iv) develops interesting characters; and (v) uses a range of literary strategies and devices to enhance the style and tone; and	5 (B) write using newly acquired basic vocabulary 5 (F) write using a variety of grade-appropriate sentence lengths, patterns, and connecting words to combine phrases, clauses, and sentences in increasingly accurate ways as more English is acquired 5 (G) narrate, describe, and explain with increasing specificity and detail to fulfill content-area writing needs as more English is acquired
(B) write a poem using: (i) poetic techniques (e.g., rhyme scheme, meter); (ii) figurative language (e.g., personification, idioms, hyperbole); and (iii) graphic elements (e.g., word position).	1 (E) internalize new, basic, and academic language by using and reusing it in meaningful ways in speaking and writing activities that build concept and language attainment 5 (B) write using newly acquired basic vocabulary
(16) Writing. Students write about their own experiences. Students are expected to write a personal narrative that has a clearly defined focus	5 (F) write using a variety of grade-appropriate sentence lengths, patterns, and connecting words to combine phrases, clauses, and sentences in increasingly accurate ways as more English is acquired

and communicates the importance of or reasons for actions and/or consequences.	5 (G) narrate, describe, and explain with increasing specificity and detail to fulfill content-area writing needs as more English is acquired
(17) Writing/Expository and Procedural Texts. Students write expository and procedural or work-related texts to communicate ideas and information to specific audiences for specific purposes. Students are expected to:	
Seventh-Grade ELAR TEKS	**ELPS**
(17) cont . . . (A) write a multiparagraph essay to convey information about a topic that: (i) presents effective introductions and concluding paragraphs; (ii) contains a clearly stated purpose or controlling idea; (iii) is logically organized with appropriate facts and details and includes no extraneous information or inconsistencies; (iv) accurately synthesizes ideas from several sources; and (v) uses a variety of sentence structures, rhetorical devices, and transitions to link paragraphs;	5 (F) write using a variety of grade-appropriate sentence lengths, patterns, and connecting words to combine phrases, clauses, and sentences in increasingly accurate ways as more English is acquired; 5 (G) narrate, describe, and explain with increasing specificity and detail to fulfill content-area writing needs as more English is acquired
(B) write a letter that reflects an opinion, registers a complaint, or requests information in a business or friendly context;	1 (G) demonstrate an increasing ability to distinguish between formal and informal English and an increasing knowledge of when to use each one commensurate with grade-level learning expectations 5 (G) narrate, describe, and explain with increasing specificity and detail to fulfill content-area writing needs as more English is acquired
(C) write responses to literary or expository texts that demonstrate the writing skills for multiparagraph essays and provide sustained evidence from the text using quotations when appropriate; and	5 (G) narrate, describe, and explain with increasing specificity and detail to fulfill content-area writing needs as more English is acquired
(D) produce a multimedia presentation involving text and graphics using available technology.	5 (F) write using a variety of grade-appropriate sentence lengths, patterns, and connecting words to combine phrases, clauses, and sentences in increasingly accurate ways as more English is acquired 5 (G) narrate, describe, and explain with increasing specificity and detail to fulfill content-area writing needs as more English is acquired
(18) Writing/Persuasive Texts. Students write persuasive texts to influence the attitudes or actions of a specific audience on specific issues. Students are expected to write a persuasive essay to the appropriate audience that:	
(A) establishes a clear thesis or position;	5 (F) write using a variety of grade-appropriate sentence lengths, patterns, and connecting words to combine phrases, clauses, and sentences in increasingly accurate ways as more English is acquired 5 (G) narrate, describe, and explain with increasing specificity and detail to fulfill content-area writing

	needs as more English is acquired
(B) considers and responds to the views of others and anticipates and answers reader concerns and counterarguments; and	5 (F) write using a variety of grade-appropriate sentence lengths, patterns, and connecting words to combine phrases, clauses, and sentences in increasingly accurate ways as more English is acquired 5 (G) narrate, describe, and explain with increasing specificity and detail to fulfill content-area writing needs as more English is acquired

Seventh-Grade ELAR TEKS	**ELPS**
(18) cont . . . (C) includes evidence that is logically organized to support the author's viewpoint and that differentiates between fact and opinion.	5 (F) write using a variety of grade-appropriate sentence lengths, patterns, and connecting words to combine phrases, clauses, and sentences in increasingly accurate ways as more English is acquired 5 (G) narrate, describe, and explain with increasing specificity and detail to fulfill content-area writing needs as more English is acquired
(19) Oral and Written Conventions/Conventions. Students understand the function of and use the conventions of academic language when speaking and writing. Students will continue to apply earlier standards with greater complexity. Students are expected to:	
(A) identify, use, and understand the function of the following parts of speech in the context of reading, writing, and speaking: (i) verbs (perfect and progressive tenses) and participles; (ii) appositive phrases; (iii) adverbial and adjectival phrases and clauses; (iv) conjunctive adverbs (e.g., consequently, furthermore, indeed); (v) prepositions and prepositional phrases and their influence on subject-verb agreement; (vi) relative pronouns (e.g., whose, that, which); (vii) subordinating conjunctions (e.g., because, since); and (viii)transitions for sentence to sentence or paragraph to paragraph coherence;	5 (E) employ increasingly complex grammatical structures in content-area writing commensurate with grade-level expectations, such as: (i) using correct verbs, tenses, and pronouns / antecedents (ii) using possessive case (apostrophes) correctly (iii) using negatives and contractions correctly 5 (F) write using a variety of grade-appropriate sentence lengths, patterns, and connecting words to combine phrases, clauses, and sentences in increasingly accurate ways as more English is acquired
(B) write complex sentences and differentiate between main versus subordinate clauses; and	5 (F) write using a variety of grade-appropriate sentence lengths, patterns, and connecting words to combine phrases, clauses, and sentences in increasingly accurate ways as more English is acquired
(C) use a variety of complete sentences (e.g., simple, compound, complex) that include properly placed modifiers, correctly identified antecedents, parallel structures, and consistent tenses.	5 (F) write using a variety of grade-appropriate sentence lengths, patterns, and connecting words to combine phrases, clauses, and sentences in increasingly accurate ways as more English is acquired
(20) Oral and Written Conventions/Handwriting, Capitalization, and Punctuation. Students write legibly and use appropriate capitalization and	

punctuation conventions in their compositions. Students are expected to:	
(A) use conventions of capitalization; and	5 (C) spell familiar English words with increasing accuracy, and employ English spelling patterns and rules with increasing accuracy as more English is acquired
Seventh-Grade ELAR TEKS	**ELPS**
(20) cont . . . (B) recognize and use punctuation marks including: (i) commas after introductory words, phrases, and clauses; and (ii) semicolons, colons, and hyphens.	5 (E) employ increasingly complex grammatical structures in content-area writing commensurate with grade-level expectations, such as: (i) using correct verbs, tenses, and pronouns / antecedents (ii) using possessive case (apostrophe s) correctly (iii) using negatives and contractions correctly
(21) Oral and Written Conventions/Spelling. Students spell correctly. Students are expected to spell correctly, including using various resources to determine and check correct spellings.	1 (B) monitor oral and written language production and employ self-corrective techniques or other resources 5 (C) spell familiar English words with increasing accuracy, and employ English spelling patterns and rules with increasing accuracy as more English is acquired
Oral and Written Conventions/Spelling – No Correlation	**5 (A) learn relationships between sounds and letters of the English language to represent sounds when writing in English**
(22) Research/Research Plan. Students ask open-ended research questions and develop a plan for answering them. Students are expected to:	
(A) brainstorm, consult with others, decide upon a topic, and formulate a major research question to address the major research topic; and	1 (E) internalize new, basic, and academic language by using and reusing it in meaningful ways in speaking and writing activities that build concept and language attainment 3 (F) ask and give information ranging from using a very limited bank of high-frequency, high-need, concrete vocabulary, including key words and expressions needed for basic communication in academic and social contexts, to using abstract and content-based vocabulary during extended speaking assignments 3 (G) express opinions, ideas, and feelings ranging from communicating single words and short phrases to participating in extended discussions on a variety of social and grade-appropriate academic topics

(B) apply steps for obtaining and evaluating information from a wide variety of sources and create a written plan after preliminary research in reference works and additional text searches.	4 (J) demonstrate English comprehension and expand reading skills by employing inferential skills such as predicting, making connections between ideas, drawing inferences and conclusions from text and graphic sources, and finding supporting text evidence commensurate with content-area needs 4 (K) demonstrate English comprehension and expand reading skills by employing analytical skills such as evaluating written information and performing critical analyses commensurate with content-area and grade-level needs 5 (G) narrate, describe, and explain with increasing specificity and detail to fulfill content-area writing needs as more English is acquired

Seventh-Grade ELAR TEKS	**ELPS**
(23) Research/Gathering Sources. Students determine, locate, and explore the full range of relevant sources addressing a research question and systematically record the information they gather. Students are expected to:	
(A) follow the research plan to gather information from a range of relevant print and electronic sources using advanced search strategies;	2 (F) listen to and derive meaning from a variety of media such as audio tape, video, DVD, and CD-ROM to build and reinforce concept and language attainment 4 (J) demonstrate English comprehension and expand reading skills by employing inferential skills such as predicting, making connections between ideas, drawing inferences and conclusions from text and graphic sources, and finding supporting text evidence commensurate with content-area needs 4 (K) demonstrate English comprehension and expand reading skills by employing analytical skills such as evaluating written information and performing critical analyses commensurate with content-area and grade-level needs
(B) categorize information thematically in order to see the larger constructs inherent in the information;	4 (J) demonstrate English comprehension and expand reading skills by employing inferential skills such as predicting, making connections between ideas, drawing inferences and conclusions from text and graphic sources, and finding supporting text evidence commensurate with content-area needs 4 (K) demonstrate English comprehension and expand reading skills by employing analytical skills such as evaluating written information and performing critical analyses commensurate with content-area and grade-level needs
(C) record bibliographic information (e.g., author, title, page number) for all notes and sources according to a standard format; and	*No ELPS Correlation*
(D) differentiate between paraphrasing and plagiarism and identify the importance of citing valid and reliable sources.	*No ELPS Correlation*

(24) Research/Synthesizing Information. Students clarify research questions and evaluate and synthesize collected information. Students are expected to:	
(A) narrow or broaden the major research question, if necessary, based on further research and investigation; and	4 (K) demonstrate English comprehension and expand reading skills by employing analytical skills such as evaluating written information and performing critical analyses commensurate with content-area and grade-level needs
(B) utilize elements that demonstrate the reliability and validity of the sources used (e.g., publication date, coverage, language, point of view) and explain why one source is more useful than another.	4 (K) demonstrate English comprehension and expand reading skills by employing analytical skills such as evaluating written information and performing critical analyses commensurate with content-area and grade-level needs

Seventh-Grade ELAR TEKS	ELPS
(25) Research/Organizing and Presenting Ideas. Students organize and present their ideas and information according to the purpose of the research and their audience. Students are expected to synthesize the research into a written or an oral presentation that:	
(A) draws conclusions and summarizes or paraphrases the findings in a systematic way;	4 (G) demonstrate comprehension of increasingly complex English by participating in shared reading, retelling or summarizing material, responding to questions, and taking notes commensurate with content-area and grade-level needs 4 (J) demonstrate English comprehension and expand reading skills by employing inferential skills such as predicting, making connections between ideas, drawing inferences and conclusions from text and graphic sources, and finding supporting text evidence commensurate with content-area needs
(B) marshals evidence to explain the topic and gives relevant reasons for conclusions;	4 (J) demonstrate English comprehension and expand reading skills by employing inferential skills such as predicting, making connections between ideas, drawing inferences and conclusions from text and graphic sources, and finding supporting text evidence commensurate with content-area needs
(C) presents the findings in a meaningful format; and	5 (G) narrate, describe, and explain with increasing specificity and detail to fulfill content-area writing needs as more English is acquired
(D) follows accepted formats for integrating quotations and citations into the written text to maintain a flow of ideas.	5 (F) write using a variety of grade-appropriate sentence lengths, patterns, and connecting words to combine phrases, clauses, and sentences in increasingly accurate ways as more English is acquired

(26) Listening and Speaking/Listening. Students will use comprehension skills to listen attentively to others in formal and informal settings. Students will continue to apply earlier standards with	

greater complexity. Students are expected to:	
(A) listen to and interpret a speaker's purpose by explaining the content, evaluating the delivery of the presentation, and asking questions or making comments about the evidence that supports a speaker's claims;	2 (D) monitor understanding of spoken language during classroom instruction and interactions and seek clarification as needed 2 (I) demonstrate listening comprehension of increasingly complex spoken English by following directions, retelling or summarizing spoken messages, responding to questions and requests, collaborating with peers, and taking notes commensurate with content and grade-level needs 3 (F) ask and give information ranging from using a very limited bank of high-frequency, high-need, concrete vocabulary, including key words and expressions needed for basic communication in academic and social contexts, to using abstract and content-based vocabulary during extended speaking assignments

Seventh-Grade ELAR TEKS	ELPS
(26) cont . . . (B) follow and give complex oral instructions to perform specific tasks, answer questions, or solve problems; and	2 (G) understand the general meaning, main points, and important details of spoken language ranging from situations in which topics, language, and contexts are familiar to unfamiliar 2 (H) understand implicit ideas and information in increasingly complex spoken language commensurate with grade-level learning expectations 2 (I) demonstrate listening comprehension of increasingly complex spoken English by following directions, retelling or summarizing spoken messages, responding to questions and requests, collaborating with peers, and taking notes commensurate with content and grade-level needs 3 (F) ask and give information ranging from using a very limited bank of high-frequency, high-need, concrete vocabulary, including key words and expressions needed for basic communication in academic and social contexts, to using abstract and content-based vocabulary during extended speaking assignments
(C) draw conclusions about the speaker's message by considering verbal communication (e.g., word choice, tone) and nonverbal cues (e.g., posture, gestures, facial expressions).	2 (E) use visual, contextual, and linguistic support to enhance and confirm understanding of increasingly complex and elaborated spoken language 2 (I) demonstrate listening comprehension of increasingly complex spoken English by following directions, retelling or summarizing spoken messages, responding to questions and requests, collaborating with peers, and taking notes commensurate with content and grade-level needs 2 (H) understand implicit ideas and information in increasingly complex spoken language commensurate with grade-level learning expectations
Listening and Speaking/Listening – No Correlation	**2 (A) distinguish sounds and intonation patterns of English with increasing ease**
	2 (B) recognize elements of the English sound system in newly acquired vocabulary such as long and short vowels, silent letters, and consonant clusters
(27) *Listening and Speaking/Speaking. Students speak*	1 (D) speak using learning strategies such as requesting

clearly and to the point, using the conventions of language. Students will continue to apply earlier standards with greater complexity. Students are expected to present a critique of a literary work, film, or dramatic production, employing eye contact, speaking rate, volume, enunciation, a variety of natural gestures, and conventions of language to communicate ideas effectively.	assistance, employing nonverbal cues, and using synonyms and circumlocution 2 (C) learn new language structures, expressions, and basic and academic vocabulary heard during classroom instruction and interactions 3 (B) expand and internalize initial English vocabulary by learning and using high-frequency English words necessary for identifying and describing people, places, and objects, by retelling simple stories and basic information represented or supported by pictures, and by learning and using routine language needed for classroom communication 3 (C) speak using a variety of grammatical structures, sentence lengths, sentence types, and connecting words with increasing accuracy and ease as more English is acquired 3 (D) speak using grade-level content-area vocabulary in context to internalize new English words and build academic language proficiency
Seventh-Grade ELAR TEKS	**ELPS**
(27) cont . . .	3 (G) express opinions, ideas, and feelings ranging from communicating single words and short phrases to participating in extended discussions on a variety of social and grade-appropriate academic topics 3 (H) narrate, describe, and explain with increasing specificity and detail as more English is acquired 3 (I) adapt spoken language appropriately for formal and informal purposes 3 (J) respond orally to information presented in a wide variety of print, electronic, audio, and visual media to build and reinforce concept and language attainment
Listening and Speaking/Speaking – No Correlation	**3 (A) practice producing sounds of newly acquired vocabulary such as long and short vowels, silent letters, and consonant clusters to pronounce English words in a manner that is increasingly comprehensible**
(28) Listening and Speaking/Teamwork. Students work productively with others in teams. Students will continue to apply earlier standards with greater complexity. Students are expected to participate productively in discussions, plan agendas with clear goals and deadlines, set time limits for speakers, take notes, and vote on key issues.	1 (B) monitor oral and written language production and employ self-corrective techniques or other resources 1 (G) demonstrate an increasing ability to distinguish between formal and informal English and an increasing knowledge of when to use each one commensurate with grade-level learning expectations 2 (I) demonstrate listening comprehension of increasingly complex spoken English by following directions, retelling or summarizing spoken messages, responding to questions and requests, collaborating with peers, and taking notes 3 (E) share information in cooperative learning interactions

ELAR TEKS and ELPS Side-by-Side

Eighth-Grade

Eighth-Grade ELAR TEKS	ELPS
(1) Reading/Fluency. Students read grade-level text with fluency and comprehension. Students are expected to adjust fluency when reading aloud grade-level text based on the reading purpose and the nature of the text.	4 (E) read linguistically accommodated content-area material with a decreasing need for linguistic accommodations as more English is learned 4 (H) read silently with increasing ease and comprehension for longer periods
(2) Reading/Vocabulary Development. Students understand new vocabulary and use it when reading and writing. Students are expected to:	
(A) determine the meaning of grade-level academic English words derived from Latin, Greek, or other linguistic roots and affixes;	4 (A) learn relationships between sounds and letters of the English language and decode (sound out) words using a combination of skills such as recognizing sound-letter relationships and identifying cognates, affixes, roots, and base words 4 (C) develop basic sight vocabulary, derive meaning of environmental print, and comprehend English vocabulary and language structures used routinely in written classroom materials
(B) use context (within a sentence and in larger sections of text) to determine or clarify the meaning of unfamiliar or ambiguous words or words with novel meanings;	1 (F) use accessible language and learn new and essential language in the process 4 (F) use visual and contextual support and support from peers and teachers to read grade-appropriate content-area text, to enhance and confirm understanding, to develop vocabulary, to grasp language structures, and to tap background knowledge needed to comprehend increasingly challenging language
(C) complete analogies that describe a function or its description (e.g., pen:paper as chalk: ______ or soft:kitten as hard: ______);	1 (C) use strategic learning techniques such as concept mapping, drawing, memorizing, comparing, contrasting, and reviewing to acquire basic and grade-level vocabulary
(D) identify common words or word parts from other languages that are used in written English (e.g., phenomenon, charisma, chorus, passé, flora, fauna); and	1 (H) develop and expand repertoire of learning strategies such as reasoning inductively or deductively, looking for patterns in language, and analyzing sayings and expressions commensurate with grade-level learning expectations
(E) use a dictionary, a glossary, or a thesaurus (printed or electronic) to determine the meanings, syllabication, pronunciations, alternate word choices, and parts of speech of words.	1 (B) monitor oral and written language production and employ self-corrective techniques or other resources
(3) Comprehension of Literary Text/Theme and Genre. Students analyze, make inferences, and draw conclusions about theme and genre in different cultural, historical, and contemporary contexts and provide evidence from the text to support their understanding. Students are expected to:	

Eighth-Grade ELAR TEKS	ELPS
(3) cont . . . (A) analyze literary works that share similar themes across cultures;	4 (K) demonstrate English comprehension and expand reading skills by employing analytical skills such as evaluating written information and performing critical analyses commensurate with content-area and grade-level needs
(B) compare and contrast the similarities and differences in mythologies from various cultures (e.g., ideas of afterlife, roles and characteristics of deities, purposes of myths); and	1 (C) use strategic learning techniques such as concept mapping, drawing, memorizing, comparing, contrasting, and reviewing to acquire basic and grade-level vocabulary 4 (K) demonstrate English comprehension and expand reading skills by employing analytical skills such as evaluating written information and performing critical analyses commensurate with content-area and grade-level needs
(C) explain how the values and beliefs of particular characters are affected by the historical and cultural setting of the literary work.	4 (J) demonstrate English comprehension and expand reading skills by employing inferential skills such as predicting, making connections between ideas, drawing inferences and conclusions from text and graphic sources, and finding supporting text evidence commensurate with content-area needs
(4) Comprehension of Literary Text/Poetry. Students understand, make inferences, and draw conclusions about the structure and elements of poetry and provide evidence from text to support their understanding. Students are expected to compare and contrast the relationship between the purpose and characteristics of different poetic forms (e.g., epic poetry, lyric poetry).	1 (C) use strategic learning techniques such as concept mapping, drawing, memorizing, comparing, contrasting, and reviewing to acquire basic and grade-level vocabulary 1 (H) develop and expand repertoire of learning strategies such as reasoning inductively or deductively, looking for patterns in language, and analyzing sayings and expressions commensurate with grade-level learning expectations 4 (J) demonstrate English comprehension and expand reading skills by employing inferential skills such as predicting, making connections between ideas, drawing inferences and conclusions from text and graphic sources, and finding supporting text evidence commensurate with content-area needs
(5) Comprehension of Literary Text/Drama. Students understand, make inferences, and draw conclusions about the structure and elements of drama and provide evidence from text to support their understanding. Students are expected to analyze how different playwrights characterize their protagonists and antagonists through the dialogue and staging of their plays.	4 (J) demonstrate English comprehension and expand reading skills by employing inferential skills such as predicting, making connections between ideas, drawing inferences and conclusions from text and graphic sources, and finding supporting text evidence commensurate with content-area needs 4 (K) demonstrate English comprehension and expand reading skills by employing analytical skills such as evaluating written information and performing critical analyses commensurate with content-area and grade-level needs

Eighth-Grade ELAR TEKS	ELPS
(6) Comprehension of Literary Text/Fiction. Students understand, make inferences, and draw conclusions about the structure and elements of fiction and provide evidence from text to support their understanding. Students are expected to:	
(A) analyze linear plot developments (e.g., conflict, rising action, falling action, resolution, subplots) to determine whether and how conflicts are resolved;	4 (J) demonstrate English comprehension and expand reading skills by employing inferential skills such as predicting, making connections between ideas, drawing inferences and conclusions from text and graphic sources, and finding supporting text evidence commensurate with content-area needs 4 (K) demonstrate English comprehension and expand reading skills by employing analytical skills such as evaluating written information and performing critical analyses commensurate with content-area and grade-level needs
(B) analyze how the central characters' qualities influence the theme of a fictional work and resolution of the central conflict; and	4 (K) demonstrate English comprehension and expand reading skills by employing analytical skills such as evaluating written information and performing critical analyses commensurate with content-area and grade-level needs
(C) analyze different forms of point of view, including limited versus omniscient, subjective versus objective.	4 (K) demonstrate English comprehension and expand reading skills by employing analytical skills such as evaluating written information and performing critical analyses commensurate with content-area and grade-level needs
(7) Comprehension of Literary Text/Literary Nonfiction. Students understand, make inferences, and draw conclusions about the varied structural patterns and features of literary nonfiction and provide evidence from text to support their understanding. Students are expected to analyze passages in well-known speeches for the author's use of literary devices and word and phrase choice (e.g., aphorisms, epigraphs) to appeal to the audience.	4 (J) demonstrate English comprehension and expand reading skills by employing inferential skills such as predicting, making connections between ideas, drawing inferences and conclusions from text and graphic sources, and finding supporting text evidence commensurate with content-area needs 4 (K) demonstrate English comprehension and expand reading skills by employing analytical skills such as evaluating written information and performing critical analyses commensurate with content-area and grade-level needs
(8) Comprehension of Literary Text/Sensory Language. Students understand, make inferences, and draw conclusions about how an author's sensory language creates imagery in literary text and provide evidence from text to support their understanding. Students are expected to explain the effect of similes and extended metaphors in literary text.	4 (J) demonstrate English comprehension and expand reading skills by employing inferential skills such as predicting, making connections between ideas, drawing inferences and conclusions from text and graphic sources, and finding supporting text evidence commensurate with content-area needs

Eighth-Grade ELAR TEKS	ELPS
(9) Comprehension of Informational Text/Culture and History. Students analyze, make inferences, and draw conclusions about the author's purpose in cultural, historical, and contemporary contexts and provide evidence from the text to support their understanding. Students are expected to analyze works written on the same topic and compare how the authors achieved similar or different purposes.	4 (J) demonstrate English comprehension and expand reading skills by employing inferential skills such as predicting, making connections between ideas, drawing inferences and conclusions from text and graphic sources, and finding supporting text evidence commensurate with content-area needs 4 (K) demonstrate English comprehension and expand reading skills by employing analytical skills such as evaluating written information and performing critical analyses commensurate with content-area and grade-level needs
(10) Comprehension of Informational Text/Expository Text. Students analyze, make inferences, and draw conclusions about expository text and provide evidence from text to support their understanding. Students are expected to:	
(A) summarize the main ideas, supporting details, and relationships among ideas in text succinctly in ways that maintain meaning and logical order;	4 (I) demonstrate English comprehension and expand reading skills by employing basic reading skills such as demonstrating understanding of supporting ideas and details in text and graphic sources, summarizing text, and distinguishing main ideas from details commensurate with content-area needs
(B) distinguish factual claims from commonplace assertions and opinions and evaluate inferences from their logic in text;	4 (J) demonstrate English comprehension and expand reading skills by employing inferential skills such as predicting, making connections between ideas, drawing inferences and conclusions from text and graphic sources, and finding supporting text evidence commensurate with content-area needs 4 (K) demonstrate English comprehension and expand reading skills by employing analytical skills such as evaluating written information and performing critical analyses commensurate with content-area and grade-level needs
(C) make subtle inferences and draw complex conclusions about the ideas in text and their organizational patterns; and	1 (H) develop and expand repertoire of learning strategies such as reasoning inductively or deductively, looking for patterns in language, and analyzing sayings and expressions 4 (J) demonstrate English comprehension and expand reading skills by employing inferential skills such as predicting, making connections between ideas, drawing inferences and conclusions from text and graphic sources, and finding supporting text evidence commensurate with content-area needs
(D) synthesize and make logical connections between ideas within a text and across two or three texts representing similar or different genres and support those findings with textual evidence.	1 (H) develop and expand repertoire of learning strategies such as reasoning inductively or deductively, looking for patterns in language, and analyzing sayings and expressions 4 (J) demonstrate English comprehension and expand reading skills by employing inferential skills such as predicting, making connections between ideas, drawing inferences and conclusions from text and graphic sources, and finding supporting text evidence commensurate with content-area need

Eighth-Grade ELAR TEKS	ELPS
(11) Comprehension of Informational Text/Persuasive Text. Students analyze, make inferences, and draw conclusions about persuasive text and provide evidence from text to support their analyses. Students are expected to:	
(A) compare and contrast persuasive texts that reached different conclusions about the same issue and explain how the authors reached their conclusions through analyzing the evidence each presents; and	1 (C) use strategic learning techniques such as concept mapping, drawing, memorizing, comparing, contrasting, and reviewing to acquire basic and grade-level vocabulary 4 (K) demonstrate English comprehension and expand reading skills by employing analytical skills such as evaluating written information and performing critical analyses commensurate with content-area and grade-level needs
(B) analyze the use of such rhetorical and logical fallacies as loaded terms, caricatures, leading questions, false assumptions, and incorrect premises in persuasive texts.	1 (H) develop and expand repertoire of learning strategies such as reasoning inductively or deductively, looking for patterns in language, and analyzing sayings and expressions 4 (J) demonstrate English comprehension and expand reading skills by employing inferential skills such as predicting, making connections between ideas, drawing inferences and conclusions from text and graphic sources, and finding supporting text evidence commensurate with content-area needs 4 (K) demonstrate English comprehension and expand reading skills by employing analytical skills such as evaluating written information and performing critical analyses commensurate with content-area and grade-level needs
(12) Comprehension of Informational Text/Procedural Texts. Students understand how to glean and use information in procedural texts and documents. Students are expected to:	
(A) analyze text for missing or extraneous information in multistep directions or legends for diagrams; and	4 (K) demonstrate English comprehension and expand reading skills by employing analytical skills such as evaluating written information and performing critical analyses commensurate with content-area and grade-level needs
(B) evaluate graphics for their clarity in communicating meaning or achieving a specific purpose.	4 (D) use prereading supports such as graphic organizers, illustrations, and pretaught topic-related vocabulary and other prereading activities to enhance comprehension of written text 4 (F) use visual and contextual support and support from peers and teachers to read grade-appropriate content-area text, to enhance and confirm understanding, to develop vocabulary, to grasp language structures, and to tap background knowledge needed to comprehend increasingly challenging language

Eighth-Grade ELAR TEKS	ELPS
(12) (B) cont . . .	4 (I) demonstrate English comprehension and expand reading skills by employing basic reading skills such as demonstrating understanding of supporting ideas and details in text and graphic sources, summarizing text, and distinguishing main ideas from details commensurate with content-area needs
(13) Reading/Media Literacy. Students use comprehension skills to analyze how words, images, graphics, and sounds work together in various forms to impact meaning. Students will continue to apply earlier standards with greater depth in increasingly more complex texts. Students are expected to:	
(A) evaluate the role of media in focusing attention on events and informing opinion on issues;	4 (J) demonstrate English comprehension and expand reading skills by employing inferential skills such as predicting, making connections between ideas, drawing inferences and conclusions from text and graphic sources, and finding supporting text evidence commensurate with content-area needs 4 (K) demonstrate English comprehension and expand reading skills by employing analytical skills such as evaluating written information and performing critical analyses commensurate with content-area and grade-level needs
(B) interpret how visual and sound techniques (e.g., special effects, camera angles, lighting, music) influence the message;	2 (F) listen to and derive meaning from a variety of media such as audio tape, video, DVD, and CD-ROM to build and reinforce concept and language attainment 4 (K) demonstrate English comprehension and expand reading skills by employing analytical skills such as evaluating written information and performing critical analyses commensurate with content-area and grade-level need
(C) evaluate various techniques used to create a point of view in media and the impact on audience; and	4 (J) demonstrate English comprehension and expand reading skills by employing inferential skills such as predicting, making connections between ideas, drawing inferences and conclusions from text and graphic sources, and finding supporting text evidence commensurate with content-area needs 4 (K) demonstrate English comprehension and expand reading skills by employing analytical skills such as evaluating written information and performing critical analyses commensurate with content-area and grade-level needs
(D) assess the correct level of formality and tone for successful participation in various digital media.	1 (G) demonstrate an increasing ability to distinguish between formal and informal English and an increasing knowledge of when to use each one commensurate with grade-level learning expectations; 2 (F) listen to and derive meaning from a variety of media such as audio tape, video, DVD, and CD-ROM to build and reinforce concept and language attainment

Eighth-Grade ELAR TEKS	ELPS
(13) (D) cont . . .	4 (K) demonstrate English comprehension and expand reading skills by employing analytical skills such as evaluating written information and performing critical analyses commensurate with content-area and grade-level needs
Reading/Media Literacy – No Correlation	**4(B) recognize directionality of English reading such as left to right and top to bottom**
(14) Writing/Writing Process. Students use elements of the writing process (planning, drafting, revising, editing, and publishing) to compose text. Students are expected to:	
(A) plan a first draft by selecting a genre appropriate for conveying the intended meaning to an audience, determining appropriate topics through a range of strategies (e.g., discussion, background reading, personal interests, interviews), and developing a thesis or controlling idea;	1 (A) use prior knowledge and experiences to understand meanings in English 3 (G) express opinions, ideas, and feelings ranging from communicating single words and short phrases to participating in extended discussions on a variety of social and grade-appropriate academic topics 5 (B) write using newly acquired basic vocabulary and content-based grade-level vocabulary
(B) develop drafts by choosing an appropriate organizational strategy (e.g., sequence of events, cause and effect, compare/contrast) and building on ideas to create a focused, organized, and coherent piece of writing;	1 (C) use strategic learning techniques such as concept mapping, drawing, memorizing, comparing, contrasting, and reviewing to acquire basic and grade-level vocabulary 5 (F) write using a variety of grade-appropriate sentence lengths, patterns, and connecting words to combine phrases, clauses, and sentences in increasingly accurate ways as more English is acquired
(C) revise drafts to ensure precise word choice and vivid images; consistent point of view; use of simple, compound, and complex sentences; internal and external coherence; and the use of effective transitions after rethinking how well questions of purpose, audience, and genre have been addressed;	5 (D) edit writing for standard grammar and usage, including subject-verb agreement, pronoun agreement, and appropriate verb tenses commensurate with grade-level expectations as more English is acquired 5 (F) write using a variety of grade-appropriate sentence lengths, patterns, and connecting words to combine phrases, clauses, and sentences in increasingly accurate ways as more English is acquired
(D) edit drafts for grammar, mechanics, and spelling; and	5 (D) edit writing for standard grammar and usage, including subject-verb agreement, pronoun agreement, and appropriate verb tenses commensurate with grade-level expectations as more English is acquired
(E) revise final draft in response to feedback from peers and teacher and publish written work for appropriate audiences.	4 (F) use visual and contextual support and support from peers and teachers to read grade-appropriate content-area text, to enhance and confirm understanding, to develop vocabulary, to grasp language structures, and to tap background knowledge needed to comprehend increasingly challenging language 5 (D) edit writing for standard grammar and usage, including subject-verb agreement, pronoun agreement, and appropriate verb tenses commensurate with grade-level expectations as more English is acquired

Eighth-Grade ELAR TEKS	ELPS
(15) Writing/Literary Texts. Students write literary texts to express their ideas and feelings about real or imagined people, events, and ideas. Students are expected to:	
(A) write an imaginative story that: (i) sustains reader interest; (ii) includes well-paced action and an engaging story line; (iii) creates a specific, believable setting through the use of sensory details; (iv) develops interesting characters; and (v) uses a range of literary strategies and devices to enhance the style and tone; and	5 (B) write using newly acquired basic vocabulary and content-based grade-level vocabulary 5 (F) write using a variety of grade-appropriate sentence lengths, patterns, and connecting words to combine phrases, clauses, and sentences in increasingly accurate ways as more English is acquired 5 (G) narrate, describe, and explain with increasing specificity and detail to fulfill content-area writing needs as more English is acquired
(B) write a poem using: (i) poetic techniques (e.g., rhyme scheme, meter); (ii) figurative language (e.g., personification, idioms, hyperbole); and (iii) graphic elements (e.g., word position).	1 (E) internalize new, basic, and academic language by using and reusing it in meaningful ways in speaking and writing activities that build concept and language attainment 5 (B) write using newly acquired basic vocabulary and content-based grade-level vocabulary
(16) Writing. Students write about their own experiences. Students are expected to write a personal narrative that has a clearly defined focus and includes reflections on decisions, actions, and/or consequences.	5 (F) write using a variety of grade-appropriate sentence lengths, patterns, and connecting words to combine phrases, clauses, and sentences in increasingly accurate ways as more English is acquired 5 (G) narrate, describe, and explain with increasing specificity and detail to fulfill content-area writing needs as more English is acquired
(17) Writing/Expository and Procedural Texts. Students write expository and procedural or work-related texts to communicate ideas and information to specific audiences for specific purposes. Students are expected to:	
(A) write a multiparagraph essay to convey information about a topic that: (i) presents effective introductions and concluding paragraphs; (ii) contains a clearly stated purpose or controlling idea; (iii) is logically organized with appropriate facts and details and includes no extraneous information or inconsistencies; (iv) accurately synthesizes ideas from several sources; and (v) uses a variety of sentence structures, rhetorical devices, and transitions to link paragraphs;	5 (F) using a variety of grade-appropriate sentence lengths, patterns, and connecting words to combine phrases, clauses, and sentences in increasingly accurate ways as more English is acquired 5 (G) narrate, describe, and explain with increasing specificity and detail to fulfill content-area writing needs as more English is acquired
(B) write a letter that reflects an opinion, registers a complaint, or requests information in a business or friendly context;	5 (G) narrate, describe, and explain with increasing specificity and detail to fulfill content-area writing needs as more English is acquired

Eighth-Grade ELAR TEKS	ELPS
(17) cont . . . (C) write responses to literary or expository texts that demonstrate the use of writing skills for a multi-paragraph essay and provide sustained evidence from the text using quotations when appropriate; and	5 (G) narrate, describe, and explain with increasing specificity and detail to fulfill content-area writing needs as more English is acquired
(D) produce a multimedia presentation involving text, graphics, images, and sound using available technology.	1 (G) demonstrate an increasing ability to distinguish between formal and informal English and an increasing knowledge of when to use each one commensurate with grade-level learning expectations; 5 (F) write using a variety of grade-appropriate sentence lengths, patterns, and connecting words to combine phrases, clauses, and sentences in increasingly accurate ways as more English is acquired; and 5 (G) narrate, describe, and explain with increasing specificity and detail to fulfill content-area writing needs as more English is acquired
(18) Writing/Persuasive Texts. Students write persuasive texts to influence the attitudes or actions of a specific audience on specific issues. Students are expected to write a persuasive essay to the appropriate audience that:	
(A) establishes a clear thesis or position;	5 (F) write using a variety of grade-appropriate sentence lengths, patterns, and connecting words to combine phrases, clauses, and sentences in increasingly accurate ways as more English is acquired 5 (G) narrate, describe, and explain with increasing specificity and detail to fulfill content-area writing needs as more English is acquired
(B) considers and responds to the views of others and anticipates and answers reader concerns and counterarguments; and	5 (G) narrate, describe, and explain with increasing specificity and detail to fulfill content-area writing needs as more English is acquired
(C) includes evidence that is logically organized to support the author's viewpoint and that differentiates between fact and opinion.	1 (H) develop and expand repertoire of learning strategies such as reasoning inductively or deductively, looking for patterns in language, and analyzing sayings and expressions 5 (G) narrate, describe, and explain with increasing specificity and detail to fulfill content-area writing needs as more English is acquired
(19) Oral and Written Conventions/Conventions. Students understand the function of and use the conventions of academic language when speaking and writing. Students will continue to apply earlier standards with greater complexity. Students are expected to:	

Eighth-Grade ELAR TEKS	ELPS
(19) cont . . . (A) use and understand the function of the following parts of speech in the context of reading, writing, and speaking: (i) verbs (perfect and progressive tenses) and participles; (ii) appositive phrases; (iii) adverbial and adjectival phrases and clauses; (iv) relative pronouns (e.g., whose, that, which); and (v) subordinating conjunctions (e.g., because, since);	5 (E) employ increasingly complex grammatical structures in content-area writing commensurate with grade-level expectations, such as: (i) using correct verbs, tenses, and pronouns / antecedents (ii) using possessive case (apostrophes) correctly (iii) using negatives and contractions correctly 5 (F) write using a variety of grade-appropriate sentence lengths, patterns, and connecting words to combine phrases, clauses, and sentences in increasingly accurate ways as more English is acquired
(B) write complex sentences and differentiate between main versus subordinate clauses; and	5 (F) write using a variety of grade-appropriate sentence lengths, patterns, and connecting words to combine phrases, clauses, and sentences in increasingly accurate ways as more English is acquired
(C) use a variety of complete sentences (e.g., simple, compound, complex) that include properly placed modifiers, correctly identified antecedents, parallel structures, and consistent tenses.	5 (F) write using a variety of grade-appropriate sentence lengths, patterns, and connecting words to combine phrases, clauses, and sentences in increasingly accurate ways as more English is acquired
(20) Writing/Conventions of Language/Handwriting. Students write legibly and use appropriate capitalization and punctuation conventions in their compositions. Students will continue to apply earlier standards with greater complexity. Students are expected to:	
(A) use conventions of capitalization; and	5 (C) spell familiar English words with increasing accuracy, and employ English spelling patterns and rules with increasing accuracy as more English is acquired
(B) use correct punctuation marks, including: (i) commas after introductory structures and dependent adverbial clauses, and correct punctuation of complex sentences; and (ii) semicolons, colons, hyphens, parentheses, brackets, and ellipses.	5 (C) spell familiar English words with increasing accuracy, and employ English spelling patterns and rules with increasing accuracy as more English is acquired
(21) Oral and Written Conventions/Spelling. Students spell correctly. Students are expected to spell correctly, including using various resources to determine and check correct spellings.	1 (B) monitor oral and written language production and employ self-corrective techniques or other resources 5 (C) spell familiar English words with increasing accuracy, and employ English spelling patterns and rules with increasing accuracy as more English is acquired
Oral and Written Conventions/Spelling – No Correlation	**5 (A) learn relationships between sounds and letters of the English language to represent sounds when writing in English**
(22) Research/Research Plan. Students ask open-ended research questions and develop a plan for answering them. Students are expected to:	

Eighth-Grade ELAR TEKS	ELPS
(22) cont . . . (A) brainstorm, consult with others, decide upon a topic, and formulate a major research question to address the major research topic; and	1 (E) internalize new, basic, and academic language by using and reusing it in meaningful ways in speaking and writing activities that build concept and language attainment 3 (F) ask and give information ranging from using a very limited bank of high-frequency, high-need, concrete vocabulary, including key words and expressions needed for basic communication in academic and social contexts, to using abstract and content-based vocabulary during extended speaking assignments 3 (G) express opinions, ideas, and feelings ranging from communicating single words and short phrases to participating in extended discussions on a variety of social and grade-appropriate academic topics
(B) apply steps for obtaining and evaluating information from a wide variety of sources and create a written plan after preliminary research in reference works and additional text searches.	4 (J) demonstrate English comprehension and expand reading skills by employing inferential skills such as predicting, making connections between ideas, drawing inferences and conclusions from text and graphic sources, and finding supporting text evidence commensurate with content-area needs 4 (K) demonstrate English comprehension and expand reading skills by employing analytical skills such as evaluating written information and performing critical analyses commensurate with content-area and grade-level needs 5 (G) narrate, describe, and explain with increasing specificity and detail to fulfill content-area writing needs as more English is acquired
(23) Research/Gathering Sources. Students determine, locate, and explore the full range of relevant sources addressing a research question and systematically record the information they gather. Students are expected to:	
(A) follow the research plan to gather information from a range of relevant print and electronic sources using advanced search strategies;	2 (F) listen to and derive meaning from a variety of media such as audio tape, video, DVD, and CD-ROM to build and reinforce concept and language attainment 4 (K) demonstrate English comprehension and expand reading skills by employing analytical skills such as evaluating written information and performing critical analyses commensurate with content-area and grade-level needs
(B) categorize information thematically in order to see the larger constructs inherent in the information;	4 (K) demonstrate English comprehension and expand reading skills by employing analytical skills such as evaluating written information and performing critical analyses commensurate with content-area and grade-level needs
(C) record bibliographic information (e.g., author, title, page number) for all notes and sources according to a standard format; and	*No ELPS Correlation*
(D) differentiate between paraphrasing and plagiarism and identify the importance of using valid and reliable sources.	*No ELPS Correlation*

Eighth-Grade ELAR TEKS	ELPS
(24) Research/Synthesizing Information. Students clarify research questions and evaluate and synthesize collected information. Students are expected to:	
(A) narrow or broaden the major research question, if necessary, based on further research and investigation; and	4 (K) demonstrate English comprehension and expand reading skills by employing analytical skills such as evaluating written information and performing critical analyses commensurate with content-area and grade-level needs
(B) utilize elements that demonstrate the reliability and validity of the sources used (e.g., publication date, coverage, language, point of view) and explain why one source is more useful and relevant than another.	4 (K) demonstrate English comprehension and expand reading skills by employing analytical skills such as evaluating written information and performing critical analyses commensurate with content-area and grade-level needs
(25) Research/Organizing and Presenting Ideas. Students organize and present their ideas and information according to the purpose of the research and their audience. Students are expected to synthesize the research into a written or an oral presentation that:	
(A) draws conclusions and summarizes or paraphrases the findings in a systematic way;	4 (G) demonstrate comprehension of increasingly complex English by participating in shared reading, retelling or summarizing material, responding to questions, and taking notes commensurate with content-area and grade-level needs 4 (J) demonstrate English comprehension and expand reading skills by employing inferential skills such as predicting, making connections between ideas, drawing inferences and conclusions from text and graphic sources, and finding supporting text evidence commensurate with content-area needs
(B) marshals evidence to explain the topic and gives relevant reasons for conclusions;	4 (J) demonstrate English comprehension and expand reading skills by employing inferential skills such as predicting, making connections between ideas, drawing inferences and conclusions from text and graphic sources, and finding supporting text evidence commensurate with content-area needs
(C) presents the findings in a meaningful format; and	5 (G) narrate, describe, and explain with increasing specificity and detail to fulfill content-area writing needs as more English is acquired
(D) follows accepted formats for integrating quotations and citations into the written text to maintain a flow of ideas.	5 (F) write using a variety of grade-appropriate sentence lengths, patterns, and connecting words to combine phrases, clauses, and sentences in increasingly accurate ways as more English is acquired

Eighth-Grade ELAR TEKS	ELPS
(26) *Listening and Speaking/Listening. Students will use comprehension skills to listen attentively to others in formal and informal settings. Students will continue to apply earlier standards with greater complexity. Students are expected to:*	
(A) listen to and interpret a speaker's purpose by explaining the content, evaluating the delivery of the presentation, and asking questions or making comments about the evidence that supports a speaker's claims;	2 (D) monitor understanding of spoken language during classroom instruction and interactions and seek clarification as needed 2 (I) demonstrate listening comprehension of increasingly complex spoken English by following directions, retelling or summarizing spoken messages, responding to questions and requests, collaborating with peers, and taking notes commensurate with content and grade-level needs 3 (F) ask and give information ranging from using a very limited bank of high-frequency, high-need, concrete vocabulary, including key words and expressions needed for basic communication in academic and social contexts, to using abstract and content-based vocabulary during extended speaking assignments
(B) follow and give complex oral instructions to perform specific tasks, answer questions, or solve problems; and	2 (E) use visual, contextual, and linguistic support to enhance and confirm understanding of increasingly complex and elaborated spoken language 2 (G) understand the general meaning, main points, and important details of spoken language ranging from situations in which topics, language, and contexts are familiar to unfamiliar 2 (H) understand implicit ideas and information in increasingly complex spoken language commensurate with grade-level learning expectations 2 (I) demonstrate listening comprehension of increasingly complex spoken English by following directions, retelling or summarizing spoken messages, responding to questions and requests, collaborating with peers, and taking notes commensurate with content and grade-level needs 3 (F) ask and give information ranging from using a very limited bank of high-frequency, high-need, concrete vocabulary, including key words and expressions needed for basic communication in academic and social contexts, to using abstract and content-based vocabulary during extended speaking assignments
(C) summarize formal and informal presentations, distinguish between facts and opinions, and determine the effectiveness of rhetorical devices.	1 (G) demonstrate an increasing ability to distinguish between formal and informal English and an increasing knowledge of when to use each one commensurate with grade-level learning expectation 2 (H) understand implicit ideas and information in increasingly complex spoken language commensurate with grade-level learning expectations 2 (I) demonstrate listening comprehension of increasingly complex spoken English by following directions, retelling or summarizing spoken messages, responding to questions and requests, collaborating with peers, and taking notes commensurate with content and grade-level needs

Eighth-Grade ELAR TEKS	ELPS
Listening and Speaking/Listening – No Correlation	**2 (A) distinguish sounds and intonation patterns of English with increasing ease** **2 (B) recognize elements of the English sound system in newly acquired vocabulary such as long and short vowels, silent letters, and consonant clusters**
(27) *Listening and Speaking/Speaking. Students speak clearly and to the point, using the conventions of language. Students will continue to apply earlier standards with greater complexity. Students are expected to advocate a position using anecdotes, analogies, and/or illustrations, and use eye contact, speaking rate, volume, enunciation, a variety of natural gestures, and conventions of language to communicate ideas effectively.*	1 (D) speak using learning strategies such as requesting assistance, employing nonverbal cues, and using synonyms and circumlocution 2 (C) learn new language structures, expressions, and basic and academic vocabulary heard during classroom instruction and interactions 3 (B) expand and internalize initial English vocabulary by learning and using high-frequency English words necessary for identifying and describing people, places, and objects, by retelling simple stories and basic information represented or supported by pictures, and by learning and using routine language needed for classroom communication 3 (C) speak using a variety of grammatical structures, sentence lengths, sentence types, and connecting words with increasing accuracy and ease as more English is acquired 3 (D) speak using grade-level content-area vocabulary in context to internalize new English words and build academic language proficiency 3 (G) express opinions, ideas, and feelings ranging from communicating single words and short phrases to participating in extended discussions on a variety of social and grade-appropriate academic topics 3 (H) narrate, describe, and explain with increasing specificity and detail as more English is acquired; 3 (I) adapt spoken language appropriately for formal and informal purposes 3 (J) respond orally to information presented in a wide variety of print, electronic, audio, and visual media to build and reinforce concept and language attainment
Listening and Speaking / Speaking – No Correlation	**3 (A) practice producing sounds of newly acquired vocabulary such as long and short vowels, silent letters, and consonant clusters to pronounce English words in a manner that is increasingly comprehensible**
(28) *Listening and Speaking/Teamwork. Students work productively with others in teams. Students will continue to apply earlier standards with greater complexity. Students are expected to participate productively in discussions, plan agendas with clear goals and deadlines, set time limits for speakers, take notes, and vote on key issues.*	1 (B) monitor oral and written language production and employ self-corrective techniques or other resources; 1 (G) demonstrate an increasing ability to distinguish between formal and informal English and an increasing knowledge of when to use each one commensurate with grade-level learning expectations 2 (I) demonstrate listening comprehension of increasingly complex spoken English by following directions, retelling or summarizing spoken messages, responding to questions and requests, collaborating with peers, and taking notes 3 (E) share information in cooperative learning interactions

ELAR TEKS and ELPS Side-by-Side
Ninth-Grade

Ninth-Grade ELAR TEKS	ELPS
(1) Reading/Vocabulary Development. Students understand new vocabulary and use it when reading and writing. Students are expected to:	
(A) determine the meaning of grade-level technical academic English words in multiple content-areas (e.g., science, mathematics, social studies, the arts) derived from Latin, Greek, or other linguistic roots and affixes;	4 (A) learn relationships between sounds and letters of the English language and decode (sound out) words using a combination of skills such as recognizing sound-letter relationships and identifying cognates, affixes, roots, and base words 4 (C) develop basic sight vocabulary, derive meaning of environmental print, and comprehend English vocabulary and language structures used routinely in written classroom materials
(B) analyze textual context (within a sentence and in larger sections of text) to distinguish between the denotative and connotative meanings of words;	4 (F) use visual and contextual support and support from peers and teachers to read grade-appropriate content-area text, enhance and confirm understanding, and develop vocabulary, grasp of language structures, and background knowledge needed to comprehend increasingly challenging language 4 (K) demonstrate English comprehension and expand reading skills by employing analytical skills such as evaluating written information and performing critical analyses commensurate with content-area and grade-level needs
(C) produce analogies that describe a function of an object or its description;	1 (C) use strategic learning techniques such as concept mapping, drawing, memorizing, comparing, contrasting, and reviewing to acquire basic and grade-level vocabulary
(D) describe the origins and meanings of foreign words or phrases used frequently in written English (e.g., caveat emptor, carte blanche, tete a tete, pas de deux, bon appetit, quid pro quo); and	1 (H) develop and expand repertoire of learning strategies such as reasoning inductively or deductively, looking for patterns in language, and analyzing sayings and expressions
(E) use a dictionary, a glossary, or a thesaurus (printed or electronic) to determine or confirm the meanings of words and phrases, including their connotations and denotations, and their etymology.	1 (B) monitor oral and written language production and employ self-corrective techniques or other resources
(2) Reading/Comprehension of Literary Text/Theme and Genre. Students analyze, make inferences, and draw conclusions about theme and genre in different cultural, historical, and contemporary contexts and provide evidence from the text to support their understanding. Students are expected to:	
(A) analyze how the genre of texts with similar themes shapes meaning;	4 (K) demonstrate English comprehension and expand reading skills by employing analytical skills such as evaluating written information and performing critical analyses commensurate with content-area and grade-level needs

Ninth-Grade ELAR TEKS	ELPS
(2) cont . . . (B) analyze the influence of mythic, classical and traditional literature on 20th and 21st century literature; and	4 (K) demonstrate English comprehension and expand reading skills by employing analytical skills such as evaluating written information and performing critical analyses commensurate with content-area and grade-level needs
(C) relate the figurative language of a literary work to its historical and cultural setting.	4 (J) demonstrate English comprehension and expand reading skills by employing inferential skills such as predicting, making connections between ideas, drawing inferences and conclusions from text and graphic sources, and finding supporting text evidence commensurate with content-area needs
(3) *Reading/Comprehension of Literary Text/Poetry. Students understand, make inferences, and draw conclusions about the structure and elements of poetry and provide evidence from text to support their understanding. Students are expected to analyze the effects of diction and imagery (e.g., controlling images, figurative language, understatement, overstatement, irony, paradox) in poetry.*	4 (E) read linguistically accommodated content-area material with a decreasing need for linguistic accommodations as more English is learned 4 (J) demonstrate English comprehension and expand reading skills by employing inferential skills such as predicting, making connections between ideas, drawing inferences and conclusions from text and graphic sources, and finding supporting text evidence commensurate with content-area needs 4 (K) demonstrate English comprehension and expand reading skills by employing analytical skills such as evaluating written information and performing critical analyses commensurate with content-area and grade-level needs
(4) *Reading/Comprehension of Literary Text/Drama. Students understand, make inferences, and draw conclusions about the structure and elements of drama and provide evidence from text to support their understanding. Students are expected to explain how dramatic conventions (e.g., monologues, soliloquies, dramatic irony) enhance dramatic text.*	4 (E) read linguistically accommodated content-area material with a decreasing need for linguistic accommodations as more English is learned 4 (J) demonstrate English comprehension and expand reading skills by employing inferential skills such as predicting, making connections between ideas, drawing inferences and conclusions from text and graphic sources, and finding supporting text evidence commensurate with content-area needs
(5) *Reading/Comprehension of Literary Text/Fiction. Students understand, make inferences, and draw conclusions about the structure and elements of fiction and provide evidence from text to support their understanding. Students are expected to:*	
(A) analyze nonlinear plot development (e.g., flashbacks, foreshadowing, subplots, parallel plot structures) and compare it to linear plot development;	4 (J) demonstrate English comprehension and expand reading skills by employing inferential skills such as predicting, making connections between ideas, drawing inferences and conclusions from text and graphic sources, and finding supporting text evidence commensurate with content-area needs

Ninth-Grade ELAR TEKS	ELPS
(5) (A) cont . . .	4 (K) demonstrate English comprehension and expand reading skills by employing analytical skills such as evaluating written information and performing critical analyses commensurate with content-area and grade-level needs
(B) analyze how authors develop complex yet believable characters in works of fiction through a range of literary devices, including character foils;	4 (K) demonstrate English comprehension and expand reading skills by employing analytical skills such as evaluating written information and performing critical analyses commensurate with content-area and grade-level needs
(C) analyze the way in which a work of fiction is shaped by the narrator's point of view; and	4 (K) demonstrate English comprehension and expand reading skills by employing analytical skills such as evaluating written information and performing critical analyses commensurate with content-area and grade-level needs
(D) demonstrate familiarity with works by authors from non-English-speaking literary traditions with emphasis on classical literature.	*No ELPS Correlation*
(6) *Reading/Comprehension of Literary Text/Literary Nonfiction. Students understand, make inferences, and draw conclusions about the varied structural patterns and features of literary nonfiction and provide evidence from text to support their understanding. Students are expected to analyze how literary essays interweave personal examples and ideas with factual information to explain, present a perspective, or describe a situation or event.*	4 (E) read linguistically accommodated content-area material with a decreasing need for linguistic accommodations as more English is learned 4 (J) demonstrate English comprehension and expand reading skills by employing inferential skills such as predicting, making connections between ideas, drawing inferences and conclusions from text and graphic sources, and finding supporting text evidence commensurate with content-area needs 4 (K) demonstrate English comprehension and expand reading skills by employing analytical skills such as evaluating written information and performing critical analyses commensurate with content-area and grade-level needs
(7) *Reading/Comprehension of Literary Text/Sensory Language. Students understand, make inferences, and draw conclusions about how an author's sensory language creates imagery in literary text and provide evidence from text to support their understanding. Students are expected to explain the role of irony, sarcasm, and paradox in literary works.*	1 (H) develop and expand repertoire of learning strategies such as reasoning inductively or deductively, looking for patterns in language, and analyzing sayings and expressions commensurate with grade-level learning expectations 4 (J) demonstrate English comprehension and expand reading skills by employing inferential skills such as predicting, making connections between ideas, drawing inferences and conclusions from text and graphic sources, and finding supporting text evidence commensurate with content-area needs

Ninth-Grade ELAR TEKS	ELPS
(8) *Reading/Comprehension of Informational Text/Culture and History. Students analyze, make inferences, and draw conclusions about the author's purpose in cultural, historical, and contemporary contexts and provide evidence from the text to support their understanding. Students are expected to explain the controlling idea and specific purpose of an expository text and distinguish the most important from the less important details that support the author's purpose.*	4 (J) demonstrate English comprehension and expand reading skills by employing inferential skills such as predicting, making connections between ideas, drawing inferences and conclusions from text and graphic sources, and finding supporting text evidence commensurate with content-area needs 4 (K) demonstrate English comprehension and expand reading skills by employing analytical skills such as evaluating written information and performing critical analyses commensurate with content-area and grade-level needs
(9) *Reading/Comprehension of Informational Text/Expository Text. Students analyze, make inferences, and draw conclusions about expository text and provide evidence from text to support their understanding. Students are expected to:*	
(A) summarize text and distinguish between a summary that captures the main ideas and elements of a text and a critique that takes a position and expresses an opinion;	4 (I) demonstrate English comprehension and expand reading skills by employing basic reading skills such as demonstrating understanding of supporting ideas and details in text and graphic sources, summarizing text, and distinguishing main ideas from details commensurate with content-area needs
(B) differentiate between opinions that are substantiated and unsubstantiated in the text;	4 (K) demonstrate English comprehension and expand reading skills by employing analytical skills such as evaluating written information and performing critical analyses commensurate with content-area and grade-level needs
(C) make subtle inferences and draw complex conclusions about the ideas in text and their organizational patterns; and	1 (H) develop and expand repertoire of learning strategies such as reasoning inductively or deductively, looking for patterns in language, and analyzing sayings and expressions 4 (J) demonstrate English comprehension and expand reading skills by employing inferential skills such as predicting, making connections between ideas, drawing inferences and conclusions from text and graphic sources, and finding supporting text evidence commensurate with content-area needs
(D) synthesize and make logical connections between ideas and details in several texts selected to reflect a range of viewpoints on the same topic and support those findings with textual evidence.	1 (H) develop and expand repertoire of learning strategies such as reasoning inductively or deductively, looking for patterns in language, and analyzing sayings and expressions 4 (J) demonstrate English comprehension and expand reading skills by employing inferential skills such as predicting, making connections between ideas, drawing inferences and conclusions from text and graphic sources, and finding supporting text evidence commensurate with content-area needs

Ninth-Grade ELAR TEKS	ELPS
(10) Reading/Comprehension of Informational Text/Persuasive Text. Students analyze, make inferences, and draw conclusions about persuasive text and provide evidence from text to support their analysis. Students are expected to:	
(A) analyze the relevance, quality, and credibility of evidence given to support or oppose an argument for a specific audience; and	1 (H) develop and expand repertoire of learning strategies such as reasoning inductively or deductively, looking for patterns in language, and analyzing sayings and expressions 4 (K) demonstrate English comprehension and expand reading skills by employing analytical skills such as evaluating written information and performing critical analyses commensurate with content-area and grade-level needs
(B) analyze famous speeches for the rhetorical structures and devices used to convince the reader of the authors' propositions.	4 (K) demonstrate English comprehension and expand reading skills by employing analytical skills such as evaluating written information and performing critical analyses commensurate with content-area and grade-level needs
(11) Reading/Comprehension of Informational Text/Procedural Texts. Students understand how to glean and use information in procedural texts and documents. Students are expected to:	
(A) analyze the clarity of the objective(s) of procedural text (e.g., consider reading instructions for software, warranties, consumer publications); and	4 (K) demonstrate English comprehension and expand reading skills by employing analytical skills such as evaluating written information and performing critical analyses commensurate with content-area and grade-level needs
(B) analyze factual, quantitative, or technical data presented in multiple graphical sources.	4 (I) demonstrate English comprehension and expand reading skills by employing basic reading skills such as demonstrating understanding of supporting ideas and details in text and graphic sources, summarizing text, and distinguishing main ideas from details commensurate with content-area needs 4 (K) demonstrate English comprehension and expand reading skills by employing analytical skills such as evaluating written information and performing critical analyses commensurate with content-area and grade-level needs
(12) Reading/Media Literacy. Students use comprehension skills to analyze how words, images, graphics, and sounds work together in various forms to impact meaning. Students will continue to apply earlier standards with greater depth in increasingly more complex texts. Students are expected to:	

Ninth-Grade ELAR TEKS	ELPS
(12) cont . . . (A) compare and contrast how events are presented and information is communicated by visual images (e.g., graphic art, illustrations, news photographs) versus nonvisual texts;	1 (C) use strategic learning techniques such as concept mapping, drawing, memorizing, comparing, contrasting, and reviewing to acquire basic and grade-level vocabulary 4 (K) demonstrate English comprehension and expand reading skills by employing analytical skills such as evaluating written information and performing critical analyses commensurate with content-area and grade-level needs
(B) analyze how messages in media are conveyed through visual and sound techniques (e.g., editing, reaction shots, sequencing, background music);	2 (F) listen to and derive meaning from a variety of media such as audio tape, video, DVD, and CD-ROM to build and reinforce concept and language attainment 4 (K) demonstrate English comprehension and expand reading skills by employing analytical skills such as evaluating written information and performing critical analyses commensurate with content-area and grade-level needs
(C) compare and contrast coverage of the same event in various media (e.g., newspapers, television, documentaries, blogs, Internet); and	1 (C) use strategic learning techniques such as concept mapping, drawing, memorizing, comparing, contrasting, and reviewing to acquire basic and grade-level vocabulary 2 (F) listen to and derive meaning from a variety of media such as audio tape, video, DVD, and CD-ROM to build and reinforce concept and language attainment 4 (K) demonstrate English comprehension and expand reading skills by employing analytical skills such as evaluating written information and performing critical analyses commensurate with content-area and grade-level needs
(D) evaluate changes in formality and tone within the same medium for specific audiences and purposes.	4 (K) demonstrate English comprehension and expand reading skills by employing analytical skills such as evaluating written information and performing critical analyses commensurate with content-area and grade-level needs
Reading Media and Literacy – No Correlation	**4(B) recognize directionality of English reading such as left to right and top to bottom** **4 (H) read silently with increasing ease and comprehension for longer periods**
(13) Writing/Writing Process. Students use elements of the writing process (planning, drafting, revising, editing, and publishing) to compose text. Students are expected to:	
(A) plan a first draft by selecting the correct genre for conveying the intended meaning to multiple audiences, determining appropriate topics through a range of strategies (e.g., discussion, background reading, personal interests, interviews), and developing a thesis or controlling idea;	1 (A) use prior knowledge and experiences to understand meanings in English 3 (G) express opinions, ideas, and feelings ranging from communicating single words and short phrases to participating in extended discussions on a variety of social and grade-appropriate academic topics 5 (B) write using newly acquired basic vocabulary and content-based grade-level vocabulary

Ninth-Grade ELAR TEKS	ELPS
(13) cont . . . (B) structure ideas in a sustained and persuasive way (e.g., using outlines, note taking, graphic organizers, lists) and develop drafts in timed and open-ended situations that include transitions and the rhetorical devices used to convey meaning;	4 (D) use prereading supports such as graphic organizers, illustrations, and pretaught topic-related vocabulary and other prereading activities to enhance comprehension of written text 4 (G) demonstrate comprehension of increasingly complex English by participating in shared reading, retelling or summarizing material, responding to questions, and taking notes commensurate with content-area and grade level needs 5 (F) write using a variety of grade-appropriate sentence lengths, patterns, and connecting words to combine phrases, clauses, and sentences in increasingly accurate ways as more English is acquired
(C) revise drafts to improve style, word choice, figurative language, sentence variety, and subtlety of meaning after rethinking how well questions of purpose, audience, and genre have been addressed;	5 (F) write using a variety of grade-appropriate sentence lengths, patterns, and connecting words to combine phrases, clauses, and sentences in increasingly accurate ways as more English is acquired
(D) edit drafts for grammar, mechanics, and spelling; and	5 (D) edit writing for standard grammar and usage, including subject-verb agreement, pronoun agreement, and appropriate verb tenses commensurate with grade-level expectations as more English is acquired
(E) revise final draft in response to feedback from peers and teacher and publish written work for appropriate audiences.	4 (F) use visual and contextual support and support from peers and teachers to read grade-appropriate content-area text, to enhance and confirm understanding, to develop vocabulary, to grasp language structures, and to tap background knowledge needed to comprehend increasingly challenging language 5 (D) edit writing for standard grammar and usage, including subject-verb agreement, pronoun agreement, and appropriate verb tenses commensurate with grade-level expectations as more English is acquired
(14) Writing/Literary Texts. Students write literary texts to express their ideas and feelings about real or imagined people, events, and ideas. Students are responsible for at least two forms of literary writing. Students are expected to:	
(A) write an engaging story with a well-developed conflict and resolution, interesting and believable characters, and a range of literary strategies (e.g., dialogue, suspense) and devices to enhance the plot;	5 (F) write using a variety of grade-appropriate sentence lengths, patterns, and connecting words to combine phrases, clauses, and sentences in increasingly accurate ways as more English is acquired 5 (G) narrate, describe, and explain with increasing specificity and detail to fulfill content-area writing needs as more English is acquired
(B) write a poem using a variety of poetic techniques (e.g., structural elements, figurative language) and a variety of poetic forms (e.g., sonnets, ballads); and	1 (E) internalize new, basic, and academic language by using and reusing it in meaningful ways in speaking and writing activities that build concept and language attainment 5 (B) write using newly acquired basic vocabulary and content-based grade-level vocabulary
(C) write a script with an explicit or implicit theme and details that contribute to a definite mood or tone.	5 (F) write using a variety of grade-appropriate sentence lengths, patterns, and connecting words to combine phrases, clauses, and sentences in increasingly accurate ways as more English is acquired

Ninth-Grade ELAR TEKS	ELPS
(14) (C) cont . . .	5 (G) narrate, describe, and explain with increasing specificity and detail to fulfill content-area writing needs as more English is acquired
(15) Writing/Expository and Procedural Texts. Students write expository and procedural or work-related texts to communicate ideas and information to specific audiences for specific purposes. Students are expected to:	
(A) write an analytical essay of sufficient length that includes: (i) effective introductory and concluding paragraphs and a variety of sentence structures; (ii) rhetorical devices, and transitions between paragraphs; (iii) a controlling idea or thesis; (iv) an organizing structure appropriate to purpose, audience, and context; and (v) relevant information and valid inferences;	5 (F) write using a variety of grade-appropriate sentence lengths, patterns, and connecting words to combine phrases, clauses, and sentences in increasingly accurate ways as more English is acquired 5 (G) narrate, describe, and explain with increasing specificity and detail to fulfill content-area writing needs as more English is acquired
(B) write procedural or work-related documents (e.g., instructions, e-mails, correspondence, memos, project plans) that include: (i) organized and accurately conveyed information; and (ii) reader-friendly formatting techniques;	5 (F) write using a variety of grade-appropriate sentence lengths, patterns, and connecting words to combine phrases, clauses, and sentences in increasingly accurate ways as more English is acquired
(C) write an interpretative response to an expository or a literary text (e.g., essay or review) that: (i) extends beyond a summary and literal analysis; (ii) addresses the writing skills for an analytical essay and provides evidence from the text using embedded quotations; and (iii) analyzes the aesthetic effects of an author's use of stylistic or rhetorical devices; and	5 (F) write using a variety of grade-appropriate sentence lengths, patterns, and connecting words to combine phrases, clauses, and sentences in increasingly accurate ways as more English is acquired 5 (G) narrate, describe, and explain with increasing specificity and detail to fulfill content-area writing needs as more English is acquired
(D) produce a multimedia presentation (e.g., documentary, class newspaper, docudrama, infomercial, visual or textual parodies, theatrical production) with graphics, images, and sound that conveys a distinctive point of view and appeals to a specific audience.	5 (F) write using a variety of grade-appropriate sentence lengths, patterns, and connecting words to combine phrases, clauses, and sentences in increasingly accurate ways as more English is acquired; and 5 (G) narrate, describe, and explain with increasing specificity and detail to fulfill content-area writing needs as more English is acquired
(16) Writing/Persuasive Texts. Students write persuasive texts to influence the attitudes or actions of a specific audience on specific issues. Students are expected to write an argumentative essay to the appropriate audience that includes:	

Ninth-Grade ELAR TEKS	ELPS
(16) cont . . . (A) a clear thesis or position based on logical reasons supported by precise and relevant evidence;	5 (F) write using a variety of grade-appropriate sentence lengths, patterns, and connecting words to combine phrases, clauses, and sentences in increasingly accurate ways as more English is acquired 5 (G) narrate, describe, and explain with increasing specificity and detail to fulfill content-area writing needs as more English is acquired
(B) consideration of the whole range of information and views on the topic and accurate and honest representation of these views;	5 (F) write using a variety of grade-appropriate sentence lengths, patterns, and connecting words to combine phrases, clauses, and sentences in increasingly accurate ways as more English is acquired 5 (G) narrate, describe, and explain with increasing specificity and detail to fulfill content-area writing needs as more English is acquired
(C) counterarguments based on evidence to anticipate and address objections;	5 (F) write using a variety of grade-appropriate sentence lengths, patterns, and connecting words to combine phrases, clauses, and sentences in increasingly accurate ways as more English is acquired 5 (G) narrate, describe, and explain with increasing specificity and detail to fulfill content-area writing needs as more English is acquired
(D) an organizing structure appropriate to the purpose, audience, and context; and	5 (F) write using a variety of grade-appropriate sentence lengths, patterns, and connecting words to combine phrases, clauses, and sentences in increasingly accurate ways as more English is acquired 5 (G) narrate, describe, and explain with increasing specificity and detail to fulfill content-area writing needs as more English is acquired
(E) an analysis of the relative value of specific data, facts, and ideas.	1 (H) develop and expand repertoire of learning strategies such as reasoning inductively or deductively, looking for patterns in language, and analyzing sayings and expressions 5 (G) narrate, describe, and explain with increasing specificity and detail to fulfill content-area writing needs as more English is acquired
(17) Oral and Written Conventions/Conventions. Students understand the function of and use the conventions of academic language when speaking and writing. Students will continue to apply earlier standards with greater complexity. Students are expected to:	
(A) use and understand the function of the following parts of speech in the context of reading, writing, and speaking: (i) more complex active and passive tenses and verbals (gerunds, infinitives, participles); (ii) restrictive and nonrestrictive relative clauses; and (iii) reciprocal pronouns (e.g., each other, one another);	5 (E) employ increasingly complex grammatical structures in content-area writing commensurate with grade-level expectations, such as: (i) using correct verbs, tenses, and pronouns / antecedents (ii) using possessive case (apostrophe s) correctly (iii) using negatives and contractions correctly

Ninth-Grade ELAR TEKS	ELPS
(17) cont . . . (B) identify and use the subjunctive mood to express doubts, wishes, and possibilities; and	1 (H) develop and expand repertoire of learning strategies such as reasoning inductively or deductively, looking for patterns in language, and analyzing sayings and expressions
(C) use a variety of correctly structured sentences (e.g., compound, complex, compound-complex).	5 (F) write using a variety of grade-appropriate sentence lengths, patterns, and connecting words to combine phrases, clauses, and sentences in increasingly accurate ways as more English is acquired; and
(18) Oral and Written Conventions/Handwriting, Capitalization, and Punctuation. Students write legibly and use appropriate capitalization and punctuation conventions in their compositions. Students are expected to:	
(A) use conventions of capitalization; and	5 (C) spell familiar English words with increasing accuracy, and employ English spelling patterns and rules with increasing accuracy as more English is acquired
(B) use correct punctuation marks including: (i) quotation marks to indicate sarcasm or irony; (ii) comma placement in nonrestrictive phrases, clauses, and contrasting expressions; and (iii) dashes to emphasize parenthetical information.	5 (E) employ increasingly complex grammatical structures in content-area writing commensurate with grade-level expectations, such as: (i) using correct verbs, tenses, and pronouns / antecedents; (ii) using possessive case (apostrophes) correctly (iii) using negatives and contractions correctly
(19) Oral and Written Conventions/Spelling. Students spell correctly. Students are expected to spell correctly, including using various resources to determine and check correct spellings.	1 (B) monitor oral and written language production and employ self-corrective techniques or other resources 5 (C) spell familiar English words with increasing accuracy, and employ English spelling patterns and rules with increasing accuracy as more English is acquired
Oral and Written Conventions/Spelling – No Correlation	**5 (A) learn relationships between sounds and letters of the English language to represent sounds when writing in English**
(20) Research/Research Plan. Students ask open-ended research questions and develop a plan for answering them. Students are expected to:	
(A) brainstorm, consult with others, decide upon a topic, and formulate a major research question to address the major research topic; and	1 (E) internalize new, basic, and academic language by using and reusing it in meaningful ways in speaking and writing activities that build concept and language attainment 3 (F) ask and give information ranging from using a very limited bank of high-frequency, high-need, concrete vocabulary, including key words and expressions needed for basic communication in academic and social contexts, to using abstract and content-based vocabulary during extended speaking assignments

Ninth-Grade ELAR TEKS	ELPS
(20)(A) cont . . .	3 (G) express opinions, ideas, and feelings ranging from communicating single words and short phrases to participating in extended discussions on a variety of social and grade-appropriate academic topics
(B) formulate a plan for engaging in research on a complex, multifaceted topic.	1 (F) use accessible language and learn new and essential language in the process
(21) Research/Gathering Sources. Students determine, locate, and explore the full range of relevant sources addressing a research question and systematically record the information they gather. Students are expected to:	
(A) follow the research plan to compile data from authoritative sources in a manner that identifies the major issues and debates within the field of inquiry;	2 (F) listen to and derive meaning from a variety of media such as audio tape, video, DVD, and CD-ROM to build and reinforce concept and language attainment 4 (G) demonstrate comprehension of increasingly complex English by participating in shared reading, retelling or summarizing material, responding to questions, and taking notes commensurate with content-area and grade-level needs 4 (K) demonstrate English comprehension and expand reading skills by employing analytical skills such as evaluating written information and performing critical analyses commensurate with content-area and grade-level needs
(B) organize information gathered from multiple sources to create a variety of graphics and forms (e.g., notes, learning logs); and	4 (G) demonstrate comprehension of increasingly complex English by participating in shared reading, retelling or summarizing material, responding to questions, and taking notes commensurate with content-area and grade level needs 5 (B) write using newly acquired basic vocabulary and content-based grade-level vocabulary
(C) paraphrase, summarize, quote, and accurately cite all researched information according to a standard format (e.g., author, title, page number).	5 (G) narrate, describe, and explain with increasing specificity and detail to fulfill content-area writing needs as more English is acquired
(22) Research/Synthesizing Information. Students clarify research questions and evaluate and synthesize collected information. Students are expected to:	
(A) modify the major research question as necessary to refocus the research plan;	5 (G) narrate, describe, and explain with increasing specificity and detail to fulfill content-area writing needs as more English is acquired
(B) evaluate the relevance of information to the topic and determine the reliability, validity, and accuracy of sources (including Internet sources) by examining their authority and objectivity; and	4 (K) demonstrate English comprehension and expand reading skills by employing analytical skills such as evaluating written information and performing critical analyses commensurate with content-area and grade-level needs

Ninth-Grade ELAR TEKS	ELPS
(22) cont . . . (C) critique the research process at each step to implement changes as the need occurs and is identified.	4 (K) demonstrate English comprehension and expand reading skills by employing analytical skills such as evaluating written information and performing critical analyses commensurate with content-area and grade-level needs
(23) Research/Organizing and Presenting Ideas. Students organize and present their ideas and information according to the purpose of the research and their audience. Students are expected to synthesize the research into a written or an oral presentation that:	
(A) marshals evidence in support of a clear thesis statement and related claims;	4 (J) demonstrate English comprehension and expand reading skills by employing inferential skills such as predicting, making connections between ideas, drawing inferences and conclusions from text and graphic sources, and finding supporting text evidence commensurate with content-area needs
(B) provides an analysis for the audience that reflects a logical progression of ideas and a clearly stated point of view;	1 (H) develop and expand repertoire of learning strategies such as reasoning inductively or deductively, looking for patterns in language, and analyzing sayings and expressions 5 (G) narrate, describe, and explain with increasing specificity and detail to fulfill content-area writing needs as more English is acquired
(C) uses graphics and illustrations to help explain concepts where appropriate;	1 (C) use strategic learning techniques such as concept mapping, drawing, memorizing, comparing, contrasting, and reviewing to acquire basic and grade-level vocabulary
(D) uses a variety of evaluative tools (e.g., self-made rubrics, peer reviews, teacher and expert evaluations) to examine the quality of the research; and	4 (F) use visual and contextual support and support from peers and teachers to read grade-appropriate content-area text, to enhance and confirm understanding, to develop vocabulary, to grasp language structures, and to tap background knowledge needed to comprehend increasingly challenging language
(E) uses a style manual (e.g., Modern Language Association, Chicago Manual of Style) to document sources and format written materials.	1 (B) monitor oral and written language production and employ self-corrective techniques or other resources
(24) Listening and Speaking/Listening. Students will use comprehension skills to listen attentively to others in formal and informal settings. Students will continue to apply earlier standards with greater complexity. Students are expected to:	

Ninth-Grade ELAR TEKS	ELPS
(24) cont . . . (A) listen responsively to a speaker by taking notes that summarize, synthesize, or highlight the speaker's ideas for critical reflection and by asking questions related to the content for clarification and elaboration;	2 (D) monitor understanding of spoken language during classroom instruction and interactions and seek clarification as needed 2 (I) demonstrate listening comprehension of increasingly complex spoken English by following directions, retelling or summarizing spoken messages, responding to questions and requests, collaborating with peers, and taking notes commensurate with content and grade-level needs 3 (F) ask and give information ranging from using a very limited bank of high-frequency, high-need, concrete vocabulary, including key words and expressions needed for basic communication in academic and social contexts, to using abstract and content-based vocabulary during extended speaking assignments
(B) follow and give complex oral instructions to perform specific tasks, answer questions, solve problems, and complete processes; and	2 (E) use visual, contextual, and linguistic support to enhance and confirm understanding of increasingly complex and elaborated spoken language 2 (G) understand the general meaning, main points, and important details of spoken language ranging from situations in which topics, language, and contexts are familiar to unfamiliar 2 (H) understand implicit ideas and information in increasingly complex spoken language commensurate with grade-level learning expectations 2 (I) demonstrate listening comprehension of increasingly complex spoken English by following directions, retelling or summarizing spoken messages, responding to questions and requests, collaborating with peers, and taking notes commensurate with content and grade-level needs 3 (F) ask and give information ranging from using a very limited bank of high-frequency, high-need, concrete vocabulary, including key words and expressions needed for basic communication in academic and social contexts, to using abstract and content-based vocabulary during extended speaking assignments
(C) evaluate the effectiveness of a speaker's main and supporting ideas.	2 (G) understand the general meaning, main points, and important details of spoken language ranging from situations in which topics, language, and contexts are familiar to unfamiliar 2 (H) understand implicit ideas and information in increasingly complex spoken language commensurate with grade-level learning expectations
Listening and Speaking/Listening – No Correlation	**2 (A) distinguish sounds and intonation patterns of English with increasing ease** **2 (B) recognize elements of the English sound system in newly acquired vocabulary such as long and short vowels, silent letters, and consonant clusters**

Ninth-Grade ELAR TEKS	ELPS
(25) Listening and Speaking/Speaking. Students speak clearly and to the point, using the conventions of language. Students will continue to apply earlier standards with greater complexity. Students are expected to give presentations using informal, formal, and technical language effectively to meet the needs of audience, purpose, and occasion, employing eye contact, speaking rate (e.g., pauses for effect), volume, enunciation, purposeful gestures, and conventions of language to communicate ideas effectively.	1 (D) speak using learning strategies such as requesting assistance, employing nonverbal cues, and using synonyms and circumlocution 2 (C) learn new language structures, expressions, and basic and academic vocabulary heard during classroom instruction and interactions 3 (B) expand and internalize initial English vocabulary by learning and using high-frequency English words necessary for identifying and describing people, places, and objects, by retelling simple stories and basic information represented or supported by pictures, and by learning and using routine language needed for classroom communication 3 (C) speak using a variety of grammatical structures, sentence lengths, sentence types, and connecting words with increasing accuracy and ease as more English is acquired 3 (D) speak using grade-level content-area vocabulary in context to internalize new English words and build academic language proficiency 3 (G) express opinions, ideas, and feelings ranging from communicating single words and short phrases to participating in extended discussions on a variety of social and grade-appropriate academic topics 3 (H) narrate, describe, and explain with increasing specificity and detail as more English is acquired 3 (I) adapt spoken language appropriately for formal and informal purposes 3 (J) respond orally to information presented in a wide variety of print, electronic, audio, and visual media to build and reinforce concept and language attainment
Listening and Speaking/Speaking – No Correlation	3 (A) **practice producing sounds of newly acquired vocabulary such as long and short vowels, silent letters, and consonant clusters to pronounce English words in a manner that is increasingly comprehensible**
(26) Listening and Speaking/Teamwork. Students work productively with others in teams. Students will continue to apply earlier standards with greater complexity. Students are expected to participate productively in teams, building on the ideas of others, contributing relevant information, developing a plan for consensus-building, and setting ground rules for decision making.	1 (B) monitor oral and written language production and employ self-corrective techniques or other resources 1 (G) demonstrate an increasing ability to distinguish between formal and informal English and an increasing knowledge of when to use each one commensurate with grade-level learning expectations 2 (I) demonstrate listening comprehension of increasingly complex spoken English by following directions, retelling or summarizing spoken messages, responding to questions and requests, collaborating with peers, and taking notes 3 (E) share information in cooperative learning interactions

ELAR TEKS and ELPS Side-by-Side

Tenth-Grade

Tenth-Grade ELAR TEKS	ELPS
(1) *Reading/Vocabulary Development. Students understand new vocabulary and use it when reading and writing. Students are expected to:*	
(A) determine the meaning of grade-level technical academic English words in multiple content-areas (e.g., science, mathematics, social studies, the arts) derived from Latin, Greek, or other linguistic roots and affixes;	4 (A) learn relationships between sounds and letters of the English language and decode (sound out) words using a combination of skills such as recognizing sound-letter relationships and identifying cognates, affixes, roots, and base words 4 (C) develop basic sight vocabulary, derive meaning of environmental print, and comprehend English vocabulary and language structures used routinely in written classroom materials
(B) analyze textual context (within a sentence and in larger sections of text) to distinguish between the denotative and connotative meanings of words;	4 (F) use visual and contextual support and support from peers and teachers to read grade-appropriate content-area text, to enhance and confirm understanding, to develop vocabulary, to grasp language structures, and to tap background knowledge needed to comprehend increasingly challenging language 4 (K) demonstrate English comprehension and expand reading skills by employing analytical skills such as evaluating written information and performing critical analyses commensurate with content-area and grade-level needs
(C) infer word meaning through the identification and analysis of analogies and other word relationships;	1 (H) develop and expand repertoire of learning strategies such as reasoning inductively or deductively, looking for patterns in language, and analyzing sayings and expressions
(D) show the relationship between the origins and meaning of foreign words or phrases used frequently in written English and historical events or developments (e.g., glasnost, avant-garde, coup d'état); and	1 (H) develop and expand repertoire of learning strategies such as reasoning inductively or deductively, looking for patterns in language, and analyzing sayings and expressions
(E) use a dictionary, a glossary, or a thesaurus (printed or electronic) to determine or confirm the meanings of words and phrases, including their connotations and denotations, and their etymology.	1 (B) monitor oral and written language production and employ self-corrective techniques or other resources
(2) *Reading/Comprehension of Literary Text/Theme and Genre. Students analyze, make inferences and draw conclusions about theme and genre in different cultural, historical, and contemporary contexts and provide evidence from the text to support their understanding. Students are expected to:*	
(A) compare and contrast differences in similar themes expressed in different time periods;	1 (C) use strategic learning techniques such as concept mapping, drawing, memorizing, comparing, contrasting, and reviewing to acquire basic and grade-level vocabulary

Tenth-Grade ELAR TEKS	ELPS
(2) (A) cont . . .	4 (K) demonstrate English comprehension and expand reading skills by employing analytical skills such as evaluating written information and performing critical analyses commensurate with content-area and grade-level needs
(B) analyze archetypes (e.g., journey of a hero, tragic flaw) in mythic, traditional and classical literature; and	4 (K) demonstrate English comprehension and expand reading skills by employing analytical skills such as evaluating written information and performing critical analyses commensurate with content-area and grade-level needs
(C) relate the figurative language of a literary work to its historical and cultural setting.	1 (H) develop and expand repertoire of learning strategies such as reasoning inductively or deductively, looking for patterns in language, and analyzing sayings and expressions 4 (J) demonstrate English comprehension and expand reading skills by employing inferential skills such as predicting, making connections between ideas, drawing inferences and conclusions from text and graphic sources, and finding supporting text evidence commensurate with content-area needs
(3) *Reading/Comprehension of Literary Text/Poetry. Students understand, make inferences, and draw conclusions about the structure and elements of poetry and provide evidence from text to support their understanding. Students are expected to analyze the structure or prosody (e.g., meter, rhyme scheme) and graphic elements (e.g., line length, punctuation, word position) in poetry.*	1 (H) develop and expand repertoire of learning strategies such as reasoning inductively or deductively, looking for patterns in language, and analyzing sayings and expressions 4 (J) demonstrate English comprehension and expand reading skills by employing inferential skills such as predicting, making connections between ideas, drawing inferences and conclusions from text and graphic sources, and finding supporting text evidence commensurate with content-area needs 4 (K) demonstrate English comprehension and expand reading skills by employing analytical skills such as evaluating written information and performing critical analyses commensurate with content-area and grade-level needs
(4) *Reading/Comprehension of Literary Text/Drama. Students understand, make inferences, and draw conclusions about the structure and elements of drama and provide evidence from text to support their understanding. Students are expected to analyze how archetypes and motifs in drama affect the plot of plays.*	4 (J) demonstrate English comprehension and expand reading skills by employing inferential skills such as predicting, making connections between ideas, drawing inferences and conclusions from text and graphic sources, and finding supporting text evidence commensurate with content-area needs 4 (K) demonstrate English comprehension and expand reading skills by employing analytical skills such as evaluating written information and performing critical analyses commensurate with content-area and grade-level needs

Tenth-Grade ELAR TEKS	ELPS
(5) ***Reading/Comprehension of Literary Text/Fiction. Students understand, make inferences, and draw conclusions about the structure and elements of fiction and provide evidence from text to support their understanding. Students are expected to:***	
(A) analyze isolated scenes and their contribution to the success of the plot as a whole in a variety of works of fiction;	4 (K) demonstrate English comprehension and expand reading skills by employing analytical skills such as evaluating written information and performing critical analyses commensurate with content-area and grade-level needs
(B) analyze differences in the characters' moral dilemmas in works of fiction across different countries or cultures;	4 (K) demonstrate English comprehension and expand reading skills by employing analytical skills such as evaluating written information and performing critical analyses commensurate with content-area and grade-level needs
(C) evaluate the connection between forms of narration (e.g., unreliable, omniscient) and tone in works of fiction; and	4 (J) demonstrate English comprehension and expand reading skills by employing inferential skills such as predicting, making connections between ideas, drawing inferences and conclusions from text and graphic sources, and finding supporting text evidence commensurate with content-area needs
(D) demonstrate familiarity with works by authors from non-English-speaking literary traditions with emphasis on 20th century world literature.	1 (H) develop and expand repertoire of learning strategies such as reasoning inductively or deductively, looking for patterns in language, and analyzing sayings and expressions
(6) ***Reading/Comprehension of Literary Text/Literary Nonfiction. Students understand, make inferences, and draw conclusions about the varied structural patterns and features of literary nonfiction and provide evidence from text to support their understanding. Students are expected to evaluate the role of syntax and diction and the effect of voice, tone, and imagery on a speech, literary essay, or other forms of literary nonfiction.***	4 (E) read linguistically accommodated content-area material with a decreasing need for linguistic accommodations as more English is learned 4 (J) demonstrate English comprehension and expand reading skills by employing inferential skills such as predicting, making connections between ideas, drawing inferences and conclusions from text and graphic sources, and finding supporting text evidence commensurate with content-area needs 4 (K) demonstrate English comprehension and expand reading skills by employing analytical skills such as evaluating written information and performing critical analyses commensurate with content-area and grade-level needs
(7) ***Reading/Comprehension of Literary Text/Sensory Language. Students understand, make inferences, and draw conclusions about how an author's sensory language creates imagery in literary text and provide evidence from text to support their understanding. Students are expected to explain the function of symbolism, allegory, and allusions in literary works.***	1 (H) develop and expand repertoire of learning strategies such as reasoning inductively or deductively, looking for patterns in language, and analyzing sayings and expressions 4 (E) read linguistically accommodated content-area material with a decreasing need for linguistic accommodations as more English is learned; 4 (J) demonstrate English comprehension and expand reading skills by employing inferential skills such as predicting, making connections between ideas, drawing inferences and conclusions from text and graphic sources, and finding supporting text evidence commensurate with content-area needs

Tenth-Grade ELAR TEKS	ELPS
(8) *Reading/Comprehension of Informational Text/Culture and History. Students analyze, make inferences, and draw conclusions about the author's purpose in cultural, historical, and contemporary contexts and provide evidence from the text to support their understanding. Students are expected to analyze the controlling idea and specific purpose of a passage and the textual elements that support and elaborate it, including both the most important details and the less important details.*	4 (J) demonstrate English comprehension and expand reading skills by employing inferential skills such as predicting, making connections between ideas, drawing inferences and conclusions from text and graphic sources, and finding supporting text evidence commensurate with content-area needs 4 (K) demonstrate English comprehension and expand reading skills by employing analytical skills such as evaluating written information and performing critical analyses commensurate with content-area and grade-level needs
(9) *Reading/Comprehension of Informational Text/Expository Text. Students analyze, make inferences, and draw conclusions about expository text and provide evidence from text to support their understanding. Students are expected to:*	
(A) summarize text and distinguish between a summary and a critique and identify nonessential information in a summary and unsubstantiated opinions in a critique;	4 (I) demonstrate English comprehension and expand reading skills by employing basic reading skills such as demonstrating understanding of supporting ideas and details in text and graphic sources, summarizing text, and distinguishing main ideas from details commensurate with content-area needs
(B) distinguish among different kinds of evidence (e.g., logical, empirical, anecdotal) used to support conclusions and arguments in texts;	1 (C) use strategic learning techniques such as concept mapping, drawing, memorizing, comparing, contrasting, and reviewing to acquire basic and grade-level vocabulary 4 (K) demonstrate English comprehension and expand reading skills by employing analytical skills such as evaluating written information and performing critical analyses commensurate with content-area and grade-level needs
(C) make and defend subtle inferences and complex conclusions about the ideas in text and their organizational patterns; and	1 (H) develop and expand repertoire of learning strategies such as reasoning inductively or deductively, looking for patterns in language, and analyzing sayings and expressions 4 (J) demonstrate English comprehension and expand reading skills by employing inferential skills such as predicting, making connections between ideas, drawing inferences and conclusions from text and graphic sources, and finding supporting text evidence commensurate with content-area needs
(D) synthesize and make logical connections between ideas and details in several texts selected to reflect a range of viewpoints on the same topic and support those findings with textual evidence.	1 (H) develop and expand repertoire of learning strategies such as reasoning inductively or deductively, looking for patterns in language, and analyzing sayings and expressions 4 (J) demonstrate English comprehension and expand reading skills by employing inferential skills such as predicting, making connections between ideas, drawing inferences and conclusions from text and graphic sources, and finding supporting text evidence

	commensurate with content-area needs
Tenth-Grade ELAR TEKS	**ELPS**
(10) Reading/Comprehension of Informational Text/Persuasive Text. Students analyze, make inferences and draw conclusions about persuasive text and provide evidence from text to support their analysis. Students are expected to:	
(A) explain shifts in perspective in arguments about the same topic and evaluate the accuracy of the evidence used to support the different viewpoints within those arguments; and	4 (K) demonstrate English comprehension and expand reading skills by employing analytical skills such as evaluating written information and performing critical analyses commensurate with content-area and grade-level needs
(B) analyze contemporary political debates for such rhetorical and logical fallacies as appeals to commonly held opinions, false dilemmas, appeals to pity, and personal attacks.	1 (H) develop and expand repertoire of learning strategies such as reasoning inductively or deductively, looking for patterns in language, and analyzing sayings and expressions 4 (K) demonstrate English comprehension and expand reading skills by employing analytical skills such as evaluating written information and performing critical analyses commensurate with content-area and grade-level needs
(11) Reading/Comprehension of Informational Text/Procedural Texts. Students understand how to glean and use information in procedural texts and documents. Students are expected to:	
(A) evaluate text for the clarity of its graphics and its visual appeal; and	4 (K) demonstrate English comprehension and expand reading skills by employing analytical skills such as evaluating written information and performing critical analyses commensurate with content-area and grade-level needs
(B) synthesize information from multiple graphical sources to draw conclusions about the ideas presented (e.g., maps, charts, schematics).	4 (J) demonstrate English comprehension and expand reading skills by employing inferential skills such as predicting, making connections between ideas, drawing inferences and conclusions from text and graphic sources, and finding supporting text evidence commensurate with content-area needs 4 (I) demonstrate English comprehension and expand reading skills by employing basic reading skills such as demonstrating understanding of supporting ideas and details in text and graphic sources, summarizing text, and distinguishing main ideas from details commensurate with content-area needs
(12) Reading/Media Literacy. Students use comprehension skills to analyze how words, images, graphics, and sounds work together in various forms to impact meaning. Students will continue to apply earlier standards with greater depth in increasingly more complex texts.	

Students are expected to:	
Tenth-Grade ELAR TEKS	**ELPS**
(12) cont . . . (A) evaluate how messages presented in media reflect social and cultural views in ways different from traditional texts;	4 (K) demonstrate English comprehension and expand reading skills by employing analytical skills such as evaluating written information and performing critical analyses commensurate with content-area and grade-level needs
(B) analyze how messages in media are conveyed through visual and sound techniques (e.g., editing, reaction shots, sequencing, background music);	2 (F) listen to and derive meaning from a variety of media such as audio tape, video, DVD, and CD-ROM to build and reinforce concept and language attainment 4 (K) demonstrate English comprehension and expand reading skills by employing analytical skills such as evaluating written information and performing critical analyses commensurate with content-area and grade-level needs
(C) examine how individual perception or bias in coverage of the same event influences the audience; and	4 (J) demonstrate English comprehension and expand reading skills by employing inferential skills such as predicting, making connections between ideas, drawing inferences and conclusions from text and graphic sources, and finding supporting text evidence commensurate with content-area needs
(D) evaluate changes in formality and tone within the same medium for specific audiences and purposes.	4 (K) demonstrate English comprehension and expand reading skills by employing analytical skills such as evaluating written information and performing critical analyses commensurate with content-area and grade-level needs
Reading/Media Literacy – No Correlation	**4(B) recognize directionality of English reading such as left to right and top to bottom**
	4 (H) read silently with increasing ease and comprehension for longer periods
(13) Writing/Writing Process. Students use elements of the writing process (planning, drafting, revising, editing, and publishing) to compose text. Students are expected to:	
(A) plan a first draft by selecting the correct genre for conveying the intended meaning to multiple audiences, determining appropriate topics through a range of strategies (e.g., discussion, background reading, personal interests, interviews), and developing a thesis or controlling idea;	1 (A) use prior knowledge and experiences to understand meanings in English 3 (G) express opinions, ideas, and feelings ranging from communicating single words and short phrases to participating in extended discussions on a variety of social and grade-appropriate academic topics 5 (B) write using newly acquired basic vocabulary and content-based grade-level vocabulary
(B) structure ideas in a sustained and persuasive way (e.g., using outlines, note taking, graphic organizers, lists) and develop drafts in timed and open-ended situations that include transitions and rhetorical devices used to convey meaning;	4 (D) use prereading supports such as graphic organizers, illustrations, and pretaught topic-related vocabulary and other prereading activities to enhance comprehension of written text 4 (G) demonstrate comprehension of increasingly complex English by participating in shared reading, retelling or summarizing material, responding to questions, and taking notes commensurate with content-area and grade-level needs 5 (F) write using a variety of grade-appropriate sentence lengths, patterns, and connecting words to combine phrases, clauses, and sentences in increasingly

	accurate ways as more English is acquired
Tenth-Grade ELAR TEKS	**ELPS**
(13) cont . . . (C) revise drafts to improve style, word choice, figurative language, sentence variety, and subtlety of meaning after rethinking how well questions of purpose, audience, and genre have been addressed;	5 (F) write using a variety of grade-appropriate sentence lengths, patterns, and connecting words to combine phrases, clauses, and sentences in increasingly accurate ways as more English is acquired
(D) edit drafts for grammar, mechanics, and spelling; and	5 (D) edit writing for standard grammar and usage, including subject-verb agreement, pronoun agreement, and appropriate verb tenses commensurate with grade-level expectations as more English is acquired
(E) revise final draft in response to feedback from peers and teacher and publish written work for appropriate audiences.	4 (F) use visual and contextual support and support from peers and teachers to read grade-appropriate content-area text, to enhance and confirm understanding, to develop vocabulary, to grasp language structures, and to tap background knowledge needed to comprehend increasingly challenging language
(14) Writing/Literary Texts. Students write literary texts to express their ideas and feelings about real or imagined people, events, and ideas. Students are responsible for at least two forms of literary writing. Students are expected to:	
(A) write an engaging story with a well-developed conflict and resolution, interesting and believable characters, a range of literary strategies (e.g., dialogue, suspense) and devices to enhance the plot, and sensory details that define the mood or tone;	5 (B) write using newly acquired basic vocabulary and content-based grade-level vocabulary 5 (F) write using a variety of grade-appropriate sentence lengths, patterns, and connecting words to combine phrases, clauses, and sentences in increasingly accurate ways as more English is acquired 5 (G) narrate, describe, and explain with increasing specificity and detail to fulfill content-area writing needs as more English is acquired
(B) write a poem using a variety of poetic techniques (e.g., structural elements, figurative language) and a variety of poetic forms (e.g., sonnets, ballads); and	1 (E) internalize new, basic, and academic language by using and reusing it in meaningful ways in speaking and writing activities that build concept and language attainment
(C) write a script with an explicit or implicit theme and details that contribute to a definite mood or tone.	5 (F) write using a variety of grade-appropriate sentence lengths, patterns, and connecting words to combine phrases, clauses, and sentences in increasingly accurate ways as more English is acquired 5 (G) narrate, describe, and explain with increasing specificity and detail to fulfill content-area writing needs as more English is acquired
(15) Writing/Expository and Procedural Texts. Students write expository and procedural or work-related texts to communicate ideas and information to specific audiences for specific purposes. Students are expected to:	

Tenth-Grade ELAR TEKS	ELPS
(15) cont . . . (A) write an analytical essay of sufficient length that includes: (i) effective introductory and concluding paragraphs and a variety of sentence structures; (ii) rhetorical devices, and transitions between paragraphs; (iii) a thesis or controlling idea; (iv) an organizing structure appropriate to purpose, audience, and context; (v) relevant evidence and well-chosen details; and (vi) distinctions about the relative value of specific data, facts, and ideas that support the thesis statement;	5 (F) write using a variety of grade-appropriate sentence lengths, patterns, and connecting words to combine phrases, clauses, and sentences in increasingly accurate ways as more English is acquired 5 (G) narrate, describe, and explain with increasing specificity and detail to fulfill content-area writing needs as more English is acquired
(B) write procedural or work-related documents (e.g., instructions, e-mails, correspondence, memos, project plans) that include: (i) organized and accurately conveyed information; (ii) reader-friendly formatting techniques; and (iii) anticipation of readers' questions;	1 (G) demonstrate an increasing ability to distinguish between formal and informal English and an increasing knowledge of when to use each one commensurate with grade-level learning expectations 5 (F) write using a variety of grade-appropriate sentence lengths, patterns, and connecting words to combine phrases, clauses, and sentences in increasingly accurate ways as more English is acquired 5 (G) narrate, describe, and explain with increasing specificity and detail to fulfill content-area writing needs as more English is acquired
(C) write an interpretative response to an expository or a literary text (e.g., essay or review) that: (i) extends beyond a summary and literal analysis; (ii) addresses the writing skills for an analytical essay and provides evidence from the text using embedded quotations; and (iii) analyzes the aesthetic effects of an author's use of stylistic and rhetorical devices; and	5 (F) write using a variety of grade-appropriate sentence lengths, patterns, and connecting words to combine phrases, clauses, and sentences in increasingly accurate ways as more English is acquired 5 (G) narrate, describe, and explain with increasing specificity and detail to fulfill content-area writing needs as more English is acquired
(D) produce a multimedia presentation (e.g., documentary, class newspaper, docudrama, infomercial, visual or textual parodies, theatrical production) with graphics, images, and sound that conveys a distinctive point of view and appeals to a specific audience.	5 (F) write using a variety of grade-appropriate sentence lengths, patterns, and connecting words to combine phrases, clauses, and sentences in increasingly accurate ways as more English is acquired 5 (G) narrate, describe, and explain with increasing specificity and detail to fulfill content-area writing needs as more English is acquired
(16) Writing/Persuasive Texts. Students write persuasive texts to influence the attitudes or actions of a specific audience on specific issues. Students are expected to write an argumentative essay to the appropriate audience that includes:	
(A) a clear thesis or position based on logical reasons supported by precise and relevant evidence;	5 (F) write using a variety of grade-appropriate sentence lengths, patterns, and connecting words to combine phrases, clauses, and sentences in increasingly accurate ways as more English is acquired 5 (G) narrate, describe, and explain with increasing specificity and detail to fulfill content-area writing needs as more English is acquired

Tenth-Grade ELAR TEKS	ELPS
(16) cont . . . (B) consideration of the whole range of information and views on the topic and accurate and honest representation of these views (i.e., in the author's own words and not out of context);	5 (G) narrate, describe, and explain with increasing specificity and detail to fulfill content-area writing needs as more English is acquired
(C) counterarguments based on evidence to anticipate and address objections;	5 (G) narrate, describe, and explain with increasing specificity and detail to fulfill content-area writing needs as more English is acquired
(D) an organizing structure appropriate to the purpose, audience, and context;	5 (F) write using a variety of grade-appropriate sentence lengths, patterns, and connecting words to combine phrases, clauses, and sentences in increasingly accurate ways as more English is acquired 5 (G) narrate, describe, and explain with increasing specificity and detail to fulfill content-area writing needs as more English is acquired
(E) an analysis of the relative value of specific data, facts, and ideas; and	5 (G) narrate, describe, and explain with increasing specificity and detail to fulfill content-area writing needs as more English is acquired
(F) a range of appropriate appeals (e.g., descriptions, anecdotes, case studies, analogies, illustrations).	1 (H) develop and expand repertoire of learning strategies such as reasoning inductively or deductively, looking for patterns in language, and analyzing sayings and expressions 5 (G) narrate, describe, and explain with increasing specificity and detail to fulfill content-area writing needs as more English is acquired
(17) Oral and Written Conventions/Conventions. Students understand the function of and use the conventions of academic language when speaking and writing. Students will continue to apply earlier standards with greater complexity. Students are expected to:	
(A) use and understand the function of the following parts of speech in the context of reading, writing, and speaking: (i) more complex active and passive tenses and verbals (gerunds, infinitives, participles); (ii) restrictive and nonrestrictive relative clauses; and (iii) reciprocal pronouns (e.g., each other, one another);	3 (C) speak using a variety of grammatical structures, sentence lengths, sentence types, and connecting words with increasing accuracy and ease as more English is acquired 3 (D) speak using grade-level content-area vocabulary in context to internalize new English words and build academic language proficiency 3 (G) express opinions, ideas, and feelings ranging from communicating single words and short phrases to participating in extended discussions on a variety of social and grade-appropriate academic topics 5 (E) employ increasingly complex grammatical structures in content-area writing commensurate with grade-level expectations, such as: (i) using correct verbs, tenses, and pronouns / antecedents (ii) using possessive case (apostrophes) correctly (iii) using negatives and contractions correctly 5 (F) write using a variety of grade-appropriate sentence lengths, patterns, and connecting words to combine phrases, clauses, and sentences in increasingly accurate ways as more English is acquired

Tenth-Grade ELAR TEKS	ELPS
(17) cont . . . (B) identify and use the subjunctive mood to express doubts, wishes, and possibilities; and	5 (G) narrate, describe, and explain with increasing specificity and detail to fulfill content-area writing needs as more English is acquired
(C) use a variety of correctly structured sentences (e.g., compound, complex, compound-complex).	5 (F) write using a variety of grade-appropriate sentence lengths, patterns, and connecting words to combine phrases, clauses, and sentences in increasingly accurate ways as more English is acquired
(18) Oral and Written Conventions/Handwriting, Capitalization, and Punctuation. Students write legibly and use appropriate capitalization and punctuation conventions in their compositions. Students are expected to:	
(A) use conventions of capitalization; and	5 (C) spell familiar English words with increasing accuracy, and employ English spelling patterns and rules with increasing accuracy as more English is acquired
(B) use correct punctuation marks including: (i) comma placement in nonrestrictive phrases, clauses, and contrasting expressions; (ii) quotation marks to indicate sarcasm or irony; and (iii) dashes to emphasize parenthetical information.	5 (F) write using a variety of grade-appropriate sentence lengths, patterns, and connecting words to combine phrases, clauses, and sentences in increasingly accurate ways as more English is acquired
(19) Oral and Written Conventions/Spelling. Students spell correctly. Students are expected to spell correctly, including using various resources to determine and check correct spellings.	1 (B) monitor oral and written language production and employ self-corrective techniques or other resources 5 (C) spell familiar English words with increasing accuracy, and employ English spelling patterns and rules with increasing accuracy as more English is acquired
Oral and Written Conventions/Spelling – No Correlation	**5 (A) learn relationships between sounds and letters of the English language to represent sounds when writing in English**
(20) Research/Research Plan. Students ask open-ended research questions and develop a plan for answering them. Students are expected to:	
(A) brainstorm, consult with others, decide upon a topic, and formulate a major research question to address the major research topic; and	1 (E) internalize new, basic, and academic language by using and reusing it in meaningful ways in speaking and writing activities that build concept and language attainment 3 (F) ask and give information ranging from using a very limited bank of high-frequency, high-need, concrete vocabulary, including key words and expressions needed for basic communication in academic and social contexts, to using abstract and content-based vocabulary during extended speaking assignments 3 (G) express opinions, ideas, and feelings ranging from communicating single words and short phrases to participating in extended discussions on a variety of social and grade-appropriate academic topics

Tenth-Grade ELAR TEKS	ELPS
(20) cont . . . (B) formulate a plan for engaging in research on a complex, multi-faceted topic.	1 (F) use accessible language and learn new and essential language in the process
(21) Research/Gathering Sources. Students determine, locate, and explore the full range of relevant sources addressing a research question and systematically record the information they gather. Students are expected to:	
(A) follow the research plan to compile data from authoritative sources in a manner that identifies the major issues and debates within the field of inquiry;	2 (F) listen to and derive meaning from a variety of media such as audio tape, video, DVD, and CD-ROM to build and reinforce concept and language attainment 4 (K) demonstrate English comprehension and expand reading skills by employing analytical skills such as evaluating written information and performing critical analyses commensurate with content-area and grade-level needs
(B) organize information gathered from multiple sources to create a variety of graphics and forms (e.g., notes, learning logs); and	5 (B) write using newly acquired basic vocabulary and content-based grade-level vocabulary
(C) paraphrase, summarize, quote, and accurately cite all researched information according to a standard format (e.g., author, title, page number).	4 (G) demonstrate comprehension of increasingly complex English by participating in shared reading, retelling or summarizing material, responding to questions, and taking notes commensurate with content-area and grade level needs; 5 (G) narrate, describe, and explain with increasing specificity and detail to fulfill content-area writing needs as more English is acquired
(22) Research/Synthesizing Information. Students clarify research questions and evaluate and synthesize collected information. Students are expected to:	
(A) modify the major research question as necessary to refocus the research plan;	1 (B) monitor oral and written language production and employ self-corrective techniques or other resources
(B) evaluate the relevance of information to the topic and determine the reliability, validity, and accuracy of sources (including Internet sources) by examining their authority and objectivity; and	4 (K) demonstrate English comprehension and expand reading skills by employing analytical skills such as evaluating written information and performing critical analyses commensurate with content-area and grade-level needs
(C) critique the research process at each step to implement changes as the need occurs and is identified.	4 (K) demonstrate English comprehension and expand reading skills by employing analytical skills such as evaluating written information and performing critical analyses commensurate with content-area and grade-level needs

Tenth-Grade ELAR TEKS	ELPS
(23) Research/Organizing and Presenting Ideas. Students organize and present their ideas and information according to the purpose of the research and their audience. Students are expected to synthesize the research into a written or an oral presentation that:	
(A) marshals evidence in support of a clear thesis statement and related claims;	4 (J) demonstrate English comprehension and expand reading skills by employing inferential skills such as predicting, making connections between ideas, drawing inferences and conclusions from text and graphic sources, and finding supporting text evidence commensurate with content-area needs 5 (G) narrate, describe, and explain with increasing specificity and detail to fulfill content-area writing needs as more English is acquired
(B) provides an analysis for the audience that reflects a logical progression of ideas and a clearly stated point of view;	1 (H) develop and expand repertoire of learning strategies such as reasoning inductively or deductively, looking for patterns in language, and analyzing sayings and expressions 5 (G) narrate, describe, and explain with increasing specificity and detail to fulfill content-area writing needs as more English is acquired
(C) uses graphics and illustrations to help explain concepts where appropriate;	1 (C) use strategic learning techniques such as concept mapping, drawing, memorizing, comparing, contrasting, and reviewing to acquire basic and grade-level vocabulary
(D) uses a variety of evaluative tools (e.g., self-made rubrics, peer reviews, teacher and expert evaluations) to examine the quality of the research; and	4 (F) use visual and contextual support and support from peers and teachers to read grade-appropriate content-area text, to enhance and confirm understanding, to develop vocabulary, to grasp language structures, and to tap background knowledge needed to comprehend increasingly challenging language
(E) uses a style manual (e.g., Modern Language Association, Chicago Manual of Style) to document sources and format written materials.	1 (B) monitor oral and written language production and employ self-corrective techniques or other resources
(24) Listening and Speaking/Listening. Students will use comprehension skills to listen attentively to others in formal and informal settings. Students will continue to apply earlier standards with greater complexity. Students are expected to:	
(A) listen responsively to a speaker by taking notes that summarize, synthesize, or highlight the speaker's ideas for critical reflection and by asking questions related to the content for clarification and elaboration;	2 (D) monitor understanding of spoken language during classroom instruction and interactions and seek clarification as needed 2 (I) demonstrate listening comprehension of increasingly complex spoken English by following directions, retelling or summarizing spoken messages, responding to questions and requests, collaborating with peers, and taking notes commensurate with content and grade-level needs

Tenth-Grade ELAR TEKS	ELPS
(24) (A) cont . . .	3 (F) ask and give information ranging from using a very limited bank of high-frequency, high-need, concrete vocabulary, including key words and expressions needed for basic communication in academic and social contexts, to using abstract and content-based vocabulary during extended speaking assignments
(B) follow and give complex oral instructions to perform specific tasks, answer questions, solve problems, and complete processes; and	2 (E) use visual, contextual, and linguistic support to enhance and confirm understanding of increasingly complex and elaborated spoken language 2 (G) understand the general meaning, main points, and important details of spoken language ranging from situations in which topics, language, and contexts are familiar to unfamiliar 2 (H) understand implicit ideas and information in increasingly complex spoken language commensurate with grade-level learning expectations 2 (I) demonstrate listening comprehension of increasingly complex spoken English by following directions, retelling or summarizing spoken messages, responding to questions and requests, collaborating with peers, and taking notes commensurate with content and grade-level needs 3 (F) ask and give information ranging from using a very limited bank of high-frequency, high-need, concrete vocabulary, including key words and expressions needed for basic communication in academic and social contexts, to using abstract and content-based vocabulary during extended speaking assignments
(C) evaluate how the style and structure of a speech support or undermine its purpose or meaning.	2 (G) understand the general meaning, main points, and important details of spoken language ranging from situations in which topics, language, and contexts are familiar to unfamiliar 2 (H) understand implicit ideas and information in increasingly complex spoken language commensurate with grade-level learning expectations
Listening and Speaking/Listening – No Correlation	**2 (A) distinguish sounds and intonation patterns of English with increasing ease** **2 (B) recognize elements of the English sound system in newly acquired vocabulary such as long and short vowels, silent letters, and consonant clusters**
(25) *Listening and Speaking/Speaking. Students speak clearly and to the point, using the conventions of language. Students will continue to apply earlier standards with greater complexity. Students are expected to advance a coherent argument that incorporates a clear thesis and a logical progression of valid evidence from reliable sources and that employs eye contact, speaking rate (e.g., pauses for effect), volume, enunciation, purposeful gestures, and conventions of language to communicate ideas effectively.*	1 (D) speak using learning strategies such as requesting assistance, employing nonverbal cues, and using synonyms and circumlocution 2 (C) learn new language structures, expressions, and basic and academic vocabulary heard during classroom instruction and interactions 3 (B) expand and internalize initial English vocabulary by learning and using high-frequency English words necessary for identifying and describing people, places, and objects, by retelling simple stories and basic information represented or supported by pictures, and by learning and using routine language needed for classroom communication

Tenth-Grade ELAR TEKS	ELPS
(25) cont . . .	3 (C) speak using a variety of grammatical structures, sentence lengths, sentence types, and connecting words with increasing accuracy and ease as more English is acquired 3 (D) speak using grade-level content-area vocabulary in context to internalize new English words and build academic language proficiency 3 (G) express opinions, ideas, and feelings ranging from communicating single words and short phrases to participating in extended discussions on a variety of social and grade-appropriate academic topics 3 (H) narrate, describe, and explain with increasing specificity and detail as more English is acquired 3 (I) adapt spoken language appropriately for formal and informal purposes 3 (J) respond orally to information presented in a wide variety of print, electronic, audio, and visual media to build and reinforce concept and language attainment
Listening and Speaking/Speaking – No Correlation	3 (A) **practice producing sounds of newly acquired vocabulary such as long and short vowels, silent letters, and consonant clusters to pronounce English words in a manner that is increasingly comprehensible**
(26) Listening and Speaking/Teamwork. Students work productively with others in teams. Students will continue to apply earlier standards with greater complexity. Students are expected to participate productively in teams, building on the ideas of others, contributing relevant information, developing a plan for consensus-building, and setting ground rules for decision making.	1 (B) monitor oral and written language production and employ self-corrective techniques or other resources 1 (G) demonstrate an increasing ability to distinguish between formal and informal English and an increasing knowledge of when to use each one commensurate with grade-level learning expectations 2 (I) demonstrate listening comprehension of increasingly complex spoken English by following directions, retelling or summarizing spoken messages, responding to questions and requests, collaborating with peers, and taking notes 3 (E) share information in cooperative learning interactions

ELAR TEKS and ELPS Side-by-Side
Eleventh-Grade

Eleventh-Grade ELAR TEKS	ELPS
(1) Reading/Vocabulary Development. Students understand new vocabulary and use it when reading and writing. Students are expected to:	
(A) determine the meaning of grade-level technical academic English words in multiple content-areas (e.g., science, mathematics, social studies, the arts) derived from Latin, Greek, or other linguistic roots and affixes;	4 (A) learn relationships between sounds and letters of the English language and decode (sound out) words using a combination of skills such as recognizing sound-letter relationships and identifying cognates, affixes, roots, and base words 4 (C) develop basic sight vocabulary, derive meaning of environmental print, and comprehend English vocabulary and language structures used routinely in written classroom materials
(B) analyze textual context (within a sentence and in larger sections of text) to draw conclusions about the nuance in word meanings;	4 (F) use visual and contextual support and support from peers and teachers to read grade-appropriate content-area text, to enhance and confirm understanding, to develop vocabulary, to grasp language structures, and to tap background knowledge needed to comprehend increasingly challenging language 4 (K) demonstrate English comprehension and expand reading skills by employing analytical skills such as evaluating written information and performing critical analyses commensurate with content-area and grade-level needs
(C) infer word meaning through the identification and analysis of analogies and other word relationships;	1 (H) develop and expand repertoire of learning strategies such as reasoning inductively or deductively, looking for patterns in language, and analyzing sayings and expressions
(D) recognize and use knowledge of cognates in different languages and of word origins to determine the meaning of words; and	1 (H) develop and expand repertoire of learning strategies such as reasoning inductively or deductively, looking for patterns in language, and analyzing sayings and expressions 4 (A) learn relationships between sounds and letters of the English language and decode (sound out) words using a combination of skills such as recognizing sound-letter relationships and identifying cognates, affixes, roots, and base words
(E) use general and specialized dictionaries, thesauri, glossaries, histories of language, books of quotations, and other related references (printed or electronic) as needed.	1 (B) monitor oral and written language production and employ self-corrective techniques or other resources
(2) Reading/Comprehension of Literary Text/Theme and Genre. Students analyze, make inferences, and draw conclusions about theme and genre in different cultural, historical, and contemporary contexts and provide evidence from the text to support their understanding. Students are expected to:	

Eleventh-Grade ELAR TEKS	ELPS
(2) cont . . . (A) analyze the way in which the theme or meaning of a selection represents a view or comment on the human condition;	4 (K) demonstrate English comprehension and expand reading skills by employing analytical skills such as evaluating written information and performing critical analyses commensurate with content-area and grade-level needs
(B) relate the characters and text structures of mythic, traditional, and classical literature to 20th and 21st century American novels, plays, or films; and	4 (J) demonstrate English comprehension and expand reading skills by employing inferential skills such as predicting, making connections between ideas, drawing inferences and conclusions from text and graphic sources, and finding supporting text evidence commensurate with content-area needs
(C) relate the main ideas found in a literary work to primary source documents from its historical and cultural setting.	4 (I) demonstrate English comprehension and expand reading skills by employing basic reading skills such as demonstrating understanding of supporting ideas and details in text and graphic sources, summarizing text, and distinguishing main ideas from details commensurate with content-area needs 4 (J) demonstrate English comprehension and expand reading skills by employing inferential skills such as predicting, making connections between ideas, drawing inferences and conclusions from text and graphic sources, and finding supporting text evidence commensurate with content-area needs
(3) Reading/Comprehension of Literary Text/Poetry. Students understand, make inferences, and draw conclusions about the structure and elements of poetry and provide evidence from text to support their understanding. Students are expected to analyze the effects of metrics, rhyme schemes (e.g., end, internal, slant, eye), and other conventions in American poetry.	4 (E) read linguistically accommodated content-area material with a decreasing need for linguistic accommodations as more English is learned 4 (J) demonstrate English comprehension and expand reading skills by employing inferential skills such as predicting, making connections between ideas, drawing inferences and conclusions from text and graphic sources, and finding supporting text evidence commensurate with content-area needs 4 (K) demonstrate English comprehension and expand reading skills by employing analytical skills such as evaluating written information and performing critical analyses commensurate with content-area and grade-level needs
(4) Reading/Comprehension of Literary Text/Drama. Students understand, make inferences, and draw conclusions about the structure and elements of drama and provide evidence from text to support their understanding. Students are expected to analyze the themes and characteristics in different periods of modern American drama.	4 (E) read linguistically accommodated content-area material with a decreasing need for linguistic accommodations as more English is learned 4 (J) demonstrate English comprehension and expand reading skills by employing inferential skills such as predicting, making connections between ideas, drawing inferences and conclusions from text and graphic sources, and finding supporting text evidence commensurate with content-area needs 4 (K) demonstrate English comprehension and expand reading skills by employing analytical skills such as evaluating written information and performing critical analyses commensurate with content-area and grade-level needs

Eleventh-Grade ELAR TEKS	ELPS
(5) *Reading/Comprehension of Literary Text/Fiction. Students understand, make inferences, and draw conclusions about the structure and elements of fiction and provide evidence from text to support their understanding. Students are expected to:*	
(A) evaluate how different literary elements (e.g., figurative language, point of view) shape the author's portrayal of the plot and setting in works of fiction;	1 (H) develop and expand repertoire of learning strategies such as reasoning inductively or deductively, looking for patterns in language, and analyzing sayings and expressions 4 (K) demonstrate English comprehension and expand reading skills by employing analytical skills such as evaluating written information and performing critical analyses commensurate with content-area and grade-level needs
(B) analyze the internal and external development of characters through a range of literary devices;	4 (K) demonstrate English comprehension and expand reading skills by employing analytical skills such as evaluating written information and performing critical analyses commensurate with content-area and grade-level needs
(C) analyze the impact of narration when the narrator's point of view shifts from one character to another; and	4 (K) demonstrate English comprehension and expand reading skills by employing analytical skills such as evaluating written information and performing critical analyses commensurate with content-area and grade-level needs
(D) demonstrate familiarity with works by authors in American fiction from each major literary period.	*No ELPS Correlation*
(6) *Reading/Comprehension of Literary Text/Literary Nonfiction. Students understand, make inferences, and draw conclusions about the varied structural patterns and features of literary nonfiction and provide evidence from text to support their understanding. Students are expected to analyze how rhetorical techniques (e.g., repetition, parallel structure, understatement, overstatement) in literary essays, true life adventures, and historically important speeches influence the reader, evoke emotions, and create meaning.*	4 (E) read linguistically accommodated content-area material with a decreasing need for linguistic accommodations as more English is learned 4 (J) demonstrate English comprehension and expand reading skills by employing inferential skills such as predicting, making connections between ideas, drawing inferences and conclusions from text and graphic sources, and finding supporting text evidence commensurate with content-area needs 4 (K) demonstrate English comprehension and expand reading skills by employing analytical skills such as evaluating written information and performing critical analyses commensurate with content-area and grade-level needs
(7) *Reading/Comprehension of Literary Text/Sensory Language. Students understand, make inferences, and draw conclusions about how an author's sensory language creates imagery in literary text and provide evidence from text to support their understanding. Students are expected to analyze the meaning of classical, mythological, and biblical allusions in words, phrases, passages, and literary works.*	1 (H) develop and expand repertoire of learning strategies such as reasoning inductively or deductively, looking for patterns in language, and analyzing sayings and expressions 4 (E) read linguistically accommodated content-area material with a decreasing need for linguistic accommodations as more English is learned

Eleventh-Grade ELAR TEKS	ELPS
(7) cont . . .	4 (J) demonstrate English comprehension and expand reading skills by employing inferential skills such as predicting, making connections between ideas, drawing inferences and conclusions from text and graphic sources, and finding supporting text evidence commensurate with content-area needs 4 (K) demonstrate English comprehension and expand reading skills by employing analytical skills such as evaluating written information and performing critical analyses commensurate with content-area and grade-level needs
(8) Reading/Comprehension of Informational Text/Culture and History. Students analyze, make inferences, and draw conclusions about the author's purpose in cultural, historical, and contemporary contexts and provide evidence from the text to support their understanding. Students are expected to analyze how the style, tone, and diction of a text advance the author's purpose and perspective or stance.	4 (E) read linguistically accommodated content-area material with a decreasing need for linguistic accommodations as more English is learned 4 (J) demonstrate English comprehension and expand reading skills by employing inferential skills such as predicting, making connections between ideas, drawing inferences and conclusions from text and graphic sources, and finding supporting text evidence commensurate with content-area needs 4 (K) demonstrate English comprehension and expand reading skills by employing analytical skills such as evaluating written information and performing critical analyses commensurate with content-area and grade-level needs
(9) Reading/Comprehension of Informational Text/Expository Text. Students analyze, make inferences, and draw conclusions about expository text and provide evidence from text to support their understanding. Students are expected to:	
(A) summarize a text in a manner that captures the author's viewpoint, its main ideas, and its elements without taking a position or expressing an opinion;	4 (I) demonstrate English comprehension and expand reading skills by employing basic reading skills such as demonstrating understanding of supporting ideas and details in text and graphic sources, summarizing text, and distinguishing main ideas from details commensurate with content-area needs
(B) distinguish between inductive and deductive reasoning and analyze the elements of deductively and inductively reasoned texts and the different ways conclusions are supported;	1 (H) develop and expand repertoire of learning strategies such as reasoning inductively or deductively, looking for patterns in language, and analyzing sayings and expressions 4 (K) demonstrate English comprehension and expand reading skills by employing analytical skills such as evaluating written information and performing critical analyses commensurate with content-area and grade-level needs
(C) make and defend subtle inferences and complex conclusions about the ideas in text and their organizational patterns; and	1 (H) develop and expand repertoire of learning strategies such as reasoning inductively or deductively, looking for patterns in language, and analyzing sayings and expressions

Eleventh-Grade ELAR TEKS	ELPS
(9)(C) cont . . .	4 (J) demonstrate English comprehension and expand reading skills by employing inferential skills such as predicting, making connections between ideas, drawing inferences and conclusions from text and graphic sources, and finding supporting text evidence commensurate with content-area needs
(D) synthesize ideas and make logical connections (e.g., thematic links, author analyses) between and among multiple texts representing similar or different genres and technical sources and support those findings with textual evidence.	1 (H) develop and expand repertoire of learning strategies such as reasoning inductively or deductively, looking for patterns in language, and analyzing sayings and expressions 4 (J) demonstrate English comprehension and expand reading skills by employing inferential skills such as predicting, making connections between ideas, drawing inferences and conclusions from text and graphic sources, and finding supporting text evidence commensurate with content-area needs
(10) Reading/Comprehension of Informational Text/Persuasive Text. Students analyze, make inferences, and draw conclusions about persuasive text and provide evidence from text to support their analyses. Students are expected to:	
(A) evaluate how the author's purpose and stated or perceived audience affect the tone of persuasive texts; and	4 (K) demonstrate English comprehension and expand reading skills by employing analytical skills such as evaluating written information and performing critical analyses commensurate with content-area and grade-level needs
(B) analyze historical and contemporary political debates for such logical fallacies as non sequiturs, circular logic, and hasty generalizations.	1 (H) develop and expand repertoire of learning strategies such as reasoning inductively or deductively, looking for patterns in language, and analyzing sayings and expressions 4 (K) demonstrate English comprehension and expand reading skills by employing analytical skills such as evaluating written information and performing critical analyses commensurate with content-area and grade-level needs
(11) Reading/Comprehension of Informational Text/Procedural Texts. Students understand how to glean and use information in procedural texts and documents. Students are expected to:	
(A) evaluate the logic of the sequence of information presented in text (e.g., product support material, contracts); and	1 (H) develop and expand repertoire of learning strategies such as reasoning inductively or deductively, looking for patterns in language, and analyzing sayings and expressions 4 (K) demonstrate English comprehension and expand reading skills by employing analytical skills such as evaluating written information and performing critical analyses commensurate with content-area and grade-level needs

Eleventh-Grade ELAR TEKS	ELPS
(11) cont . . . (B) translate (from text to graphic or from graphic to text) complex, factual, quantitative, or technical information presented in maps, charts, illustrations, graphs, timelines, tables, and diagrams.	1 (C) use strategic learning techniques such as concept mapping, drawing, memorizing, comparing, contrasting, and reviewing to acquire basic and grade-level vocabulary 4 (I) demonstrate English comprehension and expand reading skills by employing basic reading skills such as demonstrating understanding of supporting ideas and details in text and graphic sources, summarizing text, and distinguishing main ideas from details commensurate with content-area needs
(12) Reading/Media Literacy. Students use comprehension skills to analyze how words, images, graphics, and sounds work together in various forms to impact meaning. Students will continue to apply earlier standards with greater depth in increasingly more complex texts. Students are expected to:	
(A) evaluate how messages presented in media reflect social and cultural views in ways different from traditional texts;	4 (K) demonstrate English comprehension and expand reading skills by employing analytical skills such as evaluating written information and performing critical analyses commensurate with content-area and grade-level needs
(B) evaluate the interactions of different techniques (e.g., layout, pictures, typeface in print media, images, text, sound in electronic journalism) used in multilayered media;	2 (F) listen to and derive meaning from a variety of media such as audio tape, video, DVD, and CD-ROM to build and reinforce concept and language attainment 4 (K) demonstrate English comprehension and expand reading skills by employing analytical skills such as evaluating written information and performing critical analyses commensurate with content-area and grade-level needs
(C) evaluate the objectivity of coverage of the same event in various types of media; and	2 (F) listen to and derive meaning from a variety of media such as audio tape, video, DVD, and CD-ROM to build and reinforce concept and language attainment 4 (K) demonstrate English comprehension and expand reading skills by employing analytical skills such as evaluating written information and performing critical analyses commensurate with content-area and grade-level needs
(D) evaluate changes in formality and tone across various media for different audiences and purposes.	1 (G) demonstrate an increasing ability to distinguish between formal and informal English and an increasing knowledge of when to use each one commensurate with grade-level learning expectations 4 (K) demonstrate English comprehension and expand reading skills by employing analytical skills such as evaluating written information and performing critical analyses commensurate with content-area and grade-level needs
Reading/Media Literacy – No Correlation	**4(B) recognize directionality of English reading such as left to right and top to bottom** **4 (H) read silently with increasing ease and comprehension for longer periods**

Eleventh-Grade ELAR TEKS	ELPS
(13) Writing/Writing Process. Students use elements of the writing process (planning, drafting, revising, editing, and publishing) to compose text. Students are expected to:	
(A) plan a first draft by selecting the correct genre for conveying the intended meaning to multiple audiences, determining appropriate topics through a range of strategies (e.g., discussion, background reading, personal interests, interviews), and developing a thesis or controlling idea;	1 (A) use prior knowledge and experiences to understand meanings in English 3 (G) express opinions, ideas, and feelings ranging from communicating single words and short phrases to participating in extended discussions on a variety of social and grade-appropriate academic topics 5 (B) write using newly acquired basic vocabulary and content-based grade-level vocabulary
(B) structure ideas in a sustained and persuasive way (e.g., using outlines, note taking, graphic organizers, lists) and develop drafts in timed and open-ended situations that include transitions and rhetorical devices to convey meaning;	4 (D) use prereading supports such as graphic organizers, illustrations, and pretaught topic-related vocabulary and other prereading activities to enhance comprehension of written text 4 (G) demonstrate comprehension of increasingly complex English by participating in shared reading, retelling or summarizing material, responding to questions, and taking notes commensurate with content-area and grade-level needs 5 (F) write using a variety of grade-appropriate sentence lengths, patterns, and connecting words to combine phrases, clauses, and sentences in increasingly accurate ways as more English is acquired
(C) revise drafts to clarify meaning and achieve specific rhetorical purposes, consistency of tone, and logical organization by rearranging the words, sentences, and paragraphs to employ tropes (e.g., metaphors, similes, analogies, hyperbole, understatement, rhetorical questions, irony), schemes (e.g., parallelism, antithesis, inverted word order, repetition, reversed structures), and by adding transitional words and phrases;	5 (F) write using a variety of grade-appropriate sentence lengths, patterns, and connecting words to combine phrases, clauses, and sentences in increasingly accurate ways as more English is acquired
(D) edit drafts for grammar, mechanics, and spelling; and	5 (D) edit writing for standard grammar and usage, including subject-verb agreement, pronoun agreement, and appropriate verb tenses commensurate with grade-level expectations as more English is acquired
(E) revise final draft in response to feedback from peers and teacher and publish written work for appropriate audiences.	4 (F) use visual and contextual support and support from peers and teachers to read grade-appropriate content-area text, enhance and confirm understanding, and develop vocabulary, grasp of language structures, and background knowledge needed to comprehend increasingly challenging language 5 (D) edit writing for standard grammar and usage, including subject-verb agreement, pronoun agreement, and appropriate verb tenses commensurate with grade-level expectations as more English is acquired

Eleventh-Grade ELAR TEKS	ELPS
(14) Writing/Literary Texts. Students write literary texts to express their ideas and feelings about real or imagined people, events, and ideas. Students are responsible for at least two forms of literary writing. Students are expected to:	
(A) write an engaging story with a well-developed conflict and resolution, complex and non-stereotypical characters, a range of literary strategies (e.g., dialogue, suspense) and devices to enhance the plot, and sensory details that define the mood or tone;	5 (B) write using newly acquired basic vocabulary and content-based grade-level vocabulary 5 (F) write using a variety of grade-appropriate sentence lengths, patterns, and connecting words to combine phrases, clauses, and sentences in increasingly accurate ways as more English is acquired 5 (G) narrate, describe, and explain with increasing specificity and detail to fulfill content-area writing needs as more English is acquired
(B) write a poem that reflects an awareness of poetic conventions and traditions within different forms (e.g., sonnets, ballads, free verse); and	1 (E) internalize new, basic, and academic language by using and reusing it in meaningful ways in speaking and writing activities that build concept and language attainment 5 (B) write using newly acquired basic vocabulary and content-based grade-level vocabulary
(C) write a script with an explicit or implicit theme, using a variety of literary techniques.	5 (B) write using newly acquired basic vocabulary and content-based grade-level vocabulary 5 (F) write using a variety of grade-appropriate sentence lengths, patterns, and connecting words to combine phrases, clauses, and sentences in increasingly accurate ways as more English is acquired 5 (G) narrate, describe, and explain with increasing specificity and detail to fulfill content-area writing needs as more English is acquired
(15) Writing/Expository and Procedural Texts. Students write expository and procedural or work-related texts to communicate ideas and information to specific audiences for specific purposes. Students are expected to:	
(A) write an analytical essay of sufficient length that includes: (i) effective introductory and concluding paragraphs and a variety of sentence structures; (ii) rhetorical devices, and transitions between paragraphs; (iii) a clear thesis statement or controlling idea; (iv) a clear organizational schema for conveying ideas; (v) relevant and substantial evidence and well-chosen details; and (vi) information on multiple relevant perspectives and a consideration of the validity, reliability, and relevance of primary and secondary sources;	4 (K) demonstrate English comprehension and expand reading skills by employing analytical skills such as evaluating written information and performing critical analyses commensurate with content-area and grade-level needs 5 (B) write using newly acquired basic vocabulary and content-based grade-level vocabulary 5 (F) write using a variety of grade-appropriate sentence lengths, patterns, and connecting words to combine phrases, clauses, and sentences in increasingly accurate ways as more English is acquired 5 (G) narrate, describe, and explain with increasing specificity and detail to fulfill content-area writing needs as more English is acquired

Eleventh-Grade ELAR TEKS	ELPS
(15) cont . . . (B) write procedural or work-related documents (e.g., résumés, proposals, college applications, operation manuals) that include: (i) a clearly stated purpose combined with a well-supported viewpoint on the topic; (ii) appropriate formatting structures (e.g., headings, graphics, white space); (iii) relevant questions that engage readers and consider their needs; (iv) accurate technical information in accessible language; and (v) appropriate organizational structures supported by facts and details (documented if appropriate);	5 (B) write using newly acquired basic vocabulary and content-based grade-level vocabulary 5 (F) write using a variety of grade-appropriate sentence lengths, patterns, and connecting words to combine phrases, clauses, and sentences in increasingly accurate ways as more English is acquired 5 (G) narrate, describe, and explain with increasing specificity and detail to fulfill content-area writing needs as more English is acquired
(C) write an interpretation of an expository or a literary text that: (i) advances a clear thesis statement; (ii) addresses the writing skills for an analytical essay, including references to and commentary on quotations from the text; (iii) analyzes the aesthetic effects of an author's use of stylistic or rhetorical devices; (iv) identifies and analyzes the ambiguities, nuances, and complexities within the text; and (v) anticipates and responds to readers' questions or contradictory information; and	4 (K) demonstrate English comprehension and expand reading skills by employing analytical skills such as evaluating written information and performing critical analyses commensurate with content-area and grade-level needs 5 (F) write using a variety of grade-appropriate sentence lengths, patterns, and connecting words to combine phrases, clauses, and sentences in increasingly accurate ways as more English is acquired
(D) produce a multimedia presentation (e.g., documentary, class newspaper, docudrama, infomercial, visual or textual parodies, theatrical production) with graphics, images, and sound that appeals to a specific audience and synthesizes information from multiple points of view.	5 (F) write using a variety of grade-appropriate sentence lengths, patterns, and connecting words to combine phrases, clauses, and sentences in increasingly accurate ways as more English is acquired; and 5 (G) narrate, describe, and explain with increasing specificity and detail to fulfill content-area writing needs as more English is acquired
(16) Writing/Persuasive Texts. Students write persuasive texts to influence the attitudes or actions of a specific audience on specific issues. Students are expected to write an argumentative essay (e.g., evaluative essays, proposals) to the appropriate audience that includes:	
(A) a clear thesis or position based on logical reasons supported by precise and relevant evidence, including facts, expert opinions, quotations, and/or expressions of commonly accepted beliefs;	5 (F) write using a variety of grade-appropriate sentence lengths, patterns, and connecting words to combine phrases, clauses, and sentences in increasingly accurate ways as more English is acquired 5 (G) narrate, describe, and explain with increasing specificity and detail to fulfill content-area writing needs as more English is acquired
(B) accurate and honest representation of divergent views (i.e., in the author's own words and not out of context);	5 (G) narrate, describe, and explain with increasing specificity and detail to fulfill content-area writing needs as more English is acquired
(C) an organizing structure appropriate to the purpose, audience, and context;	5 (F) write using a variety of grade-appropriate sentence lengths, patterns, and connecting words to combine phrases, clauses, and sentences in increasingly accurate ways as more English is acquired

Eleventh-Grade ELAR TEKS	ELPS
(16)(C) cont . . .	5 (G) narrate, describe, and explain with increasing specificity and detail to fulfill content-area writing needs as more English is acquired
(D) information on the complete range of relevant perspectives;	5 (G) narrate, describe, and explain with increasing specificity and detail to fulfill content-area writing needs as more English is acquired
(E) demonstrated consideration of the validity and reliability of all primary and secondary sources used; and	1 (H) develop and expand repertoire of learning strategies such as reasoning inductively or deductively, looking for patterns in language, and analyzing sayings and expressions 5 (G) narrate, describe, and explain with increasing specificity and detail to fulfill content-area writing needs as more English is acquired
(F) language attentively crafted to move a disinterested or opposed audience, using specific rhetorical devices to back up assertions (e.g., appeals to logic, emotions, ethical beliefs).	1 (H) develop and expand repertoire of learning strategies such as reasoning inductively or deductively, looking for patterns in language, and analyzing sayings and expressions 5 (B) write using newly acquired basic vocabulary and content-based grade-level vocabulary 5 (G) narrate, describe, and explain with increasing specificity and detail to fulfill content-area writing needs as more English is acquired
(17) Oral and Written Conventions/Conventions. Students understand the function of and use the conventions of academic language when speaking and writing. Students will continue to apply earlier standards with greater complexity. Students are expected to:	
(A) use and understand the function of different types of clauses and phrases (e.g., adjectival, noun, adverbial clauses and phrases); and	1 (H) develop and expand repertoire of learning strategies such as reasoning inductively or deductively, looking for patterns in language, and analyzing sayings and expressions 5 (E) employ increasingly complex grammatical structures in content-area writing commensurate with grade-level expectations, such as: (i) using correct verbs, tenses, and pronouns / antecedents (ii) using possessive case (apostrophes) correctly (iii) using negatives and contractions correctly
(B) use a variety of correctly structured sentences (e.g., compound, complex, compound-complex).	5 (E) employ increasingly complex grammatical structures in content-area writing commensurate with grade-level expectations, such as: (i) using correct verbs, tenses, and pronouns / antecedents (ii) using possessive case (apostrophes) correctly (iii) using negatives and contractions correctly

Eleventh-Grade ELAR TEKS	ELPS
(18) Oral and Written Conventions/Handwriting, Capitalization, and Punctuation. Students write legibly and use appropriate capitalization and punctuation conventions in their compositions. Students are expected to correctly and consistently use conventions of punctuation and capitalization.	5 (C) spell familiar English words with increasing accuracy, and employ English spelling patterns and rules with increasing accuracy as more English is acquired
(19) Oral and Written Conventions/Spelling. Students spell correctly. Students are expected to spell correctly, including using various resources to determine and check correct spellings.	1 (B) monitor oral and written language production and employ self-corrective techniques or other resources 5 (C) spell familiar English words with increasing accuracy, and employ English spelling patterns and rules with increasing accuracy as more English is acquired
Oral and Written Conventions/Spelling – No Correlation	**5 (A) learn relationships between sounds and letters of the English language to represent sounds when writing in English**
(20) Research/Research Plan. Students ask open-ended research questions and develop a plan for answering them. Students are expected to:	
(A) brainstorm, consult with others, decide upon a topic, and formulate a major research question to address the major research topic; and	1 (E) internalize new, basic, and academic language by using and reusing it in meaningful ways in speaking and writing activities that build concept and language attainment 3 (F) ask and give information ranging from using a very limited bank of high-frequency, high-need, concrete vocabulary, including key words and expressions needed for basic communication in academic and social contexts, to using abstract and content-based vocabulary during extended speaking assignments 3 (G) express opinions, ideas, and feelings ranging from communicating single words and short phrases to participating in extended discussions on a variety of social and grade-appropriate academic topics
(B) formulate a plan for engaging in in-depth research on a complex, multifaceted topic.	1 (F) use accessible language and learn new and essential language in the process
(21) Research/Gathering Sources. Students determine, locate, and explore the full range of relevant sources addressing a research question and systematically record the information they gather. Students are expected to:	
(A) follow the research plan to gather evidence from experts on the topic and texts written for informed audiences in the field, distinguishing between reliable and unreliable sources and avoiding over-reliance on one source;	2 (F) listen to and derive meaning from a variety of media such as audio tape, video, DVD, and CD-ROM to build and reinforce concept and language attainment 2 (G) understand the general meaning, main points, and important details of spoken language ranging from situations in which topics, language, and contexts are familiar to unfamiliar

Eleventh-Grade ELAR TEKS	ELPS
(21)(A) cont . . .	4 (K) demonstrate English comprehension and expand reading skills by employing analytical skills such as evaluating written information and performing critical analyses commensurate with content-area and grade-level needs
(B) systematically organize relevant and accurate information to support central ideas, concepts, and themes, outline ideas into conceptual maps/timelines, and separate factual data from complex inferences; and	4 (I) demonstrate English comprehension and expand reading skills by employing basic reading skills such as demonstrating understanding of supporting ideas and details in text and graphic sources, summarizing text, and distinguishing main ideas from details commensurate with content-area needs 4 (J) demonstrate English comprehension and expand reading skills by employing inferential skills such as predicting, making connections between ideas, drawing inferences and conclusions from text and graphic sources, and finding supporting text evidence commensurate with content-area needs 5 (B) write using newly acquired basic vocabulary and content-based grade-level vocabulary 5 (G) narrate, describe, and explain with increasing specificity and detail to fulfill content-area writing needs as more English is acquired
(C) paraphrase, summarize, quote, and accurately cite all researched information according to a standard format (e.g., author, title, page number), differentiating among primary, secondary, and other sources.	4 (G) demonstrate comprehension of increasingly complex English by participating in shared reading, retelling or summarizing material, responding to questions, and taking notes commensurate with content-area and grade-level needs 4 (I) demonstrate English comprehension and expand reading skills by employing basic reading skills such as demonstrating understanding of supporting ideas and details in text and graphic sources, summarizing text, and distinguishing main ideas from details commensurate with content-area needs 4 (J) demonstrate English comprehension and expand reading skills by employing inferential skills such as predicting, making connections between ideas, drawing inferences and conclusions from text and graphic sources, and finding supporting text evidence commensurate with content-area needs 5 (G) narrate, describe, and explain with increasing specificity and detail to fulfill content-area writing needs as more English is acquired
(22) Research/Synthesizing Information. Students clarify research questions and evaluate and synthesize collected information. Students are expected to:	
(A) modify the major research question as necessary to refocus the research plan;	5 (G) narrate, describe, and explain with increasing specificity and detail to fulfill content-area writing needs as more English is acquired
(B) differentiate between theories and the evidence that supports them and determine whether the evidence found is weak or strong and how that evidence helps create a cogent argument; and	4 (K) demonstrate English comprehension and expand reading skills by employing analytical skills such as evaluating written information and performing critical analyses commensurate with content-area and grade-level needs

(22) cont . . . (C) critique the research process at each step to implement changes as the need occurs and is identified.	4 (K) demonstrate English comprehension and expand reading skills by employing analytical skills such as evaluating written information and performing critical analyses commensurate with content-area and grade-level needs
(23) Research/Organizing and Presenting Ideas. Students organize and present their ideas and information according to the purpose of the research and their audience. Students are expected to synthesize the research into an extended written or oral presentation that:	
(A) provides an analysis that supports and develops personal opinions, as opposed to simply restating existing information;	5 (G) narrate, describe, and explain with increasing specificity and detail to fulfill content-area writing needs as more English is acquired
(B) uses a variety of formats and rhetorical strategies to argue for the thesis;	5 (F) write using a variety of grade-appropriate sentence lengths, patterns, and connecting words to combine phrases, clauses, and sentences in increasingly accurate ways as more English is acquired
(C) develops an argument that incorporates the complexities of and discrepancies in information from multiple sources and perspectives while anticipating and refuting counterarguments;	4 (K) demonstrate English comprehension and expand reading skills by employing analytical skills such as evaluating written information and performing critical analyses commensurate with content-area and grade-level needs
(D) uses a style manual (e.g., Modern Language Association, Chicago Manual of Style) to document sources and format written materials; and	1 (B) monitor oral and written language production and employ self-corrective techniques or other resources
(E) is of sufficient length and complexity to address the topic.	5 (G) narrate, describe, and explain with increasing specificity and detail to fulfill content-area writing needs as more English is acquired
(24) Listening and Speaking/Listening. Students will use comprehension skills to listen attentively to others in formal and informal settings. Students will continue to apply earlier standards with greater complexity. Students are expected to:	
(A) listen responsively to a speaker by framing inquiries that reflect an understanding of the content and by identifying the positions taken and the evidence in support of those positions; and	2 (D) monitor understanding of spoken language during classroom instruction and interactions and seek clarification as needed 2 (I) demonstrate listening comprehension of increasingly complex spoken English by following directions, retelling or summarizing spoken messages, responding to questions and requests, collaborating with peers, and taking notes commensurate with content and grade-level needs 3 (F) ask and give information ranging from using a very limited bank of high-frequency, high-need, concrete vocabulary, including key words and expressions needed for basic communication in academic and social contexts, to using abstract and content-based vocabulary during extended speaking assignments

Eleventh-Grade ELAR TEKS	ELPS
(B) evaluate the clarity and coherence of a speaker's message and critique the impact of a speaker's diction and syntax on an audience.	2 (E) use visual, contextual, and linguistic support to enhance and confirm understanding of increasingly complex and elaborated spoken language 2 (G) understand the general meaning, main points, and important details of spoken language ranging from situations in which topics, language, and contexts are familiar to unfamiliar 2 (H) understand implicit ideas and information in increasingly complex spoken language commensurate with grade-level learning expectations
Listening and Speaking/Listening – No Correlation	**2 (A) distinguish sounds and intonation patterns of English with increasing ease** **2 (B) recognize elements of the English sound system in newly acquired vocabulary such as long and short vowels, silent letters, and consonant clusters**
(25) Listening and Speaking/Speaking. Students speak clearly and to the point, using the conventions of language. Students will continue to apply earlier standards with greater complexity. Students are expected to give a formal presentation that exhibits a logical structure, smooth transitions, accurate evidence, well-chosen details, and rhetorical devices, and that employs eye contact, speaking rate (e.g., pauses for effect), volume, enunciation, purposeful gestures, and conventions of language to communicate ideas effectively.	1 (D) speak using learning strategies such as requesting assistance, employing nonverbal cues, and using synonyms and circumlocution 2 (C) learn new language structures, expressions, and basic and academic vocabulary heard during classroom instruction and interactions 3 (B) expand and internalize initial English vocabulary by learning and using high-frequency English words necessary for identifying and describing people, places, and objects, by retelling simple stories and basic information represented or supported by pictures, and by learning and using routine language needed for classroom communication 3 (C) speak using a variety of grammatical structures, sentence lengths, sentence types, and connecting words with increasing accuracy and ease as more English is acquired 3 (D) speak using grade-level content-area vocabulary in context to internalize new English words and build academic language proficiency 3 (G) express opinions, ideas, and feelings ranging from communicating single words and short phrases to participating in extended discussions on a variety of social and grade-appropriate academic topics 3 (H) narrate, describe, and explain with increasing specificity and detail as more English is acquired 3 (I) adapt spoken language appropriately for formal and informal purposes 3 (J) respond orally to information presented in a wide variety of print, electronic, audio, and visual media to build and reinforce concept and language attainment
Listening and Speaking / Speaking – No Correlation	**3 (A) practice producing sounds of newly acquired vocabulary such as long and short vowels, silent letters, and consonant clusters to pronounce English words in a manner that is increasingly comprehensible**

Eleventh-Grade ELAR TEKS	ELPS
(26) *Listening and Speaking/Teamwork. Students work productively with others in teams. Students will continue to apply earlier standards with greater complexity. Students are expected to participate productively in teams, offering ideas or judgments that are purposeful in moving the team toward goals, asking relevant and insightful questions, tolerating a range of positions and ambiguity in decision making, and evaluating the work of the group based on agreed-upon criteria*	1 (B) monitor oral and written language production and employ self-corrective techniques or other resources 1 (G) demonstrate an increasing ability to distinguish between formal and informal English and an increasing knowledge of when to use each one commensurate with grade-level learning expectations 2 (I) demonstrate listening comprehension of increasingly complex spoken English by following directions, retelling or summarizing spoken messages, responding to questions and requests, collaborating with peers, and taking notes 3 (E) share information in cooperative learning interactions

This page is intentionally left blank.

ELAR TEKS and ELPS Side-by-Side
Twelfth-Grade

Twelfth-Grade ELAR TEKS	ELPS
(1) Reading/Vocabulary Development. Students understand new vocabulary and use it when reading and writing. Students are expected to:	
(A) determine the meaning of technical academic English words in multiple content-areas (e.g., science, mathematics, social studies, the arts) derived from Latin, Greek, or other linguistic roots and affixes;	4 (A) learn relationships between sounds and letters of the English language and decode (sound out) words using a combination of skills such as recognizing sound-letter relationships and identifying cognates, affixes, roots, and base words 4 (C) develop basic sight vocabulary, derive meaning of environmental print, and comprehend English vocabulary and language structures used routinely in written classroom materials
(B) analyze textual context (within a sentence and in larger sections of text) to draw conclusions about the nuance in word meanings;	4 (F) use visual and contextual support and support from peers and teachers to read grade-appropriate content-area text, to enhance and confirm understanding, to develop vocabulary, to grasp language structures, and to tap background knowledge needed to comprehend increasingly challenging language 4 (K) demonstrate English comprehension and expand reading skills by employing analytical skills such as evaluating written information and performing critical analyses commensurate with content-area and grade-level needs
(C) use the relationship between words encountered in analogies to determine their meanings (e.g., synonyms/antonyms, connotation/denotation);	1 (H) develop and expand repertoire of learning strategies such as reasoning inductively or deductively, looking for patterns in language, and analyzing sayings and expressions
(D) analyze and explain how the English language has developed and been influenced by other languages; and	1 (H) develop and expand repertoire of learning strategies such as reasoning inductively or deductively, looking for patterns in language, and analyzing sayings and expressions 4 (A) learn relationships between sounds and letters of the English language and decode (sound out) words using a combination of skills such as recognizing sound-letter relationships and identifying cognates, affixes, roots, and base words
(E) use general and specialized dictionaries, thesauri, histories of language, books of quotations, and other related references (printed or electronic) as needed.	1 (B) monitor oral and written language production and employ self-corrective techniques or other resources
(2) Reading/Comprehension of Literary Text/Theme and Genre. Students analyze, make inferences, and draw conclusions about theme and genre in different cultural, historical, and contemporary contexts and provide evidence from the text to support their understanding. Students are expected to:	

Twelfth-Grade ELAR TEKS	ELPS
(2) cont . . . (A) compare and contrast works of literature that express a universal theme;	1 (C) use strategic learning techniques such as concept mapping, drawing, memorizing, comparing, contrasting, and reviewing to acquire basic and grade-level vocabulary 4 (K) demonstrate English comprehension and expand reading skills by employing analytical skills such as evaluating written information and performing critical analyses commensurate with content-area and grade-level needs
(B) compare and contrast the similarities and differences in classical plays with their modern day novel, play, or film versions; and	1 (C) use strategic learning techniques such as concept mapping, drawing, memorizing, comparing, contrasting, and reviewing to acquire basic and grade-level vocabulary 4 (K) demonstrate English comprehension and expand reading skills by employing analytical skills such as evaluating written information and performing critical analyses commensurate with content-area and grade-level needs
(C) relate the characters, setting, and theme of a literary work to the historical, social, and economic ideas of its time.	4 (J) demonstrate English comprehension and expand reading skills by employing inferential skills such as predicting, making connections between ideas, drawing inferences and conclusions from text and graphic sources, and finding supporting text evidence commensurate with content-area needs
(3) Reading/Comprehension of Literary Text/Poetry. Students understand, make inferences, and draw conclusions about the structure and elements of poetry and provide evidence from text to support their understanding. Students are expected to evaluate the changes in sound, form, figurative language, graphics, and dramatic structure in poetry across literary time periods.	4 (E) read linguistically accommodated content-area material with a decreasing need for linguistic accommodations as more English is learned 4 (J) demonstrate English comprehension and expand reading skills by employing inferential skills such as predicting, making connections between ideas, drawing inferences and conclusions from text and graphic sources, and finding supporting text evidence commensurate with content-area needs 4 (K) demonstrate English comprehension and expand reading skills by employing analytical skills such as evaluating written information and performing critical analyses commensurate with content-area and grade-level needs
(4) Reading/Comprehension of Literary Text/Drama. Students understand, make inferences, and draw conclusions about the structure and elements of drama and provide evidence from text to support their understanding. Students are expected to evaluate how the structure and elements of drama change in the works of British dramatists across literary periods.	4 (E) read linguistically accommodated content-area material with a decreasing need for linguistic accommodations as more English is learned 4 (J) demonstrate English comprehension and expand reading skills by employing inferential skills such as predicting, making connections between ideas, drawing inferences and conclusions from text and graphic sources, and finding supporting text evidence commensurate with content-area needs 4 (K) demonstrate English comprehension and expand reading skills by employing analytical skills such as evaluating written information and performing critical analyses commensurate with content-area and grade-level needs

Twelfth-Grade ELAR TEKS	ELPS
(5) *Reading/Comprehension of Literary Text/Fiction. Students understand, make inferences, and draw conclusions about the structure and elements of fiction and provide evidence from text to support their understanding. Students are expected to:*	
(A) analyze how complex plot structures (e.g., subplots) and devices (e.g., foreshadowing, flashbacks, suspense) function and advance the action in a work of fiction;	4 (K) demonstrate English comprehension and expand reading skills by employing analytical skills such as evaluating written information and performing critical analyses commensurate with content-area and grade-level needs
(B) analyze the moral dilemmas and quandaries presented in works of fiction as revealed by the underlying motivations and behaviors of the characters;	4 (K) demonstrate English comprehension and expand reading skills by employing analytical skills such as evaluating written information and performing critical analyses commensurate with content-area and grade-level needs
(C) compare and contrast the effects of different forms of narration across various genres of fiction; and	1 (C) use strategic learning techniques such as concept mapping, drawing, memorizing, comparing, contrasting, and reviewing to acquire basic and grade-level vocabulary 4 (K) demonstrate English comprehension and expand reading skills by employing analytical skills such as evaluating written information and performing critical analyses commensurate with content-area and grade-level needs
(D) demonstrate familiarity with works of fiction by British authors from each major literary period.	*No ELPS Correlation*
(6) *Reading/Comprehension of Literary Text/Literary Nonfiction. Students understand, make inferences, and draw conclusions about the varied structural patterns and features of literary nonfiction and provide evidence from text to support their understanding. Students are expected to analyze the effect of ambiguity, contradiction, subtlety, paradox, irony, sarcasm, and overstatement in literary essays, speeches, and other forms of literary nonfiction.*	1 (H) develop and expand repertoire of learning strategies such as reasoning inductively or deductively, looking for patterns in language, and analyzing sayings and expressions 4 (E) read linguistically accommodated content-area material with a decreasing need for linguistic accommodations as more English is learned; 4 (J) demonstrate English comprehension and expand reading skills by employing inferential skills such as predicting, making connections between ideas, drawing inferences and conclusions from text and graphic sources, and finding supporting text evidence commensurate with content-area needs 4 (K) demonstrate English comprehension and expand reading skills by employing analytical skills such as evaluating written information and performing critical analyses commensurate with content-area and grade-level needs

Twelfth-Grade ELAR TEKS	ELPS
(7) *Reading/Comprehension of Literary Text/Sensory Language. Students understand, make inferences, and draw conclusions about how an author's sensory language creates imagery in literary text and provide evidence from text to support their understanding. Students are expected to analyze how the author's patterns of imagery, literary allusions, and conceits reveal theme, set tone, and create meaning in metaphors, passages, and literary works.*	4 (E) read linguistically accommodated content-area material with a decreasing need for linguistic accommodations as more English is learned 4 (J) demonstrate English comprehension and expand reading skills by employing inferential skills such as predicting, making connections between ideas, drawing inferences and conclusions from text and graphic sources, and finding supporting text evidence commensurate with content-area needs 4 (K) demonstrate English comprehension and expand reading skills by employing analytical skills such as evaluating written information and performing critical analyses commensurate with content-area and grade-level needs
(8) *Reading/Comprehension of Informational Text/Culture and History. Students analyze, make inferences, and draw conclusions about the author's purpose in cultural, historical, and contemporary contexts and provide evidence from the text to support their understanding. Students are expected to analyze the consistency and clarity of the expression of the controlling idea and the ways in which the organizational and rhetorical patterns of text support or confound the author's meaning or purpose.*	4 (E) read linguistically accommodated content-area material with a decreasing need for linguistic accommodations as more English is learned 4 (J) demonstrate English comprehension and expand reading skills by employing inferential skills such as predicting, making connections between ideas, drawing inferences and conclusions from text and graphic sources, and finding supporting text evidence commensurate with content-area needs 4 (K) demonstrate English comprehension and expand reading skills by employing analytical skills such as evaluating written information and performing critical analyses commensurate with content-area and grade-level needs
(9) *Reading/Comprehension of Informational Text/Expository Text. Students analyze, make inferences, and draw conclusions about expository text and provide evidence from text to support their understanding. Students are expected to:*	
(A) summarize a text in a manner that captures the author's viewpoint, its main ideas, and its elements without taking a position or expressing an opinion;	4 (I) demonstrate English comprehension and expand reading skills by employing basic reading skills such as demonstrating understanding of supporting ideas and details in text and graphic sources, summarizing text, and distinguishing main ideas from details commensurate with content-area needs
(B) explain how authors writing on the same issue reached different conclusions because of differences in assumptions, evidence, reasoning, and viewpoints;	1 (H) develop and expand repertoire of learning strategies such as reasoning inductively or deductively, looking for patterns in language, and analyzing sayings and expressions 4 (K) demonstrate English comprehension and expand reading skills by employing analytical skills such as evaluating written information and performing critical analyses commensurate with content-area and grade-level needs

Twelfth-Grade ELAR TEKS	ELPS
(9) cont . . . (C) make and defend subtle inferences and complex conclusions about the ideas in text and their organizational patterns; and	4 (J) demonstrate English comprehension and expand reading skills by employing inferential skills such as predicting, making connections between ideas, drawing inferences and conclusions from text and graphic sources, and finding supporting text evidence commensurate with content-area needs
(D) synthesize ideas and make logical connections (e.g., thematic links, author analysis) among multiple texts representing similar or different genres and technical sources and support those findings with textual evidence.	4 (J) demonstrate English comprehension and expand reading skills by employing inferential skills such as predicting, making connections between ideas, drawing inferences and conclusions from text and graphic sources, and finding supporting text evidence commensurate with content-area needs
(10) Reading/Comprehension of Informational Text/Persuasive Text. Students analyze, make inferences, and draw conclusions about persuasive text and provide evidence from text to support their analyses. Students are expected to:	
(A) evaluate the merits of an argument, action, or policy by analyzing the relationships (e.g., implication, necessity, sufficiency) among evidence, inferences, assumptions, and claims in text; and	4 (J) demonstrate English comprehension and expand reading skills by employing inferential skills such as predicting, making connections between ideas, drawing inferences and conclusions from text and graphic sources, and finding supporting text evidence commensurate with content-area needs 4 (K) demonstrate English comprehension and expand reading skills by employing analytical skills such as evaluating written information and performing critical analyses commensurate with content-area and grade-level needs
(B) draw conclusions about the credibility of persuasive text by examining its implicit and stated assumptions about an issue as conveyed by the specific use of language.	4 (J) demonstrate English comprehension and expand reading skills by employing inferential skills such as predicting, making connections between ideas, drawing inferences and conclusions from text and graphic sources, and finding supporting text evidence commensurate with content-area needs
(11) Reading/Comprehension of Informational Text/Procedural Texts. Students understand how to glean and use information in procedural texts and documents. Students are expected to:	
(A) draw conclusions about how the patterns of organization and hierarchic structures support the understandability of text; and	1 (H) develop and expand repertoire of learning strategies such as reasoning inductively or deductively, looking for patterns in language, and analyzing sayings and expressions 4 (J) demonstrate English comprehension and expand reading skills by employing inferential skills such as predicting, making connections between ideas, drawing inferences and conclusions from text and graphic sources, and finding supporting text evidence commensurate with content-area needs

Twelfth-Grade ELAR TEKS	ELPS
(11) cont . . . (B) evaluate the structures of text (e.g., format, headers) for their clarity and organizational coherence and for the effectiveness of their graphic representations.	4 (K) demonstrate English comprehension and expand reading skills by employing analytical skills such as evaluating written information and performing critical analyses commensurate with content-area and grade-level needs
(12) Reading/Media Literacy. Students use comprehension skills to analyze how words, images, graphics, and sounds work together in various forms to impact meaning. Students will continue to apply earlier standards with greater depth in increasingly more complex texts. Students are expected to:	
(A) evaluate how messages presented in media reflect social and cultural views in ways different from traditional texts;	4 (K) demonstrate English comprehension and expand reading skills by employing analytical skills such as evaluating written information and performing critical analyses commensurate with content-area and grade-level needs
(B) evaluate the interactions of different techniques (e.g., layout, pictures, typeface in print media, images, text, sound in electronic journalism) used in multi-layered media;	2 (F) listen to and derive meaning from a variety of media such as audio tape, video, DVD, and CD-ROM to build and reinforce concept and language attainment 4 (K) demonstrate English comprehension and expand reading skills by employing analytical skills such as evaluating written information and performing critical analyses commensurate with content-area and grade-level needs
(C) evaluate how one issue or event is represented across various media to understand the notions of bias, audience, and purpose; and	2 (F) listen to and derive meaning from a variety of media such as audio tape, video, DVD, and CD-ROM to build and reinforce concept and language attainment 4 (K) demonstrate English comprehension and expand reading skills by employing analytical skills such as evaluating written information and performing critical analyses commensurate with content-area and grade-level needs
(D) evaluate changes in formality and tone across various media for different audiences and purposes.	1 (G) demonstrate an increasing ability to distinguish between formal and informal English and an increasing knowledge of when to use each one commensurate with grade-level learning expectations 4 (K) demonstrate English comprehension and expand reading skills by employing analytical skills such as evaluating written information and performing critical analyses commensurate with content-area and grade-level needs
Reading/Media Literacy – No Correlation	**4(B) recognize directionality of English reading such as left to right and top to bottom** **4 (H) read silently with increasing ease and comprehension for longer periods**

Twelfth-Grade ELAR TEKS	ELPS
(13) *Writing/Writing Process. Students use elements of the writing process (planning, drafting, revising, editing, and publishing) to compose text. Students are expected to:*	
(A) plan a first draft by selecting the correct genre for conveying the intended meaning to multiple audiences, determining appropriate topics through a range of strategies (e.g., discussion, background reading, personal interests, interviews), and developing a thesis or controlling idea;	1 (A) use prior knowledge and experiences to understand meanings in English 3 (G) express opinions, ideas, and feelings ranging from communicating single words and short phrases to participating in extended discussions on a variety of social and grade-appropriate academic topics 5 (B) write using newly acquired basic vocabulary and content-based grade-level vocabulary
(B) structure ideas in a sustained and persuasive way (e.g., using outlines, note taking, graphic organizers, lists) and develop drafts in timed and open-ended situations that include transitions and the rhetorical devices to convey meaning;	4 (D) use prereading supports such as graphic organizers, illustrations, and pretaught topic-related vocabulary and other prereading activities to enhance comprehension of written text 4 (G) demonstrate comprehension of increasingly complex English by participating in shared reading, retelling or summarizing material, responding to questions, and taking notes commensurate with content-area and grade-level needs 5 (F) write using a variety of grade-appropriate sentence lengths, patterns, and connecting words to combine phrases, clauses, and sentences in increasingly accurate ways as more English is acquired
(C) revise drafts to clarify meaning and achieve specific rhetorical purposes, consistency of tone, and logical organization by rearranging the words, sentences, and paragraphs to employ tropes (e.g., metaphors, similes, analogies, hyperbole, understatement, rhetorical questions, irony), schemes (e.g., parallelism, antithesis, inverted word order, repetition, reversed structures), and by adding transitional words and phrases;	5 (F) write using a variety of grade-appropriate sentence lengths, patterns, and connecting words to combine phrases, clauses, and sentences in increasingly accurate ways as more English is acquired
(D) edit drafts for grammar, mechanics, and spelling; and	5 (D) edit writing for standard grammar and usage, including subject-verb agreement, pronoun agreement, and appropriate verb tenses commensurate with grade-level expectations as more English is acquired
(E) revise final draft in response to feedback from peers and teacher and publish written work for appropriate audiences.	4 (F) use visual and contextual support and support from peers and teachers to read grade-appropriate content-area text, to enhance and confirm understanding, to develop vocabulary, to grasp language structures, and to tap background knowledge needed to comprehend increasingly challenging language 5 (D) edit writing for standard grammar and usage, including subject-verb agreement, pronoun agreement, and appropriate verb tenses commensurate with grade-level expectations as more English is acquired

Twelfth-Grade ELAR TEKS	ELPS
(14) Writing/Literary Texts. Students write literary texts to express their ideas and feelings about real or imagined people, events, and ideas. Students are responsible for at least two forms of literary writing. Students are expected to:	
(A) write an engaging story with a well-developed conflict and resolution, a clear theme, complex and nonstereotypical characters, a range of literary strategies (e.g., dialogue, suspense), devices to enhance the plot, and sensory details that define the mood or tone;	5 (B) write using newly acquired basic vocabulary and content-based grade-level vocabulary 5 (F) write using a variety of grade-appropriate sentence lengths, patterns, and connecting words to combine phrases, clauses, and sentences in increasingly accurate ways as more English is acquired 5 (G) narrate, describe, and explain with increasing specificity and detail to fulfill content-area writing needs as more English is acquired
(B) write a poem that reflects an awareness of poetic conventions and traditions within different forms (e.g., sonnets, ballads, free verse); and	1 (E) internalize new, basic, and academic language by using and reusing it in meaningful ways in speaking and writing activities that build concept and language attainment 5 (B) write using newly acquired basic vocabulary and content-based grade-level vocabulary
(15) Writing/Expository and Procedural Texts. Students write expository and procedural or work-related texts to communicate ideas and information to specific audiences for specific purposes. Students are expected to:	
(A) write an analytical essay of sufficient length that includes: (i) effective introductory and concluding paragraphs and a variety of sentence structures; (ii) rhetorical devices, and transitions between paragraphs; (iii) a clear thesis statement or controlling idea; (iv) a clear organizational schema for conveying ideas; (v) relevant and substantial evidence and well-chosen details; (vi) information on all relevant perspectives and consideration of the validity, reliability, and relevance of primary and secondary sources; and (vii) an analysis of views and information that contradict the thesis statement and the evidence presented for it;	4 (K) demonstrate English comprehension and expand reading skills by employing analytical skills such as evaluating written information and performing critical analyses commensurate with content-area and grade-level needs 5 (E) employ increasingly complex grammatical structures in content-area writing commensurate with grade-level expectations, such as: (i) using correct verbs, tenses, and pronouns / antecedents (ii) using possessive case (apostrophes) correctly (iii) using negatives and contractions correctly 5 (F) write using a variety of grade-appropriate sentence lengths, patterns, and connecting words to combine phrases, clauses, and sentences in increasingly accurate ways as more English is acquired 5 (G) narrate, describe, and explain with increasing specificity and detail to fulfill content-area writing needs as more English is acquired

Twelfth-Grade ELAR TEKS	ELPS
(15) cont . . . (B) write procedural and work-related documents (e.g., résumés, proposals, college applications, operation manuals) that include: (i) a clearly stated purpose combined with a well-supported viewpoint on the topic; (ii) appropriate formatting structures (e.g., headings, graphics, white space); (iii) relevant questions that engage readers and address their potential problems and misunderstandings; (iv) accurate technical information in accessible language; and (v) appropriate organizational structures supported by facts and details (documented if appropriate);	5 (B) write using newly acquired basic vocabulary and content-based grade-level vocabulary 5 (F) write using a variety of grade-appropriate sentence lengths, patterns, and connecting words to combine phrases, clauses, and sentences in increasingly accurate ways as more English is acquired 5 (G) narrate, describe, and explain with increasing specificity and detail to fulfill content-area writing needs as more English is acquired
(C) write an interpretation of an expository or a literary text that: (i) advances a clear thesis statement; (ii) addresses the writing skills for an analytical essay including references to and commentary on quotations from the text; (iii) analyzes the aesthetic effects of an author's use of stylistic or rhetorical devices; (iv) identifies and analyzes ambiguities, nuances, and complexities within the text; and (v) anticipates and responds to readers' questions and contradictory information; and	4 (K) demonstrate English comprehension and expand reading skills by employing analytical skills such as evaluating written information and performing critical analyses commensurate with content-area and grade-level needs 5 (F) write using a variety of grade-appropriate sentence lengths, patterns, and connecting words to combine phrases, clauses, and sentences in increasingly accurate ways as more English is acquired 5 (G) narrate, describe, and explain with increasing specificity and detail to fulfill content-area writing needs as more English is acquired
(D) produce a multimedia presentation (e.g., documentary, class newspaper, docudrama, infomercial, visual or textual parodies, theatrical production) with graphics, images, and sound that appeals to a specific audience and synthesizes information from multiple points of view.	5 (F) write using a variety of grade-appropriate sentence lengths, patterns, and connecting words to combine phrases, clauses, and sentences in increasingly accurate ways as more English is acquired
(16) Writing/Persuasive Texts. Students write persuasive texts to influence the attitudes or actions of a specific audience on specific issues. Students are expected to write an argumentative essay (e.g., evaluative essays, proposals) to the appropriate audience that includes:	
(A) a clear thesis or position based on logical reasons with various forms of support (e.g., hard evidence, reason, common sense, cultural assumptions);	5 (F) write using a variety of grade-appropriate sentence lengths, patterns, and connecting words to combine phrases, clauses, and sentences in increasingly accurate ways as more English is acquired 5 (G) narrate, describe, and explain with increasing specificity and detail to fulfill content-area writing needs as more English is acquired
(B) accurate and honest representation of divergent views (i.e., in the author's own words and not out of context);	5 (G) narrate, describe, and explain with increasing specificity and detail to fulfill content-area writing needs as more English is acquired
(C) an organizing structure appropriate to the purpose, audience, and context;	5 (F) write using a variety of grade-appropriate sentence lengths, patterns, and connecting words to combine phrases, clauses, and sentences in increasingly accurate ways as more English is acquired

Twelfth-Grade ELAR TEKS	ELPS
(16)(C) cont . . .	5 (G) narrate, describe, and explain with increasing specificity and detail to fulfill content-area writing needs as more English is acquired
(D) information on the complete range of relevant perspectives;	5 (G) narrate, describe, and explain with increasing specificity and detail to fulfill content-area writing needs as more English is acquired
(E) demonstrated consideration of the validity and reliability of all primary and secondary sources used;	1 (H) develop and expand repertoire of learning strategies such as reasoning inductively or deductively, looking for patterns in language, and analyzing sayings and expressions 5 (G) narrate, describe, and explain with increasing specificity and detail to fulfill content-area writing needs as more English is acquired
(F) language attentively crafted to move a disinterested or opposed audience, using specific rhetorical devices to back up assertions (e.g., appeals to logic, emotions, ethical beliefs); and	5 (B) write using newly acquired basic vocabulary and content-based grade-level vocabulary 5 (G) narrate, describe, and explain with increasing specificity and detail to fulfill content-area writing needs as more English is acquired
(G) an awareness and anticipation of audience response that is reflected in different levels of formality, style, and tone.	1 (G) demonstrate an increasing ability to distinguish between formal and informal English and an increasing knowledge of when to use each one commensurate with grade-level learning expectations 5 (G) narrate, describe, and explain with increasing specificity and detail to fulfill content-area writing needs as more English is acquired
(17) Oral and Written Conventions/Conventions. Students understand the function of and use the conventions of academic language when speaking and writing. Students will continue to apply earlier standards with greater complexity. Students are expected to:	
(A) use and understand the function of different types of clauses and phrases (e.g., adjectival, noun, adverbial clauses and phrases); and	3 (C) speak using a variety of grammatical structures, sentence lengths, sentence types, and connecting words with increasing accuracy and ease as more English is acquired 5 (E) employ increasingly complex grammatical structures in content-area writing commensurate with grade-level expectations, such as: (i) using correct verbs, tenses, and pronouns / antecedents (ii) using possessive case (apostrophes) correctly (iii) using negatives and contractions correctly
(B) use a variety of correctly structured sentences (e.g., compound, complex, compound-complex).	3 (C) speak using a variety of grammatical structures, sentence lengths, sentence types, and connecting words with increasing accuracy and ease as more English is acquired 5 (F) write using a variety of grade-appropriate sentence lengths, patterns, and connecting words to combine phrases, clauses, and sentences in increasingly accurate ways as more English is acquired

Twelfth-Grade ELAR TEKS	ELPS
(18) Oral and Written Conventions/Handwriting, Capitalization, and Punctuation. Students write legibly and use appropriate capitalization and punctuation conventions in their compositions. Students are expected to correctly and consistently use conventions of punctuation and capitalization.	*No ELPS Correlation*
(19) Oral and Written Conventions/Spelling. Students spell correctly. Students are expected to spell correctly, including using various resources to determine and check correct spellings.	1 (B) monitor oral and written language production and employ self-corrective techniques or other resources 5 (C) spell familiar English words with increasing accuracy, and employ English spelling patterns and rules with increasing accuracy as more English is acquired
Oral and Written Conventions/Spelling – No Correlation	**5 (A) learn relationships between sounds and letters of the English language to represent sounds when writing in English**
(20) Research/Research Plan. Students ask open-ended research questions and develop a plan for answering them. Students are expected to:	
(A) brainstorm, consult with others, decide upon a topic, and formulate a major research question to address the major research topic; and	1 (E) internalize new, basic, and academic language by using and reusing it in meaningful ways in speaking and writing activities that build concept and language attainment 3 (F) ask and give information ranging from using a very limited bank of high-frequency, high-need, concrete vocabulary, including key words and expressions needed for basic communication in academic and social contexts, to using abstract and content-based vocabulary during extended speaking assignments 3 (G) express opinions, ideas, and feelings ranging from communicating single words and short phrases to participating in extended discussions on a variety of social and grade-appropriate academic topics
(B) formulate a plan for engaging in in-depth research on a complex, multifaceted topic.	1 (F) use accessible language and learn new and essential language in the process
(21) Research/Gathering Sources. Students determine, locate, and explore the full range of relevant sources addressing a research question and systematically record the information they gather. Students are expected to:	

Twelfth-Grade ELAR TEKS	ELPS
(21) cont . . . (A) follow the research plan to gather evidence from experts on the topic and texts written for informed audiences in the field, distinguishing between reliable and unreliable sources and avoiding over-reliance on one source;	2 (F) listen to and derive meaning from a variety of media such as audio tape, video, DVD, and CD-ROM to build and reinforce concept and language attainment 2 (G) understand the general meaning, main points, and important details of spoken language ranging from situations in which topics, language, and contexts are familiar to unfamiliar 4 (K) demonstrate English comprehension and expand reading skills by employing analytical skills such as evaluating written information and performing critical analyses commensurate with content-area and grade-level needs
(B) systematically organize relevant and accurate information to support central ideas, concepts, and themes, outline ideas into conceptual maps/timelines, and separate factual data from complex inferences; and	4 (I) demonstrate English comprehension and expand reading skills by employing basic reading skills such as demonstrating understanding of supporting ideas and details in text and graphic sources, summarizing text, and distinguishing main ideas from details commensurate with content-area needs 4 (J) demonstrate English comprehension and expand reading skills by employing inferential skills such as predicting, making connections between ideas, drawing inferences and conclusions from text and graphic sources, and finding supporting text evidence commensurate with content-area needs 5 (B) write using newly acquired basic vocabulary and content-based grade-level vocabulary 5 (G) narrate, describe, and explain with increasing specificity and detail to fulfill content-area writing needs as more English is acquired
(C) paraphrase, summarize, quote, and accurately cite all researched information according to a standard format (e.g., author, title, page number), differentiating among primary, secondary, and other sources.	4 (I) demonstrate English comprehension and expand reading skills by employing basic reading skills such as demonstrating understanding of supporting ideas and details in text and graphic sources, summarizing text, and distinguishing main ideas from details commensurate with content-area needs 4 (J) demonstrate English comprehension and expand reading skills by employing inferential skills such as predicting, making connections between ideas, drawing inferences and conclusions from text and graphic sources, and finding supporting text evidence commensurate with content-area needs 5 (G) narrate, describe, and explain with increasing specificity and detail to fulfill content-area writing needs as more English is acquired
(22) Research/Synthesizing Information. Students clarify research questions and evaluate and synthesize collected information. Students are expected to:	
(A) modify the major research question as necessary to refocus the research plan;	5 (G) narrate, describe, and explain with increasing specificity and detail to fulfill content-area writing needs as more English is acquired

Twelfth-Grade ELAR TEKS	ELPS
(22) cont . . . (B) differentiate between theories and the evidence that supports them and determine whether the evidence found is weak or strong and how that evidence helps create a cogent argument; and	4 (K) demonstrate English comprehension and expand reading skills by employing analytical skills such as evaluating written information and performing critical analyses commensurate with content-area and grade-level needs
(C) critique the research process at each step to implement changes as the need occurs and is identified.	4 (K) demonstrate English comprehension and expand reading skills by employing analytical skills such as evaluating written information and performing critical analyses commensurate with content-area and grade-level needs
(23) Research/Organizing and Presenting Ideas. Students organize and present their ideas and information according to the purpose of the research and their audience. Students are expected to synthesize the research into an extended written or oral presentation that:	
(A) provides an analysis that supports and develops personal opinions, as opposed to simply restating existing information;	5 (G) narrate, describe, and explain with increasing specificity and detail to fulfill content-area writing needs as more English is acquired
(B) uses a variety of formats and rhetorical strategies to argue for the thesis;	5 (F) write using a variety of grade-appropriate sentence lengths, patterns, and connecting words to combine phrases, clauses, and sentences in increasingly accurate ways as more English is acquired
(C) develops an argument that incorporates the complexities of and discrepancies in information from multiple sources and perspectives while anticipating and refuting counterarguments;	4 (K) demonstrate English comprehension and expand reading skills by employing analytical skills such as evaluating written information and performing critical analyses commensurate with content-area and grade-level needs
(D) uses a style manual (e.g., Modern Language Association, Chicago Manual of Style) to document sources and format written materials; and	1 (B) monitor oral and written language production and employ self-corrective techniques or other resources
(E) is of sufficient length and complexity to address the topic.	5 (G) narrate, describe, and explain with increasing specificity and detail to fulfill content-area writing needs as more English is acquired
(24) Listening and Speaking/Listening. Students will use comprehension skills to listen attentively to others in formal and informal settings. Students will continue to apply earlier standards with greater complexity. Students are expected to:	
(A) listen responsively to a speaker by framing inquiries that reflect an understanding of the content and by identifying the positions taken and the evidence in support of those positions; and	2 (D) monitor understanding of spoken language during classroom instruction and interactions and seek clarification as needed 2 (I) demonstrate listening comprehension of increasingly complex spoken English by following directions, retelling or summarizing spoken messages, responding to questions and requests, collaborating with peers, and taking notes commensurate with content and grade-level needs

Twelfth-Grade ELAR TEKS	ELPS
(24)(A) cont . . .	3 (F) ask and give information ranging from using a very limited bank of high-frequency, high-need, concrete vocabulary, including key words and expressions needed for basic communication in academic and social contexts, to using abstract and content-based vocabulary during extended speaking assignments
(B) assess the persuasiveness of a presentation based on content, diction, rhetorical strategies, and delivery.	2 (E) use visual, contextual, and linguistic support to enhance and confirm understanding of increasingly complex and elaborated spoken language 2 (G) understand the general meaning, main points, and important details of spoken language ranging from situations in which topics, language, and contexts are familiar to unfamiliar 2 (H) understand implicit ideas and information in increasingly complex spoken language commensurate with grade-level learning expectations
Listening and Speaking /Listening – No Correlation	**2 (A) distinguish sounds and intonation patterns of English with increasing ease**
	2 (B) recognize elements of the English sound system in newly acquired vocabulary such as long and short vowels, silent letters, and consonant clusters
(25) Listening and Speaking/Speaking. Students speak clearly and to the point, using the conventions of language. Students will continue to apply earlier standards with greater complexity. Students are expected to formulate sound arguments by using elements of classical speeches (e.g., introduction, first and second transitions, body, and conclusion), the art of persuasion, rhetorical devices, eye contact, speaking rate (e.g., pauses for effect), volume, enunciation, purposeful gestures, and conventions of language to communicate ideas effectively.	1 (D) speak using learning strategies such as requesting assistance, employing nonverbal cues, and using synonyms and circumlocution 2 (C) learn new language structures, expressions, and basic and academic vocabulary heard during classroom instruction and interactions 3 (B) expand and internalize initial English vocabulary by learning and using high-frequency English words necessary for identifying and describing people, places, and objects, by retelling simple stories and basic information represented or supported by pictures, and by learning and using routine language needed for classroom communication 3 (C) speak using a variety of grammatical structures, sentence lengths, sentence types, and connecting words with increasing accuracy and ease as more English is acquired 3 (D) speak using grade-level content-area vocabulary in context to internalize new English words and build academic language proficiency 3 (G) express opinions, ideas, and feelings ranging from communicating single words and short phrases to participating in extended discussions on a variety of social and grade-appropriate academic topics 3 (H) narrate, describe, and explain with increasing specificity and detail as more English is acquired 3 (I) adapt spoken language appropriately for formal and informal purposes 3 (J) respond orally to information presented in a wide variety of print, electronic, audio, and visual media to build and reinforce concept and language attainment

Twelfth-Grade ELAR TEKS	ELPS
Listening and Speaking/Speaking – No Correlation	3 (A) practice producing sounds of newly acquired vocabulary such as long and short vowels, silent letters, and consonant clusters to pronounce English words in a manner that is increasingly comprehensible
(26) Listening and Speaking/Teamwork. Students work productively with others in teams. Students will continue to apply earlier standards with greater complexity. Students are expected to participate productively in teams, offering ideas or judgments that are purposeful in moving the team toward goals, asking relevant and insightful questions, tolerating a range of positions and ambiguity in decision making, and evaluating the work of the group based on agreed-upon criteria.	1 (B) monitor oral and written language production and employ self-corrective techniques or other resources 1 (G) demonstrate an increasing ability to distinguish between formal and informal English and an increasing knowledge of when to use each one commensurate with grade-level learning expectations 2 (I) demonstrate listening comprehension of increasingly complex spoken English by following directions, retelling or summarizing spoken messages, responding to questions and requests, collaborating with peers, and taking notes 3 (E) share information in cooperative learning interactions

This page is intentionally left blank.

Sentence Stems and Activities Aligned to Cross-Curricular Student Expectations
(subsection c)

1(A) use prior knowledge and experiences to understand meanings in English	**Prior Knowledge** • I know . . . • I want to know . . . • This word/phrase might mean . . . • This word/phrase is like . . . • This word/phrase reminds me of . . . • I think this word probably means . . . because . . .	• Anticipation Chat • Anticipation Guides • Insert Method • KWL • List/Group/Label • Pretest with a partner • Free Write
1(B) monitor oral and written language production and employ self-corrective techniques or other resources	**Self-Corrective Techniques** • I mean . . . • Let me say that again . . . • I meant to say/write . . . • Let me rephrase that . . . • How would I be able to check . . . ?	• Accountable Conversation Stems • Oral Scaffolding • Think Alouds • Total Response Signals
1(C) use strategic learning techniques such as concept mapping, drawing, memorizing, comparing, contrasting, and reviewing to acquire basic and grade-level vocabulary	**Memorizing/Reviewing** • ___ means . . . • I know/don't know the words . . . • I'm familiar/not familiar with ___ • I will need to review . . . **Concept Map/Drawing** • The main idea/key term of my concept map/drawing is . . . • Some examples/important details are . . . • I decided to represent ___ this way because . . . **Comparing/Contrasting** • ___ is the same as ___ because they are both . . . • ___ is different from ___ because . . . • ___ is similar to ___ because . . . • ___ is different from ___ because . . . • One significant similarity is ___ because . . . • One significant difference is . . . because . . .	• Concept Map • Creating Analogies • Flash Card Review • Four Corners Vocabulary • Personal Dictionary • Scanning • Six Step Vocabulary Process • Total Response Signals • TOTAL PHYSICAL RESPONSE (TPR) • Vocabulary Game Shows • Word Play
1(D) speak using learning strategies such as requesting assistance, employing non-verbal cues, and using synonyms and circumlocution (conveying ideas by defining or describing when exact English words are not known)	**Requesting Assistance** • Can you help me . . . • I don't understand . . . • Would you please repeat/rephrase that . . . ? • Would you please say that again a little slower? • Would you please explain . . . ? **Synonyms/Circumlocution** • It's the same as . . . • It has . . . • It's similar to . . . • It includes . . . • Let me rephrase that . . .	• Accountable Conversation Stems • Expert/Novice • Instructional Scaffolding • Think, Pair, Share • Total Physical Response (TPR)
1(E) internalize new, basic, and academic language by using and reusing it in meaningful ways in speaking and writing activities that build concept and language attainment	**Concept Attainment with New Words** • I think ___ is a . . . • I think ___ is not a . . . • All ___ are . . . • All ___ have . . . • All ___ are not . . . • All ___ do not have . . . • ___ is an example of ___ because. . . • ___ is not an example of ___ because . . . • Another example might be ___ because . . . • One characteristic/attribute of ___ is . . .	• Concept Attainment • Concept Definition Map • Creating Analogies • Group Response with a White Board • Instructional Conversation • Question, Signal, Stem, Share, Assess • Think, Pair, Share • Whip Around

1(E) cont . . .	**Language Attainment with New Words** • ___ means . . . • ___ does not mean . . . • I can use the word ___ when . . . • I would not use the word ___ when . . . • I might be able to use the word ___ when ___ because . . . • I probably would not use the word ___ when ___ because . . .	
1(F) use accessible language and learn new and essential language in the process	**Using Accessible Language** • If I want ___ I need to say . . . • To find out how to say ___ I can look . . . • Will you please explain what ___ means? • I can use resources such as ___ to remember how to say . . .	• Accountable Conversation Stems • CALLA Approach • Expert/Novice • Instructional Scaffolding • Think Alouds
1(G) demonstrate an increasing ability to distinguish between formal and informal English and an increasing knowledge of when to use each one commensurate with grade-level learning expectations	**Formal and Informal English** • At school we say . . . • When we talk to the whole class we should . . . • When we talk with our friends we can . . . • Scientists/Historians/Mathematicians/Writers use the word/phrase . . . to say . . . • I would describe someone outside of school by . . . • I would describe that using scientific/social studies/mathematical/literary language by saying . . .	• Brick and Mortar Cards • Discussion Starter Cards • Formal/Informal Pairs • Radio Talk Show • Same Scene Twice • Sentence Sort
1(H) develop and expand repertoire of learning strategies such as reasoning inductively or deductively, looking for patterns in language, and analyzing sayings and expressions commensurate with grade-level learning expectations	**Deductive Reasoning** • All ___ are . . . • ___ is ___ so it must an example of . . . **Inductive Reasoning** • All the ___ we saw were/had . . . • So all ___ probably are/have . . . • Every example we observed was/had . . . • So we can infer that all ___ are/have . . . **Patterns in Language** **Analyzing Sayings/Expressions** • I think the word/expression ___ means . . . • One word/expression that was used a lot was . . . • The writer chose this word/expression because . . . • Another expression the writer could have chosen might be . . . because . . . • I noticed the writer tended to use (tense, mood, structure, etc.) . . . • One pattern I noticed was . . .	• Instructional Conversation • Literature Circles • Perspective-Based Writing • Question, Signal, Stem, and Share • Structured Conversation
2(A) distinguish sounds and intonation patterns of English with increasing ease	**Sounds and Intonation Patterns** • You said the word ___. It starts with . . . • I think that word starts with the letter (is spelled) ___ because . . . • You stressed the word ___ because . . . • You did not stress the word ___ because . . . • To change the meaning of this sentence I could stress . . . • To change the tone of this sentence, I could (change the pitch, volume, speed, etc.) . . .	• CCAP • Sound Scripting • Segmental Practice • Suprasegmental Practice

2 (B) recognize elements of the English sound system in newly acquired vocabulary such as long and short vowels, silent letters, and consonant clusters	**Sound System** • The word ___ has the long/short vowel . . . • The word ___ has a silent . . . • The word ___ has the consonant blend . . . • The letter ___ in the word ___ is long because . . . • The ___ is silent in the word ___ because . . . • The word ___ is pronounced ___ because . . .	• Word Wall based on Sounds • Word Sort • Songs/Poems/Rhymes with emphasis on Sounds • Systematic Phonics Instruction • Segmental Practice
2 (C) learn new language structures, expressions, and basic and academic vocabulary heard during classroom instruction and interactions	**Language Structures/Expressions during Interactions** • I heard the new word/phrase . . . • One new phrase I used was . . . • I heard ___ use the word/phrase . . . • A new word/phrase I heard was . . . • I can use that word/phrase when . . . • I used the word/phrase ___ when I spoke with . . . • I used the word/phrase ___ to express the idea that . . .	• Oral Scaffolding • Personal Dictionary • Scanning • Self-Assessment of Levels of Word Knowledge • Think, Pair, Share, • Vocabulary Self-Collection • Word Sorts
2(D) monitor understanding of spoken language during classroom instruction and interactions and seek clarification as needed	**Clarification during Instruction and Interaction** • Can you help me to . . . ? • I don't understand what/how. . . • Would you please repeat that? • So you're saying . . . • May I please have some more information? • May I have some time to think?	• Inside/Outside Circle • Instructional Conversation • Instructional Scaffolding • Structured Conversation • Think Alouds • Think, Pair, Share • Total Physical Response (TPR)
2(E) use visual, contextual, and linguistic support to enhance and confirm understanding of increasingly complex and elaborated spoken language	**Linguistic, Visual, Textual Support** • If I want to find out ___ I can . . . • I can use ___ to check if I . . . • When I hear ___ it tells me . . . • If I don't understand ___ I can say things like . . . • Will you please explain what ___ means? • Let me see if I understand. You said . . . • Would you please show me on the (diagram/picture/organizer/notes/etc.) . . . ?	• Graphic Organizers • Inside/Outside Circle • Instructional Conversation • Instructional Scaffolding • Nonlinguistic Representations • Posted Phrases and Stems • Structured Conversation • Think, Pair, Share
2(F) listen to and derive meaning from a variety of media such as audio tape, video, DVD, and CD-ROM to build and reinforce concept and language attainment	**Concept Attainment from a Variety of Media** • I notice . . . • I heard/saw a . . . • I heard/observed ___ which makes me think . . . • I think ___ is an example of ___ because . . . • One characteristic/attribute of ___ that I heard/observed is . . . **Language Attainment from a Variety of Media** • I heard/saw the word/phrase ___. • I think the word/ phrase means/does not mean . . . • I heard/saw the word/phrase ___. I can use it when . . . • I heard/saw the word/phrase ___. I might be able to use it when ___ because . . . • I heard/saw the word/phrase ___. I probably would not use it when ___ because . . .	• Concept Attainment • Concept Mapping • Learning Logs and Journals • Chunking Input • Visual Literacy Frames • Pairs View

2(G) understand the general meaning, main points, and important details of spoken language ranging from situations in which topics, language, and contexts are familiar to unfamiliar	**Meaning in Spoken Language** • I think ___ means . . . • You said ___ . I think it means . . . • I think ___ means ___ because . . . • I heard you say ___ . Another way to say that might be . . . **Main Point in Spoken Language** • It's about . . . • I think the main idea I heard was/is . . . • Based on the information I heard in ___ . I can conclude that the main points were . . . • (The speaker) said ____ . This supports my view that the main idea is . . . **Details in Spoken Language** • I heard (the speaker) say . . . • One thing (the speaker) said was . . . • One important thing I heard (the speaker) say was . . . • (The speaker) said ____ which is important because . . . • I heard (the speaker) say ___ which supports the idea that... One thing I heard was . . .	• Instructional Conversation • Literature Circles • IEP • Question, Signal, Stem, Share, Assess • Perspective-Based Activities • Reciprocal Teaching • Story Telling • Structured Conversation • Summarization Frames
2(H) understand implicit ideas and information in increasingly complex spoken language commensurate with grade-level learning expectations	**Implicit Ideas** • I think ___ probably . . . • I can infer ___ probably . . . • I can assume ___ because . . . • Even though it doesn't say ___ I think . . . • Based on ___ I can infer that . . . • From the information found in ___ I can infer that ___ because . . .	• Instructional Conversation • Literature Circles • Perspective-Based Activities • Question, Signal, Stem, Share, Assess • Reciprocal Teaching • Socratic Dialog • Story Telling • Structured Conversation • Summarization Frames • Whip Around
2(I) demonstrate listening comprehension of increasingly complex spoken English by following directions, retelling or summarizing spoken messages, responding to questions and requests, collaborating with peers, and taking notes commensurate with content and grade-level needs	**Following Spoken Directions** • The first step is . . . • The next steps are . . . • I know I'm finished when . . . • The initial step is . . . • The next step(s) in the process is/are . . . • I know I've completed the task successfully when . . . **Retelling/Summarizing Spoken English** • It's about . . . • The main idea is . . . • First . . . Then . . . Finally . . . • I would explain the story/concept to a friend by . . . • The general idea is . . . Some ideas I heard that support the main idea include . . . **Responding to Questions/Requests** • I heard you say ___ , so I need to . . . • You asked ___ . I think . . . • I think you're asking . . . • One answer to your question might be . . .	• Framed Oral Recap • Keep, Delete, Substitute, Select • IEPT • Instructional Conversation • Literature Circles • Note Taking Strategies • Outlines • Perspective-Based Activities • Question Answer Relationship (QAR) • Question, Signal, Stem, Share, Assess • Reader/Writer/Speaker Response Triads • Reciprocal Teaching • ReQuest • Story Telling • Structured Conversation • Summarization Frames • Tiered Questions • Tiered Response Stems

<table>
<tr><td>2(I) cont . . .</td><td>Collaborating with Peers
• Can you help me understand . . . ?
• Would you please repeat that?
• Who's responsible for . . . ?
• Who should . . . ?
• My job/part/role is to . . .
• So I should . . .
• I'm responsible for . . .

Taking Notes
• I noted . . .
• The main ideas I wrote down were . . .
• Some details I wrote down were . . .
• I can organize the ideas I wrote by . . . (making an outline, concept map, Venn diagram, chart, etc.)</td><td>• W.I.T.
• Word MES Questioning</td></tr>
<tr><td>3(A) practice producing sounds of newly acquired vocabulary such as long and short vowels, silent letters, and consonant clusters to pronounce English words in a manner that is increasingly comprehensible</td><td>Producing Sounds
• The letter(s) ___ make(s) the ___ sound.
• The word ___ begins with the letter . . .
• The word ___ has the long/short vowel . . .
• The word ___ has a silent . . .
• The word ___ has the consonant blend . . .
• The letter ___ in the word ___is long because . . .
• The ___ is silent in the word ___ because . . .
• The word ___ is pronounced ___ because . . .</td><td>• Fluency Workshop
• List Stressed Words
• Recasting
• Segmental Practice:
• Suprasegmental Practice</td></tr>
<tr><td>3(B) expand and internalize initial English vocabulary by learning and using high-frequency English words necessary for identifying and describing people, places, and objects, by retelling simple stories and basic information represented or supported by pictures, and by learning and using routine language needed for classroom communication</td><td>Description and Simple Storytelling with High-Frequency Words and Visuals
• I see . . .
• I hear . . .
• I observe . . .
• ___ has/is . . .
• The picture(s) show(s) . . .
• The first thing that happened was . . . Then . . . Finally . . .
• ___ probably also has/is . . .
• ___ could be described as___ because . . .

Routine Language for Classroom Communication
• Where is/are . . . ?
• Where do I . . . ?
• How do I . . . ?
• Can you help me . . .?
• May I please have some more information?
• May I ask someone for help?
• May I go to . . . ?
• May I sharpen my pencil?
• When is it time to . . . ?</td><td>• Accountable Conversation Stems
• Conga Line
• Expert/Novice
• Inside/Outside Circle
• Instructional Conversation
• Literature Circles
• Numbered Heads Together
• Partner Reading
• Question, Signal, Stem Share Assess
• Retelling
• Summarization Frames
• Think, Pair, Share</td></tr>
</table>

3(C) speak using a variety of grammatical structures, sentence lengths, sentence types, and connecting words with increasing accuracy and ease as more English is acquired	**Speak Using a Variety of Structures** ***Description*** • ___ is/has/looks like . . . • ___ is/has/looks like ___ because . . . • ___ tends to/seems/becomes/is able to/appears to be . . . • ___ is an example of . . . because . . . • ___ shows/is/has ___ which means . . . • ___ for example/for instance/such as . . . ***Sequence*** • ___ while/before/after . . . • First . . . second . . . finally . . . • At first . . . but now/later/subsequently . . . • Previously/initially/earlier . . . however now/later . . . ***Cause and Effect*** • ___ causes . . . • When ___ then . . . • Not only ___ but also . . . • ___ was brought about by . . . • ___ was one of the causes of ___ however . . . • ___ contributed to ___ due to . . . ***Comparison*** • ___ is the same as/is different from ___ . • ___ differs from/is similar to ___ in that . . . • Although ___ still/yet . . . • ___however/ whereas/ nevertheless . . . • ___on the other hand/on the contrary . . . ***Qualification*** • Sometimes/few/many . . . • Occasionally/often/seldom/ rarely . . . • Sometimes/often___ because . . . • Many/few___ however/due to . . . • Rarely/seldom ___ yet . . . ***Emphasis*** • ___ is important. • ___ is significant due to . . . • It's important to note . . . since . . . • ___ is especially relevant due to . . . • Above all/of course/remember ___ because . . . ***Conclusion*** • Finally/therefore . . . • As a result___ should/it is necessary to . . . • ___ proves ___ because . . .	• Canned Questions • Instructional Conversation • Experiments/Labs • Discovery Learning • Literature Circles • Numbered Heads Together • IEPT (Peer Tutoring) • Perspective-Based Activities • Question, Signal, Stem, Share, Assess • R.A.F.T. • Reader/Writer/Speaker Response Triads • Signal Words • Story Telling • Structured Conversation • Summarization Frames

3(D) speak using grade-level content-area vocabulary in context to internalize new English words and build academic language proficiency	**Speak using vocabulary in context** • This word/phrase means . . . • This word/phrase is like . . . • This word/phrase reminds me of . . . • I think this word probably means . . . because . . .	• Content Specific Stems • Creating Analogies • Instructional Conversation • Perspective-Based Activities • Self-Assessment of Levels of Word Knowledge • Structured Conversation • Question, Signal, Stem, Share, Assess • Literature Circles • Reciprocal Teaching
3(E) share information in cooperative learning interactions	**Share in Cooperative Interactions** • I feel/think/believe . . . • In my opinion . . . • I wonder. . . • I like the idea that . . . • The way I would . . . • My suggestion would be . . . because . . . • I agree/disagree that . . . because . . . • After considering ___ I think . . .	• Instructional Conversation • Perspective-Based Activities • Structured Conversation • Question, Signal, Stem, Share, Assess • Literature Circles • Peer Editing • Pairs View • Partner Reading • Interview Grids
3(F) ask and give information ranging from using a very limited bank of high-frequency, high-need, concrete vocabulary, including key words and expressions needed for basic communication in academic and social contexts, to using abstract and content-based vocabulary during extended speaking assignments	**Ask and Give Information** • What is . . . ? • ___ is . . . • What did you notice about/in . . . ? • I noticed . . . • How do you . . . • First you . . . then . . . • Why do you think ___ is important? • ___ is important because . . . • What are the characteristics/attributes of . . . ? • One of the characteristics/attributes of ___ is . . . • What do you think caused . . . ? • I think ___ caused ___ because . . . • In my opinion ___ happened due to . . .	• Instructional Conversation • Interview Grids • Literature Circles • Perspective-Based Activities • Question, Signal, Stem, Share, Assess • Structured Conversation • Think, Pair, Share
3(G) express opinions, ideas, and feelings ranging from communicating single words and short phrases to participating in extended discussions on a variety of social and grade-appropriate academic topics	**Express Opinions, Ideas, and Feelings** • How do you feel when/about . . . ? • I feel . . . • What do you think about . . . ? • I think . . . • What is your opinion about . . . ? • In my opinion . . . • My view on the matter is . . . • I agree/disagree that ___ because. . . • Why do you think . . . ? • I think ___ because . . . • Is there another . . . ? • Another ___ might be___ since . . . • What else can you tell me about . . . ? • Another . . .	• Anticipation Chat • Instructional Conversation • Literature Circles • Perspective-Based Activities • Question, Signal, Stem, Share, Assess • Reciprocal Teaching • Structured Conversation • Think, Pair, Share • W.I.T. Questioning

3(H) narrate, describe, and explain with increasing specificity and detail as more English is acquired	**Narrate, Describe, and Explain with Increasing Detail** • This is a . . . • ___ is about . . . • The main idea is . . . • It's important to remember . . . • First . . . then . . . finally . . . • Initially . . . then . . . ultimately . . . • It's significant that . . . because . . . • Some of the supporting ideas are . . . • Some of the important details include . . .	• Instructional Conversation • Literature Circles • Numbered Heads Together • Question, Signal, Stem, Share, Assess • Socratic Dialog • Story Telling • Structured Conversation • Summarization Frames
3(I) adapt spoken language appropriately for formal and informal purposes	**Formal and Informal Spoken English** • At school we say . . . • When we talk to the whole class we should . . . • When we talk with our friends we can . . . • I would explain the story/concept to a friend by . . . • Scientists/Historians/ Mathematicians/Writers use the word/phrase . . . to . . . • I would describe ___ to someone outside of school by . . . • I would describe ___ using scientific/social studies/ mathematical/literary language by . . .	• Expert/Novice • Oral Scaffolding • Radio Talk Show • Sentence Sort • Word Sorts
3(J) respond orally to information presented in a wide variety of print, electronic, audio, and visual media to build and reinforce concept and language attainment	**Concept Attainment from a Variety of Media** • I see . . . • I noticed . . . • I heard/saw a . . . • I heard/observed, which makes me think . . . • I think ___ is an example of ___ because . . . • One characteristic/attribute of ___ that I heard/observed is . . . **Language Attainment from a Variety of Media** • I see/hear . . . • I heard/saw the word/phrase ___. • I think the word/phrase means/does not mean . . . • I heard/saw the word/phrase ___. I can use it when . . . • I heard/saw the word/phrase ___. I might be able to use it when ___ because . . . • I heard/saw the word/ phrase___. I probably would not use it when ___ because . . .	• Concept Attainment • Concept Definition Map • Learning Logs and Journals • Chunking Input • Visual Literacy Frames • Pairs View

4(A) learn relationships between sounds and letters of the English language and decode (sound out) words using a combination of skills such as recognizing sound-letter relationships and identifying cognates, affixes, roots, and base words	**Decoding** • The letter(s) ___ make(s) the ___ sound . . . • The word ___ has the long/short vowel . . . • The word ___ has a silent . . . • The word ___ has the consonant blend . . . • The letter ___ in the word ___ is long because . . . • The ___ is silent in the word ___ because . . . • The word ___ is pronounced ___ because . . . **Cognates** • A cognate is . . . • The word ___ sounds like ___ in my language and means . . . • The word ___ sounds like___ in my language, but does NOT mean . . . **Affixes, Roots, and Base words** • A prefix is . . . • A suffix is . . . • An affix is . . . • A root is . . . • A base word is . . . • The word ___ has the prefix ___ which means . . . • The word ___ has the suffix ___ which means . . . • The word ___ has the root ___ which means . . . • The root ____ is probably common in (history/geography/science/math/ language arts) because . . . • This word probably means ___ because . . .	• Direct Teaching of Affixes • Direct Teaching of Cognates • Direct Teaching of Roots • Self-Assessment of Levels of Word Knowledge • Word Generation • Word Sorts • Word Study Books • Word Walls
4(B) recognize directionality of English reading such as left to right and top to bottom	**Directionality of English Text** • In English, words go . . . *(students can use gestures to indicate directionality)* • In ____ (Chinese/Arabic/Hebrew etc.) words go . . . , but in English words go . . . • In ____ (Spanish/French/Russian etc.) words go . . . , and in English words also go . . .	• Total Physical Response (TPR) • Directionality Sort
4(C) develop basic sight vocabulary, derive meaning of environmental print, and comprehend English vocabulary and language structures used routinely in written classroom materials	**Sight Vocabulary/ Environmental Print** • When I see the word/phrase ___ it means . . . *(students demonstrate actions with gesture or use simple phrases to explain classroom vocabulary)* • This sign says ___ . It tells me . . . *(students demonstrate actions with gesture or use simple phrases to explain classroom vocabulary)* • My friend's name is . . . • Our logo/mascot/team is . . .	• Expert/Novice • Oral Scaffolding • Total Physical Response (TPR)

<table>
<tr>
<td>4(D) use prereading supports such as graphic organizers, illustrations, and pretaught topic-related vocabulary and other prereading activities to enhance comprehension of written text</td>
<td>Prereading Supports
• This story/article is about . . .
• This wordlist tells me this story is about . . .
• The illustrations tell me this story is about . . .
• The diagram tells me the story is about . . .
• The organizer tells me that I should pay attention to . . .
• The organizer shows me that ___ is significant because . . .
• The strategy that will help me to understand this text the best is probably. . . (note taking, scanning, surveying key text features such as bold words illustrations and headings, using the wordlist, etc.)</td>
<td>• Advance Organizers
• Anticipation Guides
• Backwards Book Walk
• Comprehension Strategies
• DRTA
• Scanning
• SQ2PRS
• Visuals
• Word Walls</td>
</tr>
<tr>
<td>4(E) read linguistically accommodated content-area material with a decreasing need for linguistic accommodations as more English is learned</td>
<td>Use of Linguistically Accommodated Material
• ___ (native language summary, native language wordlist, picture dictionary, outline, simplified English text, sentence starters, etc.) helped me to understand/write/say . . .
• I should use ____when . . .
• I don't need to use ___ when . . .</td>
<td>• Adapted Text
• Comprehension Strategies
• Hi-Lo Readers
• Insert Method
• Margin Notes
• Native Language Texts
• Outlines and Graphic Organizers
• Related Literature
• SQ2PRS
• Stop and Think
• Taped Text</td>
</tr>
<tr>
<td>4(F) use visual and contextual support and support from peers and teachers to read grade-appropriate content-area text, to enhance and confirm understanding, to develop vocabulary, to grasp language structures, and to tap background knowledge needed to comprehend increasingly challenging language</td>
<td>Using Visual/Contextual Support to Understand Text
Reading
• The illustrations tell me this text is about . . .
• The diagram tells me the text is about . . .
• The organizer tells me that I should pay attention to . . .
• The organizer shows me that ___ is significant because . . .

Confirming understanding
• I can check if I understand what I'm reading by . . .
• The strategy that will help me to understand this text the best is probably . . . (note taking, scanning, surveying key text features such as bold words illustrations and headings, using the wordlist, etc.) because . . .</td>
<td>• Anticipation Chat
• Comprehension Strategies
• DRTA
• Graphic Organizers
• Improv Read Aloud
• Insert Method
• Nonlinguistic Representations
• Perspective-Based Activities
• QtA
• Question, Signal, Stem, Share, Assess
• Scanning
• SQ2PRS</td>
</tr>
</table>

4(F) cont . . .	***Developing Vocabulary and Background Knowledge*** • I use the word wall/wordlist while I read to . . . • When I come across an unfamiliar word or phrase, I . . . ***Grasp of Language Structures*** • When I see ___ in a text, it tells me . . . • I noticed a lot of ___ in the text. It probably means . . . • I also noticed ___ in the text. I was wondering . . . because . . . • I noticed the writer tended to use (tense, mood, structure, etc.) . . . **Using Teacher/Peer Support to Understand Text** ***Reading*** • What is the main idea of . . . ? • What should I write down about . . . ? • What should I pay attention to in . . . ? • Would you please show me on the (diagram/ picture/organizer/notes/etc.) . . . ? ***Confirming understanding*** • It seems like ___ . Is that right? • Can you help me understand . . . ? • Can I please have some more information about . . . ? • Where can I find out how to . . . ? • Can I ask someone for help with . . . ? ***Developing Vocabulary and Background*** • Will you please explain what ___ means? • Does ___ also mean . . . ? • Why does the text have . . . ? ***Grasp of Language Structures*** • One word/expression that I saw was . . . • What does the word/expression ___ mean? • Why is there a lot of ___ in the text?	
4(G) demonstrate comprehension of increasingly complex English by participating in shared reading, retelling or summarizing material, responding to questions, and taking notes commensurate with content-area and grade-level needs	**Shared Reading** • Can you help me understand . . . ? • Would you please repeat that? • Who should read . . . ? • I will read . . . • My job/part/role is to . . . • So I should . . . • I'm responsible for . . . **Retelling, Summarizing** • It's about . . . • The main idea is . . . • First . . . Then . . . Finally . . . • I would explain the story/concept to a friend by . . . • The story is about___ . What happened was . . . • The general idea is . . . Some ideas I heard that support the main idea include . . .	• Cornell Notes • Guided Notes • Instructional Conversation • Keep, Delete, Substitute • Literature Circles • Numbered Heads Together • Perspective-Based Activities • Question, Signal, Stem, Share, Assess • Reciprocal Teaching • Socratic Dialog • Story Telling • Structured Conversation Summarization Frames

4(G) cont . . .	**Responding to Questions/Requests** • I heard you say___, so I need to . . . • You asked ___ . I think . . . • I think you're asking . . . • One answer to your question might be . . . **Taking Notes/ Responding to Questions** • I noted . . . • The main ideas I wrote down were . . . • Some details I wrote down were . . . • I can organize the ideas I wrote by . . . (making an outline, concept map, Venn diagram, chart, etc.)	
4(H) read silently with increasing ease and comprehension for longer periods	**Read Silently with Increasing Comprehension** • I read about . . . • I liked/didn't like . . . • The text I read today described . . . • I would describe what I read today as . . . because . . .	• Book reviews • Dialog Journal • Double Entry Journal • Idea Bookmarks • Interactive Reading Longs • SSR Program • Structured Conversation
4(I) demonstrate English comprehension and expand reading skills by employing basic reading skills such as demonstrating understanding of supporting ideas and details in text and graphic sources, summarizing text, and distinguishing main ideas from details commensurate with content-area needs	**Supporting Ideas** • The text talked about things like . . . • The text discussed different topics, for example . . . • ___ supports the idea that . . . • ___ resulted in . . . • ___ caused/led to ___ . **Details** • This talks about things/people/events like . . . • ___ could be described as . . . • I would describe ____ as___ because . . . • Some significant features/facts about ___ include . . . **Graphic Sources** • The illustrations tell me this text is about . . . • This illustration/chart/diagram shows . . . • The illustrator showed ___ by . . . • The author(s) included a diagram/graph/chart showing ___ because . . . • This illustration/diagram/graph/chart is significant because . . . **Summarizing** • This is about . . . • The main characters/ideas are . . . • The main actions/arguments/problems discussed in the passage are . . . • In my opinion, the most significant idea/conflict in this passage is ___ because . . . • **Distinguishing Main Ideas and Details** • This text is about . . . • The main idea of this text is . . . • One detail that supports the main idea is . . . • ___ supports the idea that . . . • ___ is an example of a detail because . . . • ___ is an example of a main idea because . . .	• Comprehension Strategies • DRTA • Graphic Organizers • Learning Logs • Nonlinguistic Representation • Numbered Heads Together • Perspective-Based Activities • QtA • Question, Signal, Stem, Share, Assess • Scanning • SQ2PRS • Structured Conversation • Summarization Frames

4(J) demonstrate English comprehension and expand reading skills by employing inferential skills such as predicting, making connections between ideas, drawing inferences and conclusions from text and graphic sources, and finding supporting text evidence commensurate with content-area needs	**Predicting** • I think ___ will . . . • I predict ___ will happen next because . . . • Based on the information in the passage, it seems that ___ will probably . . . • ____ supports the idea that ___ might . . . **Making Connections Between Ideas** • ___ reminds me of . . . • ___ is similar to . . . • ___ is different from . . . • ___ relates to what happened when ___ because . . . • ___ is the result of __ because . . . **Drawing Inferences and Conclusions** • I think ___ probably . . . • I can infer ___ probably . . . • I can assume ____ because . . . • Even though it doesn't say ___ I think . . . • Based on ___ I can conclude that . . . • From the information found in ___ I can infer that ___ because . . . **Finding Supporting Text Evidence** • I think___ because . . . • ____ supports the idea that . . . • I think ___ is evidence that . . . • ___ corroborates the idea that . . . • Based on the information found in ____ I can conclude that __ because . . .	• Scanning • Comprehension Strategies • Nonlinguistic Representations • Summarization Frames • Graphic Organizers • DRTA • SQ2PRS • Question, Signal, Stem, Share, Assess • Perspective-Based Activities • Structured Conversation • Learning Logs and Journals • QtA • Prediction Café • Structured Academic Controversy
4(K) demonstrate English comprehension and expand reading skills by employing analytical skills such as evaluating written information and performing critical analyses commensurate with content-area and grade-level needs	**Evaluating Written Information** • The theme of this text is . . . • The setting/plot/conflict/genre of this text is . . . • Some characters/ideas/symbols/metaphors/similes found in this text include . . . • I would describe ___ as ___ because . . . • The author used ___ in order to . . . • The author could have used ___ in order to . . . **Performing Critical Analysis** • The author wrote this to . . . • The author used the word/phrase ___ to . . . • The intended audience of this text is . . . • The writer's motive for ___ was probably . . . • The writer tried to prove ___ by . . . • ___ is an example of bias/propaganda because . . . • The author was successful/unsuccessful because . . . • I would agree/disagree with the author that ___ because . . .	• Book Reviews • Comprehension Strategies • Dialogue Journals • Double Entry Journals • DRTA • Graphic Organizers • Instructional Conversation • Learning Logs and Journals • Nonlinguistic Representations • Perspective-Based Activities • QtA • Question, Signal, Stem, Share, Assess • Scanning • SQ2PRS • Structured Academic Controversy • Structured Conversation • Summarization Frames

5(A) learn relationships between sounds and letters of the English language to represent sounds when writing in English	**Letter/Sound Relationships in Writing** • The letter(s) ___ make(s) the ___ sound. • The word ___ has the long/short vowel . . . • The word ___ has a silent . . . • The word ___ has the consonant blend . . . • The letter ___ in the word ___ is long because . . . • The ___ is silent in the word ___ because . . . • The word ___ is pronounced ___ because . . .	• Homophone/Homograph Sort • Word Sorts • Word Study Books • Word Walls
5(B) write using newly acquired basic vocabulary and content-based grade-level vocabulary	**Write Using New Vocabulary** • I learned the word . . . • ___ means . . . • I can use the word ___ to . . . • I can use the phrase ___ in order to show . . . • The phrase ___ can be used to help the reader . . . • The word/phrase ___ would/would not be appropriate for . . . • I can ___ using the word/phrase . . .	• Choose the Words • Cloze Sentences • Dialogue Journals • Double Entry Journals • Field Notes • Letters/Editorials • Learning Logs and Journals • Read, Write, Pair, Share • Self-Assessment of Levels of Word Knowledge • Think/Pair/Share • Word Sort • Word Wall • Ticket Out
5(C) spell familiar English words with increasing accuracy, and employ English spelling patterns and rules with increasing accuracy as more English is acquired	**English Spelling Patterns and Rules** • ___ is spelled . . . • ___ begins with the letter . . . • In this set of words I notice . . . • These words are all similar because . . . • The spelling rule that applies to this word is ___ because . . . • This word is spelled correctly/incorrectly because . . . • I can check my spelling by . . .	• Homophone/Homograph Sort • Peer Editing • Personal Spelling Guide • Word Analysis • Word Sorts • Word Walls
5(D) edit writing for standard grammar and usage, including subject-verb agreement, pronoun agreement, and appropriate verb tenses commensurate with grade-level expectations as more English is acquired	**Grammar and Usage** • Pronouns agree when . . . • The subject ___ agrees/disagrees with the verb ___ because . . . • The pronoun ___ agrees/disagrees with ___ because . . . • The present/past/future/conditional tense is appropriate/inappropriate in this sentence because . . .	• Contextualized Grammar Instruction • Daily Oral Language • Oral Scaffolding • Peer Editing • Reciprocal Teaching • Sentence mark Up • Sentence Sorts • Writing Process
5(E) employ increasingly complex grammatical structures in content-area writing commensurate with grade-level expectations, such as: (i) using correct verbs, tenses, and pronouns/antecedents; (ii)using possessive case (apostrophe s) correctly; and (iii)using negatives and contractions correctly	**Using Correct Verb Tenses** • A subject of a sentence is . . . • A verb is . . . • A subject and a verb agree when . . . • A verb tense is . . . • A tense is appropriate when . . . **Using Possessive Case/Contractions Correctly** • An apostrophe is . . . • Apostrophe's are used to show . . . • A contraction is . . . • The apostrophe in this contraction is correct/ incorrect because . . . • This apostrophe correctly/incorrectly shows contraction because . . .	• Contextualized Grammar Instruction • Daily Oral Language • Oral Scaffolding • Peer Editing • Reciprocal Teaching • Sentence mark Up • Sentence Sorts

5(E) cont . . .	**Using Negatives** • The word (no/not/none) is used when . . . • An example of a sentence with (no/note/none) is . . . • Neither is used when . . . • An example of a sentence with neither is . . . • Hardly, scarcely, and barely are used to show . . . • Nothing/nowhere and nobody are used to show . . .	
5(F) write using a variety of grade-appropriate sentence lengths, patterns, and connecting words to combine phrases, clauses, and sentences in increasingly accurate ways as more English is acquired	**Writing Using a Variety of Sentence Structures** ***Cause-and-Effect*** • ___ caused/led to . . . • When ___then . . . • Not only ___ but also . . . • ___ was brought about by . . . • ___ was one of the causes of ___ however . . . • ___ contributed to ___ due to . . . ***Comparison*** • ___ is the same as/is different from ___ • ___ differs from/is similar to ___ in that . . . • Although ___ still/yet . . . • ___ however/ whereas/ nevertheless . . . • ___ on the other hand/on the contrary . . . ***Qualification*** • Sometimes/few/many . . . • Occasionally/often/seldom/rarely . . . • Sometimes/often___ because . . . • Many/few___ however/due to . . . • Rarely/seldom ___ yet . . . ***Emphasis*** • ___ is important. • ___ is significant due to . . . • It's important to note . . . since . . . • ___ is especially relevant due to . . . • Above all/of course/remember ___ because . . . ***Conclusion*** • Finally/therefore . . . • As a result___ should/it is necessary to . . . • ___ proves ___ because . . .	• Dialogue Journals • Double Entry Journals • Draw & Write • Field Notes • Free Write • Genre Analysis /Imitation • Hand Motions for Connecting Words • Letters/Editorials • Learning Logs and Journals • Perspective-Based Writing • RAFT • Read, Write, Pair, Share • Sentence Frames • Summary Frames
5(G) narrate, describe, and explain with increasing specificity and detail to fulfill content-area writing needs as more English is acquired	**Narration** • First . . . second . . . finally . . . • ___ while/before/after . . . • At first . . . but now/later/subsequently . . . • Previously/initially/ earlier . . . however now/ later . . . **Description & Explanation** • ___ is/has ___ • ___ is tends to/seems/becomes/is able to/ appears to be . . . • ___ is an example of . . . because . . . • ___ shows/is/has ___ which means . . . • ___ for example/for instance/such as . . . • ___ is a characteristic or attribute of ___	• Sentence Frames • Free Write • Learning Logs and Journals • Dialogue Journals • Book Reviews • Field Notes • Double Entry Journals • Letters Editorials • Draw & Write • Perspective-Based Writing • Unit Study for ELLs • Genre Analysis/Imitation

This page is intentionally left blank.

Language Proficiency Level Descriptors

(subsection d)

§74.4. English language Proficiency Standards

http://www.tea.state.tx.us/rules/tac/chapter074/ch074a.html

(d) Proficiency level descriptors.

(1) Listening, Kindergarten - Grade 12. ELLs may be at the beginning, intermediate, advanced, or advanced high stage of English language acquisition in listening. The following proficiency level descriptors for listening are sufficient to describe the overall English language proficiency levels of ELLs in this language domain in order to linguistically accommodate their instruction.

(A) Beginning. Beginning ELLs have little or no ability to understand spoken English in academic and social settings. These students:

(i) struggle to understand simple conversations and simple discussions even when the topics are familiar and the speaker uses linguistic supports such as visuals, slower speech and other verbal cues, and gestures;

(ii) struggle to identify and distinguish individual words and phrases during social and instructional interactions that have not been intentionally modified for ELLs; and

(iii) may not seek clarification in English when failing to comprehend the English they hear; frequently remain silent, watching others for cues.

(B) Intermediate. Intermediate ELLs have the ability to understand simple, high-frequency spoken English used in routine academic and social settings. These students:

(i) usually understand simple or routine directions, as well as short, simple conversations and short, simple discussions on familiar topics; when topics are unfamiliar, require extensive linguistic supports and adaptations such as visuals, slower speech and other verbal cues, simplified language, gestures, and preteaching to preview or build topic-related vocabulary;

(ii) often identify and distinguish key words and phrases necessary to understand the general meaning during social and basic instructional interactions that have not been intentionally modified for ELLs; and

(iii) have the ability to seek clarification in English when failing to comprehend the English they hear by requiring/requesting the speaker to repeat, slow down, or rephrase speech.

(C) Advanced. Advanced ELLs have the ability to understand, with second-language acquisition support, grade-appropriate spoken English used in academic and social settings. These students:

(i) usually understand longer, more elaborated directions, conversations, and discussions on familiar and some unfamiliar topics, but sometimes need processing time and sometimes depend on visuals, verbal cues, and gestures to support understanding;

(ii) understand most main points, most important details, and some implicit information during social and basic instructional interactions that have not been intentionally modified for ELLs; and

(iii) occasionally require/request the speaker to repeat, slow down, or rephrase to clarify the meaning of the English they hear.

(D) Advanced high. Advanced high ELLs have the ability to understand, with minimal second-language acquisition support, grade-appropriate spoken English used in academic and social settings. These students:

(i) understand longer, elaborated directions, conversations, and discussions on familiar and unfamiliar topics with occasional need for processing time and with little dependence on visuals, verbal cues, and gestures; some exceptions when complex academic or highly specialized language is used;

(ii) understand main points, important details, and implicit information at a level nearly comparable to native English-speaking peers during social and instructional interactions; and

(iii) rarely require/request the speaker to repeat, slow down, or rephrase to clarify the meaning of the English they hear.

(2) Speaking, Kindergarten-Grade 12. ELLs may be at the beginning, intermediate, advanced, or advanced high stage of English language acquisition in speaking. The following proficiency level descriptors for speaking are sufficient to describe the overall English language proficiency levels of ELLs in this language domain in order to linguistically accommodate their instruction.

(A) Beginning. Beginning ELLs have little or no ability to speak English in academic and social settings. These students:

(i) mainly speak using single words and short phrases consisting of recently practiced, memorized, or highly familiar material to get immediate needs met; may be hesitant to speak and often give up in their attempts to communicate;

(ii) speak using a very limited bank of high-frequency, high-need, concrete vocabulary, including key words and expressions needed for basic communication in academic and social contexts;

(iii) lack the knowledge of English grammar necessary to connect ideas and speak in sentences; can sometimes produce sentences using recently practiced, memorized, or highly familiar material;

(iv) exhibit second-language acquisition errors that may hinder overall communication, particularly when trying to convey information beyond memorized, practiced, or highly familiar material; and

(v) typically use pronunciation that significantly inhibits communication.

(B) Intermediate. Intermediate ELLs have the ability to speak in a simple manner using English commonly heard in routine academic and social settings. These students:

(i) are able to express simple, original messages, speak using sentences, and participate in short conversations and classroom interactions; may hesitate frequently and for long periods to think about how to communicate desired meaning;

(ii) speak simply using basic vocabulary needed in everyday social interactions and routine academic contexts; rarely have vocabulary to speak in detail;

(iii) exhibit an emerging awareness of English grammar and speak using mostly simple sentence structures and simple tenses; are most comfortable speaking in present tense;

(iv) exhibit second-language acquisition errors that may hinder overall communication when trying to use complex or less familiar English; and

(v) use pronunciation that can usually be understood by people accustomed to interacting with ELLs.

(C) Advanced. Advanced ELLs have the ability to speak using grade-appropriate English, with second-language acquisition support, in academic and social settings. These students:

(i) are able to participate comfortably in most conversations and academic discussions on familiar topics, with some pauses to restate, repeat, or search for words and phrases to clarify meaning;

(ii) discuss familiar academic topics using content-based terms and common abstract vocabulary; can usually speak in some detail on familiar topics;

(iii) have a grasp of basic grammar features, including a basic ability to narrate and describe in present, past, and future tenses; have an emerging ability to use complex sentences and complex grammar features;

(iv) make errors that interfere somewhat with communication when using complex grammar structures, long sentences, and less familiar words and expressions; and

(v) may mispronounce words, but use pronunciation that can usually be understood by people not accustomed to interacting with ELLs.

(D) Advanced high. Advanced high ELLs have the ability to speak using grade-appropriate English, with minimal second-language acquisition support, in academic and social settings. These students:

(i) are able to participate in extended discussions on a variety of social and grade-appropriate academic topics with only occasional disruptions, hesitations, or pauses;

(ii) communicate effectively using abstract and content-based vocabulary during classroom instructional tasks, with some exceptions when low-frequency or academically demanding vocabulary is needed; use many of the same idioms and colloquialisms as their native English-speaking peers;

(iii) can use English grammar structures and complex sentences to narrate and describe at a level nearly comparable to native English-speaking peers;

(iv) make few second-language acquisition errors that interfere with overall communication; and

(v) may mispronounce words, but rarely use pronunciation that interferes with overall communication.

(3) Reading, Kindergarten-Grade 1. ELLs in Kindergarten and Grade 1 may be at the beginning, intermediate, advanced, or advanced high stage of English language acquisition in reading. The following proficiency level descriptors for reading are sufficient to describe the overall English language proficiency levels of ELLs in this language domain in order to linguistically accommodate their instruction and should take into account developmental stages of emergent readers.

(A) Beginning. Beginning ELLs have little or no ability to use the English language to build foundational reading skills. These students:

(i) derive little or no meaning from grade-appropriate stories read aloud in English, unless the stories are:

(I) read in short "chunks";

(II) controlled to include the little English they know such as language that is high frequency, concrete, and recently practiced; and

(III) accompanied by ample visual supports such as illustrations, gestures, pantomime, and objects and by linguistic supports such as careful enunciation and slower speech;

(ii) begin to recognize and understand environmental print in English such as signs, labeled items, names of peers, and logos; and

(iii) have difficulty decoding most grade-appropriate English text because they:

(I) understand the meaning of very few words in English; and

(II) struggle significantly with sounds in spoken English words and with sound-symbol relationships due to differences between their primary language and English.

(B) Intermediate. Intermediate ELLs have a limited ability to use the English language to build foundational reading skills. These students:

(i) demonstrate limited comprehension (key words and general meaning) of grade-appropriate stories read aloud in English, unless the stories include:

(I) predictable story lines;

(II) highly familiar topics;

(III) primarily high-frequency, concrete vocabulary;

(IV) short, simple sentences; and

(V) visual and linguistic supports;

(ii) regularly recognize and understand common environmental print in English such as signs, labeled items, names of peers, logos; and

(iii) have difficulty decoding grade-appropriate English text because they:

(I) understand the meaning of only those English words they hear frequently; and

(II) struggle with some sounds in English words and some sound-symbol relationships due to differences between their primary language and English.

(C) Advanced. Advanced ELLs have the ability to use the English language, with second-language acquisition support, to build foundational reading skills. These students:

(i) demonstrate comprehension of most main points and most supporting ideas in grade-appropriate stories read aloud in English, although they may still depend on visual and linguistic supports to gain or confirm meaning;

(ii) recognize some basic English vocabulary and high-frequency words in isolated print; and

(iii) with second-language acquisition support, are able to decode most grade-appropriate English text because they:

(I) understand the meaning of most grade-appropriate English words; and

(II) have little difficulty with English sounds and sound-symbol relationships that result from differences between their primary language and English.

(D) Advanced high. Advanced high ELLs have the ability to use the English language, with minimal second-language acquisition support, to build foundational reading skills. These students:

(i) demonstrate, with minimal second-language acquisition support and at a level nearly comparable to native English-speaking peers, comprehension of main points and supporting ideas (explicit and implicit) in grade-appropriate stories read aloud in English;

(ii) with some exceptions, recognize sight vocabulary and high-frequency words to a degree nearly comparable to that of native English-speaking peers; and

(iii) with minimal second-language acquisition support, have an ability to decode and understand grade-appropriate English text at a level nearly comparable to native English-speaking peers.

(4) Reading, Grades 2-12. ELLs in Grades 2-12 may be at the beginning, intermediate, advanced, or advanced high stage of English language acquisition in reading. The following proficiency level descriptors for reading are sufficient to describe the overall English language proficiency levels of ELLs in this language domain in order to linguistically accommodate their instruction.

(A) Beginning. Beginning ELLs have little or no ability to read and understand English used in academic and social contexts. These students:

(i) read and understand the very limited recently practiced, memorized, or highly familiar English they have learned; vocabulary predominantly includes:

(I) environmental print;

(II) some very high-frequency words; and

(III) concrete words that can be represented by pictures;

(ii) read slowly, word by word;

(iii) have a very limited sense of English language structures;

(iv) comprehend predominantly isolated familiar words and phrases; comprehend some sentences in highly routine contexts or recently practiced, highly familiar text;

(v) are highly dependent on visuals and prior knowledge to derive meaning from text in English; and

(vi) are able to apply reading comprehension skills in English only when reading texts written for this level.

(B) Intermediate. Intermediate ELLs have the ability to read and understand simple, high-frequency English used in routine academic and social contexts. These students:

(i) read and understand English vocabulary on a somewhat wider range of topics and with increased depth; vocabulary predominantly includes:

(I) everyday oral language;

(II) literal meanings of common words;

(III) routine academic language and terms; and

(IV) commonly used abstract language such as terms used to describe basic feelings;

(ii) often read slowly and in short phrases; may re-read to clarify meaning;

(iii) have a growing understanding of basic, routinely used English language structures;

(iv) understand simple sentences in short, connected texts, but are dependent on visual cues, topic familiarity, prior knowledge, pretaught topic-related vocabulary, story predictability, and teacher/peer assistance to sustain comprehension;

(v) struggle to independently read and understand grade-level texts; and

(vi) are able to apply basic and some higher-order comprehension skills when reading texts that are linguistically accommodated and/or simplified for this level.

(C) Advanced. Advanced ELLs have the ability to read and understand, with second-language acquisition support, grade-appropriate English used in academic and social contexts. These students:

(i) read and understand, with second-language acquisition support, a variety of grade-appropriate English vocabulary used in social and academic contexts:

(I) with second-language acquisition support, read and understand grade-appropriate concrete and abstract vocabulary, but have difficulty with less commonly encountered words;

(II) demonstrate an emerging ability to understand words and phrases beyond their literal meaning; and

(III) understand multiple meanings of commonly used words;

(ii) read longer phrases and simple sentences from familiar text with appropriate rate and speed;

(iii) are developing skill in using their growing familiarity with English language structures to construct meaning of grade-appropriate text; and

(iv) are able to apply basic and higher-order comprehension skills when reading grade-appropriate text, but are still occasionally dependent on visuals, teacher/peer assistance, and other linguistically accommodated text features to determine or clarify meaning, particularly with unfamiliar topics.

(D) Advanced high. Advanced high ELLs have the ability to read and understand, with minimal second-language acquisition support, grade-appropriate English used in academic and social contexts. These students:

(i) read and understand vocabulary at a level nearly comparable to that of their native English-speaking peers, with some exceptions when low-frequency or specialized vocabulary is used;

(ii) generally read grade-appropriate, familiar text with appropriate rate, speed, intonation, and expression;

(iii) are able to, at a level nearly comparable to native English-speaking peers, use their familiarity with English language structures to construct meaning of grade-appropriate text; and

(iv) are able to apply, with minimal second-language acquisition support and at a level nearly comparable to native English-speaking peers, basic and higher-order comprehension skills when reading grade-appropriate text.

(5) Writing, Kindergarten-Grade 1. ELLs in Kindergarten and Grade 1 may be at the beginning, intermediate, advanced, or advanced high stage of English language acquisition in writing. The following proficiency level descriptors for writing are sufficient to describe the overall English language

proficiency levels of ELLs in this language domain in order to linguistically accommodate their instruction and should take into account developmental stages of emergent writers.

(A) Beginning. Beginning ELLs have little or no ability to use the English language to build foundational writing skills. These students:

(i) are unable to use English to explain self-generated writing such as stories they have created or other personal expressions, including emergent forms of writing (pictures, letter-like forms, mock words, scribbling, etc.);

(ii) know too little English to participate meaningfully in grade-appropriate shared writing activities using the English language;

(iii) cannot express themselves meaningfully in self-generated, connected written text in English beyond the level of high-frequency, concrete words, phrases, or short sentences that have been recently practiced and/or memorized; and

(iv) may demonstrate little or no awareness of English print conventions.

(B) Intermediate. Intermediate ELLs have a limited ability to use the English language to build foundational writing skills. These students:

(i) know enough English to explain briefly and simply self-generated writing, including emergent forms of writing, as long as the topic is highly familiar and concrete and requires very high-frequency English;

(ii) can participate meaningfully in grade-appropriate shared writing activities using the English language only when the writing topic is highly familiar and concrete and requires very high-frequency English;

(iii) express themselves meaningfully in self-generated, connected written text in English when their writing is limited to short sentences featuring simple, concrete English used frequently in class; and

(iv) frequently exhibit features of their primary language when writing in English such as primary language words, spelling patterns, word order, and literal translating.

(C) Advanced. Advanced ELLs have the ability to use the English language to build, with second-language acquisition support, foundational writing skills. These students:

(i) use predominantly grade-appropriate English to explain, in some detail, most self-generated writing, including emergent forms of writing;

(ii) can participate meaningfully, with second-language acquisition support, in most grade-appropriate shared writing activities using the English language;

(iii) although second-language acquisition support is needed, have an emerging ability to express themselves in self-generated, connected written text in English in a grade-appropriate manner; and

(iv) occasionally exhibit second-language acquisition errors when writing in English.

(D) Advanced high. Advanced high ELLs have the ability to use the English language to build, with minimal second-language acquisition support, foundational writing skills. These students:

(i) use English at a level of complexity and detail nearly comparable to that of native English-speaking peers when explaining self-generated writing, including emergent forms of writing;

(ii) can participate meaningfully in most grade-appropriate shared writing activities using the English language; and

(iii) although minimal second-language acquisition support may be needed, express themselves in self-generated, connected written text in English in a manner nearly comparable to their native English-speaking peers.

(6) Writing, Grades 2-12. ELLs in Grades 2-12 may be at the beginning, intermediate, advanced, or advanced high stage of English language acquisition in writing. The following proficiency level descriptors for writing are sufficient to describe the overall English language proficiency levels of ELLs in this language domain in order to linguistically accommodate their instruction.

(A) Beginning. Beginning ELLs lack the English vocabulary and grasp of English language structures necessary to address grade-appropriate writing tasks meaningfully. These students:

(i) have little or no ability to use the English language to express ideas in writing and engage meaningfully in grade-appropriate writing assignments in content-area instruction;

(ii) lack the English necessary to develop or demonstrate elements of grade-appropriate writing such as focus and coherence, conventions, organization, voice, and development of ideas in English; and

(iii) exhibit writing features typical at this level, including:

(I) ability to label, list, and copy;

(II) high-frequency words/phrases and short, simple sentences (or even short paragraphs) based primarily on recently practiced, memorized, or highly familiar material; this type of writing may be quite accurate;

(III) present tense used primarily; and

(IV) frequent primary language features (spelling patterns, word order, literal translations, and words from the student's primary language) and other errors associated with second-language acquisition may significantly hinder or prevent understanding, even for individuals accustomed to the writing of ELLs.

(B) Intermediate. Intermediate ELLs have enough English vocabulary and enough grasp of English language structures to address grade-appropriate writing tasks in a limited way. These students:

(i) have a limited ability to use the English language to express ideas in writing and engage meaningfully in grade-appropriate writing assignments in content-area instruction;

(ii) are limited in their ability to develop or demonstrate elements of grade-appropriate writing in English; communicate best when topics are highly familiar and concrete, and require simple, high-frequency English; and

(iii) exhibit writing features typical at this level, including:

(I) simple, original messages consisting of short, simple sentences; frequent inaccuracies occur when creating or taking risks beyond familiar English;

(II) high-frequency vocabulary; academic writing often has an oral tone;

(III) loosely connected text with limited use of cohesive devices or repetitive use, which may cause gaps in meaning;

(IV) repetition of ideas due to lack of vocabulary and language structures;

(V) present tense used most accurately; simple future and past tenses, if attempted, are used inconsistently or with frequent inaccuracies;

(VI) undetailed descriptions, explanations, and narrations; difficulty expressing abstract ideas;

(VII) primary language features and errors associated with second-language acquisition may be frequent; and

(VIII) some writing may be understood only by individuals accustomed to the writing of ELLs; parts of the writing may be hard to understand even for individuals accustomed to ELL writing.

(C) Advanced. Advanced ELLs have enough English vocabulary and command of English language structures to address grade-appropriate writing tasks, although second-language acquisition support is needed. These students:

(i) are able to use the English language, with second-language acquisition support, to express ideas in writing and engage meaningfully in grade-appropriate writing assignments in content-area instruction;

(ii) know enough English to be able to develop or demonstrate elements of grade-appropriate writing in English, although second-language acquisition support is particularly needed when topics are abstract, academically challenging, or unfamiliar; and

(iii) exhibit writing features typical at this level, including:

(I) grasp of basic verbs, tenses, grammar features, and sentence patterns; partial grasp of more complex verbs, tenses, grammar features, and sentence patterns;

(II) emerging grade-appropriate vocabulary; academic writing has a more academic tone;

(III) use of a variety of common cohesive devices, although some redundancy may occur;

(IV) narrations, explanations, and descriptions developed in some detail with emerging clarity; quality or quantity declines when abstract ideas are expressed, academic demands are high, or low-frequency vocabulary is required;

(V) occasional second-language acquisition errors; and

(VI) communications are usually understood by individuals not accustomed to the writing of ELLs.

(D) Advanced high. Advanced high ELLs have acquired the English vocabulary and command of English language structures necessary to address grade-appropriate writing tasks with minimal second-language acquisition support. These students:

(i) are able to use the English language, with minimal second-language acquisition support, to express ideas in writing and engage meaningfully in grade-appropriate writing assignments in content-area instruction;

(ii) know enough English to be able to develop or demonstrate, with minimal second-language acquisition support, elements of grade-appropriate writing in English; and

(iii) exhibit writing features typical at this level, including:

(I) nearly comparable to writing of native English-speaking peers in clarity and precision with regard to English vocabulary and language structures, with occasional exceptions when writing about academically complex ideas, abstract ideas, or topics requiring low-frequency vocabulary;

(II) occasional difficulty with naturalness of phrasing and expression; and

(III) errors associated with second-language acquisition are minor and usually limited to low-frequency words and structures; errors rarely interfere with communication.

(e) Effective date. The provisions of this section supersede the ESL standards specified in Chapter 128 of this title (relating to Texas Essential Knowledge and Skills for Spanish Language Arts and English as a Second-language) upon the effective date of this section.

Source: http://www.tea.state.tx.us/rules/tac/chapter074/ch074a.html

ELPS Linguistic Accommodation by Proficiency Level Self-Assessment

Rate the current level of awareness of the English Language Proficiency standards at your district or campus.

A: Always
M: Mostly
S: Sometimes
N: Never

Indicator	A	M	S	N	Comments/Questions
I am aware of the level of language proficiency of the English learners I teach.					
I am aware of specific instructional strategies to support ELLs at various levels of English language proficiency.					
I am aware of specific English language district and classroom resources that enhance comprehension for ELLs at various levels of proficiency.					
I am aware of specific native language district and classroom resources that enhance comprehension for ELLs at various levels of proficiency.					
I differentiate instruction to meet students' needs at various levels of language proficiency.					
I provide a variety of resources for English learners at various levels of proficiency.					

Summaries of ELPS Proficiency Level Descriptors*

Please refer to actual proficiency level descriptors to plan instruction.

Level	Listening *(d1: K-12)* *The student comprehends . . .*	Speaking *(d2: K-12)* *The student speaks . . .*	Reading *(d4: 2-12)* *The student reads . . .*	Writing *(d6: 2-12)* *The student writes . . .*
Beginning **(A)**	1A(i) few **simple conversations** with linguistic support 1A(ii) **modified conversation** 1A(iii) few words, **does not seek clarification,** watches others for cues	2A(i) using **single words and short phrases** with practiced material; tends to give up on attempts 2A(ii) using **limited bank of key vocabulary** 2A(iii) with **recently practiced familiar material** 2A(iv) with frequent **errors** that hinder communication 2A(v) with **pronunciation that inhibits communication**	4A(i) little except recently practiced terms, **environmental print,** high-frequency words, **concrete words represented by pictures** 4A(ii) **slowly, word by word** 4A(iii) with very limited sense of English structure 4A(iv) with comprehension of **practiced, familiar text** 4A(v) with need for **visuals and prior knowledge** 4A(vi) modified and **adapted text**	6A(i) with **little ability to use English** 6A(ii) **without focus** and coherence, conventions, organization, voice 6A(iii) labels, lists, and copies of printed text and **high-frequency words/phrases,** short and simple, practiced sentences primarily in **present tense with frequent errors** that hinder or prevent understanding
Intermediate **(B)**	1B(i) unfamiliar language with **linguistic supports** and adaptations 1B(ii) unmodified conversation with **key words** and phrases 1B(iii) with **requests for clarification** by asking speaker to repeat, slow down, or rephrase speech	2B(i) **with simple messages** and hesitation to think about meaning 2B(ii) using **basic vocabulary** 2B(iii) with **simple sentence structures** and present tense 2B(iv) with **errors** that inhibit unfamiliar communication 2B(v) with **pronunciation generally understood** by those familiar with English Language Learners	4B(i) **wider range of topics:** and everyday academic language 4B(ii) **slowly** and **rereads** 4B(iii) basic language structures 4B(iv) simple sentences **with visual cues, pretaught vocabulary** and **interaction** 4B(v) **grade-level texts** with difficulty 4B(vi) at high level with **linguistic accommodation**	6B(i) with **limited ability to use English** in content-area writing 6B(ii) best on **topics that are highly familiar** with simple English 6B(iii) with **simple oral tone in messages,** high-frequency vocabulary, loosely connected text, repetition of ideas, **mostly in the present tense,** undetailed descriptions, and **frequent errors**
Advanced ***(C)***	1C(i) with some processing time, **visuals, verbal cues, and gestures; for unfamiliar conversations** 1C(ii) most unmodified interaction 1C(iii) with occasional **requests** for the speaker to slow down, repeat, rephrase, and **clarify meaning**	2C(i) in conversations with some **pauses to restate, repeat, and clarify** 2C(ii) using **content-based and abstract terms** on familiar topics 2C(iii) with **past, present, and future** 2C(iv) using **complex sentences** and grammar with some errors 2C(v) with **pronunciation usually understood** by most	4C(i) abstract grade-appropriate text 4C(ii) **longer phrases and familiar sentences** appropriately 4C(iii) while developing the ability to construct meaning from text 4C(iv) at **high-comprehension** level with **linguistic support** for unfamiliar topics and to clarify meaning	6C(i) grade-appropriate **ideas with second-language support** 6C(ii) with extra need for second-language **support when topics are technical and abstract** 6C(iii) with a grasp of basic English usage and some understanding of complex usage with **emerging grade-appropriate vocabulary** and a more academic tone
Advanced High ***(D)***	1D(i) longer **discussions on unfamiliar topics** 1D(ii) spoken information nearly **comparable to native speaker** 1D(iii) with few requests for speaker to slow down, repeat, or rephrase	2D(i) in **extended discussions** with few pauses 2D(ii) using **abstract content-based vocabulary** except low-frequency terms; using idioms 2D(iii) with grammar **nearly comparable to native speaker** 2D(iv) with **few errors** blocking communication 2D(v) **occasional mispronunciation**	4D(i) **nearly comparable to native speakers** 4D(ii) **grade-appropriate familiar text** appropriately 4D(iii) while constructing meaning at near native ability level 4D(iv) with high-level comprehension with **minimal linguistic support**	6D(i) grade appropriate **content-area ideas with little need for** linguistic **support** 6D(ii) develop and demonstrate **grade-appropriate** writing 6D (iii) nearly **comparable to native speakers** with clarity and precision, with **occasional difficulties** with naturalness of language.

***These summaries are not appropriate to use in formally identifying student proficiency levels for TELPAS. TELPAS assessment and training materials are provided by the Texas Education Agency Student Assessment Division**: http://www.tea.state.tx.us/index3.aspx?id=3300&menu_id3=793*

Linguistic Accommodations for each Proficiency Level*

Sequence of Language Development	Communicating and Scaffolding Instruction			
	Listening *Teachers . . .*	**Speaking** *Teachers . . .*	**Reading** *Teachers . . .*	**Writing** *Teachers . . .*
Beginning Students (A)	• Allow use of same language peer and **native language support** • Expect student to struggle to understand simple conversations • Use **gestures and movement** and other linguistic support to communicate language and expectations	• Provide short **sentence stems** and single words for practice before conversations • **Allow some nonparticipation** in simple conversations • Provide **word bank** of key vocabulary • Model **pronunciation of social and academic language**	• Organize reading in **chunks** • Practice **high-frequency, concrete terms** • Use **visual and linguistic supports** • Explain classroom **environmental print** • Use adapted text	• Allow **drawing and use of native language** to express concepts • Allow student to use high-frequency recently memorized, and **short, simple, sentences** • Provide **short, simple sentence stems** with present tense and high frequency vocabulary
Intermediate (B)	• Provide **visuals, slower speech, verbal cues, simplified language** • **Preteach vocabulary** before discussions and lectures • **Teach phrases** for student to request speakers repeat, slow down, or rephrase speech	• Allow extra **processing time** • Provide **sentence stems** with simple sentence structures and tenses • Model and provide practice in **pronunciation of academic terms**	• Allow wide range of reading • Allow grade-level comprehension and **analysis of tasks** including **drawing** and use of **native language** and peer collaboration • Provide high level of **visual and linguistic supports** with adapted text and **pretaught vocabulary**	• Allow **drawing and use of native language** to express academic concepts • Allow writing on **familiar, concrete topics** • **Avoid assessment of language errors** in content-area writing • Provide simple **sentence stems and scaffolded writing assignments**
Advanced (C)	• Allow some **processing time, visuals, verbal cues, and gestures** for unfamiliar conversations • Provide opportunities for student to **request clarification,** repetition and rephrasing	• **Allow extra time** after pauses • Provide **sentence stems** with past, present, future, and **complex grammar,** and vocabulary with **content-based and abstract terms**	• Allow abstract grade-level reading comprehension and analysis with **peer support** • Provide **visual and linguistic supports** including **adapted text** for unfamiliar topics	• Provide **grade-level appropriate writing tasks** • Allow abstract and technical writing with linguistic support including teacher **modeling and student interaction** • Provide complex **sentence stems** for **scaffolded writing assignments**
Advanced High (D)	• Allow some **extra time** when academic material is complex and unfamiliar • Provide **visuals, verbal cues, and gestures** when material is complex and unfamiliar	• Opportunities for extended **discussions** • Provide **sentence stems with** past, present, future, and **complex grammar** and vocabulary with **content-based and abstract terms**	• Allow abstract grade-level reading • Provide minimal **visual and linguistic supports** • Allow grade-level comprehension and **analysis tasks** with **peer collaboration**	• Provide complex **grade-level appropriate writing tasks** • Allow abstract and technical writing with **minimal linguistic support** • Use **genre analysis** to identify and use features of advanced English writing

**Guidelines at specific proficiency levels may be beneficial for students at all levels of proficiency depending on the context of instructional delivery, materials, and students' background knowledge.*

Differentiating by Language Level
Instructional Planning Guide

Advanced/Advanced High	Intermediate	Beginners
• Visuals for academic vocabulary and concepts • Grade-level text • Complex sentence stems • Preteaching low-frequency academic vocabulary • Peer interaction • Verbal scaffolding as needed • Grade-level writing tasks • Gestures for memorization of academic concepts • Modeling • Graphic organizers • Manipulatives	• Visuals for academic vocabulary and concepts • Adapted grade-level text • Sentence stems • Preteaching academic vocabulary • Peer interaction • Verbal scaffolding • Adapted writing tasks with scaffolding • Gestures for memorization of academic concepts • Modeling • Graphic organizers • Manipulatives	• Visuals for classroom vocabulary and academic concepts • Native language and adapted grade-level text • Short, simple sentence stems • Preteaching social and academic vocabulary • Peer interaction (same language peer as needed) • Extensive verbal scaffolding • Adapted writing tasks with drawing and scaffolding • Gestures (basic and academic concepts) • Modeling • Graphic organizers • Manipulatives • Preteaching functional language (stems for social interaction) • Pronunciation of social/academic language • Slower, simplified speech • Instruction in high-frequency concrete social vocabulary • Use of native language for key concepts • Verbal cues • Chunking use of information in print • Word bank

Differentiating by Language Level
Instructional Planning Template

Grade Level/Topic: Key Vocabulary & Concepts:	Content Objective: Language Objective:	
Tasks and Accommodations for Advanced/Advanced High	Accommodation to Support Intermediate Students	Accommodations to Support Beginners

Guide to Terms and Activities

Accountable Conversation Questions:
Place the following poster in your room:

> **What to say instead of "I Don't Know"**
>
> - **May I please have some more information?**
> - **May I have some time to think?**
> - **Would you please repeat the question?**
> - **Where could I find information about that?**
> - **May I ask a friend for help?**

Model the way students can use the poster questions when they are unsure about what to say when called on by the teacher. (Seidlitz & Perryman, 2008). Explain that when they are called on for a response, they can either respond, or ask for help and then respond. Newcomer English Language Learners should not be pressured to speak in front of the class if they have not yet begun to show early production levels of speech proficiency. Students should be encouraged, but not forced to speak when in the silent period of language development (Krashen, 1982).

Academic language: Specialized vocabulary and structures tend to be more abstract, complex, and challenging and are found with high frequency in classroom oral and written discourse.

Adapted Text: Adaptations in text helps struggling students comprehend academic language. Some methods include: graphic organizers, outlines, highlighted text, taped text, margin notes, native language texts, native language glossaries, and word lists (Echevarria, Vogt & Short, 2008)

Advance Organizers: Information given to students prior to reading or instruction help them organize information they encounter during instruction (Mayer, 2003). Advance organizers should involve both activating prior knowledge and organizing new information. Examples include: graphic organizers, anticipation guides, KWL, guided notes, etc.

Anticipation Chat: Prior to instruction, a teacher facilitates a conversation between students about the content to be learned. The teacher opens the discussion by having the students make inferences about what they are going to learn based on prior knowledge, experiences and limited information about the new concepts (Zwiers, 2008).

Anticipation Guides: This is a structured series of statements given to students before instruction. Students choose to agree or disagree with the statements either individually or in groups. After instruction, students revisit the statements and discuss whether have changed their minds about the statements, based on what they have learned. (Head, M. H. & Readence, J. 1986).

Backwards Book Walk: Students scan a non-fiction text, briefly looking at headings, illustrations, captions, key words, and other text features before reading a book. After the scan, students discuss what they believe they will learn from the text. (Echevarria & Vogt, 2008)

Book Reviews: After being immersed in the book review genre, English Language Learners write short reviews which can then be published for others to read. (Samway, K., 2006)

Brick words: Brick words are content specific vocabulary. (Dutro, S., & Moran, C., 2003).

Brick and Mortar Cards: Students are given five "brick" cards with academic vocabulary (content area terms) and are instructed to organize them in a way they think makes sense. Afterward, they have to link the cards together using the language. They write the language they are using on "mortar" cards that tie the concepts together. Students may need lists of sentence terms and connecting words to facilitate the process. (Zwiers, 2008)

CALLA Approach: This is an approach to teaching English Language Learners that involves the explicit teaching of language learning strategies, academic content, and language skills with scaffolding, active engaged learning, and language use. (Chamot, A. & O'Malley, J., 1994)

CCAP (Communicative Cognitive Approach to Pronunciation): This is a five-step process for assisting English Language Learners in improving pronunciation. (Celce-Murcia, M., Brinton, D. & Goodwin. J, 1996 as cited in Flores M., 1998)

- Description and analysis of the pronunciation feature
- Listening/Discrimination activities (see segmental/supra segmental practice below).
- Controlled practice and feedback
- Guided practice and feedback
- Communicative practice

Canned Questions: Students are given a series of question stems ranging from the lowest to the highest level of Bloom's Taxonomy so that they can participate in discussions about a topic. For example:

- "What is..."
- "How do..."
- What would be a better approach to..."
- "How do you know that..." (Echevarria & Vogt, 2008)

Choose the Words: During this activity, students select words from a word wall or word list to use in a conversation or in writing.

Chunking Input: Chunking means to break up material into smaller units for easier comprehension. Visual and auditory information can be chunked so that students have time to discuss new information, pay attention to details, and create schema for organizing new information.

Cloze Sentences: Fill in the blank sentences help students process academic text. (Taylor, 1953; Gibbons, 2002)

Compare, Contrast, Analogy & Metaphor Frames: These sentence frames help students organize schema for new words (Marzano, 2001 & Hill, J. & Flynn, K. 2006)

For example:

- Compare: ___ is similar to ___ in that both....
- Contrast: ___ is different from ___ in that ...
- Analogy: ___ is to ___ as ___ is to ____
- Metaphor: I think ___ is like/is... because...

Comprehension Strategies: Strategies help proficient readers understand what they read. These strategies are used in different kinds of text, can be taught, and when they are taught, students are likely to use them. Strategies include: prediction, self-questioning, monitoring, determining importance, and summarizing. (Echevarria, Vogt, & Short, 2008; Dole, Duffy, Roehler, & Pearson, 1991; Baker, 2004)

Concept Attainment: This Jerome Bruner strategy instructs teachers to provide examples and non-examples of concepts to students. Then teachers can ask students to categorize the examples. Over time, students develop conceptual categories at increasing levels of depth and understanding. (Boulware, B.J., & Crow, M., 2008; Bruner, J., 1967)

Concept Definition Map: This visual organizer enables students to process a term. (Echevarria, Vogt, & Short, 2008.) Four questions are asked:

- What is the term?
- What is it?
- What is it like?
- What are some examples?

Concept Mapping: This is a technique for making a visual diagram of the relationship between concepts. Concept maps begin with a single concept written in a square or circle. New concepts are listed and connected with lines and shapes creating a web that shows the relationship between the ideas. (Novak, J.D., 1995)

Content Specific Stems: In this activity, incomplete sentences are directly tied to content concepts to scaffold the development of language structures that provide the opportunity for conversation and writing.

Conga Line: During this activity, students form two lines facing one another. Students in each row share ideas, review concepts, or ask one another questions. After the first discussion, one row moves and the other remains stationary so that each student now has a new partner. (Echevarria & Vogt, 2008)

Content-Specific Stems: In this activity, sentence stems using content specific vocabulary are provided to students. For example, instead of a general stem such as, "In my opinion..." a content specific stem would be, "In my opinion the Declaration of Independence is significant because..."

Contextualized Grammar Instruction: Teaching grammar in mini-lessons demonstrates specific, meaningful tasks that students will perform. The purpose of the grammar instruction is to enable students to communicate verbally or to write more effectively. (Weaver, 1996)

Cornell Notes: Students use this method of note-taking in which a paper is divided into two columns. In one large column students take traditional notes in modified outline form. In the other column, students write key vocabulary terms and questions. (Paulk, Walter, 2000).

Creating Analogies: This method is used to

generate comparisons using the frame: ____ is to ____ as ___ is to ____. (Marzano, R., Pickering, D., & Pollock, J, 2001)

Daily Oral Language: This strategy for teaching English usage involves five minute mini-lessons where students view a list of sentences with incorrect English usage. Students learn correct usage by correcting the mistakes in the sentences. (Vail, N. & Papenfuss, J., 1993).

Dialogue Journal: A dialogue journal is exchanged between the student and teacher or between two or more students. The journal focuses on academic topics, and the language used by the teacher and student should be content focused and academic. (Samway, K., 2006)

Direct Teaching of Affixes: Lessons on prefixes and suffixes build knowledge of English word structure. (White, Sowell, & Yanagihara, 1989)

Direct Teaching of Cognates: Lessons on words that sound the same in the primary language and the target language help students learn quickly. For a list of Spanish and English cognates see: http://www.colorincolorado.org/pdfs/articles/cognates.pdf . Students must be careful of false cognates, words that sound the same in the primary and target language, but do not have the same meaning. For a list of false Spanish/English cognates see: http://www.platiquemos-letstalk.com/Extras/Articles/FalseCognates/FalseCongnatesMain.htm

Direct Teaching of Word Roots: In this activity, students learn Greek and Latin roots that form the base of many words in English. A partial list of roots can be found here: https://www.msu.edu/~defores1/gre/roots/gre_rts_afx2.htm

Directionality Sort: In groups, students are given copies of texts in various languages. Each group must sort the texts based on perceived directionality. Is the text written from top to bottom then left to right? Is the text written right to left, then top to bottom? For newspapers showing letters and characters used in a variety of languages see: www.newoxxo.com

Discovery Learning: This is an inquiry-based approach to instruction in which teachers create problems and dilemmas through which students construct knowledge and representations of knowledge. Ideas, hypotheses, and explanations continue to be revised as learning takes place. (Bruner, J.S. 1967). This discovery approach has been criticized by some (Marzano, 2001; Kirschner, P. A., Sweller, J. & Clark, R. E. (2006) for teaching skills to novices who don't have adequate background and language to be able to learn new content. Teachers of English Language Learners must be careful to preteach content area functional language and set goals and objectives for the lesson when teaching English Language Learners using a discovery approach.

Discussion Starter Cards: Small cards containing sentence starters are given to students to use when beginning an academic conversation or when seeking ways to extend a conversation. For example: In my opinion..., I think..., Another possibility is ... etc. (Thornberry, 2005)

Double Entry Journals: This is a two-column journal used for reflective writing about texts. In one column, students write words, phrases, or ideas they found interesting or significant while reading. In the other column, students write the reasons they found the words significant, or they list ways they could use them in their own writing. (Samway, K, 2006)

Draw & Write: This exercise allows English Language Learners to express their knowledge of academic content while drawing and writing. Students may use their native language to express ideas but are encouraged to express new concepts using English. (Adapted from: Samway, K., 2006)

DRTA (Directed Reading-Thinking Activity): In this activity, the teacher stops regularly during reading to have students make and justify predictions. Questions might be: What do you think is going to happen? Why do you think that will happen next? Is there another possibility? What made you think that? (Echevarria, Vogt, & Short, 2008)

Experiments/Labs: This is a form of discovery learning in science where students directly encounter the scientific process: making an observation, forming a hypothesis, testing the hypothesis, and coming to a conclusion. Teachers of ELLs need to make sure to preteach necessary content and functional vocabulary to enable full participation of English Language Learners.

Expert/Novice: This is a simulation involving two students. One student takes on the role of an expert and the other a novice in a particular situation. The expert responds to questions asked by the novice. The procedure can be used for lower level cognitive activities such as having students introduce one another to classroom procedures, and higher level activities such as explaining content area concepts at greater degrees of depth. The procedure can also be used to model the difference between formal and informal English, with the expert speaking formally and the novice informally. (Seidlitz & Perrryman, 2008)

Field Notes: In this activity, students take notes and write reflections in a journals about what they are learning and experiencing. Field journals can be written or drawn and should be content focused, yet they can contain both social and academic language. (Samway, K., 2006)

Flash Card Review: To engage in this exercise, students make flash cards, preferably including images with explanations of the meanings of words. Students study, play games, and sort the flash cards in various ways.

Fluency Workshop: Students have three opportunities to talk and listen to another student about the same topic during this workshop. They alternate between listening and speaking. When listening, students may ask questions, but cannot contribute an opinion on the speaker's words. After the activity, students reflect on their level of fluency in the first and third discussion. (Maurice, K., 1983).

Formal/Informal Pairs: The teacher writes a statement on two strips of paper; one with formal English, one with informal English. The teacher distributes one strip to each student. Students have to find their match in the classroom. As an alternate activity, give pairs of strips to students. Have students match the pairs. This can be done individually or in small groups.

Four Corners Vocabulary: This is a way of processing vocabulary with a paper or note card divided into four sections: the term, a definition, a sentence, and an illustration. (Developed by D. Short, Center for Applied Linguistics. Described in: Echevarria & Vogt, 2008)

Framed Oral Recap: This is an oral review involving two students using sentence starters. Students are given stems such as: "Today I realized...," "Now I know....," and "The most significant thing I learned was ...." Students pair up with a partner to discuss what they have learned in a lesson or unit. (Adapted from Zwiers, 2008)
Free Write: During free write, students write nonstop about a topic for five to ten minutes. The goal is to keep writing, even if they can't think of ideas. They may write "I don't know what to write" if they are unable to think of new ideas during the free write. English Language Learners can sketch and write in their native language although they should be encouraged to write in English. (Elbow, P. 1998) Writing with Power, Oxford University Press, 1981, 1998.

General Stems: These are incomplete sentences that scaffold the development of language structures to provide the opportunity for conversation and writing in any academic context.

Genre Analysis/Imitation: Students read high quality selections from a genre of literature during this activity. They note particular words, phrases, and ideas they found interesting or effective and record those in a journal. Students then use their notes and observations as a resource when writing in that genre. (Adapted from Samway, K., 2006)

Glossary Circles: Based on the idea of Literature Circles (Daniels, 1994) In this activity, students work collaboratively on a set of related terms. They are given one glossary page per term, using a template that includes 4 squares labeled Vocabulary Enrichment, Illustration, Connections, and Discussion Questions. During learning, students share terms , illustrations, definitions, connections, and questions that have been added to the glossary page. (ie. study on polygons)

Graffiti Write: In small groups, students are asked to simultaneously list academic words tied to a particular concept, within a short time frame.

Graphic Organizers: Graphic organizers provide a way of developing a learner's schema by organizing information visually. Examples include the T-Chart, Venn diagram, Concept Map, Concept Web, Timeline, etc. Graphic organizers are a form of nonlinguistic representation that can help students process and retain new information. (Marzano, R., Pickering., D. & Pollock., J., 2001)

Group Response with a White Board: Students write responses to questions on white boards using dry erase markers during this activity. These can be made from card stock slipped into report covers, or with shower board cut into squares that fit on student's desks. White boards are a form of active response signal shown to be highly effective in improving achievement for struggling learners.

Guided Notes: Teacher prepared notes used as a scaffold help students practice note-taking skills during lectures. For examples of guided note formats see: http://www.studygs.net/guidednotes.htm

Hand Motions for Connecting Words: Gestures representing transition/signal words that students use to visually model the function of connecting words in a sentence. For example, students might bring their hands together for terms like: also, including, as well as, etc. For terms such as excluding, neither, without, no longer, etc., students could bring their hands together. Students can come up with their own signals for various categories including: comparing, contrasting, cause and effect, sequence, description, and emphasis. (Adapted from: Zwiers, 2008)

Hi-Lo Readers: Readers published on a variety of reading levels while having the same content focus and objectives. For example National Geographic Explorer Books can be found here: http://new.ngsp.com/Products/SocialStudies/nbspnbspNationalGeographicExplorerBooks/tabid/586/Default.aspx And http://www.kidbiz3000.com/

Homophone/Homograph Sort: The teacher prepares homophone/homograph cards, listing words that sound the same, but are spelled differently, e.g., know/no, hear/here. The teacher asks the students to group the words that sound the same together and then explain the meanings of each.

IEPT (Inter-Ethnolingusitic Peer Tutoring): This is a research based method for increasing fluency in English Language Learners by pairing them with fluent English speakers. Tasks are highly structured and fluent English speakers are trained to promote more extensive interaction with English Language Learners (Johnson. D. 1995).

Idea Bookmarks: For this activity, students take reflective notes from the books they are reading on bookmark size pieces of paper. The bookmarks include quotes, observations, and words that strike the reader as interesting or effective. The bookmarks can be divided into boxes as quotes are added with page numbers written in each box. (Davies., K, 2006)

Improv Read Aloud: During this exercise, students act out a story silently that the teacher or another student reads aloud. Each student has a role and has to discover how to act out the story while it is being read. Afterward, students discuss how each student played their part during the improv. (Zwiers, 2008)

Insert Method: In this activity, students read text with a partner and mark the texts with the following coding system: a check to show a concept or fact already known, a question mark to show a concept that is confusing, an exclamation mark to show something new or surprising, or a plus to show an idea or concept that is new. (Echevarria & Vogt, 2008)

Inside/Outside Circle: Students form two concentric circles facing one another, an inside circle and an outside circle. Students can then participate in short, guided discussion or review with their partner. After the discussion, the outside circle rotates one person to the right while the inside circle remains still. All students now have a new partner to speak with. This exercise facilitates student conversations. (Kagan, 1990)

Instructional Conversation: During this activity, students engage in conversation about literature through open- ended dialogue with the teacher or with students in small groups. Instructional conversations have few "known answer" questions and promote complex language and expression. (Goldenberg, C., 1992)

Instructional Scaffolding: This is model of teaching that helps students achieve increasing levels of independence following the pattern: teach, model, practice, and apply. (Echevarria, Vogt & Short, 2008)

Interactive Reading Logs: Reading logs are used by students during silent reading to reflect on the text. These logs can be exchanged with other students or with the teacher for questions , comments, or responses. These logs are ideal components of an SSR program.

Interview Grids: Interview grids help students record other student's responses to various questions. Students wander around the room and search for their partners who will respond to their questions. (Zwiers, 2008)

Keep, Delete, Substitute, Select: Students learn a strategy for summarizing developed by Brown, Campoine, and Day (1981) discussed in Classroom Instruction That Works (Marzano. R, Pickering D., & Pollock J., 2001) Students keep important information, delete unnecessary and redundant material, substitute general terms for specific terms (e.g. birds for robins, crows, etc.), and select or invent a topic sentence. For ELLs, Hill and Flynn (2006) recommend using gestures to represent each phase of the process and to explain the difference between high frequency and low frequency terms.

KID: Keyword, Information, Drawing In this activity, students list a word, important information about the word, and then a drawing of the word.

KIM Chart: A graphic organizer for students to organize what they are learning, have learned or for review. In the K section of the organizer students jot down key points that are being taught or that they have learned. In the I section students list important information that supports those points. And in the M section they come up with a visual representation that sums up the point and that will remind them of what was learned (Castillo ,2007)

KWL: This is a prereading strategy used to access prior knowledge and set up new learning experiences (Ogle, 1986). The teacher creates a chart where students respond to three questions: What do you know? What do you want to know? What have you learned? The first two questions are discussed prior to reading and the third is discussed afterward.

Language proficiency level: This is a measure of a student's ability to listen, speak, read, and write in English.

Learning Logs and Journals: Students can record observations and questions about what they are learning in a particular content area with learning logs or journals. The teacher can provide general or specific sentence starters to help students reflect on their learning.. (Samway, K., 2006)

Letters/Editorials: For this activity, students can write letters and editorials from their own point of view or from the point of view of a character in a novel, person from history, or a physical object (sun, atom, frog, etc.) Teachers of ELLs should remember to scaffold the writing process by providing sentence frames, graphic organizers, wordlists, and other writing supports. Newcomers may use the Draw/Write method discussed above.

Linguistic accommodations: The ways to provide access to curriculum and opportunities for language development for English Language Learners are: comprehensible input, differentiating based on language proficiency level, and scaffolding.

Literacy: To be literate, students have to have the ability to use and process printed and written material in a specific affective filter.

List Stressed Words: Students take a written paragraph and highlight words that would be stressed, focusing on stressing content English words such as nouns, verbs, adverbs over process words such as articles, prepositions, linking-verbs/modals and auxiliaries.

List/Group/Label: Students are given a list of words or students brainstorm a list of words as they engage in listing, grouping, and labeling. They sort the words on this list into similar piles and create labels for each pile. This can be done by topic (planets, stars, scientific laws, etc.) or by word type (those beginning with a particular letter, those with a particular suffix, those in a particular tense) (Taba, Hilda, 1967)

Literature Circles: In this activity students form small groups similar to "book clubs" to discuss literature. Roles include: discussion facilitators, passage pickers, illustrators, connectors, summarizers, vocabulary enrichers, travel tracers, investigators, and figurative language finders. ELLs will need to be supported with sentence starters, wordlists, and adapted text as necessary, depending on language level. (Schlick, N. & Johnson, N., 1999). For support in starting literature circles see: http://www.litcircles.org/.

Margin Notes: This is a way of adapting text. Teachers, students, or volunteers write key terms, translations of key terms, or short native language summaries, text clarifications, or hints for understanding in the margins of a text book. (Echevarria, Vogt & Short, 2008)

Native Language Texts: Native language translations, chapter summaries, wordlists, glossaries, or related literature can be used to understand texts from content area classes. Many text book companies include Spanish language resources with the adoption.

Native Language Brainstorm: This method allows students to think about and list ideas related to a concept in their native language.

Nonlinguistic Representations: Nonverbal means of representing knowledge include illustrations, graphic organizers, physical models, and kinesthetic activities (Marzano, R., Pickering, D., & Pollock, J, 2001). Hill, J and Flynn, K. (2006) advocate integrating Total Physical Response (Asher J., 1967) as a means of integrating nonlinguistic representations because it engages learners in the early stages of language development.

Note Taking Strategies: Students learn strategies for organizing information presented in lectures and in texts during note-taking. English Language Learners, at the early stages of language development, benefit from guided notes (see above), native language wordlists, summaries, and opportunities to clarify concepts with peers. Strategies include informal outlines, concept webbing, Cornell Note taking, and combination notes. Research seems to indicate that students should write more rather than less when taking notes (Marzano, R., Pickering, D., and Pollock, J., 2001). ELLs in pre-production phases can respond to teacher notes through gesture. Those in early production and speech emergent phases can communicate about information in teacher prepared notes using teacher provided sentence frames. (Hill., J. & Flynn., K, 2006)

Numbered Heads Together: This strategy enables all students, in small groups, a chance to share with the whole class over time. Each student in a group is assigned a number (1, 2, 3 and 4). When asking questions the teacher will ask all the Ones to speak first, and then open the discussion to the rest of the class. For the next question, the teacher will ask the Twos to speak, then the Threes, and finally the Fours. The teacher can also randomize which number will speak in which order. When doing numbered heads with English Language Learners, teachers should provide sentence starters for the students. (Kagan, 1995).

Oral Scaffolding: This the process of:

- teaching academic language explicitly
- modeling academic language
- providing opportunities in structured ways for students to use language orally
- writing and using the language students have seen modeled and used in the classroom. (Adapted from Gibbons, 2002)

Outlines: This traditional note-taking method involves Roman numerals, Arabic numerals, and upper/lowercase letters.

Pairs View: This strategy keeps students engaged and focused while they process viewed material at a deeper level. When watching a video clip or movie, each pair of students is assigned a role. For example, one partner might be responsible for identifying key dates while another is listing for important people and their actions. (Kagan, S., 1992). Cooperative Learning. San Juan Capistrano, CA: Kagan Cooperative Learning.)

Paragraph Frames: Incomplete paragraphs are provided for students to scaffold the development of language structures that offer the opportunity for students to develop academic writing and communication skills.

Partner Reading: This strategy for processing text requires that two students read a text. Each can alternate a paragraph while the other summarizes or one can read and the other student summarize and ask questions. (Johnson, D., 1995)

Peer Editing: During this activity, students review one another's work using a rubric. Research shows that English Language Learners benefit from peer editing when trained using peer response strategies. (Berg, C., 1999)

Personal Dictionary: To engage in this activity, students choose words from the word wall, wordlists, or words encountered in texts. Words are recorded on note cards or in notebooks which become personal dictionaries. Students are encouraged to draw, reflect, or use their native language when defining the meaning of terms. (Adapted from Echevarria, Vogt, & Short, 2008)

Personal Spelling Guide: In this activity, students record correct spellings of misspelled words on note cards. As the number of cards grows, students sort the words, based on each word's characteristics. Students should generate the categories. For example, students may develop lists like: contractions, big words, words with "ie" or "ei", words that are hard to say, words I never used. Encourage students to look for patterns in the spellings of the words as they make lists. To assess their knowledge of spelling words, students can select a number of words to review and have a partner quiz them orally their self-selected words.

Perspective-Based Writing: This activity requires students to write from an assigned point of view using specific academic language. For example, students in a social studies class could write from the perspective of Martin Luther King , Jr., to explain his participation in the Montgomery bus boycott to a fellow pastor. Students should be given specific words and phrases to integrate into the writing assignment. Students can also write from the point of view of inanimate objects such as rocks, water, molecules, etc. and describe processes from an imaginative perspective. In addition, students can take on the role of an expert within a field: math, science, social studies, or literature, and use the language of the discipline to write about a particular topic. Genre studies can be particularly helpful as a way of preparing students for perspective-based writing activities. (Seidlitz & Perryman, 2008).

Posted Phrases and Stems: Sentence frames posted in clearly visible locations in the classroom to enable students to have easy access to functional language during a task. For example, during a lab the teacher might post the stems: How do I record...., Can you help me (gather, mix, measure, identify, list...., Can you explain what you mean by ...? Frames should be posted in English but can be written in the native language as well.

Prediction Café: This activity is a way to have students participate in mini-discussions about prediction. Pick out important headings, quotes, or captions from a text (about eight quotes for a class of 24). Students discuss what they think the text is about or what they think will happen in the text. (Note: Even though some students may receive the same card, predictions will vary.) Students should be given frames to facilitate the development of academic language during the activity such as: __makes me think that.., I believe ___ because..., etc.). (Zwiers, J., 2008)

Pretest with a partner: Students are given a pretest, in pairs. Students take turns reading the questions. After each question they try to come to consensus , and then they record an answer. (Echevarria, J. & Vogt. M., 2008)

QtA (Question the Author): This is a strategy for deepening the level of thinking about literature (Beck,. I. & McKeown, M., Hamilton, R., & Kugan. L., 1997). Instead of staying within the realm of the text, the teacher prompts the students to think about the author's purpose. For example:

- What do you think the author is trying to say?
- Why do you think the author chose that word or phrase?
- Would you have chosen a different word or phrase?

Question Answer Relationship (QAR): This is a way of teaching students to analyze the nature of questions they are asked about a text. Questions are divided into four categories (Echevarria J., & Vogt M., 2008)

- Right there (found in the text)
- Think and Search (requires thinking about relationships between ideas in the text)
- Author and Me (requires making an inference about the text)
- On My Own (requires reflection on experience and knowledge)

Question, Signal, Stem, Share, Assess: This is a strategy to get students to use new academic language during student-student interactions. The teacher asks a question and then asks students to show a signal when they are ready to respond to the question, using a particular sentence stem provided by the teacher. Students share their answers. Students are then assessed orally or in writing (Seidlitz, J., & Perryman B., 2008).

Quick Write: Within a short time period, students are asked to respond in writing to a specific content concept.

Radio Talk Show: Students create a radio talk show about a particular topic. This can be a good opportunity for students to practice using academic language as they take on the role of an expert. It can also provide an opportunity for students to identify the distinctions between formal and informal use of English as they play different roles. (Wilhelm., J., 2002)

R.A.F.T.: This social studies writing strategy enables students to write from various points of view (Fisher, D. & Frey, N., 2004). The letters stand for Role (the perspective the students take, Audience (the individuals the author is addressing), Format (the type of writing that will take place), Topic (the subject).

Read, Write, Pair, Share: This strategy encourages students to share their writing and ideas during interactions. Students read a text, write their thoughts using a sentence starter, pair up with another student, and share their writing. Students can also be given suggestions about responding to one another's writing. (Fisher, D. & Frey, N., 2007).

Reader/Writer/Speaker Response Triads: This is a way of processing text in cooperative groups. Students form groups of three. One student reads the text aloud; one writes the group's reactions or responses to questions about the text, a third reports the answers to the group. After reporting to the group, the students switch roles. (Echevarria J., & Vogt M., 2007)

Recasting: For this activity, repeat an English Language Learner's incorrect statement or question correctly. Do not chang the meaning or the low risk environment Be sure the learner feels comfortable during the interaction. Recasts have been shown to have a positive impact on second language acquisition (Leeman, J., 2003).

Reciprocal Teaching: This is a student-student interaction involving collaboration to create meaning from texts (Palincsar & Brown, 1985). Hill and Flynn (2006) suggest adapting reciprocal teaching for use among English Language Learners by providing vocabulary, modeling language use, and using pictorial representation during the discussion. Reciprocal teaching involves a student leader who guides the class through stages: Summarizing, Question Generating, Clarifying, and Predicting.

Related Literature: These are texts connected to and supportive of text used in class content areas. These texts can be fiction or nonfiction, in the native language, or in the target language. (Echevarria, J., & Vogt, M., Short. D., 2008)

ReQuest: This is a variation of reciprocal teaching (see above). The teacher asks questions using particular stems following a period of SSR. After another period of SSR, the teacher provides stems for students to use when responding to text.. (Manzo, A., 1969: as cited in Fisher, D. & Frey, N., 2007)

Retelling: Students can retell a narrative text in their own words or summarize an expository text in their own words when they engage in this activity.

Same Scene Twice: Students perform a skit that involves individuals discussing a topic. The first time, the individuals are novices who use informal language to discuss the topic. The second time, they are experts who discuss the topic using correct academic terminology and academic English. (adapted from Wilhelm, J., 2002)

Scanning: Students scan through a text backwards looking for unfamiliar terms. The teacher then provides quick, brief definitions for the terms, giving only the meaning of the word as it appears in context. Marzano, Pickering, and Pollock (2001) state that "even superficial instruction on words greatly enhances the probability that students will learn the words from context when they encounter them in their reading and that, "the effects of vocabulary instruction are even more powerful when the words selected are those that students most likely will encounter when they learn new content."

Segmental Practice: Listening/Discrimination activities that help learners listen for and practice pronouncing individual combinations of syllables. There are several ways to engage in segmental practice. Tongue twisters and comparisons with native language pronunciations can help English Language Learners practice English pronunciation. The activity "syllable, storm, say" involves students brainstorming syllables that begin with a particular sound for example: pat, pen, pal, pas, pon, pen, etc. Long and short vowel sounds can be used as well as diphthongs. Students then practice in partners pronouncing the terms. (Celce-Murcia, M., Brinton. D. & Goodwin. J, 1996).

Self-Assessment of Levels of Word Knowledge: Students rank their knowledge of new words on the word wall and other word lists using total response signals (see below) or sentence starters. Responses range from no familiarity with the word to understanding a word well enough to explain it to others. (Diamond & Gutlohn, 2006: as cited in Echevarria, Vogt, Short, 2008)

Sentence frames: Incomplete sentences are provided for students to scaffold the development of language structures that provide the opportunity for students to develop academic language.

Sentence Mark Up: Students use colored pencils to mark texts for cause and effect, opposing thoughts, connecting words, and other features of sentences. This helps students understand the relationship between clauses. (Zwiers, J., 2008)

Sentence Sort: This activity requires students to sort various sentences based on characteristics. The teacher provides the sentences and students sort them. This can be done with an open sort where students create the categories or a closed sort where the teacher creates the categories. It can also be done by taking a paragraph from a textbook or from class literature. Possible categories include:

- Description sentences
- Complex sentences
- Simple sentences
- Sentences connecting ideas
- Sentences comparing ideas
- Sentences opposing ideas
- Sentences with correct usage
- Sentences with incorrect usage
- Sentences in formal English
- Sentences in informal English

Sentence Stems: Incomplete sentences are provided for students to scaffold the development of specific language structures and to facilitate entry into conversation and writing. For example "In my opinion..." or "One characteristic of annelids is...

Signal Words: Signal words determine a text pattern such as generalization, cause and effect, process, sequence, etc. A sample of signal words can be found at:
www.nifl.gov/readingprofiles/Signal_Words.pdf

Six Step Vocabulary Process: This research based process, developed by Marzano (2004) helps teachers employ methods develop academic vocabulary. The steps are: Teacher provides a description. Students restate the explanation in their own words. Students create a nonlinguistic representation of the term. Students periodically do activities that help them add to their knowledge of vocabulary terms. Periodically students are asked to discuss the terms with each other. Periodically, students are involved in games that allow them to "play" with the terms.

Sound Scripting: This is a way for students to mark text showing pauses and stress. Students use a writing program to write a paragraph, enter a paragraph break to show pauses, and use capital and bold letters to show word stress. (Powell, M., 1996)

SQP2RS (Squeepers): This classroom reading strategy trains students to use cognitive/metacognitive strategies to process nonfiction text. The following steps are involved (Echevarria, Vogt, Short, 2008):

- Survey: students scan the visuals, headings, and other text features.
- Question: students write a list of questions they might find answers to while reading
- Predict: student write predictions about what they will learn
- Read: students read the text
- Respond: students revisit their questions and think through responses to reading

SSR Program (Sustained, Silent Reading): This program encourages students to read books of their choice during a silent reading period of 15-20 minutes per day. Pilgreen (2000) discusses eight features of high quality SSR programs: access to books, book appeal, conducive reading environment, encouragement to read, non-accountability, distributed reading time, staff training, and follow up activities. (Pilgreen, 2000).

Story Telling: In this activity, students retell narratives in their native language.

Structured Academic Controversy: This is a way of structuring classroom discussion to promote deep thinking and to understand multiple perspectives. Johnson & Johnson (1995) outline five steps.

- Organizing Information And Deriving Conclusions
- Presenting And Advocating Positions
- Uncertainty Created By Being Challenged By Opposing Views
- Epistemic Curiosity And Perspective Taking
- Reconceptualizing, Synthesizing, and Integrating

Structured Conversation: In this activity, student/student interaction is explicitly planned. Students are given sentence frames to begin the conversation as well as specific questions and sentence starters for the purpose of elaboration.

Summarization Frames: This is a way of structuring summaries of content area text. The frames involve specific questions that help students summarize different kinds of texts. Marzano (2001 p. 27-42) and Flynn & Hill (2006) discuss seven frames:

- narrative frame
- topic restriction frame
- illustration frame
- definition frame;
- argumentation frame;
- problem solution frame
- conversation frame

Suprasegmental Practice: This pronunciation practice involves units and groups of syllables. Some techniques include: sound scripting (see above), recasting (see above), a pronunciation portfolio, and content/function word comparisons. (Wennerstrom, A., 1993).

Systematic Phonics Instruction: This activity teaches sound-spelling relationships and how to use those relationships when reading. The national literacy panel (Francis, D.J., Lesaux, N.K., & August, D.L., 2006) reported that instruction in phonemic awareness, phonics, and fluency had "clear benefits for language minority students."

Taped Text: Recordings of text can be used as a way of adapting text for English Language Learners. (Echevarria, Vogt, & Short, 2008)

Think Alouds: Thinking aloud allows teachers to scaffold cognitive and metacognitive thinking by verbalizing the thought process. (Bauman, Jones, & Seifert-Kessell, 1993)

Think, Pair, Share: This method encourages student-student interaction. The teacher asks a question and then provides wait time. The students then find a partner and compare their answers. Afterward, selected students share their thoughts with the whole class. (Lyman, 1981)

Ticket Out: For this activity, students write a short reflection at the end of a lesson. Teachers can ask students to reflect on what they have learned. As students write they can use new vocabulary learned during the lesson.

Tiered Questions: In this activity, a varying types of questions to students, based on their level of language development. (Hill & Flynn, 2006)

Tiered Response Stems: this activity, ask a single question, but allow students to choose from a variety of stems to construct responses. Students can choose a stem based on their level of language knowledge and proficiency. (Seidlitz & Perryman, 2008)

Total Physical Response (TPR): This is a way of teaching that uses gesture and movement to make content comprehensible to ESL newcomers. (Asher, J., 1967)

Total Response Signals (Also called active response signals): Active responses such as thumbs up/down, white boards, and response cards can be used by students. Response signals enable teachers to check for understanding instantly, and students can self-assess current levels of understanding.

Unit Study for ELLs: This is a modified approach to writers workshop advocated by Samway (2006). The steps involve:

- Teachers gather high quality samples of the genre
- Teachers provide time for immersion in books
- Sifting between books that students can model and those that they can't
- Students immerse themselves a second time in the books
- Students try the "writing moves" used by accomplished writers
- Students write and publish
- Students reflect and assess

Visual Literacy Frames: This is a framework for improving visual literacy focusing on affective, compositional, and critical dimensions of visual information processing.
(Callow, J., 2008).

Visuals: Illustrations, graphic organizers, manipulatives, models, and real world objects are used to make content comprehensible for English Language Learners.

Vocabulary Game Shows: Using games like Jeopardy, Pictionary, and Who Wants to be a Millionaire etc., allows students a chance to practice academic vocabulary.

Vocabulary Self-Collection: This ia a research-based method of vocabulary instruction involving student collection of words for class study. Students share where the word was found, the definition, and why the class should study that particular word.
(Ruddell, M., & Shearer, B., 2002)

W.I.T. Questioning: This is a questioning strategy that trains students to use three stems to promote elaboration in discussion (Seiditz & Perryman, 2008):

- Why do you think...?
- Is there another...?
- Tell me more about...

Whip Around: This is a way of getting input from all students during a class discussion. The teacher asks students to write a bulleted list in response to an open- ended question. Students write their responses to the question and then stand up. The teacher then calls on students, one at a time, to respond to the question. If students have the same answer they mark it off on their papers. The teacher continues to call on students, and students continue to mark their answers. When all their answers have been marked, the students sit down. The activity continues until all students are seated. (Fisher, D. & Frey, N., 2007)

Word Analysis: In this activity, students study the parts, origins, and structures of words for the purpose of improving spelling (Harrington, 1996).

Word Generation: In this activity, students brainstorm words having particular roots. Teachers then have students predict the meaning of the word based on the roots. (Echevarria, Vogt & Short, 2008)

Word MES Questioning: This is a method of differentiating instruction for ELLs developed by Hill & Flynn (2006). The mnemonic device stands for "Word, Model, Expand, and Sound." Teachers work on word selection with pre-production students. "Model for early production. Expand what speech emergence students have said or written and help intermediate and advanced fluency students sound like a book" by working on fluency.

Word Play: In this activity, students manipulate words through various word games to increase understanding. Johnson, von Hoff Johnson, & Shlicting (2004) divide word games into eight categories: onomastics (name games), expressions, figures of speech, word associations, word formations, word manipulations, word games, and ambiguities.

Word Sorts: Sorting words based on structure and spelling can improve orthography (Bear, D. & Invernizzi, M., 2004).

Word Splash: Identify what you want students to know about a certain concept (key vocabulary or words connected to the concept). Write the words randomly and in all directions. Tell students you wrote the words in no particular order (called a splash). After presenting the lesson have students begin to place the words in some logical order and use the words in either speaking or writing.

Word Study Books: In this activity, students organize words in a notebook based on spelling, affixes and roots. (Bear D., & Invernizzi, M., 2004).

Word Walls: This is a collection of words posted on a classroom wall. Word walls are organized by topic, sound, or spelling and help improve literacy. (Eyraud et al., 2000)

Written Conversation: Using planned language and content, students interact during writing conversation. In pairs, students respond to one another's specific questions and sentence starters.

This page is intentionally left blank.

Bibliography

Asher, J. and Price, B. "The Learning Strategy of Total Physical Response: Some Age Differences." *Child Development*, 38, 1219-1227. 1967.

Asher, J. "The Total Physical Response Approach to Second Language Learning." *The Modern Language Journal* (53) 1. 1969.

August, D. and Shanahan, T. "Developing Literacy in Second Language Learners: Report of the National Literacy Panel on Language-Minority Children and Youth." *Center for Applied Linguistics*, Lawrence Erlbaum Associates: Mahwah, NJ. 2006.

Ausubel, D. P. "The Use of Advance Organizers in the Learning and Retention of Meaningful Verbal Material." *Journal of Educational Psychology*, 51, 267-272. 1960.

Baker, L. "Reading Comprehension and Science Inquiry: Metacognitive Connections." In E.W.Saul (Ed.), "Crossing Borders in Literacy and Science Instruction: Perspectives on Theory and Practice." Newark, DE: *International Reading Association*; Arlington, VA: *National Science Teachers Association* (NSTA) Press. 2004.

Bauman, J. F., Russell, N. S., and Jones, L. A. "Effects of Think-aloud Instruction on Elementary Students' Comprehension Abilities. *Journal of Reading Behavior*, 24 (2), 143-172. 1992.

Bear, D.R., Invernizzi, M., Templeton, S., & Johnson, F. *Words their Way: Word Study for Phonics, Vocabulary, and Spelling Instruction (2nd Ed.).* Upper Saddle River, NJ: Merrill Prentice Hall. 2004.

Beck, I.L., McKeown, M.G., Hamilton, R.L., & Kugan, L. "Questioning the Author: An Approach for Enhancing Student Engagement with Text." Newark, DE: International Reading Association. 1997.

Berg, C. "The Effects of Trained Peer Response on ESL Students' Revision Types and Writing Quality." *Journal of Second Language Writing,* Volume 8, Issue 3, 215-241. September 1999,

Boulware, B.J., & Crow, M. "Using the Concept Attainment Strategy to Enhance Reading Comprehension." *The Reading Teacher, 61*(6), 491–495. March, 2008.

Brown, A., Campoine, J., and Day, J. "Learning to Learn: On Training Students to Learn from Texts." *Educational Researcher, 10,* 14-24. 1981.

Bruner, J., Goodnow, J. & Austin, G. A. *A Study of Thinking*. New York: Science Editions. 1967.

Chamot, A.U. & O'Malley, *J.M. The Calla Handbook: Implementing the Cognitive Academic Language Learning Approach*. White Plains, NY: Addison Wesley Longman. 1994.

Callow, J. Show Me: "Principles for Assessing Students' Visual Literacy." *The Reading Teacher, 61*(8), 616–626. May, 2008.

Celce-Murcia, M., Brinton, D. & Goodwin, J. *Teaching Pronunciation: A Reference for Teachers of English to Speakers of Other Languages.* Cambridge: Cambridge University Press. 1996.

Cunningham-Flores, M. *Improving Adult ESL Learners' Pronunciation Skills*. National Center for ESL Literacy Education. 1998.

Dole, J., Duffy, G., Roehler, L., & Pearson, P. "Moving from the Old to the New: Research in Reading Comprehension Instruction." *Review of Educational Research, 61,* 239-264. 1991.

Echevarria, J., Short, D & Vogt, M. *Making Content Comprehensible. The Sheltered Instruction Observation Protocol.* Boston, MA: Pearson. 2008.

Elbow, P. *Writing with Power*. Oxford: Oxford University Press. 1998.

Eyraud, K., Giles, G., Koenig, S., & Stoller, F. "The Word Wall Approach: Promoting L2 Vocabulary Learning". *English Teaching Forum*, 38, 2-11. 2000.

Fisher, D., & Frey, N. *Checking for Understanding: Formative Assessment Techniques for your Classroom.* Alexandria, VA: Association for Supervision and Curriculum Development. 2007.

Francis, D., Lesaux, N., & August, D. "Language of Instruction for Language Minority Learners." In D. L. August & T. Shanahan (Eds.) *Developing Literacy in a Second Language: Report of the National Literacy Panel.* (pp.365-414). Mahwah, NJ: Lawrence Erlbaum Associates. 2006.

Gibbons, P. *Scaffolding Language, Scaffolding Learning.* Portsmouth, NH: Heinemann. 2002.

Goldenberg, C., "Instructional Conversations: Promoting Comprehension through Discussion, *The Reading Teacher, 46 (4),* 316-326. 1992-1993.

Harrington, M. J. "Basic Instruction in Word Analysis Skills to Improve Spelling Competence." *Education,* 117, 22. Available: http://www.questia.com/ 1996.

Head, M., & Readence, J. "Anticipation Guides: Meaning through Prediction." In E. Dishner, T. Bean, J. Readence, & D. Moore (Eds.), *Reading in the Content Areas,* Dubuque, IA: Kendall/Hunt. 1986.

High, Julie. *Second Language Learning through Cooperative Learning.* San Clemente, CA: Kagan Publishing. 1993.

Hill, J., & Flynn, K. *Classroom Instruction that Works with English Language Learners.* Alexandria, VA: Association for Supervision and Curriculum Development. 2006.

Johnson, D., & Johnson, R. *Creative Controversy: Intellectual Challenge in the Classroom* (3rd ed.). Edina, MN: Interaction Book Company. 1995.

Kagan, S. *Cooperative learning for students limited in language proficiency.* in M. Brubacher, R. Payne & K. Rickett (Eds.), *Perspectives on Small Group Learning.* Oakville, Ontario, Canada. 1990.

Kagan, S. *Cooperative Learning.* San Juan Capistrano, CA: Kagan Cooperative Learning. 1992.

Kirschner, P., Sweller, J., & Clark, R. "Why Minimal Guidance during Instruction Does Not Work: An Analysis of the Failure of Constructivist, Discovery, Problem-based, Experiential, and Inquiry-based Teaching". *Educational Psychologist* 41 (2): 75–86. 2006.

Krashen, S. *Principles and Practices in Second Language Acquisition.* Oxford: Pergamon. 1982.

Leeman, J. Recasts and Second Language Development: Beyond Negative Evidence. *Studies in Second Language Acquisition, 25,* 37-63. 2003.

Lyman, F. T. "The Responsive Classroom Discussion: The Inclusion of All Students." In A. Anderson (Ed.), *Mainstreaming Digest* (pp. 109-113). College Park: University of Maryland Press. 1981.

Marzano, R. *Building Academic Background.* Alexandria, VA: MCREL, ASCD. 2004.

Marzano, R., Pickering, D. J., & Pollock, J. E. *Classroom Instruction that Works.* Alexandria, VA: MCREL, ASCD. 2001.

Maurice, K. "The Fluency Workshop." *TESOL Newsletter,* 17, 4. 1983.

Mayer, R. *Learning and Instruction.* New Jersey: Pearson Education, Inc. 2003.

"Principles and Standards for School Mathematics." *National Council of Teachers of Mathematics* NCTM. Reston, VA: NCTM. 2000.

Novak, J.D. "Concept Mapping: A Strategy for Organizing Knowledge." in Glynn, S.M. & Duit, R. (eds.), *Learning Science in the Schools: Research Reforming Practice,* Lawrence Erlbaum Associates, Mahwah, NJ. 1995.

Ogle, D. S. "K-W-L Group Instructional Strategy." In A. S. Palincsar, D. S. Ogle, B. F. Jones, & E. G. Carr (Eds.), *Teaching Reading as Thinking* (Teleconference Resource Guide, pp. 11-17). Alexandria, VA: Association for Supervision and Curriculum Development. 1986.

Palincsar, A.S., & Brown, A.L. "Reciprocal Teaching: Activities to Promote Reading with Your Mind." In T.L. Harris & E.J. Cooper (Eds.), *Reading, Thinking and Concept Development: Strategies for the Classroom*. New York: The College Board. 1985.

Paulk, W. *How to Study in College*. Boston: Houghton Mifflin, 2000.

Pilgreen, J. *The SSR Handbook: How to Organize and Maintain a Sustained Silent Reading Program.* Portsmouth, NH: Heinemann. 2000.

Pilgreen, J. and Krashen, S. "Sustained Silent Reading with English as a Second Language with High School Students: Impact on Reading Comprehension, Reading Frequency, and Reading Enjoyment." *School Library Media Quarterly* 22: 21-23. 1993.

Powell, M. *Presenting in English*. Hove: Language Teaching Publications. 1996.

Chamot, A., & O'Malley, J. "The Calla Handbook: Implementing the Cognitive Academic Language Learning Approach." *Reading,* MA: Addison-Wesley 1994.

Ruddell, M.R., & Shearer, B.A. "'Extraordinary,' 'tremendous,' 'exhilarating,' 'magnificent': Middle school At-Risk Students Become Avid Word Learners with the Vocabulary Self-Collection Strategy (VSS). *Journal of Adolescent and Adult Literacy, 45*(4), 352-363. 2002.

Samway, K. *When English Language Learners Write: Connecting Research to Practice.* Portsmouth: Heineman. 2006.

Schlick Noe, K. & Johnson, N. *Getting Started with Literature Circles*. Norwood, MA: Christopher-Gordon Publishers, Inc. 1999.

Seidlitz, J. & Perryman, B. *Seven Steps to Building an Interactive Classroom: Engaging All Students in Academic Conversation.* San Clemente, CA: Canter Press. 2008.

Taba, H. *Curriculum Development: Theory and Practice.* New York: Harcourt Brace & World. 1962.

Taba, Hilda. *Teachers' Handbook for Elementary Social Studies*. Reading, MA: Addison-Wesley. 1967.

Taylor, W. "Cloze Procedure, A New Tool for Measuring Readability." *Journalism Quarterly.* 30, 415-433. 1953.

Thornburry, S. *How to Teach Speaking.* Essex, England: Pearson. 2005.

Vail, Neil J. and Papenfuss, J. *Daily Oral Language Plus.* Evanston, IL: McDougal, Littell. 1993.

Weaver, C. *Teaching Grammar in Context.* Portsmouth, NH: Boynton, Cook Publishers. 1996.

Wennerstrom, A. "Content-Based Pronunciation." *TESOL Journal*, 1(3), 15-18. 1993.

White, T., Sowell, J., & Yanagihara, A. "Teaching Elementary Students to Use Word-Part Clues." *The Reading Teacher, 42*, 302-308. 1989.

Willhelm., J *Action Strategies for Deepening Comprehension.* New York: Scholastic. 2002.

Zwiers, J. *Building Academic Language.* Newark, DE: Jossey-Bass/International Reading Association. 2008.